ROCK-FORMING MINERALS

ROCK-FORMING MINERALS

Vol. 3   Sheet Silicates

W. A. Deer, M.Sc., Ph.D., F.G.S.
Professor of Mineralogy and Petrology, Cambridge University

R. A. Howie, M.A., Ph.D., F.G.S.

and

J. Zussman, M.A., Ph.D., F.Inst.P.
Department of Geology, Manchester University

1724

LONGMANS

LONGMANS, GREEN AND CO LTD
48 GROSVENOR STREET, LONDON W I
RAILWAY CRESCENT, CROYDON, VICTORIA, AUSTRALIA
AUCKLAND, KINGSTON (JAMAICA), LAHORE, NAIROBI
LONGMANS SOUTHERN AFRICA (PTY) LTD
THIBAULT HOUSE, THIBAULT SQUARE, CAPE TOWN
JOHANNESBURG, SALISBURY
LONGMANS OF NIGERIA LTD
W. R. INDUSTRIAL ESTATE, IKEJA
LONGMANS OF GHANA LTD
INDUSTRIAL ESTATE, RING ROAD SOUTH, ACCRA
LONGMANS GREEN (FAR EAST) LTD
443 LOCKHART ROAD, HONG KONG
LONGMANS OF MALAYA LTD
44 JALAN AMPANG, KUALA LUMPUR
ORIENT LONGMANS LTD
CALCUTTA, BOMBAY, MADRAS
DELHI, HYDERABAD, DACCA
LONGMANS CANADA LTD
137 BOND STREET, TORONTO 2

MADE AND PRINTED IN GREAT BRITAIN BY
WILLIAM CLOWES AND SONS, LIMITED, LONDON AND BECCLES

PREFACE

In writing these volumes the primary aim has been to provide a work of reference useful to advanced students and research workers in the geological sciences. It is hoped, however, that it will also prove useful to workers in other sciences who require information about minerals or their synthetic equivalents. Each mineral has been treated in some detail, and it has thus been necessary to restrict the coverage to a selection of the more important minerals. The principle in this selection is implied in the title *Rock-Forming Minerals*, as, with a few exceptions, only those minerals are dealt with which, by their presence or absence, serve to determine or modify the name of a rock. Some may quarrel with the inclusion or omission of particular minerals; once committed, however, to the discussion of a mineral or mineral series the less common varieties have also been considered.

Most of the information contained in this text is available in the various scientific journals. An attempt has been made to collect, summarize and group these contributions under mineral headings, and the source of information is given in the references at the end of each section. The bibliography is not historically or otherwise complete, but the omission of reference to work which has been encompassed by a later and broader study does not belittle the importance of earlier investigations; where many papers have been published on a given topic, only a limited number have been selected to illustrate the scope and results of the work they report.

The collection of data and references should bring a saving of time and labour to the research worker embarking on a mineralogical study, but it is hoped also that the presentation of the results of study from many different aspects, and in particular their correlation, will further the understanding of the nature and properties of the minerals. Determinative properties are described and tabulated, but the intended function of this work is the understanding of minerals as well as their identification, and to this end, wherever possible, correlation has been attempted, optics with composition, composition with paragenesis, physical properties with structure, and so on. For each mineral the body of well-established data is summarized, but unsolved and partially solved problems are also mentioned.

The rock-forming minerals are dealt with in five volumes. The silicates are allocated on a structural basis: vol. 1. *Ortho- and Ring Silicates*, vol. 2. *Chain Silicates*, vol. 3. *Sheet Silicates*, vol. 4. *Framework Silicates*. *Non-silicates* are grouped chemically in the various sections of volume 5.

With a few exceptions, the treatment of each mineral or mineral group is in five sub-sections. In the *Structure* section, in addition to a brief description of the atomic structure, descriptions of X-ray methods for determining chemical composition and any other applications of X-rays to the study of the mineral are given. The *Chemistry* section describes the principal variations in chemical composition and includes a table of analyses representative, wherever possible, of the range of chemical and paragenetic variation. From most analyses a structural formula has been calculated. The chemistry sections also consider the synthesis and breakdown of the minerals and the phase equilibria in relevant chemical systems, together with d.t.a. observations and alteration products. The third section lists *Optical and Physical Properties* and discusses them in relation to structure and chemistry. The fourth section contains *Distinguishing Features* or tests by which each mineral may be recognized and in particular distinguished from those with which it is most likely to be confused. The *Paragenesis* section gives the principal rock types in which the mineral occurs and some typical mineral assemblages : possible derivations of the minerals are discussed and are related wherever possible to the results of phase equilibria studies. The five sub-sections for each mineral are preceded by a condensed table of properties together with an orientation sketch for biaxial minerals and an introductory paragraph, and are followed by a list of references to the literature. The references are comprehensive to 1959 but later additions extend the coverage for some sections to 1961. In the present text, mineral data are frequently presented in diagrams, and those which can be used determinatively have been drawn to an exact centimetre scale, thus enabling the reader to use them by direct measurement : numbers on such diagrams refer to the number of the analysis of the particular mineral as quoted in the tables.

The dependence of these volumes upon the researches and reports of very many workers will be so obvious to the reader as to need no emphasis, but we wish especially to record our indebtedness to those authors whose diagrams have served as a basis for the illustrations and thus facilitated our task. In this connection we would thank also the many publishers who have given permission to use their diagrams, and Mr H. C. Waddams, the artist who has so ably executed the versions used in the present text. *Mineralogical Abstracts* have been an indispensable starting point for bringing many papers to our attention : in by far the majority of cases reference has been made directly to the original papers; where this has not been possible the *Mineralogical Abstracts* reference is also given *e.g.* (M.A. 13–351). Our warmest thanks are due also to our colleagues in the Department of Geology, Manchester University, who have been helpful with discussions and information, and who have tolerated, together with the publishers, repeatedly over-optimistic reports about the work's progress and completion. We wish to thank Miss J. I. Norcott who has executed so efficiently the preparation of the typescript and also Longmans Green & Co. for their continued co-operation.

Department of Geology, The University, Manchester 13.   *October 1961*

CONTENTS *Vol. 3* *Sheet Silicates*

ACKNOWLEDGEMENTS

For permission to redraw diagrams we are indebted to the following:

The Editors, *Acta. Cryst., Amer. Journ. Sci.*; The Carnegie Institute of Washington for diagrams from *Ann. Rep. Dir. Geophys. Lab.*; The Mineralogical Society of America for diagrams from *Amer. Min.*; The Geological Society of America for diagrams from *Bull. Geol. Soc. Amer.*; Pergamon Press Ltd. for diagrams from *Geochim. et Cosmochim. Acta.*; The Mineralogical Society of London for diagrams from *Min. Mag., X-ray Identification and Crystal Structures of Clay Minerals, The Differential Thermal Investigation of Clays*; The Royal Society of Edinburgh for a diagram from *Trans. Roy. Soc. Edin.*; U.S. Geological Survey for a diagram from *Prof. Paper. 205-B.*; Akademische Verlagsgesellschaft mbH, Frankfurt, for diagrams from *Zeit. Krist.*

Plate 1(a) is reproduced from *Amer. Min.* by permission of Prof. Nagy and Mr. Faust and Plate 1(b) from *Kolloid. Zeits.* by permission of Dr. Noll and Verlag Dr. Dietrich Steinkopf, Darmstadt.

Cell parameters, interplanar and interatomic distances are generally given in Ångstrom Units. The factor 1·00202 has been used to convert kX to Å units and this factor has also been applied to all data published before 1944 which were then stated as being in Å units.

ABBREVIATIONS AND SYMBOLS

The following abbreviations have been used in the text except where otherwise stated.

A	Ångstrom units (10^{-8} cm.)
a	cell edge in the x direction
a_{rh}	rhombohedral cell edge
a_{hex}	hexagonal cell edge
anal.	analysis or analyst
b	cell edge in the y direction
Bx_a	acute bisectrix
C	(in association with λ) red light (656 mμ)
c	cell edge in the z direction
calc.	calculated
D	specific gravity
D	(in association with λ) sodium (yellow) light (589 mμ)
d	interplanar spacing
d.t.a.	differential thermal analysis
2E	apparent optic axial angle measured in air
F	(in association with λ) blue light (486 mμ)
H	hardness (Mohs scale)
Li	(in association with λ) lithium (red) light (671 mμ)
mμ	millimicron
M.A.	*Mineralogical Abstracts*
max.	maximum
min.	minimum
m. eq./g.	milliequivalents per gram (cation exchange capacity)
n	refractive index (for a cubic mineral)
O.A.P.	optic axial plane
P	pressure
R	metal ions
$r < v$ (or $r > v$)	the optic axial angle in red light is less than (or greater than) that in violet light
rh	rhombohedral
T	temperature
Tl	(in association with λ) thallium (green) light (535 mμ)
2V	the optic axial angle
x, y, z	the crystal axes
Z	number of formula units per unit cell
α, β, γ	least, intermediate and greatest refractive indices

α, β, γ	angles between the positive directions of the y and z, x and z, and x and y crystal axes
α, β, γ	the vibration directions of the slow, intermediate and fast ray; also these rays
δ	birefringence
ϕ	polar coordinate: azimuth angle measured clockwise from [010]
ρ	polar coordinate: polar angle measured from z
λ	wavelength
ϵ	extraordinary ray, refractive index
ω	ordinary ray, refractive index

MICA GROUP

$X_2Y_{4-6}[(Si,Al)_8O_{20}](OH,F)_4$

MONOCLINIC $(-)$

α 1·525 (lepidolite)–1·625 (biotite)
β 1·551 (lepidolite)–1·696 (biotite)
γ 1·554 (lepidolite)–1·696 (biotite)
δ 0·014 (glauconite)–0·08 (biotite)
$2V_\alpha$ 0°–58°

α nearly perpendicular to (001).

O.A.P. $\perp$(010) in muscovite, paragonite and some biotites.

O.A.P. (010) in glauconite, lepidolite, most biotites and phlogopites, and zinnwaldite.

Dispersion :   Weak.
Cleavage :   {001} perfect.
Twinning :   Composition plane {001}, twin axis [310].
Colour :   Various.
Pleochroism :   Strong for coloured micas; absorption greatest for vibration directions in plane of cleavage.
Unit cell : $a \simeq 5·3$, b 8·9–9·2, $c \simeq 10$, 20 or 30 Å.
    for 1M: $\beta \simeq 100°$, Z=1. Space group Cm or $C2/m$.
    for 2M$_1$: $\beta \simeq 95°$, Z=2. Space group $C2/c$.

The mica minerals as a whole show considerable variation in chemical and physical properties, but all are characterized by a platy morphology and perfect basal cleavage which is a consequence of their layered atomic structure.   Of the micas, muscovite, phlogopite and lepidolite are of considerable economic importance.   The following sections deal with the most common micas, muscovite, paragonite, glauconite, lepidolite, phlogopite, biotite and zinnwaldite (the brittle micas margarite, clintonite and xanthophyllite are considered separately).   For the most part each of these is a distinct mineral which does not form a complete solid solution series with any of the others, but phlogopite and biotite are separated merely for convenience in dealing with otherwise so large a group.   Other distinct mineral species, *e.g.* taeniolite, fuchsite, etc., because they are comparatively rare and have not been extensively investigated, have been included in the section on the mica they most resemble.   Among the most important contributions to the study of the chemical and physical properties of micas and their classification are those of Hallimond (1925, 1926, 1927), Winchell (1932, 1935, 1942, etc.), Kunitz (1924), Jakob (1925, 1926, etc.), Stevens (1938), Volk (1939), Serdiuchenko (1948), Heinrich *et al.* (1953), Smith and Yoder (1956).

STRUCTURE

The first X-ray studies of the mica structure were by Mauguin (1927, 1928), Pauling (1930) and by Jackson and West (1930, 1933). The principal polymorphic variations were investigated by Hendricks and Jefferson (1939) and more recently by Heinrich *et al.* (1953) and by Smith and Yoder (1956).

The basic structural feature of a mica is a composite sheet in which a layer of octahedrally coordinated cations is sandwiched between two identical layers of linked $(Si,Al)O_4$ tetrahedra. Two of these tetrahedral sheets (of composition $(Si,Al)_2O_5$) are illustrated in Fig. 1. On the left is a sheet in which all tetrahedra are pointing upwards as may be seen from the "elevation" drawing

o *Basal*
  oxygens
⊙ Si *with*
  oxygen
  above it

o *Basal*
  oxygens
⊛ Si *with*
  oxygen
  below it

• Si
o *Oxygen*

• Si
o *Oxygen*

FIG. 1(i). Mica structure. Plan of tetrahedral layer (Si_4O_{10}) with tetrahedra pointing upwards, and end view of layer looking down y axis.
FIG. 1(ii). Mica structure. Plan and elevation of tetrahedral layer with tetrahedra pointing downwards.

below it, and on the right is a sheet of tetrahedra which point downwards. The two sheets are superimposed and are linked by a plane of cations as shown in Figs. 2 and 3. Additional hydroxyl ions (marked A in Fig. 2), together with the apical oxygens of the inward pointing tetrahedra, complete the octahedral coordination of the sandwiched cations. Alternatively the structure may be regarded as having a central brucite layer $Mg_3(OH)_6$ (in phlogopite) or gibbsite layer $Al_2(OH)_6$ (in muscovite), in which four out of six (OH) ions are replaced by apical oxygens of the tetrahedral layers (two on each side). The remaining (OH) ions are then situated at the centres of hexagons formed by the tetrahedral vertices. The central Y ions determine the positions of the two tetrahedral sheets so that they are displaced relative to one another by $a/3$ in the [100] direction (Figs. 2 and 3). The composite layers have a centred plane group with a symmetry plane PP′, and repeat on a rectangular network with dimensions approximately $5 \cdot 3 \times 9 \cdot 2$ Å. In the micas these layers have a net

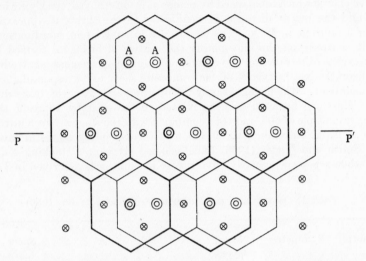

⊗ *Octahedrally coordinated cations; mainly* MgAl *or* Fe   ○ *Additional hydroxyl ions*

◎ *X ions below bottom layer* (K, Na, Ca)   ◯ *X ions above upper layer* (K, Na, Ca)

Thick lines :- bottom Si_2O_5 *layer*   *Thin lines :- upper* Si_2O_5 *layer*

FIG. 2. Mica structure. Plan of (i) and (ii) of Fig. 1 superimposed and linked by a layer of cations.

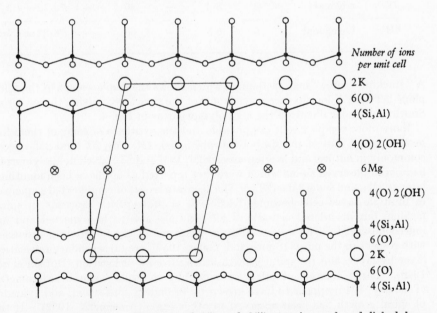

Number of ions per unit cell

2 K

6 (O)

4 (Si, Al)

4 (O) 2 (OH)

6 Mg

4 (O) 2 (OH)

4 (Si, Al)

6 (O)

2 K

6 (O)

4 (Si, Al)

FIG. 3. Mica structure. Elevation of 1(i) and 1(ii) superimposed and linked by a plane of octahedrally coordinated cations. Composite layers are shown linked by potassium ions, and the simplest unit cell is outlined. View is along *y* axis.

negative charge which is balanced by planes of X ions (K, Na, etc.) lying between them, and the repeat distance perpendicular to the sheets is approximately 10 Å or a multiple of 10 Å.   The X ions are in twelve-fold coordination since they lie centrally on the line joining the centres of hexagons formed by the basal oxygens of tetrahedral layers, and no lateral displacement is introduced in going from the basal oxygens of one composite sheet to corresponding oxygens of its neighbour.   The hexagons may be superimposed, however, in six different ways.   Thus one hexagon may be related to the next by rotation through 0° or by a multiple of 60°, and this, combined with the stagger of $a/3$ introduced by the Y layer, determines the location of corresponding atoms in successive cells.   Smith and Yoder (1956) have selected six simple stacking sequences which when repeated regularly, give rise to the unit cells described in Table 1.

Table 1.   SOME MICA POLYMORPHS (Smith and Yoder, 1956)

Polymorph	Symmetry	No. of layers	a Å	b Å	c Å	$\beta°$	Space group
1M	monoclinic	1	5·3	9·2	10	100°	$C2/m$ or Cm
$2M_1$	monoclinic	2	5·3	9·2	20	95°	$C2/c$
$2M_2$	monoclinic	2	9·2	5·3	20	98°	$C2/c$
2O	orthorhombic	2	5·3	9·2	20	90°	$Ccm2$
3T	trigonal	3	5·3	—	30	—	$P3_112$ or $P3_212$
6H	hexagonal	6	5·3	—	60	—	$P6_122$ or $P6_522$

A "stacking vector" may be defined which shows the displacement in the (001) plane between X ions in successive layers of the structure.   Using these vectors Smith and Yoder illustrate the six polymorphs as in Fig. 4.

Many more complex cells are possible and the existence of some of them has been reported, but of the six polymorphs listed, 1M, $2M_1$, 3T (and $2M_2$) occur commonly in nature, and in a few cases 12M, 18M and 8Tc (triclinic) polymorphs have been observed (some which were first reported as 6M have been identified later as $2M_2$, and some 3M as 3T).   The accurate repeat of complicated sequences in multiple layer cells becomes feasible if crystal growth proceeds in spiral fashion, but disordered crystals of all sorts are also to be expected and are indeed observed.   The two possible mechanisms of crystal growth, discussed with respect to the micas (Smith and Yoder, 1956), are (a) secondary nucleation layer by layer, and (b) spiral growth arising from a dislocation (Burton *et al.*, 1949).   Large crystals of mica examined by multiple beam interferometry (Tolansky, 1945) appear to have grown by secondary nucleation, and evidence of spiral growth has been observed in other cases (Amelinckx, 1952).   If the component layers of mica possessed the perfect three-fold symmetry of the ideal structure, the position adopted by one layer upon another would be almost arbitrary and the process of secondary nucleation should produce only disordered structures. If the deviation from the ideal is of sufficient magnitude, however, then one mode of stacking might be energetically more favourable than another. Accurate structure analysis of a mica crystal has not been

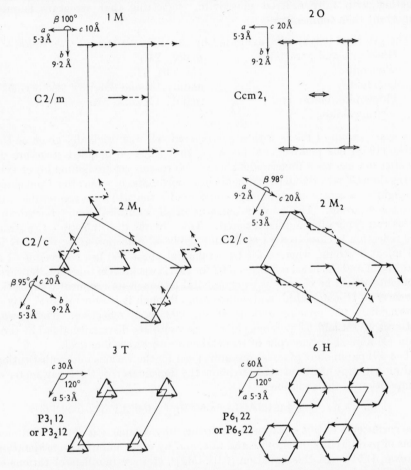

FIG. 4. The six simple ways of stacking mica layers in an ordered manner. The arrows are the inter-layer stacking vectors. Full line vectors show the layer stacking in one unit cell, whereas broken line vectors show the positions of layers in the next unit cell. The base of the unit cell is shown by thin lines, and the space group and lattice parameters are listed by the side of the diagram in each case (after Smith and Yoder, 1956).

undertaken[1], but the X-ray diffraction patterns give evidence in some cases of considerable distortion from the ideal. In muscovite, for example, the distortion is large and the majority of muscovites adopt the $2M_1$ configuration. For biotites, and for tri-octahedral micas generally (see p. 55), there is less distortion and different polymorphs commonly occur, so that distortion appears to be associated with the partial filling of the octahedral sites in the di-octahedral micas. Probably for similar reasons, stacking disorder is also more common

[1] But see Radoslovich (1960).

among phlogopites and biotites than among muscovites. According to Dekeyser and Amelinckx (1953), temperature and degree of saturation are the dominant factors in determining polymorphism and degree of order, but Smith and Yoder (1956) point out that partially ordered phlogopite and biotite occur together with fully ordered muscovite, suggesting that structure is more important than temperature.

The principal polymorphs exhibited by the different micas are as follows:

Muscovite and paragonite: mainly $2M_1$
Glauconite: 1M, $2M_1$, 3T.
Lepidolite: mainly 1M and $2M_2$; 3T also occurs.
Phlogopite, biotite and zinnwaldite: mainly 1M; also $2M_1$ and 3T.

The space group of micas with a one-layered cell was originally given as *Cm*. Pabst (1955) has pointed out, however, that since no detailed structure determination has been undertaken there is no reason yet to assume lower symmetry than *C2/m*. Small adjustments in x coordinates of some atoms and choice of origin at a centre of symmetry would render the structure compatible with this space group. The powder patterns of di-octahedral and tri-octahedral micas can generally be differentiated. Thus for the di-octahedrals the strong 060 reflection is close to $d = 1.50$ Å, and the basal reflection at $d \simeq 5$ Å (004 for 2M mica) is strong, whereas for tri-octahedral micas 060 lies between $d = 1.53$ and 1.55 Å and the basal reflection (002 for 1M) is weak. On this basis, however, lepidolite would be classed as di-octahedral although its chemical composition is nearer to tri-octahedral, and glauconite, although it is di-octahedral, has an intermediate 060 spacing and no strong 002 basal reflection. The powder patterns of 1M and 3T polymorphs of muscovite are distinguishable but those from 1M and 3T polymorphs of tri-octahedral micas are identical.

The cell parameters of micas are influenced by the various ionic substitutions and an attempt has been made to show the dependence of the b parameter on composition in the equation:

$$b \text{ (in kX)} = 8.90 + 0.12[\text{Al}]^4 + 0.066[\text{Mg}]^6 + 0.083[\text{Fe}]^6 + 0.022[\text{Ti}]^6$$

The coefficients of this equation were deduced by comparison of the cell dimensions of pyrophyllite, muscovite and talc, and by other empirical considerations (Brown, 1951). In this equation $[\text{Al}]^4$, $[\text{Mg}]^6$, etc. are numbers of cations for 12(O,OH); all iron is treated as ferrous, and lithium is grouped with aluminium. Although approximately correct values for b may be obtained in this manner, the equation is of limited usefulness for determining composition from cell parameters since it contains too many variables. Another approach to this problem is through the intensity relationships between basal reflections. Grim *et al.* (1951) show the variation of five basal reflections with composition of the octahedral layer for di- and tri-octahedral micas (substitution of Si$\rightleftharpoons$Al in the Z positions has little effect on intensities). For di-octahedral micas, only the effect of substituting ferrous or ferric iron for Al is considered since Mg and Al have similar scattering powers, and it is assumed that Li and Ti are not present in appreciable amounts. The effect is best recognized in the ratio of the second to either the first or third order of the 10 Å basal reflection. Since few muscovites have a high iron content this relationship is of limited value. More useful is that for tri-octahedral micas, in which intensities of fourth and fifth orders are compared to give an estimate of the $Mg:Fe^{+2}$ ratio (see also page 56).

CHEMISTRY

The general formula which describes the chemical composition of micas is $X_2Y_{4-6}Z_8O_{20}(OH,F)_4$ where

X is mainly K, Na or Ca but also Ba, Rb, Cs, etc.
Y is mainly Al, Mg or Fe but also Mn, Cr, Ti, Li, etc.
Z is mainly Si or Al but perhaps also Fe^{+3} and Ti.

The micas can be subdivided into di-octahedral and tri-octahedral classes in which the number of Y ions is 4 and 6 respectively. A further subdivision can be made according to the nature of the principal X constituent. In the common micas X is largely K or Na but in so-called "brittle micas" X is largely Ca; these are dealt with separately in the present text. Further subdivisions of the common micas are made according to the principal constituents in the categories X, Y and Z and these are depicted with approximate formulae in Table 2. More precise representation of formulae will be found later in the relevant sections. For the di-octahedral common micas, substitution of silicon for

Table 2. APPROXIMATE CHEMICAL FORMULAE OF MICAS

Di-octahedral

		X	Y	Z
Common Micas	Muscovite	K_2	Al_4	Si_6Al_2
	Paragonite	Na_2	Al_4	Si_6Al_2
	Glauconite	$(K,Na)_{1\cdot2-2\cdot0}$	$(Fe,Mg,Al)_4$	$Si_{7-7\cdot6}Al_{1\cdot0-0\cdot4}$
Brittle micas	Margarite	Ca_2	Al_4	Si_4Al_4

Tri-octahedral

		X	Y	Z
Common micas	Phlogopite	K_2	$(Mg,Fe^{+2})_6$	Si_6Al_2
	Biotite	K_2	$(Mg,Fe,Al)_6$	$Si_{6-5}Al_{2-3}$
	Zinnwaldite	K_2	$(Fe,Li,Al)_6$	$Si_{6-7}Al_{2-1}$
	Lepidolite	K_2	$(Li,Al)_{5-6}$	$Si_{6-5}Al_{2-3}$
Brittle micas	Clintonite and Xanthophyllite	Ca_2	$(Mg,Al)_6$	$Si_{2\cdot5}Al_{5\cdot5}$

aluminium in tetrahedral coordination is generally balanced electrostatically by equivalent substitution of divalent ions for aluminium in octahedral sites.   Thus Foster (1956) considers that the substituted di-octahedral potassium micas form a series with the general formula ranging from trisilicic $XR_2^{+3}Si_3AlO_{10}(OH)_2$ to tetrasilicic $XR^{+3}R^{+2}Si_4O_{10}(OH)_2$.

The minerals talc and pyrophyllite are closely related structurally to the micas but differ in having no X ions and no Al in Z positions.

A chemical feature which most micas have in common is their water content; analyses, except for those with high fluorine content, show approximately 4–5 per cent. H_2O^+.   Both di- and tri-octahedral micas are found in fine-grained "clay mica" form, often with higher water content and other characteristic features discussed elsewhere (p. 15).

There seems to be no *a priori* reason why micas with Y ions numbering anything between 4 and 6 per formula unit, should not exist.   Opinions range, however, from the extreme view that all intermediate compositions are possible to the contention that all specimens ostensibly showing intermediate compositions are in fact physical mixtures of di- and tri-octahedral components. Taking account of chemical and X-ray evidence it would seem that biotites and lepidolites may have between 6 and 5 ions in Y sites, covering only half the range towards di-octahedral composition, and that lithian muscovites may have between 4 and 5 Y ions, coming half-way towards tri-octahedral composition. Muscovites and phlogopites are more closely confined to being di- and tri-octahedral respectively.

The various sheet minerals can be identified by their dehydration characteristics.   Kiefer (1949) describes these by four temperatures corresponding to (a) onset of dehydration, (b) and (c) beginning and end of rapid dehydration, and (d) end of dehydration (see Table 3).   Thermal stability is greater for micas than for 1:1 sheet minerals (kaolinite and serpentine), and is greater for tri-octahedral than for di-octahedral minerals of a given type (see also DeVries and Roy, 1958).   The size of ion in Y positions also influences stability, so that, for example, manganophyllite is less stable than phlogopite or biotite, and nontronite is less stable than montmorillonite (Fe^{+3} for Al).

Table 3.   THERMAL DEHYDRATION CHARACTERISTICS OF SHEET MINERALS
(Kiefer, 1949)

	Tri-octahedral					Di-octahedral			
	(a)	(b)	(c)	(d)		(a)	(b)	(c)	(d)
Phlogopite	1120°	1140°–1210°		1230°C.	Muscovite	765°	785°	905°	940°C.
Talc	900°	925°–1010°		1030°C.	Pyrophyllite	640°	690°	780°	850°C.
Antigorite	590°	665°–750°		800°C.	Kaolinite	430°	490°	570°	730°C.

OPTICAL AND PHYSICAL PROPERTIES

The optical properties of micas cover a wide range but all have negative sign and have α approximately perpendicular to their perfect (001) cleavage.   Most are biaxial, with 2V moderate for di-octahedral and generally small for tri-octahedral micas; relatively few specimens appear to be strictly uniaxial.   Birefringence is generally very weak in the plane of cleavage flakes but strong in transverse sections; pleochroism is strong in coloured micas and the absorption is greatest for vibration directions parallel to the cleavage. In thin sections relief relative to balsam is low for lepidolite and phlogopite but moderate to high for other micas. The di-octahedral micas generally have their optic axial planes perpendicular to (010) while others (with the exception of certain biotites which have the $2M_1$ structure) have the optic axial plane parallel to (010). All micas may show twinning on the "mica twin law" with composition plane {001} and twin axis [310], and well formed crystals often show {110} faces and therefore pseudo-hexagonal outline. The Mohs hardness index quoted for micas is generally an average for directions parallel to the cleavage plane. Considerable anisotropy of hardness was shown by Switzer (1941) who gave $H = 2.5$ and 4.0 parallel and perpendicular to (001) respectively, for both muscovite and biotite. Further anisotropy has been revealed by indentation hardness tests executed in various directions in the (001) plane (Bloss *et al.*, 1959). Greatest hardness was found for the direction parallel to y, and least hardness in the x direction for both fluorphlogopite and muscovite. The hardness of synthetic fluor-micas was found to be greater than that of their natural hydroxy counterpart, and natural muscovites were harder than the natural phlogopites and biotites examined. Anisotropy of hardness in the (001) plane is made use of in the percussion figure test, which may be applied to determine the orientation of crystallographic axes and their relation to optical orientation. A blow with a dull point on a cleavage plate produces a six-rayed percussion figure, the most prominent line of which is parallel to (010), the others being at 60° intervals. Thus for 1M micas the optic axial plane is parallel to one of the percussion rays, while for the $2M_1$ micas it bisects the angle between two rays. This method, however, is only useful for flakes of large area, and in some cases does not yield a conclusive result.

PARAGENESIS

The paragenesis of each variety of mica is discussed in the appropriate section; the following list, however, outlines the principal occurrences in igneous, metamorphic and sedimentary rocks.

Igneous

Muscovite: granites and granitic pegmatites.
Phlogopite: peridotites.
Biotite: gabbros, norites, diorites, granites, pegmatites.
Lepidolite and zinnwaldite: pegmatites and high-temperature veins.

Metamorphic

Muscovite, paragonite and biotite: phyllites, schists and gneisses.
Phlogopite: metamorphosed limestones and dolomites.

Sedimentary

Muscovite and paragonite: detrital and authigenic sediments.
Glauconite: greensands.

REFERENCES

Amelinckx, S., 1952. La croissance hélicoïdale de cristaux de biotite. *Compt. Rend. Acad. Sci. Paris*, vol. 234, p. 971.
Bloss, F. D., Shekarchi, E. and Shell, H. R., 1959. Hardness of synthetic and natural micas. *Amer. Min.*, vol. 44, p. 33.

Brown, G., 1951. Nomenclature of the mica clay minerals, in *X-ray identification and crystal structure of the clay minerals*. Min. Soc., Chap. V, p. 155.

Burton, W. K., Cabrera, N. and **Frank, F. C.**, 1949. The growth of crystals and the equilibrium of their surfaces. *Phil. Trans. Roy. Soc. London*, Ser. A., vol. 243, p. 299 (M.A. 12–312).

Dekeyser, W. and **Amelinckx, S.**, 1953. Le polytypisme des minéraux micacés et argileux. Deuxième partie: discussion et extension. *Compt. Rend. XIX Congr. Géol. Internat. Alger*, 1952, fasc. XVIII, p. 9 (M.A. 12–520).

DeVries, R. C. and **Roy, R.**, 1958. Influences of ionic substitution on the stability of micas and chlorites. *Econ. Geol.*, vol. 53, p. 458.

Foster, M. D., 1956. Correlation of dioctahedral potassium micas on the basis of their charge relations. A contribution to geochemistry. *U.S. Geol. Surv., Bull.* 1036-D., p. 57.

Grim, R. E., Bradley, W. F. and **Brown, G.**, 1951. The mica clay minerals, in *X-ray identification and crystal structure of the clay minerals*. Min. Soc., Chap. V, p. 138.

Hallimond, A. F., 1925. On the chemical classification of the mica group. I. The acid micas. *Min. Mag.*, vol. 20, p. 305.

—— 1926. On the chemical classification of the mica group. II. The basic micas. *Min. Mag.*, vol. 21, p. 25.

—— 1927. Studies in the mica group. *Amer. Min.*, vol. 12, p. 413.

Heinrich, E. W., Levinson, A. A., Levandowski, D. W. and **Hewitt, C. H.**, 1953. *Studies in the natural history of micas*. University of Michigan Engineering Research Institute project M.978; final report.

Hendricks, S. B. and **Jefferson, M.**, 1939. Polymorphism of the micas, with optical measurements. *Amer. Min.*, vol. 24, p. 729.

Jackson, W. W. and **West, J.**, 1930. The crystal structure of muscovite. *Zeit. Krist.*, vol. 76, p. 211.

—— —— 1933. The crystal structure of muscovite. *Zeit. Krist.*, vol. 85, p. 160.

Kiefer, C., 1949. Déshydration thermique des minéraux phylliteux. *Compt. Rend. Acad. Sci. Paris*, vol. 229, p. 1021.

Kunitz, W., 1924. Die Beziehungen zwischen der chemischen Zusammensetzung und den physikalisch-optischen Eigenschaften innerhalb der Glimmergruppe. *Neues Jahrb.*, Bl. Bd. 50, p. 365.

Mauguin, 1927. Étude des micas au moyens des rayons X. *Compt. Rend. Acad. Sci. Paris*, vol. 185, p. 288.

—— 1928. Étude des micas au moyens des rayons X. *Bull Soc. Franç. Min.*, vol. 51, p. 285.

Pabst, A., 1955. Redescription of the single layer structure of the micas. *Amer. Min.*, vol. 40, p. 967.

Pauling, L., 1930. The structure of micas and related minerals. *Proc. Nat. Acad. Sci. U.S.A.*, vol. 16, p. 123 (M.A. 4-368).

Radoslovich, E. W., 1960. The structure of muscovite, $KAl_2Si_3AlO_{10}(OH)_2$. *Acta Cryst.*, vol. 13, p. 919.

Serdiuchenko, D. P., 1948. The chemical composition and classification of micas. *Doklady Akad. Sci. U.S.S.R.*, vol. 59, p. 545.

Smith, J. V. and **Yoder, H. S.**, 1956. Experimental and theoretical studies of the mica polymorphs. *Min. Mag.*, vol. 31, p. 209.

Tolansky, S., 1945. The topography of cleavage faces of mica and selenite. *Proc. Roy. Soc. London*, ser. A., vol. 184, p. 51.

Volk, G. W., 1939. Optical and chemical studies of muscovite. *Amer. Min.*, vol. 24, p. 255.

Winchell, A. N., 1932. The lepidolite system. *Amer. Min.*, vol. 17, p. 551.

—— 1935. The biotite system. *Amer. Min.*, vol. 20, p. 173.

—— 1942. Further studies in the lepidolite system. *Amer. Min.*, vol. 27, p. 114.

Muscovite

$K_2Al_4[Si_6Al_2O_{20}](OH,F)_4$

MONOCLINIC $(-)$

α	1·552–1·574
β	1·582–1·610
γ	1·587–1·616
δ	0·036–0·049
$2V_\alpha$	30°–47°

$\alpha:z=0°-5°,\ \beta:x=1°-3°$

$\gamma=y$, O.A.P. $\perp(010)$

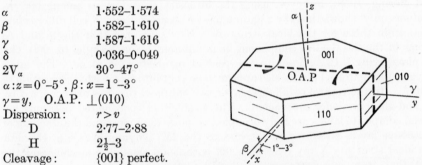

Dispersion:	$r>v$
D	2·77–2·88
H	$2\frac{1}{2}$–3
Cleavage:	{001} perfect.
Twinning:	Composition plane {001}, twin axis [310].
Colour:	Colourless, or light shades of green, red or brown; colourless in thin section.
Pleochroism:	Weak; absorption greater for vibration directions in the plane of cleavage.
Unit cell:	The most common polymorph has a 5·19, b 9·04, c 20·08 Å, β 95° 30'. $Z=2$. Space group $C2/c$.

Insoluble in acids.

Muscovite is one of the most common of the micas and occurs in a wide variety of geological environments. Its well known properties of electrical and thermal insulation have made it a mineral of industrial importance, and in technical applications the perfect lamellar cleavage of mica and the mechanical strength of its cleavage sheets are additional assets. Muscovite and phlogopite are the most transparent of the micas, and being comparatively free from iron they have the best electrical insulating properties. They often occur in large blocks (books) in which the area of cleavage sheet is a prime factor in their economic value, but the absence of structural defects and inclusions (mostly iron oxides) is also important. The name muscovite is derived from the name "muscovy glass" which was used for this mineral when first described from the Russian province of Muscovy. Among the many other synonyms for muscovite are the names adamsite, cat gold, cat silver, common mica, didymite and isinglass. These are of doubtful use, but other names such as phengite, fuchsite, etc., denote varieties of muscovite which differ chemically from the ideal composition given above. Terms such as illite, hydromuscovite, sericite, etc., denote less well defined differences and are discussed below, and in the sections on clay minerals.

STRUCTURE[1]

The micas in general are known to crystallize in many polymorphic forms, but muscovite itself shows least variation in that the majority of specimens adopt one form, the structure of which was determined by Jackson and West (1930, 1933). Its unit cell is monoclinic with a 5·19, b 9·04, c 20·08 Å, β 95° 30'; space group $C2/c$, $Z = 2$. One quarter of the tetrahedral sites are occupied by Al and three quarters by Si, but little is known at present about the ordering of the Si–Al distribution. A recent study of the structure of muscovite (Gatineau and Méring, 1958), however, using the intensity relationships among 00l reflections only, shows that the z parameters of atoms in the unit cell differ somewhat from those for the ideal structure. It is suggested that the Si and Al atoms in the tetrahedral component lie in different planes parallel to (00l), the Si plane lying 0·12 Å closer to the central octahedral Al plane. The inner oxygen and hydroxyl planes also appear to be split into two, with a separation of 0·06 Å. In the central octahedral layer two thirds of the sites are occupied by Al and the remainder are vacant. The twelve-fold coordinated positions between composite layers are fully occupied by potassium ions, and the stacking of successive layers gives rise in this case to the 2M₁ polymorph (see p. 4). For the ideal structure X-ray reflections 06l with l odd should be absent, and the fact that from muscovite some reflections of this category are quite strong indicates that the structure is considerably distorted, but no detailed investigation has yet been undertaken.[2] In the lithian muscovites where there is partial occupation of the otherwise vacant octahedral sites, these reflections are weaker and they are weaker still in patterns from biotite and phlogopite, in which octahedral sites are completely filled. It seems, therefore, that distortion decreases with increasing tri-octahedral character. Further evidence of distortion in muscovite is the value of β (95° 30') compared with $\beta = 94°$ 55' for the ideal structure. The distortion in muscovite is probably the reason why it nearly always adopts the 2M₁ stacking sequence and not others, and rarely shows the disordered stacking frequently found for other micas. In the latter cases the close approach of each layer to trigonal symmetry makes any of the alternative positions for its neighbouring layers equally favourable.

Polymorphism in natural muscovite has been studied extensively. Hendricks and Jefferson (1939) examined twenty muscovites, all of which had the 2M₁ structure. Heinrich *et al.* (1953) found that most specimens were 2M₁, and of those with higher than normal content of silica, most were 2M₁ but a few were 3T.[3] Five muscovites examined by Smith and Yoder (1956) were 2M₁, and one which previously had been described as having a three-layered monoclinic cell (Axelrod and Grimaldi, 1949) was found to be 3T (this specimen had also been described as 3H). 1M (cell parameters: a 5·208, b 8·995, c 10·275 Å, β 101° 35'), 1Md (disordered), and 2M₁ muscovites have been synthesized by Yoder and Eugster (1955), who have drawn attention to the existence of 1M and 1Md types in nature, mainly in fine-grained specimens from sediments and low grade metamorphic rocks. These have generally been described as sericites, illites or

---

[1] General features of the structures of all micas are described on p. 2.

[2] But see Radoslovich, E. W., 1960, *Acta Cryst.*, vol. 13, p. 919.

[3] The symbol T in the present text signifies a stacking arrangement with trigonal symmetry (see p. 4) whereas other writers have used T to indicate triclinic polymorphs.

hydromuscovites, and are often found to be mixtures of the 1M muscovite with other polymorphs and/or montmorillonite. The various polymorphs of muscovite yield characteristic powder X-ray patterns, 1M being distinguished from 1M*d* by the absence in the latter of *hkl* reflections. The part of the powder pattern most useful for distinguishing the polymorphs is that for spacings between 4·4 and 2·6 Å (Grim *et al.*, 1951). Lithian muscovites generally crystallize in the 2M$_1$ polymorph but when the lithium content is higher than about 3·3 per cent. (lepidolites; see p. 858,) 1M, 2M$_2$ and 3T structures are adopted. Manganoan muscovite has the 1M structure (Heinrich and Levinson, 1955*b*). Of the possible simple polymorphs, 2–O and 6–H have not been observed at all among the micas. The effects of various ionic substitutions (Al, Mg, Fe, Ti) on the *b* cell parameter, and on the relative intensities of basal reflections, have been discussed on page 6.

CHEMISTRY

The principal isomorphous replacements which occur in muscovite are as follows:

For K: Na, Rb, Cs, Ca, Ba.
For octahedral Al: Mg, Fe^{+2}, Fe^{+3}, Mn, Li, Cr, Ti, V.
For (OH): F.
(Si$_6$Al$_2$) can vary to (Si$_7$Al).

The rose-coloured muscovites (rose-muscovites) have very nearly the ideal composition, with low manganese and lithium content, and total iron usually lower than manganese. The varieties of muscovite which result from various substitutions are discussed below, but certain replacements and combinations of replacements result in chemical formulae and structures which can no longer be regarded as belonging to muscovite; these are dealt with more fully in sections on other micas.

Calcium, rubidium and caesium occur in small amounts and there has been no suggestion that their substitution for potassium results in a change from the normal muscovite structure. Sodium does not occur often in high percentage (average about 1 per cent. Na$_2$O, *i.e.* approximately 12 per cent. of the sodium molecule), but when sodium is dominant the name *paragonite* is used and this should be regarded as a separate mineral species (Schaller and Stevens, 1941). Optical properties of paragonite are similar to those of normal muscovite, however, and the structure is 2M$_1$ which is the commonest for muscovite. Experimental data obtained by Eugster and Yoder (1955) indicate that the limit of solid solution of paragonite in muscovite (24 mol. per cent. at 30,000 lb./in.^{2}) is reached at 660°C. Small amounts of barium, substituting for potassium, appear to be accommodated in the 2M$_1$ structure: muscovites with substantial barium content are rare and are known as *oellacherites*. X-ray examination of an oellacherite (Table 5, anal. 5) with 9·89 per cent. BaO showed that it had the 1M structure (Heinrich and Levinson, 1955). The case quoted above is, however, the only one identified by X-rays, and other "oellacherites" reported may be barium biotites.

Vanadium substitutes for octahedral aluminium in small amounts in normal 2M$_1$ muscovites. That it can enter to a larger extent is shown by the existence of the mineral *roscoelite* in which there may be as much as 17 per cent. V_2O_3. Calculation of atomic ratios from analyses shows that vanadium and octahedral aluminium together total four atoms per formula unit. Roscoelites which have been studied by X-ray diffraction are seen to have the 1M structure (Heinrich and Levinson, 1955) and contain more than 15 per cent. V_2O_3. It is probable that roscoelite and oellacherite are distinct chemical and structural species and that there is not a complete series between each of them and muscovite, but too few specimens have been studied for a definite conclusion to be reached. Barium-rich roscoelites have been described and their mica-like character confirmed by X-ray methods, but their polymorphic form has not been identified.

Muscovites have often been reported with between 2 and 4 per cent. Fe_2O_3, and some with equally high FeO content which is usually associated with high SiO_2. Most muscovites contain less than 1 per cent. MnO but purple and blue specimens have been described which contain about 2 per cent. MnO (Eskola, 1914). X-ray examination of one such specimen showed it to be a 1M polymorph (Heinrich and Levinson, 1955) which is unusual for a di-octahedral mica except among phengites, sericites, etc. (see below). A manganoan barian muscovite with 3·49 per cent. MnO and 4·14 per cent. BaO (Hirowatari, 1957) has the $2M_1$ structure with a 5·25, b 9·10, c 19·90 Å, β 95° 40′. Chromium is normally present in muscovites only in trace amounts but chromian muscovites are known with as much as 6 per cent. Cr_2O_3, and these are generally called *fuchsite* or *mariposite*. It has been suggested that the term mariposite be abandoned and that chromium-bearing potassium micas containing more than 1 per cent. Cr_2O_3 should be called fuchsite. Those called mariposite appear to have high SiO_2 and so can be considered as chromian phengites. Fuchsite has the same structure as muscovite with the $2M_1$ cell (Whitmore *et al.*, 1946). Micas with high lithium content are known as *lepidolites* and are discussed as a separate mineral species. Up to about 3·5 per cent. of Li_2O may enter, however, without changing the $2M_1$ muscovite structure (such micas are called lithian muscovites) but 06l reflections with l odd are weaker, indicating less distortion. It may be that rather than replacing aluminium, lithium enters vacant octahedral sites, as in the lepidolites which have a higher lithium content and do not crystallize in the $2M_1$ polymorph.

The average fluorine content of natural muscovite is about 0·6 per cent. and one of the highest recorded is 1·28 per cent. (Lokka, 1943). Fluormuscovite has been synthesized (Eitel, 1954) in which all (OH) is replaced by fluorine and this gives the 1M muscovite powder pattern (Yoder and Eugster, 1955). Fluorine content generally increases with lithium.

Sericite is a term which is used to describe fine-grained white mica (muscovite or paragonite).[1] Sericites are not necessarily chemically different from muscovite although they often have high SiO_2, MgO and H_2O, and low K_2O. Fine-grained specimens which deviate chemically from muscovite in some or all of these respects can be classified further as phengites, hydromuscovites or illites, as described below.

The name *phengite* is used to describe muscovites in which the Si : Al ratio is greater than 3 : 1 and in which increase of Si is accompanied by substitution of Mg or Fe^{+2} for Al in octahedral sites. Schaller (1950), using selected analyses of sericites, illustrates this variation from muscovite to the end-member

---

[1] Material described in the field as "sericite" is sometimes really pyrophyllite.

leucophyllite, $K_2Al_2Mg_2Si_8O_{20}(OH)_4$, in which (Al,Mg) replaces 2Al, and Si replaces (Si,Al). Mariposite is a particular type of phengite with high Cr content (though not as high as fuchsite), and the term *alurgite* has been applied to phengites with appreciable Mn content. Alurgite (with 1·53 per cent. MnO) described by Bilgrami (1956), however, while containing as much as 7·42 per cent. MgO, does not have the high SiO_2 content of a phengite. The 3T polymorph is most common among phengites but $2M_1$ and 1M are also found. No satisfactory correlation has been established between compositional or environmental factors and the occurrence of one or other of the possible polymorphs among phengites.

Table 4. Principal substitutions in the muscovite structure

	K replaced by	Octahedral Al replaced by	Tetrahedral Al replaced by
(a) Muscovite	—	—	—
(a) Paragonite	Na	—	—
(b) Oellacherite	Ba	—	—
(c) Hydromuscovite	$(H_3O)^+$	—	—
(c) Lithian muscovite	—	Li	Si
(a) Lepidolite	—	Li	Si
(b) Roscoelite	—	V	—
(b) Fuchsite	—	Cr	—
Mariposite	—	Cr	Si
(b) Manganoan muscovite	—	Mn	—
Alurgite	—	Mn	Si
(c) Phengite	—	Mg or Fe^{+2}	Si

(a) Distinct mineral species.
(b) Probably a distinct mineral species.
(c) Solid solution with pure muscovite.

Hydromuscovites have high H_2O and low K_2O content, and exhibit the 3T, 1M, 1M*d* and $2M_1$ polymorphs. Some evidence has been produced (Ganguly, 1951; Brown and Norrish, 1952) which shows that extra hydrogen is present in $(H_3O)^+$ ions replacing K^+. Sometimes magnesium is also present to a greater extent than in normal muscovite, apparently as an exchangeable cation (Foster, 1951) although the magnesium may be in the octahedral sites (2Mg replacing K, Al). The small grain size, hence large percentage of unsatisfied surface valencies, may account for the exchangeability of the magnesium (Yoder and Eugster, 1955). A fibrous magnesium-bearing hydromuscovite called *gümbelite* was investigated by Aruja (1944). Its formula is approximately $(K,H_2O)_2(Al_3Mg)Si_6Al_2O_{18}(OH)_6$ and it crystallizes in the $2M_1$ polymorph.

Illite is perhaps the least well defined term commonly applied to mica minerals (see under Clay Minerals, p. 213), and it has often been used to describe mixtures of mica layers with other clay minerals. Chemical analyses show some substitution of silicon for aluminium giving a high Si:Al ratio, accompanied by a deficit of potassium. This may be a case of solid solution replacement in the muscovite structure but it could also be due to a mixed layer muscovite-montmorillonite structure. The four polymorphs mentioned above for hydromuscovite have been identified among specimens classed as illites.

The principal substitutions in the muscovite structure are summarized in Table 4 and some typical analyses of pure muscovites and of chemical variants are given in Table 5.

Table 5. MUSCOVITE ANALYSES

	1.	2.	3.	4.	5.
SiO_2	45·87	45·24	46·01	46·77	41·37
TiO_2	—	0·01	0·00	0·21	—
Al_2O_3	38·69	36·85	35·64	34·75	32·64
Cr_2O_3	—	—	—	—	—
Fe_2O_3	—	0·09	0·13	0·71	—
ZnO	—	—	—	—	1·84
FeO	tr.	0·02	0·00	0·77	—
MnO	tr.	0·12	0·09	—	0·62
MgO	0·10	0·08	0·04	0·92	1·55
CaO	tr.	0·00	1·12	0·13	0·36
BaO	—	—	—	0·13	9·89
Na_2O	0·64	0·64	1·88	0·47	1·51
K_2O	10·08	10·08	8·19	10·61	6·33
Rb_2O	—	0·93	1·20	0·05	—
Cs_2O	—	0·20	0·20	—	—
Li_2O	—	0·49	0·69	0·02	—
F	0·00	0·91	0·54	0·16	—
H_2O^+	4·67	4·12	4·65	4·48	4·05
H_2O^-	—	0·46	0·08	—	—
	100·05	100·24	100·46	100·18	100·16
$O \equiv F$	0·00	0·38	0·23	0·07	—
Total	100·05	99·86	100·23	100·11	100·16
α	1·5595	—	—	1·555	mean
β	1·5930	1·586	—	1·589	R.I.
γ	1·5991	1·589	—	1·590	1·59
$2V\alpha$	45° 38′	46°	—	15°	—
D	2·84	—	2·865	2·82	—

NUMBERS OF IONS ON THE BASIS OF 24(O,OH,F)

	1.	2.	3.	4.	5.
Si	6·093 † }8·00	6·050 }8·00	6·090 }8·00	6·210 }8·00	5·912 }8·00
Al	1·907	1·950	1·910	1·790	2·088
Al	3·975	3·860	3·649	3·650	3·412
Ti	—	—	—	0·021	—
Cr	—	—	—	—	—
Fe^{+3}	—	0·093	0·013	0·071	0·194
Zn	— }4·00	— }4·26	— }4·05	— }4·01	— }4·01
Fe^{+2}	—	0·002	—	0·085	—
Mn	—	0·014	0·010	—	0·075
Mg	0·020	0·022	0·008	0·182	0·330
Li	—	0·264	0·366	0·005	—
Ca	—	—	0·159	0·018	0·055
Ba	—	—	—	0·006	0·554
Na	0·164 }1·87	0·166 }1·98	0·476 }2·13	0·121 }1·95	0·419 }2·18
K	1·706	1·720	1·384	1·800	1·154
Rb	—	0·080	0·102	—	—
Cs	—	0·012	0·012	—	—
(H_3O)	—	—	—	—	—
F	— }4·14	0·385 }4·06	0·113 }4·22	0·067 }4·04	— }3·86
OH	4·136	3·676	4·106	3·968	3·861

1. Muscovite (clear flawless crystal), Methuen Township, Ontario (Hurlbut, 1956). Anal. F. A. Gonyer. *a* 5·18, *b* 8·99, *c* 20·01 Å, β 96°, 2M₁ structure.
2. Rose-muscovite, Pittlite pegmatite, Rociada, New Mexico (Heinrich and Levinson, 1953). Anal. E. H. Oslund. 2M₁ structure.
3. Rose-muscovite, Varuträsk pegmatite, Sweden (Berggren, 1940). Anal. Th. Berggren; rare alkalis spectrographically by C. G. Lindkvist. 2M₁ structure.
4. White muscovite, replacement veins in granodiorite, Sultan Basin, Snohomish Co., Washington (Axelrod and Grimaldi, 1949). 3T structure.
5. Pink barium muscovite (oellacherite), Franklin, New Jersey (Bauer and Berman, 1933). Anal. L. H. Bauer. 1M structure.

† Numbers of ions in this case calculated empirically using density and cell volume.

Table 5. MUSCOVITE ANALYSES—*continued*

	6.	7.	8.	9.	10.
SiO_2	44·4	45·97	46·30	49·16	56·00
TiO_2	2·1	—	0·00	—	—
Al_2O_3	31·7	31·67	33·08	30·81	23·52
Cr_2O_3	2·1	4·81	—	—	0·78
Fe_2O_3	—	2·56	0·00	—	3·30
ZnO	—	—	—	—	—
FeO	2·3	0·53	1·20	1·43	0·51
MnO	0·05	—	0·28	—	—
MgO	0·7	0·31	0·14	2·22	2·12
CaO	0·1	0·15	0·00	—	0·37
BaO	—	—	—	—	—
Na_2O	1·1	1·03	0·63	0·48	2·72
K_2O	10·7	9·07	10·09	10·90	7·03
Rb_2O	—	—	1·37	—	—
Cs_2O	—	—	0·41	—	—
Li_2O	—	—	1·80	—	—
F	—	—	2·06	—	—
H_2O^+	4·7	3·48	3·06	4·73	3·52
H_2O^-	—	0·51	0·34	0·15	—
	99·95	100·09	100·76	100·07	99·87
$O \equiv F$	—	—	0·87	—	—
Total	99·95	100·09	99·89	100·07	99·87
α	1·566	—	—	—	—
β	1·597	1·602	—	—	1·624
γ	1·602	1·603	—	—	—
$2V_\alpha$	38°	36°	—	—	very small
D	2·85	2·88	2·803	—	—

NUMBERS OF IONS ON THE BASIS OF 24(O,OH,F)

	6.	7.	8.	9.	10.
Si	6·033 ⎫8·00	6·268 ⎫8·00	6·270 ⎫8·00	6·536 ⎫8·00	7·421 ⎫8·00
Al	1·967 ⎭	1·732 ⎭	1·730 ⎭	1·464 ⎭	0·579 ⎭
Al	3·113	3·360	3·552	3·365	3·096
Ti	0·172	—	—	—	—
Cr	0·226	0·518	—	—	0·081
Fe^{+3}	—	0·262	—	—	0·330
Zn	— ⎬3·92	— ⎬4·26	— ⎬4·73	— ⎬3·96	— ⎬3·98
Fe^{+2}	0·261	0·061	0·136	0·159	0·057
Mn	0·006	—	0·032	—	—
Mg	0·142	0·063	0·028	0·440	0·419
Li	—	—	0·980	—	—
Ca	0·015	0·022	—	—	0·053
Ba	—	—	—	—	—
Na	0·290 ⎫2·16	0·272 ⎫1·87	0·166 ⎫2·05	0·124 ⎫1·97	0·700 ⎫1·94
K	1·856	1·578	1·742	1·850	1·190
Rb	—	—	0·118	—	—
Cs	—	—	0·024	—	—
(H_3O)	—	—	—	—	—
F	— ⎫4·26	— ⎫3·17	0·882 ⎫3·65	— ⎫4·20	— ⎫3·11
OH	4·262 ⎭	3·166 ⎭	2·766 ⎭	4·196 ⎭	3·112 ⎭

6. Emerald-green fuchsite, quartz conglomerate in staurolite zone of metamorphism, Acworth Township, New Hampshire (Clifford, 1957). Anal. J. Ito.
7. Fuchsite (chrome-muscovite), Pointe du Boise, Manitoba (Whitmore *et al.*, 1946). Anal. D. R. E. Whitmore. *a* 5·20, *b* 9·05, *c* 20·01 Å, $\beta = 95°$. $2M_1$ structure.
8. Grey "lepidolite", Varuträsk pegmatite, Sweden (Berggren, 1940). Anal. Th. Berggren. Rare alkalis, spectrographically by C. G. Lindkvist. $2M_1$ structure.
9. Yellow sericite, Amelia, Virginia (Schaller, 1950). Anal. R. E. Stevens (Includes 0·19% other components).
10. Mariposite, Ross Mine, Hislop township, Ontario (Moore, 1936). Anal. Moorehouse.

Sheet Silicates

Table 5. MUSCOVITE ANALYSES—*continued*

	11.	12.	13.	14.	15.
SiO$_2$	51·22	53·3	48·42	46·17	45·49
TiO$_2$	0·53	0·01	0·87	1·07	0·89
Al$_2$O$_3$	25·91	26·0	27·16	33·85	37·51
Cr$_2$O$_3$	—	—	—	—	—
Fe$_2$O$_3$	4·59	2·5	6·57	0·99	tr.
ZnO	—	—	—	—	—
FeO	1·70	—	0·81	0·99	0·00
MnO	—	—	—	tr.	0·00
MgO	2·84	4·4	tr.	1·44	0·20
CaO	0·16	0·2	tr.	0·00	0·50
BaO	—	—	—	—	—
Na$_2$O	0·17	0·3	0·35	1·08	1·72
K$_2$O	6·09	8·3	11·23	9·60	8·86
Rb$_2$O	—	—	—	—	—
Cs$_2$O	—	—	—	—	—
Li$_2$O	—	—	—	—	—
F	—	—	tr.	—	—
H$_2$O$^+$	7·14	5·7	4·31	4·52	4·92
H$_2$O$^-$	—	—	0·19	0·07	—
	100·35	100·71	99·91	'99·75'	100·09
O≡F	—	—	—	—	—
Total	100·35	100·71	99·91	'99·75'	100·09
α	—	—	—	—	—
β	—	—	—	—	—
γ	1·588	—	—	—	1·600
2V$_\alpha$	5°	—	—	—	30°–40°
D	—	—	—	—	—

NUMBERS OF IONS ON THE BASIS OF 24(O,OH,F)

	11.		12.		13.		14.		15.	
Si	6·750	}8·00	6·885	}8·00	6·597	}8·00	6·151	}8·00	5·958	}8·00
Al	1·250		1·115		1·403		1·849		2·042	
Al	2·773		2·868		2·959		3·467		3·750	
Ti	0·052		0·001		0·089		0·107		0·087	
Cr	—		—		—		—		—	
Fe^{+3}	0·454		0·243		0·672		0·100		—	
Zn	—	}4·02	—	}3·82	—	}3·81	—	}4·07	—	}3·88
Fe^{+2}	0·188		—		0·091		0·110		—	
Mn	—		—		—		—		—	
Mg	0·557		0·709		—		0·285		0·039	
Li										
Ca	0·023		0·026		—		—		0·070	
Ba	0·043		—		—		—		—	
Na	—		0·074	}1·47	0·092	}2·04	0·278	}1·91	0·436	}1·99
K	1·023	}1·85	1·370		1·952		1·632		1·482	
Rb	—		—		—		—		—	
Cs	—		—		—		—		—	
(H$_2$O)	0·757		—		—		—		—	
F	—	}4·00	—	}4·92	—	}3·92	—	}4·02	—	}4·30
OH	4·000		4·918		3·916		4·018		4·300	

11. Hydrous muscovite (fine colloid fraction), Pennsylvanian Underclay, Vermilion Co., Illinois (Grim *et al.*, 1937). Formula according to Brown and Norrish (1952).

12. Illite, St. Austell, Cornwall (Levinson, 1955). Anal. English Clays, Lovering Pochin & Co., Ltd., St. Austell.

13. Muscovite, low grade psammitic schist, Morar, Inverness-shire (Lambert, 1959). Anal. R. St J. Lambert (Ga 25, Cr 30, V 85, Li 30, Ni 15, Co 7, Zr 15, Sr 10, Ba 650, Rb 1750 p.p.m. by Nockolds and Allen).

14. Muscovite, medium grade garnet-mica schist, Morar, Inverness-shire (Lambert, 1959). Anal. R. St J. Lambert (Ga 22, Cr 50, V 100, Li 40, Sc 10, Sr 125, Pb 20, Ba 1800, Rb 1000 p.p.m. by Nockolds and Allen).

15. Muscovite, sillimanite zone, Lake Hammersley, Clove quadrangle, Dutchess County, New York (Barth, 1936). Anal. T. F. W. Barth (Recalculated after subtracting 7 per cent. sillimanite, and 2 per cent. quartz).

When muscovite is decomposed by heating in air no major structural change occurs until about 1000 °C. Zwetsch (1934) reported that α-alumina, γ-alumina and leucite were formed at 1050 °C.: other workers have found spinel, and above 1100 °C. mullite. The study of the K_2O–Al_2O_3–SiO_2 system by Schairer and Bowen (1955) was made under equilibrium conditions and thus the phases found by them are not those reported by others (as above) for non-equilibrium conditions. Sheet muscovite exposed to water vapour at 100 atmospheres at 315 °C. and with pH 11–11·5, develops within it small crystals of diaspore, boehmite, haematite and a spinel (Holser, 1956). The muscovite structure is disrupted comparatively easily by grinding (Mackenzie and Milne, 1953), and the change, which is accompanied by an increase in base exchange capacity, can be followed by X-ray powder photography. Evidence of re-crystallization after prolonged grinding reported by Mackenzie and Milne has been refuted by Yoder and Eugster (1955). The d.t.a. curves of muscovites are variable since they depend very much upon the physical state (particularly grain size) of the specimens. Coarse-grained muscovites show no low temperature endothermic peak, whereas finely ground specimens show a small peak corresponding to the expulsion of adsorbed water below 200 °C. An endothermic peak is sometimes shown at 800°–900 °C. corresponding to the expulsion of structural water and may be followed by exothermic peaks at various temperatures according to the nature of the recrystallization product (leucite, γ-Al_2O_3, spinel, etc.). The d.t.a. curves for illites are discussed elsewhere in the section on clay minerals; hydromuscovites yield similar results. Decomposition of muscovite in acid solution takes place between 300 °C. and 400 °C. but is prevented by the presence of excess KCl, and the synthesis of muscovite from solutions of $Al(OH)_3$, SiO_2, and KCl at 400 °C. is favoured if the KCl concentration is high (Gruner, 1939, 1944). Muscovite has been synthesized also from kaolinite with excess KCl in acid solution (Gruner, *loc. cit.*) and sericite was among the clay minerals produced by heating felspars and other aluminosilicates in CO_2 charged water at 300 °C. (Norton, 1939). Morey and Chen (1955) found that 1M muscovite and boehmite are produced on the surface of orthoclase when water vapour at 350 °C. and 5000 lb./in.^{2} is passed over it for 103 days, and muscovite is formed similarly on an albite with only 0·20 per cent. K_2O.

The hydrothermal synthesis of muscovite has been achieved using a wide variety of initial materials with compositions lying within the K_2O–Al_2O_3–SiO_2–H_2O system (Yoder and Eugster, 1955). These materials were in various forms: synthetic minerals, natural analysed minerals (*e.g.* kaolinite), glasses of potassium felspar composition, synthetic glasses of the anhydrous muscovite composition, and decomposed natural muscovite (fine-grained clay muscovites and large crystals of known polymorphic form). The products were identified by X-ray diffraction and electron microscopy and it was found that muscovite could be formed in all cases at suitable temperature and pressure. The upper stability limit of muscovite is represented by the curve (Fig. 7) above which sanidine, corundum and water vapour are the stable phases. 2M, 1M and 1M*d* polymorphs were synthesized but their separate stability ranges could be established only qualitatively. 1M*d* was generally obtained in the runs at lowest temperature and of shortest duration, 1M at higher and 2M at the highest temperatures, thus indicating the order of increasing stability at high temperatures. This was further confirmed when 3T and 1M muscovites were seen to invert to 2M on heating, although the 2M polymorph generally persists at lower temperatures, indicating a very sluggish inversion. Yoder and Eugster have also determined the equilibrium curve for the reaction muscovite + quartz ⇌ potassium felspar + sillimanite + vapour, which is seen to lie only 15°C. below the muscovite breakdown curve. This reaction has some bearing on the breakdown of muscovite in nature, but other reactions involving muscovite and the formation of felspar may occur, and furthermore, the presence of chemical substituents in natural muscovites may give rise to considerably different breakdown conditions. Some preliminary work in the investigation of the system $KAlSi_3O_8$–$NaAlSi_3O_8$–Al_2O_3–H_2O has been reported (Eugster and Yoder, 1955; see pp. 25 and 32): the mineral assemblages are illustrated in Fig. 5. Muscovite is regarded as one of the minerals most stable to weathering, but illites are readily altered. The weathering of muscovite may proceed through illite and hydro-

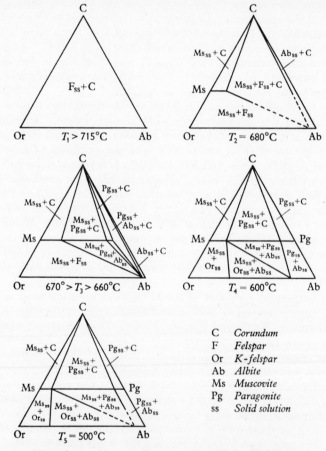

FIG. 5. Mineral assemblages in the system $NaAlSi_3O_8$–$KAlSi_3O_8$–Al_2O_3–H_2O at selected temperatures and 30,000 lbs./in.^{2} water pressure. The hydrous phases are projected on to the albite–potassium felspar–corundum plane (after Eugster and Yoder, 1955).

muscovite to montmorillonite and eventually kaolinite, by loss of potassium and increase of water and silica, but it has not been established that this sequence involves a continuous structural rearrangement. Fluormuscovite has been synthesized (Eitel, 1952; Yoder and Eugster, 1955; and others), but its stability field has not been determined.

OPTICAL AND PHYSICAL PROPERTIES

All muscovites are optically negative, but refractive indices, birefringence and 2V vary with chemical and structural differences. The refractive indices generally fall within the ranges shown in Table 6 column 1, but values as low as 1·542, 1·578 and 1·579 have been reported for α, β and γ respectively. 2V generally lies between 30° and 47° but the micas with the 3T structure are uniaxial, and many phengites show 2V between 0° and 20°. The optic axial plane in most muscovites is perpendicular to (010) with $\gamma = y$ and $\alpha : z = 0°$ to 20°, $\beta : x = 1°$ to 3°.

Table 6. OPTICAL DATA FOR MUSCOVITES, FUCHSITE AND ROSCOELITE

	Normal muscovites	Rose muscovites	Lithian muscovites	Fuchsite	Roscoelite
α	1·552–1·574	1·555	1·532	1·559–1·569	1·610
β	1·582–1·610	1·586	1·552	1·593–1·604	1·685
γ	1·587–1·616	1·592	1·556	1·597–1·611	1·704
δ	0·036–0·049	0·037	0·024	0·035–0·042	0·094
$2V_\alpha$	30°–47°	45°	34°	30°–46°	$24\frac{1}{2}°$–$39\frac{1}{2}°$
O.A.P.	$\perp$(010)	$\perp$(010)	$\perp$(010)	$\perp$(010)	—
Pleochroism:					
α	—	—	—	blue	green-brown
β	—	—	—	yellow-green	olive-green
γ	—	—	—	green	olive-green

The refractive indices of rose muscovites are lower than the averages for all muscovites, and their 2V is higher. This is in accordance with a trend throughout the muscovites for refractive indices (and birefringence) to increase with increase in iron (particularly Fe^{+3}) and Mn content, and for those with least Mg and Fe to have the largest 2V. Refractive indices increase also with decreasing Al content. In the most recent survey of the optical properties of muscovite (Heinrich *et al.*, 1953), using data from many available analyses, it was found that no convincing direct or inverse relationship (other than a general trend) was shown between optical properties and percentages of given oxides, or combinations of oxides. Such correlation has been attempted by Volk (1939), Winchell and Winchell (1951) and others. Although the colour of rose muscovite is similar to that of lepidolite there is in fact no correlation between colour and Li content. It seems that the pink colour of rose muscovite and of lepidolite is due to the small amount of Mn present perhaps as Mn^{+3}, its preponderance over Fe^{+3}, and the absence of Fe^{+2} (Heinrich *et al.*, 1953). The colour of pale green muscovites is probably due to Fe^{+2}, and the buff or brown specimens have more Fe^{+3}. A close balance of Fe^{+2} and Mn may occur in colourless muscovite, and ruby muscovites have greater refractive indices and greater Fe^{+3} and Ti contents. The fuchsite of Table 5, anal. 6, is pleochroic, with α colourless to light emerald-green, β green, and γ dark emerald-green. Refractive indices of chromian muscovites increase with increasing Cr content. The rather rare manganoan muscovite is blue, has 2V about 40°, and a mean refractive index of 1·59. Lithian muscovites have lower refractive indices, but their optical properties are influenced more by the content of iron and manganese than by the percentage of Li_2O. Optical properties of roscoelite are shown in Table 6, while the manganoan barian muscovite (Hirowatari, 1957) has α 1·566, β 1·598, γ 1·602, $2V_\alpha$ 36°. Muscovites of the high silica variety often have the 3T structure and are hence uniaxial and should show $2V = 0°$; some, however, have a small 2V (about 11°). Those with the $2M_1$ structure have the normal larger 2V, and some specimens with intermediate 2V are seen by X-rays to be mixtures of 3T and $2M_1$. The refractive indices of phengites, illites and hydrous muscovites are higher than those of normal muscovites because of the replacement of $[Al]^4$ by Si and of $[Al]^6$ by Fe^{+2} or Mg. The interference figure produced by superposition of thin plates of muscovite rotated with respect to one another may be indistinct, or may be similar to the uniaxial figure obtained from quartz; this may explain why some muscovites with $2M_1$ structure nevertheless show nearly uniaxial interference figures. Colour zoning and the zoning of inclusions sometimes occur in muscovites and can be of the core–margin, or oscillatory type, the darker zones generally having higher refractive indices and higher 2V. Zones often follow pseudo-symmetry hexagonal outlines in a sheet but may also alternate along the *z*-axis direction.

Inclusions of magnetite and haematite are common in muscovite and are usually concentrated at the cores of "books". It has been suggested that at the initial temperature of crystallization, muscovite can have a high iron content which on cooling exsolves as iron oxide. The cores of crystals were originally hotter than the margins and so held more iron which is subsequently exsolved. Where muscovite and biotite occur together the iron is all taken by the biotite and the muscovite is free from inclusions. Other minerals sometimes occur as inclusions, *e.g.* quartz, albite, apatite, staurolite, zircon and garnet; gas bubbles and organic material are not uncommon (Heinrich *et al.*, 1953). The only good cleavage is {001} but planes of parting {110} and {010} also occur, and some specimens of muscovite show in addition to these a pseudo-cleavage parallel to a lamellar structure similar to the perthitic lamellae of alkali felspar; this suggests that the muscovite has been formed by replacement of felspar. Parallel intergrowths of muscovite with biotite are not uncommon and in most cases their respective optic axial planes are mutually inclined at 60°. Much information about the topology of mica crystal surfaces has been obtained by the use of multiple beam interferometry (Tolansky, 1948). By this method spiral growth proceeding from screw dislocations can be observed, and the presence of inclusions and vacuoles is easily recognized. Steps in the surface of muscovite are frequently observed, the thickness of which is a multiple of the 002 spacing ($\simeq 10$ Å), but in some specimens even the smallest surface irregularities are absent. A recent application of such sheets is in the construction of interference filters to produce strictly monochromatic light with high intensity; the thickness of sheet needs to be constant within very fine limits. The hardness of muscovite is usually given as $2\frac{1}{2}$–3 on the Mohs scale, but as would be expected from the sheet-like structure, hardness varies with direction. Switzer (1941) gave for muscovite and biotite a hardness of $2\frac{1}{2}$ parallel to (001) and 4 perpendicular to (001). Further anisotropy of hardness when measured in various directions parallel to (001) has been recorded (Bloss *et al.*, 1959), using the Knoop indentation method. Maximum hardness on (001) in mica is observed when the long axis of the indentation is parallel to the *y* axis.

Age determinations have been made for muscovites using the potassium argon method and in some cases the ^{87}Rb$\rightarrow$^{87}Sr decay.

DISTINGUISHING FEATURES

Muscovite differs from phlogopite and biotite in having its optic axial plane perpendicular to (010). It may be possible to determine the [010] direction by a percussion figure (see p. 9); if not, X-ray methods may be used. Biotite specimens are generally much darker. Muscovite usually has a higher 2V than phlogopite, biotite and talc, and this serves to distinguish it from the latter mineral for which the optic axial plane is also perpendicular to (010). The high birefringence of muscovites distinguishes them from kaolinites, chlorites and other platy silicates with the exception of pyrophyllite which, however, has a higher 2V. X-ray powder patterns may be used to distinguish between dioctahedral and tri-octahedral micas, and they can also be used to distinguish between the different polymorphs of muscovite (see for example Yoder and Eugster, 1955).

PARAGENESIS

Muscovite occurs in a wide range of regionally metamorphosed sediments and is found in rocks belonging to each of the zones of progressive regional metamorphism. In the chlorite zone the formation of muscovite is due essentially to the recrystallization of the original sericitic mica of the sediment, and in many argillaceous rocks its appearance is the first overt sign of metamorphism (Jakob *et al.*, 1933). In the chlorite zone, muscovite is a characteristic constituent of the albite–chlorite–sericite schists. At slightly higher grades of metamorphism, and particularly where the mica is segregated into bands, sericite phyllites are typical products of the metamorphic recrystallization. In the biotite zone muscovite is generally less abundant than in rocks of corresponding compositions in the chlorite zone, due to reactions of the type:

$$5(OH)_4Mg_3Si_2O_5 + 3(OH)_2KAl_3Si_3O_{10} \rightarrow$$
serpentine   muscovite

$$3(OH)_2KMg_3AlSi_3O_{10} + 3(OH)_4Mg_2Al_2SiO_5 + 7SiO_2 + 4H_2O$$
phlogopite   amesite

Where the original sediments were richer in aluminium, muscovite is often associated with chlorite and chloritoid (Snelling, 1957). Muscovite is often present throughout the almandine zone in which it is commonly represented in the garnetiferous mica schists. In other almandine zone rocks, however, muscovite and biotite react to form potassium felspar and almandine:

$$(OH)_2KAl_3Si_3O_{10} + (OH)_2K(Fe^{+2},Mg)_3AlSi_3O_{10} + 3SiO_2 \rightarrow$$
muscovite   biotite

$$2KAlSi_3O_8 + (Fe^{+2},Mg)_3Al_2Si_3O_{12} + 2H_2O$$
potassium   almandine
felspar

Muscovite (Table 5, anal. 15) may also occur in schists and gneisses of the sillimanite zone but at this grade of metamorphism it is commonly dissociated to form potassium felspar and sillimanite. Thus, although the assemblage muscovite–quartz is stable over a large part of the PT-range of regional metamorphism, at temperatures $\simeq 600°$–$650°$C. it is replaced by felspar and sillimanite:

$$(OH)_2KAl_3Si_3O_{10} + SiO_2 \rightarrow Al_2SiO_5 + KAlSi_3O_8 + H_2O$$

muscovite ⎯⎯⎯⎯⎯ sillimanite ⎯⎯ potassium felspar

Muscovite is extremely rare in the Pre-Cambrian Grenville gneisses of south-western Quebec. It is absent from potassium felspar- and sillimanite-bearing rocks containing quartz, and Kretz (1959) has suggested that the lack of muscovite in other assemblages is probably due to its instability in combination with garnet and hornblende:

$$(OH)_2KAl_3Si_3O_{10} + (Mg,Fe^{+2})_3Al_2Si_3O_{12} \rightarrow$$

muscovite ⎯⎯⎯⎯⎯⎯⎯ garnet

$$(OH)_2K(Mg,Fe^{+2})_3AlSi_3O_{10} + 2Al_2SiO_5 + SiO_2$$

biotite ⎯⎯⎯⎯⎯ sillimanite ⎯ quartz

$$3(OH)_2KAl_3Si_3O_{10} + Ca_4[(Mg,Fe^{+2})_9Al](AlSi_{15})O_{44}(OH)_4 \rightarrow$$

muscovite ⎯⎯⎯⎯⎯⎯⎯ hornblende

$$3(OH)_2K(Mg,Fe^{+2})_3AlSi_3O_{10} + 4CaAl_2Si_2O_8 + 7SiO_2 + 2H_2O$$

biotite ⎯⎯⎯⎯⎯ anorthite ⎯ quartz

Other reactions involving the breakdown of muscovite during metamorphism have been proposed by Turner and Verhoogen (1951) and Ramberg (1952).

Lambert (1959) has shown that the composition of the white mica (Table

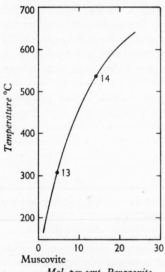

FIG. 6. The paragonite content of muscovites from metamorphic rocks of varying grade (after Lambert, 1959). Numbers 13 and 14 refer to analyses in Table 5.

5, anals. 13, 14) changes with increasing metamorphic grade. Muscovites in rocks of the garnet zone have a lower Si, Fe^{+3}, Fe^{+2} and a higher Al and Na content than those of the biotite zone and show a marked trend from the phengite to the muscovite composition. The paragonite content of muscovites from some psammitic and pelitic Moine schists of increasing grade, in relation to the muscovite–paragonite equilibrium curve (Yoder and Eugster, 1955), is shown in Fig. 6. Earlier Miyashiro (1958) demonstrated likewise, on the basis of their refractive indices, that the Fe^{+2} content of the muscovites in the higher grade rocks of the Abukuma Plateau, Japan, is lower than that in the muscovites of the rocks of lower grade.

Muscovite is also formed during the metamorphism of intermediate and acid rocks, those of intermediate composition giving rise to calcite–albite–sericite–chlorite schists, and those of acid composition to muscovite–quartz schists. This sericitization may begin, and be complete, at an early stage of the metamorphism, and although the reverse reaction muscovite→potassium felspar takes place at an advanced stage, there is a wide temperature range in which muscovite and potassium felspar occur together as a stable assemblage.

Muscovite is much less common as a product of thermal metamorphism, and in argillaceous sediments the formation of muscovite does not usually occur until the rocks have reached a medium grade of metamorphism. Under conditions in which there is a sufficiency of water, muscovite may remain stable at higher grades, but in general, with increasing metamorphism, it diminishes in amount and is replaced by potassium felspar and andalusite:

$$(OH)_2KAl_3Si_3O_{10} + SiO_2 \rightarrow KAlSi_3O_8 + Al_2SiO_5 + H_2O$$

muscovite   potassium   andalusite
felspar

Muscovite is less common than biotite in acid igneous rocks, but occurs in the muscovite and muscovite–biotite granites. It is the most common mica in aplites and has been reported as a constituent of some rhyolite porphyries. Most muscovite-bearing granites contain both potassium felspar and plagioclase, and are also often rich in quartz (Chayes, 1952). In such granites muscovite occurs in interstitial crystals as well as in small dispersed flakes within felspar. A similar relationship is also common in the quartz- and mica-rich rock, greisen, which is generally considered to have been derived from a granite modified by autometasomatic changes that occurred during the last phase of its crystallization. Some greisen, however, *e.g.* Grainsgill, may represent a filter press differentiate of normal granite (Harker, 1895). The textural relationships of muscovites in granites are generally considered to indicate two generations of muscovite crystallization. The *PT* stability curve of muscovite (Yoder and Eugster, 1955) intersects the *PT* minimum melting curve of granite (Tuttle and Bowen, 1953) at approximately 1500 atmospheres pressure and 700°C.

(Fig. 7). Thus muscovite can crystallize from a liquid of granite composition at pressures above 1500 atmospheres, but below this pressure muscovite can form only in the solid state. The larger interstitial muscovite crystals in granites could thus have formed in equilibrium with the liquid, or have crystallized in the solid state at any pressure or temperature, below the stability curve of muscovite. The smaller flakes of muscovite commonly dispersed within the felspar probably crystallized by the leaching of $K_2O \cdot 6SiO_2$ from the felspar at temperatures below the granite liquidus. In the

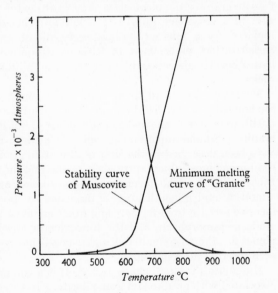

Fig. 7. Stability curve of muscovite (after Yoder and Eugster, 1955).

muscovite-rich granites of New England the greatest amount of muscovite present with plagioclase, recorded by Chayes (1952), is 12·2 per cent. The amount of normative corundum in granite analyses indicates that the muscovite content of granites is probably limited; moreover the investigation of the system K_2O–Al_2O_3–SiO_2 by Schairer and Bowen (1955) showed that granite magmas are unlikely to contain much more alumina than is required by the felspar, and granites with a high muscovite content probably owe their mineralogical constitution to metasomatic reactions.

Some muscovite-bearing granites contain cordierite, *e.g.* the Dartmoor granite (Brammall and Harwood, 1932), and in such granites the muscovite may, in part or whole, have been derived from the alteration of xenocrystal cordierite. Muscovite occurs abundantly in some argillaceous rocks in the inner aureoles of muscovite-bearing granites, and its crystallization is probably due to the diffusion of potassium into kyanite- or andalusite-bearing rocks:

$$3Al_2SiO_5 + K_2O + 3SiO_2 + 2H_2O \rightarrow 2KAl_3Si_3O_{10}(OH)_2$$

Muscovite is the characteristic product of fluorine metasomatism (greisenization) at granite–slate contacts, and the production of the white mica at the expense of such minerals as felspar, andalusite and cordierite is a reversal of the processes by which these minerals are formed in thermal metamorphism. Greisenization is especially typical in the inner aureoles of muscovite-bearing granites, *e.g.* Dartmoor, Skiddaw and Leinster granites. The greisenization of the St. Austell granite has been described by Exley (1958). In the biotite, muscovite, lithionite (zinnwaldite), and fluorite granites of this complex the potassium felspar, particularly along joint planes, is replaced by mica and secondary silica released by the conversion of the felspar to mica. In the fluorite granites the plagioclase, An_7, is altered marginally and along the cleavages to a secondary mica with a low birefringence, and finally is completely replaced by a microcrystalline aggregate of secondary mica and kaolinite. Sericitization, particularly of felspars, is common in the early stages of the hydrothermal alteration of many igneous (Vitaliano, 1957) and metamorphic rocks.

Muscovite occurs in fissure and replacement veins in the granodiorite of Snohomish County, Washington, and is considered by Axelrod and Grimaldi (1949) to be due to the metasomatic effect of hot gases along the sheeting in the granite. Similar replacement veins, of an iron-rich mica, topaz and quartz, have been described in the Mourne Mountain granites, Northern Ireland, where they occur most abundantly close to the margin of the granite (Nockolds and Richey, 1939). The formation of hydromica associated with hydrothermal alteration and mineralization is discussed by Bonorino (1959). The development of sericite from felspars and other minerals is a common feature of retrograde metamorphism, and the formation of sericite along fractures and shear planes in otherwise unaltered rocks shows that its development is favoured by such internal movements.

Muscovite (Table 5, anals. 1, 2, 3, 4) is a common constituent of pegmatites associated with granite and granodiorite. In this paragenesis muscovite occurs both as large crystalline "books" and as fine-grained sericite; the latter often replaces felspar, tourmaline, spodumene, beryl, topaz or kyanite, and is usually located in the wall rock at the pegmatite margins; dendritic intergrowths with quartz are not uncommon.

An investigation by Whitmore *et al.* (1946) of the paragenesis of chromium-bearing muscovites has shown that they occur most commonly in hydrothermal carbonate replacement zones and associated with quartz–sulphide gold deposits. Fuchsite together with corundum and kyanite has been recorded by Hutton (1940) in a corundum-bearing schist from Mikonui, New Zealand. Other metamorphic occurrences of fuchsite (Table 5, anal. 6) from a staurolite zone quartz conglomerate have been described by Clifford (1957) and from quartzites and conglomerates by Padget (1956). Lithian muscovites are generally associated with late stage hydrothermal crystallization and are common in pegmatites. Rose-muscovite (Table 5, anal. 2) is restricted to pegmatites and is located in zones of replacement of Na–Li type. It is commonly associated with cleavelandite, lepidolite, spodumene, topaz, beryl and tantalum-bearing minerals, and is often pseudomorphous after spodumene and topaz. Rose muscovite may also replace cleavelandite and beryl, and often occurs as oriented overgrowths on lepidolite and normal muscovite (Heinrich and Levinson, 1953).

The muscovites of pegmatites almost invariably have the $2M_1$ structure, but various polymorphs are found in muscovites of hydrothermal and metamorphic paragenesis.

Muscovite is less common in sediments than was originally believed, and much of the fine-grained micaceous material of these rocks has been shown to consist of mixed-layer structures of muscovite and montmorillonite, mixtures of 2M-muscovite, pyrophyllite and kaolinite, and illite. The growth of authigenic illites in sediments may result from the recrystallization of montmorillonite and kaolinite, potassium being obtained from sea water (Grim *et al.*, 1949)

$$3Al_2Si_4O_{10}(OH)_2 + 2K^+ \rightarrow 2KAl_3Si_3O_{10}(OH)_2 + 6SiO_2 + 2H^+$$

$$3Al_4Si_4O_{10}(OH)_8 + 4K^+ \rightarrow 4KAl_3Si_3O_{10}(OH)_2 + 6H_2O + 4H^+$$

The alteration and weathering of muscovite and the authigenic growth of muscovite in sediments has been reviewed by Yoder and Eugster (1955).

REFERENCES

Aruja, E., 1944. An X-ray study on the crystal structure of gümbelite. *Min. Mag.*, vol. 27, p. 11.

Axelrod, J. M. and Grimaldi, F. S., 1949. Muscovite with small optic axial angle. *Amer. Min.*, vol. 34, p. 559.

Barth, T. F. W., 1936. Structural and petrologic studies in Dutchess County, New York. Pt. II. *Bull. Geol. Soc. Amer.*, vol. 47, p. 776.

Bauer, L. H. and Berman, H., 1933. Barium-muscovite from Franklin, N. J. *Amer. Min.*, vol. 18, p. 30.

Berggren, T., 1940. Minerals of the Varuträsk pegmatite. XV. Analyses of the mica minerals and their interpretation. *Geol. För. Förh. Stockholm*, vol. 62, p. 182.

Bilgrami, S. A., 1956. Manganese silicate minerals from Chikla, Bhandara District, India. *Min. Mag.*, vol. 31, p. 236.

Bloss, F. D., Shekarchi, E. and Shell, H. R., 1959. Hardness of synthetic and natural micas. *Amer. Min.*, vol. 44, p. 33.

Bonorino, F. G., 1959. Hydrothermal alteration in the Front Ranges mineral belt. *Bull. Geol. Soc. Amer.*, vol. 70, p. 53.

Brammall, A. and **Harwood, H. F.**, 1932. The Dartmoor granites. *Quart. Journ. Geol. Soc.*, vol. 88, p. 171.

Brown, G. and **Norrish, K.**, 1952. Hydrous micas. *Min. Mag.*, vol. 29, p. 929.

Chayes, F., 1952. The finer-grained calcalkaline granites of New England. *Journ. Geol.*, vol. 60, p. 207.

Clifford, T. N., 1957. Fuchsite from a Silurian quartz conglomerate, Acworth Township, New Hampshire. *Amer. Min.*, vol. 42, p. 566.

Eitel, W., 1952. Synthesis of fluorosilicates of the mica and amphibole group. *Proc. Internat. Symp. on the Reactivity of Solids, Gothenburg*, p. 335.

Eskola, P., 1914. On the petrology of the Orijärvi region in south-western Finland. *Bull. Comm. géol. Finlande*, No. 40, p. 37.

Eugster, H. P. and **Yoder, H. S., Jr.**, 1955. The join muscovite–paragonite. *Carnegie Inst. Washington, Ann. Rep. Dir. Geophys. Lab.*, 1954–1955, p. 124.

Exley, C. S., 1958. Magmatic dfferentiation and alteration in the St. Austell granite. *Quart. Journ. Geol. Soc.*, vol. 114, p. 197.

Foster, M. D., 1951. The importance of the exchangeable magnesium and cation-exchange capacity in the study of montmorillonitic clays. *Amer. Min.*, vol. 36, p. 717.

Ganguly, A. K., 1951. Hydration of exchangeable cations in silicate minerals. *Soil. Sci.*, vol. 71, p. 239.

Gatineau, L. and **Méring, J.**, 1958. Précisions sur la structure de la muscovite. *Clay Min. Bull.*, vol. 3, p. 238.

Grim, R. E., Bradley, W. F. and **Brown, G.**, 1951. The mica clay minerals, in *X-ray identification and crystal structures of clay minerals*. Min. Soc., Chap. 5, p. 138.

—— **Bray, R. H.** and **Bradley, W. F.**, 1937. The mica in argillaceous sediments. *Amer. Min.*, vol. 22, p. 813.

—— **Dietz, R. S.** and **Bradley, W. F.**, 1949. Clay mineral composition of some sediments from the Pacific Ocean off the California coast and the Gulf of California. *Bull. Geol. Soc. Amer.*, vol. 60, p. 1785.

Gruner, J. W., 1939. Formation and stability of muscovite in acid solutions at elevated temperatures. *Amer. Min.*, vol. 24, p. 624.

—— 1944. The hydrothermal alteration of feldspars in acid solutions between 300 and 400°C. *Econ. Geol.*, vol. 39, p. 578.

Harker, A., 1895. Carrock Fell : a study in the variation of igneous rock-magmas— Part III. The Grainsgill greisen. *Quart. Journ. Geol. Soc.*, vol. 51, p. 139.

Heinrich, E. W. and **Levinson, A. A.**, 1953. Studies in the mica group; mineralogy of the rose muscovites. *Amer. Min.*, vol. 38, p. 25.

—— and **Levinson, A. A.**, 1955a. Studies in the mica group; polymorphism among the high silica sericites. *Amer. Min.*, vol. 40, p. 983.

—— —— 1955b. Studies in the mica group; manganoan-muscovite from Mattkär, Finland. *Amer. Min.*, vol. 40, p. 1132.

—— —— 1955c. Studies in the mica group; X-ray data on roscoelite and barium-muscovite. *Amer. Journ. Sci.*, vol. 253, p. 39.

—— —— **Levandowski, D. W.** and **Hewitt, C. H.**, 1953. *Studies in the natural history of micas*. University of Michigan Engineering Research Institute. Project M.978 ; final report.

Hendricks, S. B. and **Jefferson, M. E.**, 1939. Polymorphism of the micas. *Amer. Min.*, vol. 24, p. 729.

Hirowatari, F., 1957. Manganobarian muscovite from the manganese deposit of the Muramatsu mine, Nagasaki Prefecture, Japan. *Mem. Fac. Sci. Kyushu Univ., Ser. D. Geol.*, vol. 5, No. 4, p. 191.

Holser, W. T., 1956. Hydrothermal alteration of muscovite in steam gage-glasses. *Amer. Min.*, vol. 41, p. 799.

Hurlbut, C. S., Jr., 1956. Muscovite from Methuen Township, Ontario. *Amer. Min.*, vol. 41, p. 892.

Hutton, C. O., 1940. Optical properties and chemical composition of two micas from Westland, South Island, New Zealand. *New Zealand Journ. Sci. Tech.*, B, vol. 21, p. 330.

Jackson, W. W. and West, J., 1930. The crystal structure of muscovite—KAl$_2$ (AlSi$_3$)O$_{10}$(OH)$_2$. *Zeit. Krist.*, vol. 76, p. 221.

—— —— 1933. The crystal structure of muscovite—KAl$_2$(AlSi$_3$)O$_{10}$(OH)$_2$. *Zeit. Krist.*, vol. 85, p. 160.

Jakob, J., Friedlaender, C. and Brandenberg, E., 1933. Über Neubildung von Sericit. *Schweiz. Min. Petr. Mitt.*, vol. 13, p. 74.

Kretz, R., 1959. Chemical study of garnet, biotite and hornblende from gneisses of southwestern Quebec, with emphasis on distribution of elements in coexisting minerals. *Journ. Geol.*, vol. 67, p. 371.

Lambert, R. St J., 1959. The mineralogy and metamorphism of the Moine Schists of the Morar and Knoydart districts of Inverness-shire. *Trans. Roy. Soc. Edin.*, vol. 63, p. 553.

Levinson, A. A., 1953. Studies in the mica group: relationship between polymorphism and composition in the muscovite–lepidolite series. *Amer. Min.*, vol. 38, p. 88.

—— 1955. Studies in the mica group: polymorphism among illites and hydrous micas. *Amer. Min.*, vol. 40, p. 41.

—— and Heinrich, E. W., 1954. Studies in the mica group: single crystal data on phlogopites, biotites and manganophyllites. *Amer. Min.*, vol. 39, p. 937.

Lokka, L., 1943. Beiträge zur Kenntnis des Chemismus der finnischen Minerale. *Bull. Comm. géol. Finlande*, No. 129.

Mackenzie, R. C. and Milne, A. A., 1953. The effect of grinding on micas. I. Muscovite. *Min. Mag.*, vol. 30, p. 178.

Miyashiro, A., 1958. Regional metamorphism of the Gosaisyo–Takanuki district in the central Abukuma Plateau. *Journ. Fac. Sci., Univ. Tokyo, Sec. II*, vol. 11, p. 219.

Moore, E. S., 1936. Ann. Rept. Ontario Dept. Mines, vol. 45, p. 16.

Morey, G. W. and Chen, W. T., 1955. The action of hot water on some feldspars. *Carnegie Inst. Washington, Ann. Rep. Dir. Geophys. Lab.*, 1954–1955, p. 143.

Nockolds, S. R. and Richey, J. E., 1939. Replacement veins in the Mourne Mountains granites, N. Ireland. *Amer. Journ. Sci.*, vol. 237, p. 27.

Norton, F. H., 1939. Hydrothermal formation of clay minerals in the laboratory. *Amer. Min.*, vol. 24, p. 1.

Padget, P., 1956. The Pre-Cambrian geology of West Finmark. *Norsk. Geol. Tids.*, vol. 36, p. 80.

Roy, R., 1949. Decomposition and resynthesis of the micas. *Journ. Amer. Ceram. Soc.*, vol. 32, p. 204.

Schairer, J. F. and Bowen, N. L., 1945. The system K$_2$O–Al$_2$O$_3$–SiO$_2$. *Amer. Journ. Sci.*, vol. 253, p. 681.

Schaller, W. T., 1950. An interpretation of the composition of high-silica sericites. *Min. Mag.*, vol. 29, p. 406.

—— and Stevens, R. E., 1941. The validity of paragonite as a mineral species. *Amer. Min.*, vol. 26, p. 541.

Smith, J. V. and Yoder, H. S., 1956. Experimental and theoretical studies of the mica polymorphs. *Min. Mag.*, vol. 31, p. 209.

Snelling, N. J., 1957. Notes on the petrology and mineralogy of the Barrovian metamorphic zones. *Geol. Mag.*, vol. 94, p. 297.

Switzer, G., 1941.   Hardness of micaceous minerals.   *Amer. Journ. Sci.,* vol. 239, p. 316.

Tilley, C. E., 1926.   Some mineralogical transformations in crystalline schists.   *Min. Mag.,* vol. 21, p. 34.

Tolansky, S., 1948.   *Multiple-beam interferometry of surfaces and films.*   The Clarendon Press, Oxford.

Vitaliano, C. J., 1957.   Wall-rock alteration in the Broken Hills Range, Nevada.   *Journ. Geol.,* vol. 65, p. 167.

Volk, G. W., 1939.   Optical and chemical studies of muscovite.   *Amer. Min.,* vol. 24, p. 255.

Whitmore, D. R. E., Berry, L. G. and **Hawley, J. E.,** 1946.   Chrome micas.   *Amer. Min.,* vol. 31, p. 1.

Winchell, A. N. and **Winchell, H.,** 1951.   *Elements of optical mineralogy.*   Part II, New York.

Wright, F. E., 1914.   The optical properties of roscoelite.   *Amer. Journ. Sci.,* ser. 4, vol. 38, p. 305.

Yoder, H. S. and **Eugster, H. P.,** 1955.   Synthetic and natural muscovites.   *Geochim. et Cosmochim. Acta.,* vol. 8, p. 225.

Zwetsch, A., 1934.   Röntgenuntersuchungen in der Keramik.   *Ber. deut. keram. Ges.,* vol. 14, p. 2.

Paragonite

$Na_2Al_4[Si_6Al_2O_{20}](OH)_4$

MONOCLINIC $(-)$

α	1·564–1·580
β	1·594–1·609
γ	1·600–1·609
δ	0·028–0·038
$2V_\alpha$	0°–40°

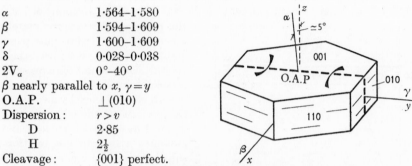

β nearly parallel to x, $\gamma = y$
O.A.P. $\perp(010)$
Dispersion: $r > v$
     D   2·85
     H $2\frac{1}{2}$
Cleavage: {001} perfect.
Colour: Colourless, pale yellow; colourless in thin section.
Unit cell: a 5·13, b 8·89, $c \sin \beta$ 18·99 Å, β 95°.
               $Z = 2$.   Space group probably $C2/c$.
Not attacked by cold HCl or H_2SO_4.

The chemical composition of paragonite differs from that of muscovite in that sodium replaces potassium. The name is from the Greek *paragon*, misleading, and was used because the mineral was originally mistaken for talc. Paragonite usually occurs in massive scaly aggregates, the fine-grained nature of which makes purification and study difficult, so that comparatively little is known about the mineral.

STRUCTURE

The cell parameters quoted above are those measured by Bannister (1943) for paragonite from Monte Campione (*cf.* anal. 1, Table 7) which contains 6·28 per cent. Na_2O and 2·17 per cent. K_2O (Schaller and Stevens, 1941). Gruner (1942) gave b 8·92 Å and $c \sin \beta$ 19·37 Å for a synthetic paragonite. The substitution of potassium by the smaller sodium ion results in a smaller unit cell than that of muscovite, particularly in the z direction, but the similarity between the cells of paragonite and of a $2M_1$ muscovite is evident. A paragonite has been reported, however, which has a 3-layered trigonal (3T) unit cell (Dietrich, 1956). Finely-ground paragonite shows an increase of basal spacing d_{002} from approximately 9·5 Å to 12·9 Å after hydration, and another increase to 14·3 Å on further wetting with water or after treatment with glycerine: muscovite does not exhibit swelling properties.

Brammallite is a clay mineral which bears a similar relation to paragonite as illite does to muscovite. Its cell parameters, a 5·2, b 9·0, $c \sin \beta$ 19·2 Å (Bannister, 1943) are similar to those given by Gruner (1942) for a synthetic paragonite. The powder pattern of brammallite, like that of illite, shows comparatively few lines some of which are broadened, but the two may be distinguished by the positions of basal reflections.

CHEMISTRY

Analyses of natural muscovites show a maximum Na_2O content of about 2 per cent., a figure consistent with the experimental results obtained by Eugster and Yoder (1955), who showed that the limit of solid solution of paragonite in muscovite (Fig. 8) is 24 mol. per cent. at 30,000 lb./in.^{2} and at about 665°C. :

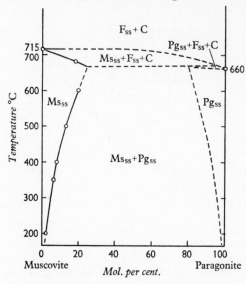

this corresponds to approximately 2 per cent. Na_2O, while pure paragonite contains 8·1 per cent. Na_2O. The amount of paragonite in solid solution at a given temperature was obtained by measuring the position of the 006 reflection in an X-ray powder pattern and assuming a straight line relationship between the *c* parameters of the two end-members. The breakdown temperature (muscovite→felspar + corundum) is lowered with increasing Na_2O content but is always above the breakdown temperature for pure paragonite. The maximum amount of muscovite which can enter into solid solution with paragonite is shown in Fig. 8 as approximately 18 mol. per cent., but analyses of natural paragonites have between 10 and 30 mol. per cent. of muscovite (approximately 1·3 to 4 per

FIG. 8. Provisional phase diagram for the subsolidus region of the muscovite–paragonite join (after Eugster and Yoder, 1955). C corundum, F felspar, Ms muscovite, Pg paragonite.

cent. K_2O). The experimental work shows clearly that there is not a continuous range of solid solution between muscovite and paragonite[1] and that paragonite must therefore be regarded as a separate mineral. The muscovite–paragonite solvus can be used to determine temperatures of formation of muscovite–paragonite assemblages.

In some preliminary studies on the system $KAlSi_3O_8$–$NaAlSi_3O_8$–Al_2O_3–H_2O, Eugster and Yoder (1955) have shown that the reaction potassium felspar + paragonite⇌albite + muscovite, over the temperature range between 300° and 600°C., is displaced towards the right (see also Fig. 5, p. 20). This is an indication that in felspar–mica assemblages, sodium enters the felspar structure in preference to that of the mica. It has previously been noted (Gruner, 1942) that the small ionic size of sodium makes it less appropriate than potassium for the positions of twelve-fold co-ordination in micas.

[1] A continuous series of solid solution exists at pressures higher than 70,000 lb./in.^{2} (Eugster, 1956).

Table 7. PARAGONITE ANALYSES

	1.	2.	3.
SiO_2	46·81	46·67	44·41
TiO_2	—	—	0·22
Al_2O_3	40·06	39·02	40·09
Fe_2O_3	tr.	2·01	1·72
FeO	—	—	0·28
MnO	—	—	0·02
MgO	0·65	—	0·16
CaO	1·26	—	0·67
Na_2O	6·40†	6·37†	5·80
K_2O	tr.†	1·36†	2·22
H_2O^+	4·82	4·91	4·45
F	—	—	0·08
Total	100·00	100·34	100·12
$O \equiv F$	—	—	0·03
	100·00	100·34	100·09
α	—	—	$\simeq 1\cdot580$
β	1·600	1·599	1·609
γ	1·605	1·604	1·609
2V	—	—	0°
D	—	2·896	—

NUMBERS OF IONS ON THE BASIS OF 24(O,OH,F)

	1.	2.	3.
Si	5·942 }8·00	5·957 }8·00	5·754 }8·00
Al	2·058	2·043	2·246
Ti	—	—	0·022
Al	3·943	3·839	3·879
Fe^{+3}	— }4·07	0·193 }4·03	0·168 }4·13
Mg	0·123	—	0·031
Fe^{+2}	—	—	0·030
Ca	0·172	—	0·093
Na	1·574 }1·75	1·576 }1·80	1·458 }1·92
K	—	0·222	0·368
OH	4·082 }4·08	4·182 }4·18	3·846 }3·88
F	—	—	0·032

1. Paragonite, Monte Campione, Switzerland (Dana's "System of Mineralogy", 6th Edit., p. 623).
2. Paragonite, Borgofranco, Piedmont, Italy (Dana's "System of Mineralogy", 6th Edit., p. 623).
3. Paragonite, chlorite–sericite schist, Glebe Mountain, southern Vermont (Rosenfeld, 1956). Anal. F. A. Gonyer.

† Redetermination of alkalis (Schaller and Stevens, 1941) gave:
  1. Na_2O 6·28, K_2O 2·17 per cent.
  2. Na_2O 7·26 K_2O 1·01 per cent.

A number of old analyses of assumed paragonites were found to be in error (Schaller and Stevens, 1941); they contained far less Na_2O and more K_2O than had been reported. For two specimens, for which chemical analyses are given in Table 7 (anals. 1, 2), redetermination of alkalis confirmed that they were paragonites.

OPTICAL AND PHYSICAL PROPERTIES

Paragonite and muscovite are very similar in optical properties and the ranges of their refractive indices overlap. A brammallite with 5·22 per cent. Na_2O and 2·58 per cent. K_2O has refractive indices α 1·561 and γ 1·579 (Bannister, 1943). For some $2M_1$ paragonites $2V_\alpha$ is about 40°, a value similar to that for $2M_1$ muscovite, but a sericite (Table 7, anal. 3) which has been identified as paragonite appears to crystallize with the $2M_1$ structure and yet has $2V \simeq 0°$ (Rosenfeld, 1956). The 3T paragonite described by Dietrich (1956) has $2V_\alpha$ less than 5°.

DISTINGUISHING FEATURES

Muscovite and paragonite can be distinguished from one another by chemical analysis for alkalis, or by X-ray diffraction, paragonite having smaller cell dimensions.

PARAGENESIS

Paragonite has been regarded as a mineral of rare occurrence, but it may have been mistaken sometimes for muscovite, since the properties of the two minerals are very similar. In recent years experimental studies and natural occurrences have shown that paragonite can and does form in a wide range of conditions. It has been reported in metamorphic areas in schists and phyllites (sometimes with kyanite and staurolite), in muscovite–biotite gneisses, in quartz veins, and in fine-grained sediments.

REFERENCES

Bannister, F. A., 1943.   Brammallite (sodium illite), a new mineral from Llandebie, South Wales.   *Min. Mag.*, vol. 26, p. 304.
Barshad, I., 1950.   The effect of the interlayer cations on the expansion of the mica type of crystal lattice.   *Amer. Min.*, vol. 35, p. 225.
Dietrich, R. V., 1956.   Trigonal paragonite from Campbell and Franklin Counties, Virginia.   *Amer. Min.*, vol. 41, p. 940.
Eugster, H. P., 1956.   Muscovite–paragonite join and its use as a geologic thermometer.   *Bull. Geol. Soc. Amer.*, vol. 67, p. 1693.
—— and Yoder, H. S., 1955.   The join muscovite–paragonite.   *Carnegie Inst. Washington, Ann. Rep. Dir. Geophys. Lab.* 1954–1955, p. 124.
Gruner, J. W., 1942.   Conditions for the formation of paragonite.   *Amer. Min.*, vol. 27, p. 131.
Rosenfeld, J. L., 1956.   Paragonite in the schist of Glebe Mountain, southern Vermont.   *Amer. Min.*, vol. 41, p. 144.
Schaller, W. T. and Stevens, R. E. 1941.   The validity of paragonite as a mineral species.   *Amer. Min.*, vol. 26, p. 541.

Glauconite

$(K,Na,Ca)_{1\cdot2-2\cdot0}(Fe^{+3},Al,Fe^{+2},Mg)_{4\cdot0}[Si_{7-7\cdot6}Al_{1-0\cdot4}O_{20}](OH)_4 \cdot n(H_2O)$

MONOCLINIC $(-)$

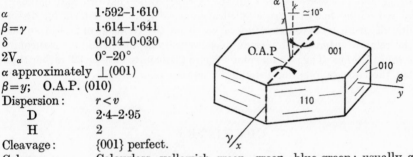

α	$1\cdot592-1\cdot610$
$\beta=\gamma$	$1\cdot614-1\cdot641$
δ	$0\cdot014-0\cdot030$
$2V_\alpha$	$0°-20°$

α approximately $\perp(001)$
$\beta=y$; O.A.P. (010)

Dispersion: $r<v$

D	$2\cdot4-2\cdot95$
H	2

Cleavage: {001} perfect.
Colour: Colourless, yellowish green, green, blue-green; usually green in thin section.
Pleochroism: α yellowish green or green.
$\beta=\gamma$ deeper yellow or bluish green.
Unit cell: $a\ 5\cdot25,\ b\ 9\cdot09,\ c\ 10\cdot03$ Å, $\beta\simeq100°$.
Z=1. Space group Cm or $C2/m$.
Readily attacked by HCl.

Glauconite is a mica mineral which occurs almost exclusively[1] in marine sediments, particularly in greensands. It is generally found in rounded fine-grained aggregates of ill-formed platelets, but better formed crystals do occur and these allow a fairly complete characterization of the mineral. Thus although in many respects glauconite can validly be considered as a clay mineral (*cf.* illite), it is here included among the micas. The term "glauconite" un-fortunately tends to be used to describe not only the mineral but also the rounded pellets in which it occurs, although the latter may contain other clay and non-clay minerals. While glauconite is of minor importance mineralogically, the conditions and manner of its formation are somewhat enigmatic and con-sequently it has been the subject of considerable investigation. The name glauconite is from the Greek *glaucos*, bluish green.

[1] Until recently it has been held that glauconite forms only in marine sediments (see p. 40), but the mineral celadonite with similar composition and properties occurs in an entirely different environment, and glauconite itself, replacing felspar and other minerals, has been reported in alluvial and eluvial deposits in the Ukraine (Dyadchenko and Khatuntzeva, 1956).

STRUCTURE[1]

The powder patterns given by glauconites were reported by Gruner (1935) to be similar to those from biotites rather than muscovites. They were indexed on the basis of a two-layered monoclinic cell ($2M_1$) with parameters a 5·23 to 5·25, b 9·05 to 9·10, c 19·96 to 20·06 Å, $\beta = 95°$. Later X-ray investigation of the micas showed that the most common cell for biotites is one-layered (1M) and it is now recognized that glauconites also have the 1M or 1Md structure (Burst, 1958). The unit cell described at the beginning of this chapter is based on Gruner's data but takes account of the more recent work. Although glauconite is a di-octahedral mica (see chemistry section), it differs from muscovite in having a considerable proportion of divalent ions in Y sites. This affects the intensities and positions of lines on the X-ray powder pattern and makes it appear more like that of a tri-octahedral mica.[2] Thus the criteria for distinguishing di- from tri-octahedral micas based on the position of reflection 060 and the relative intensities of certain basal reflections are invalid for glauconite (Grim *et al.*, 1951). The polymorphic form of glauconite may be 3T rather than 1M, but the two are indistinguishable by powder photographs.

CHEMISTRY

A large number of chemical analyses of glauconites have been published but many are of doubtful value because of the presence of impurities (*e.g.* calcium phosphate, silica, iron oxides). Although structurally most like a biotite it is clear from the more reliable analyses that glauconite is a di-octahedral mineral, and its composition is best discussed in relation to that of muscovite. The Y sites in glauconite are occupied by Fe^{+3}, Fe^{+2}, Mg and Al (Hallimond, 1922, 1928), and the total number of these ions is usually very close to four. Many workers (*e.g.* Schneider, 1927; Gruner, 1935; Hutton and Seelye, 1941; Hendricks and Ross, 1941) have derived from analyses representative empirical and structural formulae most of which lie within the ranges indicated in the formula above. This is derived from a recent detailed survey of data on glauconites by Smulikowski (1954), who suggests the following further relations between the different ions in the structure. The number of inter-layer cations (those in X sites) is always less than two but is greater than the number of Al ions in tetrahedral positions (Z sites). The excess of X ions over the number of aluminium ions in Z sites (these are equal in muscovite) is compensated in glauconite by the presence of divalent instead of trivalent ions in Y positions. Burst (1958) sets a lower limit of $\frac{2}{3}$ (*i.e.* $X_{1·33}$) to the fraction of X sites which must be occupied in a true glauconite. Below this value the crystal structure becomes disordered (1Md rather than 1M) and there is a tendency towards montmorillonite chemical composition. Of the trivalent ions in Y positions, iron predominates, Fe^{+3}:Al being greater than three in typical glauconites: others with a lower Fe^{+3}:Al ratio are termed skolites or aluminous glauconites.

---

[1] General features of the structures of all micas are described on p. 2.

[2] Three analysed glauconites from the Eocene sand of Ghent, however, give X-ray powder data similar to those of di-octahedral micas (Hoebeke and Dekeyser, 1955).

Typical values are $Fe^{+3}_{2-2\cdot 2}$, $[Al]^6_{0\cdot 6-0\cdot 8}$, $[Al]^4_{0\cdot 4-1\cdot 0}$ and $(K,Ca,Na)_{1\cdot 2-2\cdot 0}$. The relation of glauconites to other micas and clay minerals is illustrated in Fig. 9; it is seen that well crystallized glauconite is approximately a ferriferous analogue of illite. Glauconites are always low in sodium, and even lower in calcium

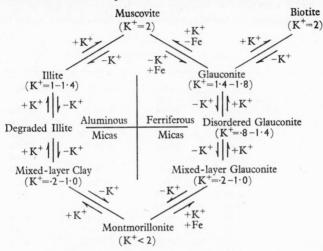

K^+ *numbers = Potassium ions per formula unit*

Fig. 9. The relation of glauconites to other micas and clay minerals (after Burst, 1958).

content: TiO_2 is rarely present in more than trace amounts, and while MgO is appreciable it does not vary greatly from one specimen to another. Celadonite is a mineral with average composition and properties indistinguishable from those of glauconite, but it occurs mainly in different environments, *e.g.* in cavities in basalts (Hendricks and Ross, 1941; Savich-Zablotzky, 1954; Schuller and Wohlmann, 1951; and others). Glauconites exhibit cation and base exchange properties similar to those of the illites, and consequently are useful as water-softeners and as decolorizing agents.

The role of water in the glauconite structure remains uncertain. The high water content sometimes found is often, in part, adsorbed water which may not be driven off completely until about 200°C. It has been suggested that the remaining water in excess of that required to furnish $4(OH)^-$ per formula unit (about 4 per cent. H_2O^+) is in the form of water molecules accompanying potassium ions between the structural layers. Glauconites also have excess silica and a deficit of potassium in comparison with most micas, so that their chemistry may be explained, like that of the illites, in terms of a mixture of mica and montmorillonite layers. Although either of these conjectures may have application in certain cases, they are not compatible with those glauconite specimens which show the X-ray powder pattern of well-defined mica. The existence of a specific homogeneous mineral is also supported by the relatively narrow ranges within which glauconite compositions fall. A third possible explanation of the excess water is that $(H_3O)^+$ ions may occupy inter-layer positions in the manner suggested by Brown and Norrish (1952) for hydro-muscovites. When structural formulae are calculated from analyses using this assumption a satisfactory result is obtained in some cases. Thus anal. 3, Table 8, gives a formula $(K,H_3O^+)_{2\cdot00}Y_{4\cdot00}Z_{8\cdot00}O_{20}(OH)_4$. For others the number of $(H_3O)^+$ ions does not balance the deficit of potassium so well. Because of the uncertainty in the figures for $(H_2O)^+$, the calculations for Table 8 were made assuming $20(O)+4(OH)$ per formula unit, disregarding the value of $(H_2O)^+$.

The dehydration curve for glauconite shows two distinct water loss processes.

Table 8. GLAUCONITE ANALYSES

	1.	2.	3.	4.	5.	6.
SiO_2	49·09	49·07	48·54	49·29	47·42	43·33
TiO_2	0·21	0·15	0·10	0·12	0·10	0·20
Al_2O_3	18·17	10·95	7·82	3·17	7·19	7·27
Fe_2O_3	6·42	15·86	17·50	21·72	22·64	24·87
Cr_2O_3	—	0·07	0·03	—	0·04	—
FeO	2·56	1·36	3·07	3·19	3·39	2·90
MnO	tr.	tr.	tr.	tr.	tr.	tr.
MgO	3·10	4·49	3·26	3·85	2·28	2·95
CaO	1·03	0·07	0·68	0·74	0·27	0·10
Na_2O	0·23	0·13	0·22	0·12	0·05	0·02
K_2O	5·62	7·51	5·87	6·02	7·46	6·00
P_2O_5	tr.	0·19	0·14	0·32	0·22	0·15
S	—	0·06	0·05	—	0·05	—
H_2O^+	}13·47	6·63	6·00	7·21	6·07	6·22
H_2O^-		3·66	6·71	4·60	3·01	5·94
Total	99·90	100·20	99·99	100·35	100·19	99·95
α	1·559	1·601	1·600	1·592	1·602	1·610
γ	1·586	1·615	1·621	1·614	1·627	1·634
δ	0·027	0·014	0·021	0·022	0·025	0·024
$2V_\alpha$	variable	10°	13°	10°	12°	10°
D	—	2·687	2·555	2·580	2·790	2·735

NUMBERS OF CATIONS ON THE BASIS OF $20(O)$ AND $4(OH)$

	1.		2.		3.		4.		5.		6.	
Si	7·222	}8·00	7·265	}8·00	7·472	}8·00	7·634	}8·00	7·216	}8·00	6·874	}8·00
Al	0·778		0·735		0·528		0·366		0·784		1·126	
Al	2·373		1·176		0·891		0·213		0·505		0·233	
Ti	0·023		0·017		0·012		0·014		0·012		0·024	
Fe^{+3}	0·711	}4·10	1·765	}4·13	2·027	}4·07	2·532	}4·06	2·591	}4·06	2·969	}4·31
Cr	—		0·008		—		—		—		—	
Fe^{+2}	0·315		0·168		0·395		0·413		0·432		0·385	
Mg	0·680		0·991		0·747		0·889		0·517		0·698	
Ca	0·163		0·021		0·112		0·123		0·044		0·016	
Na	0·066	}1·29	0·038	}1·48	0·064	}1·33	0·036	}1·35	0·014	}1·51	0·006	}1·24
K	1·056		1·416		1·152		1·190		1·448		1·214	

1. Skolite, Skole, eastern Carpathians (Smulikowski, 1936). Anal. K. Smulikowski.
2. Glauconite, limestone, Milburn, Table Hill, Otago, New Zealand.
3. Glauconite, sandstone, Kakako Creek, Otepopo, Otago.
4. Glauconite, sandstone, Whare Flat, East Taieri, Otago.
5. Glauconite, sandstone, Otepopo tunnel, Otago.
6. Glauconite, sandstone, Elephant Hill, Canterbury, New Zealand.
    Analyses 2–6: Hutton and Seelye (1941). Anal. F. T. Seelye.

The first, up to 200°C., is reversible and corresponds to adsorbed water. On heating beyond 200°C. specimens become discoloured, and from 400°C. upwards lose structurally bound water, the amount of which does not vary much from one sample to another (Sabatier, 1949). The d.t.a. curves of glauconite bear some resemblance to those of illite and montmorillonite; they show endothermic peaks at 150°–200°C. and at 550°–600°C. corresponding to the loss of adsorbed and constitutional water respectively. Illite has in addition an exothermic peak at 950°C., and the corresponding peak for glauconite though not recorded is probably at a higher temperature (Grim and Rowland, 1942).

OPTICAL AND PHYSICAL PROPERTIES

In optical properties as well as in structure, glauconite resembles biotite rather than muscovite, as its optic axial plane is parallel to (010). Refractive indices are available for a number of analysed specimens and are seen to be related to the content of ferric iron. When γ is plotted against the number of ferric ions an approximately linear relationship is apparent (Fig. 10). The relationship is not seriously upset, as it is in the biotites for example, by the influence of other ions such as Ti, Mn or F, since these are absent, or present in minor amounts, in glauconites. Refractive indices are considerably affected, however, by the variable content of adsorbed water in the crystals (Sabatier, 1949) and this may explain why the indices of the specimen of Table 8, anal. 4, falls below the line in Fig. 10. The refractive indices are nevertheless

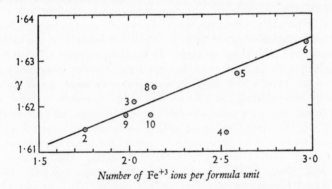

FIG. 10. γ refractive indices of some glauconites plotted against number of Fe^{+3} ions per formula unit. Nos. 2, 3, 5, 6 and 7 are as given in Table 8. Nos. 8 and 9 are from Hutton and Seelye, 1941 (their nos. 7 and 2). No. 10 is given by Smulikowski, 1954 (his no. 60).

generally higher than those of muscovites, phengites and illites. The colour of glauconite is related to the Fe^{+3} content, more Fe^{+3} resulting in deeper shades of green; skolite (Table 8, anal. 1), a glauconite with a very low Fe^{+3}:Al ratio, is almost colourless. Glauconites from older sediments tend to contain less ferric iron and so are paler green than the more recent ones (Smulikowski, 1936).

The density of glauconite might be expected to vary with Fe:Al ratio but this is masked by the effect of adsorbed water which results in a very wide range of values. Thus the density of a specimen measured before and after drying over H_2SO_4 may change by as much as 0·30 gm./c.c. (Sabatier, 1949). Glauconite is highly paramagnetic and this property may be exploited in its separation from less iron-rich micas. Electron micrographs show that well ordered glauconites (generally those with higher K content) usually have lath-like morphology, whereas the particles of disordered glauconites are irregularly shaped (Burst, 1958).

DISTINGUISHING FEATURES

Other green minerals which might be mistaken for glauconite include chlorites, which generally have a lower birefringence. Thuringite has a higher and chamosite a lower mean refractive index than glauconite.

PARAGENESIS

The relatively narrow range of chemical composition exhibited by glauconites is consistent with their formation within a very restricted set of physico-chemical and geological environments. It is generally accepted that they are formed from a variety of starting materials by marine diagenesis in shallow water and at a time of slow or negative sedimentation. They are found in impure limestones, sandstones and siltstones; greensands are so called because of the high proportion of glauconite which they contain. From their content of both ferric and ferrous iron it may be deduced that they are formed under moderately reducing conditions of the type which may, in some cases at least, occur through the action of sulphate-reducing bacteria on decaying organisms. Some weight is lent to this thesis by the frequent association of glauconite with ferrous sulphide minerals, or with foraminifera, or in pellets assumed to be coprolites. While the conditions necessary for glauconite formation are generally agreed, there is much controversy as to the parent material (Hadding, 1932; Galliher, 1935; Hendricks and Ross, 1941; Smulikowski, 1954; and others). Glauconite sometimes occurs together with partly altered biotite, but a variety of detrital minerals are equally likely to provide the materials for glauconite formation, among them illite, felspars and pyroxenes, opaline silica and volcanic glass. Hendricks and Ross (1941) point out that although much of the material may come from mud constituents, the potassium and magnesium is probably supplied by sea water. Smulikowski (1954) and others have suggested that glauconites may form by coagulation of suspended colloidal particles derived from various sources, eventually consolidating into a stable crystal structure. A process of this kind has been used in the laboratory to synthesize a poorly crystalline glauconite (Birdsall, 1951).

Since glauconite is a mineral of sedimentary origin it is particularly well suited for determination of the age of sediments by estimation of its $^{40}K/^{40}A$ ratio (Lipson, 1958; Curtis and Reynolds, 1958).

REFERENCES

Birdsall, M., 1951. Recherches sur les conditions de formations des alumino-silicates ferreux d'origine secondaire. *Compt. Rend. Acad. Sci. Paris*, vol. 233, p. 1371.

Brown, G. and **Norrish, K.,** 1952. Hydrous micas. *Min. Mag.*, vol. 29, p. 929.

Burst, J. F., 1958. Mineral heterogeneity in "glauconite" pellets. *Amer. Min.*, vol. 43, p. 481.

Curtis, G. H. and **Reynolds, J. H.,** 1958. Notes on the potassium-argon dating of sedimentary rocks. *Bull. Geol. Soc. Amer.*, vol. 69, p. 151.

Dyadchenko, M. G. and **Khatuntzeva, A. Y.,** 1956. Cases of formation of glauconite in a continental environment. *Mém. Soc. Russe Min.*, Ser. 2, vol. 85, p. 49 (M.A. 13–287).

Galliher, E. W., 1935. Glauconite genesis. *Bull. Geol. Soc. Amer.*, vol. 46, p. 1351.

Grim, R. E., Bradley, W. F. and **Brown, G.,** 1951. The mica clay minerals, in *X-ray identification and crystal structures of the clay minerals.* Min. Soc., Chap. V, p. 138.

—— and **Roland, R. A.,** 1942. Differential thermal analysis of clay minerals and other hydrous materials. *Amer. Min.*, vol. 27, p. 746.

Gruner, J. W., 1935. The structural relationship of glauconite and mica. *Amer. Min.*, vol. 20, p. 699.

Hadding, A., 1932. The pre-Quaternary sedimentary rocks of Sweden. IV. Glauconite and glauconitic rocks. *Medd. Lunds. Geol.-Min. Inst.*, No. 51 (M.A. 5–378).

Hallimond, A. F., 1922. On the classification of glauconite. *Min. Mag.*, vol. 19, p. 333.

—— 1928. The formula of glauconite. *Amer. Min.* vol. 13, p. 589.

Hendricks, S. B. and **Ross, C. S.,** 1941. The chemical composition and genesis of glauconite and celadonite. *Amer. Min.*, vol. 26, p. 683.

Hoebeke, F. and **Dekeyser, W.,** 1955. La glauconite. *C.R. Recherches, I.R.S.I.A. Brussels*, No. 18, p. 103 (M.A. 13–369).

Hutton, C. O. and **Seelye, F. T.,** 1941. Composition and properties of some New Zealand glauconites. *Amer. Min.*, vol. 26, p. 593.

Lipson, J., 1958. Potassium-argon dating of sedimentary rocks. *Bull. Geol. Soc. Amer.*, vol. 69, p. 137.

Nagelschmidt, G., 1937. X-ray investigations on clays, Part 3. *Zeit. Krist.*, vol. 97, p. 514.

Sabatier, M., 1949. Recherches sur la glauconie. *Bull. Soc. franç Min.*, vol. 72, p. 473.

Savich-Zablotzky, K. N., 1954. On the question of chemical composition and genesis of celadonite from Karadagh. *Miner. Sbornik, Lvov Geol. Soc.*, no. 8, p. 213 (M.A. 13–121).

Schneider, H., 1927. A study of glauconite. *Journ. Geol.*, vol. 35, p. 289.

Schuller, A. and **Wohlmann, E.,** 1951. Über Seladonit und seine systematische Stellung. *Neues Jahrb. Min., Abhandl.*, vol. 82, p. 111.

Smulikowski, K., 1936. Skolite, un nouveau minéral du groupe de glauconie. *Arc. Min., Warsaw*, vol. 12, p. 144 (M.A. 6–345).

—— 1954. The problem of glauconite. *Arc. Min., Warsaw*, vol. 18, p. 21.

Phlogopite

$K_2(Mg,Fe^{+2})_6[Si_6Al_2O_{20}](OH,F)_4$

MONOCLINIC $(-)$

α	1·530–1·590
β	1·557–1·637
γ	1·558–1·637
δ	0·028–0·049
$2V_\alpha$	0°–15°
$\beta=y$ $\gamma:x=0°$–5°	
O.A.P. (010)	
Dispersion:	$r<v$
D	2·76–2·90
H	2–2½
Cleavage:	{001} perfect.
Twinning:	Composition plane {001}, twin axis [310].
Colour:	Colourless, yellowish brown, green, reddish brown, dark brown; colourless, pale yellow or pale green in thin section.
Pleochroism:	α yellow, $\beta=\gamma$ brownish red, green, or yellow.
Unit cell:	a 5·3, b 9·2, c 10·3 Å, β 100°.
	$Z=1$. Space group Cm (1M polymorph).

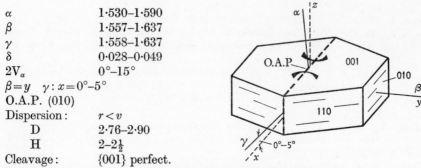

Attacked by concentrated H_2SO_4.

Phlogopite is an important member of the mica group and, as the above formula shows, it belongs to the tri-octahedral class of minerals with layered structures. The name phlogopite is used here in the manner suggested by Heinrich *et al.* (1953); this specifies that the ratio of magnesium to iron atoms in phlogopite must be greater than two to one. A more restricted application of the term phlogopite would be to the end-member $K_2Mg_6(Si_6Al_2)O_{20}(OH)_4$ which forms a solid solution series with annite $K_2Fe_6^{+2}(Si_6Al_2)O_{20}(OH)_4$. In the present usage if the Mg:Fe ratio falls below 2:1 the mineral is called biotite. Biotites, however, often have some further substitution of Al in octahedral and tetrahedral sites, tending towards compositions in the range between eastonite $K_2Mg_5Al(Si_5Al_3)O_{20}(OH)_4$ and the iron-rich siderophyllite $K_2Fe_5Al(Si_5Al_3)O_{20}(OH)_4$ (see Fig. 13, p. 57). Since there appears to be no break in these solid solution series the terminology is somewhat arbitrary and is adopted solely for the convenience of subdividing a very large range of compositions and properties. There have been other suggestions for defining phlogopite and biotite, as, for example, by their colours, since generally the more iron-rich members of the series are darker. Phlogopites with very little iron, manganese, etc., are almost colourless, and like muscovite are important economically for their properties of electrical insulation. The name is derived from the Greek *phlogopos*, fire-like, which refers to the reddish tinge which specimens often display. Its principal occurrences are in metamorphosed limestones and ultrabasic rocks.

STRUCTURE[1]

In phlogopite the octahedral sites of the mica structure are completely filled. The most common polymorph is 1M but 2M and 3T polymorphs sometimes occur, as do disordered structures which give rise to streaky diffuse scattering on X-ray diffraction photographs. The occurrence of any one of the three polymorphs or of the disordered crystals does not appear to be related to the various chemical substitutions discussed below, neither can they be correlated with paragenesis. The tri-octahedral and di-octahedral micas can readily be distinguished from one another by X-ray powder photographs (Nagelschmidt, 1937), and within the tri-octahedral group the 2M polymorph gives a characteristic pattern: 3T and 1M polymorphs in the phlogopite–biotite series are not distinguishable by powder patterns. The cell dimensions of various polymorphs of synthetic phlogopite (pure magnesium end-member) and fluorphlogopite are given in Table 9.

Table 9.   CELL PARAMETERS OF SYNTHETIC PHLOGOPITE AND FLUORPHLOGOPITE
(Yoder and Eugster, 1954)

	Phlogopite			Fluorphlogopite	
	1M	3T	2M$_1$	1M	3T
a Å	5·314	5·314	5·347	5·310	5·310
b Å	9·204	—	9·227	9·195	—
c Å	10·314	30·480	20·252	10·136	29·943
β	99° 54′	—	95° 1′	100° 4′	—
Space group	Cm	$P3_112$ or $P3_212$	$C2/c$	Cm	$P3_112$ or $P3_212$

The parameters for fluorphlogopite are significantly different from those of (hydroxy)phlogopite, and give rise to differences in X-ray powder patterns of the two minerals. Powder patterns cannot, however, be used reliably to identify fluorphlogopite since other substitutions in the structure can cause parameter changes of a similar magnitude. Thus d_{001} is reduced as F$^-$ substitutes for (OH)$^-$, but the effect may be masked by substitution of Al for Si which increases d_{001}.

Since single-crystal X-ray photographs have not been obtained it is uncertain which of the two polymorphs (1M and 3T) is adopted by synthetic phlogopite. Manganese-bearing phlogopites crystallize mainly in the 1M polymorph (Levinson and Heinrich, 1954).

The c parameter of phlogopites decreases as iron content increases although the ionic radius of Fe^{+2} is greater than that of Mg^{+2}. It is assumed that this

[1] General features of the structures of all micas are described on p. 2.

apparent anomaly is due to the greater polarizing power of the Fe^{+2} ion. The change in c parameter does not, however, provide a suitable method for determining the $Fe:Mg$ ratio because of the effect of other substitutions, Al for Si and Mg, Na for K, F for (OH), on cell parameters. The iron-magnesium ratio can be evaluated with an accuracy of about ± 5 per cent. by measuring the ratio of intensities of the 004 and 005 reflections on a powder pattern (see Fig. 12, p. 56). This ratio is highly sensitive to iron-magnesium substitution and is relatively unaffected by others (Gower, 1957).

CHEMISTRY

In Table 10 some selected phlogopite analyses are arranged in order of decreasing $Mg:Fe$ ratio. Other substitutions which may occur are discussed in turn below.

A greater amount of sodium can be incorporated in the phlogopite structure than in muscovite (*e.g.* Table 10, anal. 3, has $Na:K \simeq 1:1$); minor amounts of Rb, Cs and Ba also occur. Phlogopites often contain small amounts of manganese; those in which the manganese content is appreciable (*e.g.* Table 10, anal. 12) are called manganophyllites. Since these generally are magnesium-rich they can be regarded as manganoan phlogopites rather than manganoan biotites. Specimens with as much as 18 per cent. $(MnO + Mn_2O_3)$ have been reported (Jakob, 1925). Common minor replacements in octahedral sites include Fe^{+3}, Ti, Al and, more rarely, Li.

In one phlogopite as much as 8·97 per cent. TiO_2 occurs, and the analysis by Prider (1939) shows that most of the Ti is in octahedral coordination: (OH,F) is unusually low (anal. 7). In natural phlogopites fluorine often substitutes for (OH), the highest content recorded being 6·74 per cent. F (anal. 2). Synthetic fluorphlogopites have all the (OH) replaced by F (anal. 1).

It is generally assumed that there is only very limited solid solution between muscovite and the phlogopite–biotite series. A mica studied by Ramaseshan (1945) and Venkayya (1949), however, has too high an MgO content to be muscovite and too high an Al_2O_3 content to be phlogopite (anal. 11) and it was suggested on the basis of chemical and optical data that it is an intermediate between the two micas. It has since been shown (Heinrich *et al.*, 1953) that this specimen has the 1M structure and small 2V typical of a phlogopite. Its high Al content brings it close to the eastonite composition $K_2(Mg_5Al)[Si_5Al_3O_{20}](OH)_4$, and the deficiency in octahedral ions below the theoretical value of six is not uncommon among biotites (see p. 61). A manganophyllite described by Bilgrami (Table 10, anal. 12) also has a low content of octahedral ions.

The importance of mica as a strategic mineral has provided great impetus to the study of its artificial preparation. The difficulties of working with the high pressures required for retention of the vapour phase makes synthesis of phlogopite or of any hydroxy-mica, on a commercial scale, a very difficult proposition. Fluorphlogopite can be synthesized, however, at atmospheric pressure, and many processes were investigated in Russia (Grigoriev, 1934, 1944), Japan (Noda and Sugiyama, 1943), Germany, and in the U.S.A. (Van Valkenburg and Pike, 1952; Eitel *et al.*, 1953). Early methods employed fluorite as a source of fluorine and resulted in a calcium-bearing phlogopite. Calcium-free fluorphlogopites have been obtained by using fluorine compounds such as MgF_2, NH_4F, AlF_3 or K_2SiF_6. Thus fusion at 1350°C. of K_2CO_3, MgO, Al_2O_3 and SiO_2 in appropriate proportions with 25 per cent. NH_4F produced phlogopite with α 1·518, γ 1·554 (Grigoriev, 1944). Large crystals of fluorphlogopite with very little impurity have been produced on a commercial scale by the methods described by Hatch *et al.* (1956). They used an internal resistance method to melt batches weighing several hundred pounds, of composition $K_2SiF_6 +$ $6MgO + Al_2O_3 + 5SiO_2$. Slow cooling between 1300°C. and 1000°C. produced crystals of fluorphlogopite near the centre of the charge, the outer unmelted "mix" acting as a containing vessel to retain volatile fluoride phases. Synthetic fluorphlogopite has a much higher thermal stability than phlogopite (withstanding heating up to about 1200°C. as compared with 600°–700°C. for phlogopite); it is equally resistant to weathering and to acids, and has equally good dielectric and mechanical properties. No method has been found to produce a substitute for natural mica in the form of large blocks from which undistorted sheets may be split, but the synthetic fluorphlogopite is well suited for the manufacture of glass-bonded ceramics and reconstituted synthetic mica sheet.

Since micas occur in a very wide variety of geological environments, knowledge of their properties and of the stability conditions of hydroxy-micas is of fundamental importance. Roy (1949) reconstituted phlogopite after decomposing natural phlogopite by heating. Hydrothermal synthesis of fluorine-free phlogopite has been achieved using a variety of starting materials (Yoder and Eugster, 1954). For example, well formed crystals were prepared from MgO, γ-alumina and a glass of composition $K_2O \cdot 6SiO_2$, heated in a bomb to about 950°C. at 15,000 lb./in.[2] for five to twenty-four hours. The stability curve for synthetic phlogopite (derived experimentally except at low pressures) is reproduced in Fig. 20, p. 79. Above the stability curve, breakdown is very slow, yielding forsterite, leucite, orthorhombic $KAlSiO_4$ and vapour. The optical properties and density of the synthetic phlogopite are very close to those of natural phlogopite of similar composition and its X-ray powder pattern is that of the 1M or 3T polymorph. Phlogopite synthesized at the lowest temperatures, *i.e.* below 400°C., gives the powder pattern of the disordered 1M*d* structure. Noda and Roy (1956) have shown that hydroxy-phlogopite can be produced from fluorphlogopite by hydrothermal treatment with dilute KOH solutions, and that conversion proceeds best at about 425°C. Their experiments indicate that little or no solid solution exists between the two end-members below 450°C., and that the reaction is one of ion exchange, thus:

$$KMg_3AlSi_3O_{10}F_2 + 2(OH)^- \rightleftharpoons KMg_3AlSi_3O_{10}(OH)_2 + 2(F)^-$$

The fixation of fluorine by muscovite (Romo and Roy, 1957) is more probably an indication of decomposition and the formation of non-clay insoluble fluorides, rather than evidence of partial substitution of F for (OH) in the mica structure. Phlogopites have been synthesized with Ni substituting for Mg and with Ga for Al. The nickel phlogopite (3T or 1M polymorph) has a stability curve similar to that of Mg phlogopite, but substitution of Ga for Al lowers the equilibrium dissociation temperature by about 100°C. (Klingsberg and Roy, 1957; DeVries and Roy, 1958). The stability of phlogopite and other tri-octahedral micas is seen to be greater than that of corresponding di-octahedral micas.

Weathering of minerals in the phlogopite–biotite series generally produces a

Table 10. Phlogopite analyses

	1.	2.	3.	4.	5.	6.
SiO_2	42·70	41·18	35·64	38·63	40·95	40·22
TiO_2	—	0·39	2·83	1·11	0·82	0·27
Al_2O_3	12·21	12·52	15·13	16·80	17·28	14·21
Fe_2O_3	0·06	0·00	2·65	1·68	0·43	1·93
FeO	—	0·30	1·55	2·79	2·38	4·90
MnO	—	0·04	—	0·26	tr.	0·05
MgO	28·58	27·32	27·62	23·78	22·95	24·83
CaO	0·00	0·00	tr.	0·00	0·00	0·32
BaO	—	—	—	—	0·03	1·11
Na_2O	0·06	0·88	3·58	0·68	0·16	0·00
K_2O	10·92	11·93	6·49	10·83	9·80	7·58
F	9·20	6·74	—	0·56	0·62	2·10
H_2O^+	0·20	1·06	4·23	3·21	4·23	3·03
H_2O^-	—	0·00	0·81	0·00	0·48	0·04
	103·93	102·90	100·53	100·33	100·13	100·84
$O \equiv F$	3·87	2·84	—	0·24	0·26	0·93
Total	100·06	100·06	100·53	100·09	99·87	99·91
α	1·522	—	1·549	—	1·546	1·546
β	1·548 (calc.)	—	1·583	—	1·588–1·590	1·586
γ	1·549	—	1·585	—	1·590	1·586
$2V_\alpha$	$14° \pm 5°$	—	—	—	$0°–13°$	$0°–5°$
D	$2·88_2$	—	2·714	—	2·78	—

Numbers of ions on the basis of 24(O,OH,F)

	1.		2.		3.		4.		5.		6.	
Si	5·961	⎫7·971	5·833	⎫	5·047	⎫	5·528	⎫8·00	5·724	⎫8·00	5·737	⎫8·00
Al	2·010	⎭	2·090	⎬8·00	2·526	⎪	2·472	⎭	2·276	⎭	2·263	⎭
Al	—		—		—	⎬8·00	0·363		0·562		0·127	
Ti	—		0·106†	⎫	0·301		0·120		0·084		0·029	
Fe^{+3}	—		—		0·283	⎭	0·181		0·340		0·207	
Fe^{+2}	—	⎫5·947	0·036	⎬5·84	0·184	⎫	0·334	⎫6·10	0·276	⎫6·04	0·585	⎫6·23
Mn	—		0·005		—	⎬6·17	0·032	⎭	—	⎭	0·006	⎭
Mg	5·974	⎭	5·767	⎭	5·830	⎭	5·072		4·776		5·278	
Ca	—		—		—		—		—		0·049	⎫
Na	0·017	⎫1·96	0·242	⎫2·40	0·982	⎫2·15	0·190	⎫2·17	0·034	⎫1·78	—	⎬1·49‡
K	1·946	⎭	2·158	⎭	1·172	⎭	1·978	⎭	1·746	⎭	1·380	⎭
F	4·062	⎫4·229	3·020	⎫4·02	—	⎫4·00	0·252	⎫3·32	3·946	⎫4·22	0·860	⎫3·80§
OH	0·167	⎭	1·000	⎭	3·997	⎭	3·066	⎭	0·278	⎭	2·880	⎭

1. Synthetic fluorphlogopite (Kohn and Hatch, 1955). Anal. H. R. Shell and R. L. Craig. IM structure.
2. Phlogopite, Burgess, Ontario (Jakob and Parga-Pondal, 1932). Anal. J. Jakob. IM structure (Includes 0·54 Ti_2O_3).
3. Phlogopite, violet-brown plates, crystalline limestone, Monte Braccio, Val Malenco, Italy (Pagliani, 1940). IM structure.
4. Phlogopite, Saharakara, Madagascar (Jakob and Parga-Pondal, 1932). Anal. J. Jakob. 2M structure.
5. Phlogopite, marble, Anxiety Point, Nancy Sound, New Zealand (Hutton, 1947). Anal. F. T. Seelye. IM structure.
6. Platy phlogopite, replacing hornblende, River Leglier region, southern Yakutia, U.S.S.R. (Serdyuchenko, 1954) (Includes 0·25 Cl).

† Includes 0·065 Ti^{+3}.
‡ Includes 0·060 Ba.
§ Includes 0·060 Cl.

Table 10. PHLOGOPITE ANALYSES—*continued*

7.	8.	9.	10.	11.	12.	
40·78	40·16	40·65	38·56	36·51	38·32	SiO$_2$
8·97	0·45	0·33	4·95	—	1·54	TiO$_2$
10·95	12·65	19·88	14·12	27·38	16·51	Al$_2$O$_3$
2·18	5·52	tr.	5·51	2·78	5·76	Fe$_2$O$_3$
3·73	4·39	7·89	8·25	1·77	1·20	FeO
tr.	0·03	0·12	0·20	—	6·24	MnO
19·66	22·68	15·66	15·59	17·21	14·82	MgO
0·11	0·24	0·14	1·06	0·53	0·95	CaO
0·35	—	—	0·43	—	—	BaO
0·11	—	0·83	0·81	—	1·37	Na$_2$O
10·59	9·62	9·46	8·68	9·98	9·23	K$_2$O
0·66	—	2·57	1·25	—	—	F
1·87	3·00	2·90	1·03	3·80	4·22	H$_2$O+
0·19	—	—	—	—	0·25	H$_2$O−
100·15	98·74	101·08	100·44	99·96	100·41	
0·27	—	1·19	0·53	—	—	O ≡ F
99·88	98·74	99·89	99·91	99·96	100·41	Total
1·599	—	—	1·592	—	1·575	α
—	—	1·630	1·650	1·586	1·617	β
1·643	—	1·637	1·651	—	1·621	γ
38°	—	—	22°–35°	<5°	30°	2V$_\alpha$
—	—	—	2·984	—	2·98	D

NUMBERS OF IONS ON THE BASIS OF 24(O,OH,F)

7.	8.	9.	10.	11.	12.	
5·972 ⎫	5·917 ⎫	5·793 ⎫	5·816 ⎫	4·996 ⎫	5·562 ⎫	Si
1·880 ⎬ 8·00	2·083 ⎬ 8·00	2·207 ⎬ 8·00	2·184 ⎬ 8·00	3·004 ⎬ 8·00	2·438 ⎬ 8·00	Al
— ⎫	0·114 ⎫	1·133 ⎫	0·327 ⎫	1·693 ⎫	0·388 ⎫	Al
0·992 ⎪	0·050 ⎪	0·035 ⎭	0·562 ⎪	—	0·168 ⎪	Ti
0·246 ⎪	0·613 ⎪	—	0·625 ⎪	0·299 ⎫	0·630 ⎪	Fe+3
0·448 ⎬ 5·85	0·541 ⎬ 5·50	0·940 ⎬ 5·61‡	1·041 ⎬ 6·09	0·226 ⎬ 5·66	0·146 ⎬ 5·31	Fe+2
—	0·004 ⎪	0·015 ⎪	0·025 ⎪	—	0·768 ⎪	Mn
4·312 ⎭	4·180 ⎭	3·327 ⎭	3·505 ⎭	3·439 ⎭	3·206 ⎭	Mg
0·018 ⎫	0·038 ⎫	0·021 ⎫	0·171 ⎫	0·112 ⎫	0·147 ⎫	Ca
0·036 ⎬ 2·06†	— ⎬ 1·85	0·230 ⎬ 2·00§	0·238 ⎬ 2·34‖	— ⎬ 2·08	0·386 ⎬ 2·24	Na
1·984 ⎭	1·810 ⎭	1·722 ⎭	1·672 ⎭	1·970 ⎭	1·710 ⎭	K
0·298 ⎫ 2·16	— ⎫ 2·95	1·158 ⎫ 3·91	0·596 ⎫ 1·63	—	—	F
1·862 ⎭	2·984 ⎭	2·756 ⎭	1·037 ⎭	3·502 ⎬ 3·50	4·086	OH

7. Titaniferous phlogopite, phlogopite–leucite lamproite, Howes Hill, Western Australia (Prider, 1939). Anal. H. C. G. Vincent. 1M structure.

8. Phlogopite, associated with olivine and diopsidic augite, kimberlite, Frank Smith Mine, Cape Province, South Africa (Williams, 1932).

9. Phlogopite, "pneumatolytic block", Monte Somma, Italy (Pieruccini, 1950). (Includes Li$_2$O 0·28, Rb$_2$O 0·37, Cs$_2$O tr.).

10. Phlogopite, with pyroxene, glassy rhyolite, San Juan region, Colorado (Larsen *et al.*, 1937).

11. Mahadevite, East Godavari district, India (Venkayya, 1949). 1M structure.

12. Manganophyllite, pegmatite in manganese ore band, Chikla, Bhandara district, India (Bilgrami, 1956). Anal. S. A. Bilgrami.

† Includes 0·020 Ba.
‡ Includes 0·162 Li.
§ Includes 0·030 Rb.
‖ Includes 0·254 Ba.

"clay mica" analogous to the illites produced from muscovite, and further weathering of "clay biotites" converts them to vermiculites (Lacroix, 1940; Walker, 1950). Laboratory "weathering" by boiling with 40 per cent. $MgCl_2$ for 135 hours also yields vermiculite (Caillère *et al.*, 1949). That the product of weathering differs, however, for phlogopites with different iron contents, is suggested by Roy and Mumpton (1958) who record the weathering of an iron-poor phlogopite to a septechlorite mineral (chlorite composition but 7 Å type of structure; see p. 164).

OPTICAL AND PHYSICAL PROPERTIES

The upper limits of the ranges of refractive indices given above are derived somewhat arbitrarily through the definition that in phlogopites Mg:Fe is greater than 2:1. Increase of iron content (particularly ferric) within this range and beyond it into the biotites is generally associated with an increase in refractive indices. An attempt to correlate refractive index with total iron content (FeO + Fe_2O_3) gave poor results and a plot of γ against MgO was even less successful (Heinrich, 1946). This may be attributed to the considerable influence on optical properties of substituents other than iron, particularly manganese, titanium and fluorine. Table 11 presents for comparison the optical data for phlogopites with a high percentage of these substituents together with those of a natural and synthetic phlogopite approaching the composition $K_2Mg_6Al_2Si_6O_{20}(OH)_4$. It is estimated that the presence of 1 per cent. TiO_2 raises γ by about 0·005 and that replacement of all (OH) by F lowers it by 0·02. These effects are comparable with the increase of γ by about 0·15 when magnesium is completely replaced by iron. By plotting γ against FeO + 2(Fe_2O_3 + TiO_2) Heinrich (1946) obtained an approximate straight line relationship (Fig. 11), showing that the effect of Fe^{+3} and Ti on refractive index is greater than that of Fe^{+2}. For

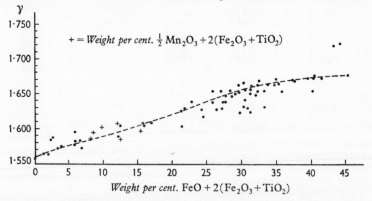

FIG. 11. The relationship between refractive index and chemical composition in the phlogopite–biotite series (after Heinrich, 1946).

manganophyllite, the best result was obtained by plotting γ against $\frac{1}{2}(Mn_2O_3 + MnO) + 2(Fe_2O_3 + TiO_2)$, indicating that the effect of manganese is less than that of ferrous iron. Both Hall (1941b) and Heinrich (1946) concluded that no accurate correlation can be found between optical constants and composition of the phlogopite–biotite minerals. Only in the rare circumstance of a suite of micas having all but one of the critical constituents nearly invariable could a simple relation be established.

Manganophyllite and titaniferous phlogopite have a larger 2V than phlogopite. The titaniferous phlogopite shows strong dispersion ($r < v$) and has the pleochroic scheme: α pale salmon-pink, β light yellow, γ reddish brown (Prider, 1940). The colours of phlogopites are influenced mainly by iron and titanium content. Those rich in titanium are usually reddish brown regardless of their Mg:Fe ratio: those poor in titanium and rich in ferrous iron tend to be blue-green or shades of brown according to the ferric iron content. As with refractive indices, a strict correlation between colour and composition is not discernible (Hall, 1941a).

Table 11. OPTICAL CONSTANTS OF SOME PHLOGOPITES

	Natural phlogopite (Winchell, 1951)	Synthetic phlogopite (Yoder and Eugster, 1954)	Fluorphlog-opite (Kohn and Hatch, 1955)	Titaniferous phlogopite (Prider, 1940)	Mangano-phyllite. (Heinrich *et al.*, 1953)
α	1·535	1·548	1·522	1·599	1·548–1·573
β	1·564	—	1·548	—	1·581–1·636
γ	1·565	1·588	1·549	1·643	1·581–1·636
δ	0·030	0·040	0·027	0·044	0·024–0·040
$2V_\alpha$	10°	0° or small	14 ± 5°	38°	0°–34°

Dispersion may be high for some phlogopites; one is reported (Ostrovsky and Petrov, 1939) which has its optic axial plane perpendicular to (010) for blue light ($2V \simeq 8°$), parallel to (010) for red light ($2V \simeq 8°$), and has $2V = 0°$ for yellow light. Acicular inclusions of rutile, and sometimes of tourmaline, occur in some phlogopites, aligned in specific directions (perpendicular to (010) and at 60° intervals). These are responsible for the phenomenon of "asterism" observed when a small light source is viewed through a thin sheet of the mica. Inclusions and colours are sometimes arranged in zones, with inclusion-free zones showing no asterism. Colour zoning may be either alternating (*e.g.* light and dark green) or of the core–margin type (*e.g.* medium brown core, pale yellow margin) (Watson, 1955). In most cases the cores of zoned phlogopites are darker than the rims and if the refractive indices differ at all, those of the darker zones are higher.

In appearance and in physical properties phlogopite is typical of the mica minerals. Prolonged grinding disrupts its crystal structure less than that of muscovite, yet sheets of muscovite have greater mechanical strength. A study of the anisotropy of hardness of synthetic fluorphlogopite (Bloss *et al.*, 1959) shows that, like muscovite, for the (001) plane, it has minimum hardness in the direction of the x axis and maximum hardness parallel to y. Substitution of boron for aluminium in tetrahedral sites decreases the hardness of fluor-phlogopite whereas substitution of barium for potassium results in considerably increased hardness. Synthetic fluorphlogopite was found to be slightly harder than natural (hydroxy)phlogopite, an effect attributed to the greater polariz-ability of the hydroxyl ion.

Phlogopite is often found as tabular pseudo-hexagonal crystals which cleave perfectly on {001} sometimes showing luminescence in the process. As with muscovites, extremely thin uniform cleavage flakes are separable and these have been studied interferometrically (Tolansky, 1948). On heating to 200°C. phlogopite develops a mosaic structure and suffers a decrease in its thermal conductivity, but muscovite does not show these effects (Powell *et al.*, 1937).

DISTINGUISHING FEATURES

Phlogopite can usually be distinguished from muscovite which has a greater 2V, and from the more iron-rich biotites which have higher refractive indices. Lepidolite can be similar to phlogopite in appearance and optical properties, and is best distinguished from it by a lithium flame test, or by an X-ray powder photograph.

PARAGENESIS

The relation between paragenesis and composition in the phlogopite–biotite series as a whole is illustrated in Fig. 21, p. 80; the two main occurrences of phlogopite are in metamorphosed limestones and in ultrabasic rocks. Phlogopite is a very common constituent of the dolomite marbles in the contact zone of the Quérigut granite, French Pyrenees (Struwe, 1958). The mineral occurs scattered through the rock as well as in lenses, layers and irregular aggregates; the crystal dimensions vary between 0·1 mm. and 1 cm., and the crystal boundaries may be either perfectly pseudo-hexagonal or irregular in outline. Intimate intergrowths with the carbonate matrix are common, and some crystals are elongated in the direction of the z axis, and may be as much as five times greater in length than in width. The metamorphism of these marbles is considered to be essentially isochemical but in common with other thermally metamorphosed limestones they give little evidence of the mechanism by which the phlogopite was formed. The source of potassium in the limestones is uncertain and some of the suggested reactions for the formation of phlogopite involve illite and dolomite, illite and chlorite, or dolomite and detrital felspar.

The formation of phlogopite in many areas of thermal metamorphism is the result of fluorine metasomatism. Thus at Mansjö Mountain (Eckermann, 1922) phlogopite enclosing remnants of calcite occurs in a chondrodite–spinel limestone at the contact with fluor-diopside pegmatite dykes. Other minerals associated with phlogopite at this locality include pargasite, scapolite, vesuvianite, prehnite, apatite and sphene. At Carlingford, Co. Louth, Eire, Osborne (1932) has described phlogopite associated with monticellite, spinel, apatite, vesuvianite and cuspidine ($Ca_4Si_2O_7F_2$) in thermally metamorphosed and metasomatized Carboniferous Limestone. In the hydrothermal contact metamorphosed marbles of Iron Hill, Colorado (Larsen, 1942), phlogopite occurs with aegirine and a sodium-rich tremolite. An unusual phlogopite-pyroxene skarn at the contact of serpentinite and epidiorite at Ardgour, Argyllshire, has been noted by Drever (1940).

Phlogopite is also a characteristic product of the regional metamorphism of impure magnesium limestone, and there it is generally considered to have been derived by reaction between dolomite and earlier formed potassium felspar or muscovite:

$$3CaMg(CO_3)_2 + KAlSi_3O_8 + H_2O \rightarrow (OH)_2KMg_3AlSi_3O_{10} + 3CaCO_3 + 3CO_2$$
dolomite   potassium   phlogopite
felspar

$$3CaMg(CO_3)_2 + (OH)_2KAl_3Si_3O_{10} \rightarrow (OH)_2KMg_3AlSi_3O_{10} + 3CaCO_3$$
dolomite   muscovite   phlogopite
$$+ 3CO_2 + Al_2O_3$$

The excess alumina in the second reaction may be used to form spinel. The association of calcite and phlogopite in marble belonging to the amphibolite facies has been considered by Ramberg (1952) who concluded that the association is stable only in the absence of excess silica impurity:

$$(OH)_2KMg_3AlSi_3O_{10} + 3CaCO_3 + 6SiO_2 \rightleftharpoons KAlSi_3O_8 + 3CaMgSi_2O_6 + 3CO_2$$
phlogopite   calcite   potassium   diopside
felspar
$$+ H_2O$$

In the amphibolite facies siliceous magnesium limestones of Glen Urquhart, Inverness-shire, however, phlogopite is associated with microcline and diopside as well as with plagioclase, tremolite and epidote, and Francis (1958) considered that the phlogopite forms equilibrium assemblages with both calcite and microcline, and with calcite and quartz.

In igneous rocks the main occurrence of phlogopite is in ultrabasic rocks. It is a particularly characteristic constituent of kimberlite (Table 10, anal. 8) in which it is commonly present in amounts of 6 to 8 per cent. In some kimberlites phlogopite displays reaction rims of ore, chlorite and calcite, and occurs also as rims attached to corroded grains of chromium-rich diopside. Inclusions of phlogopite rock and other less phlogopite-rich inclusions are known from some kimberlite pipes (Holmes, 1936). The origin of the phlogopite is uncertain but it is probably derived by a metasomatic replacement of peridotite associated with the introduction of F, P, Ti and CO_2. The kimberlite of Bachelor Lake, Quebec (Watson, 1955) is particularly rich in phlogopite and generally contains between 20 and 25 per cent. of the magnesium mica; olivine and calcite are the other major constituents and the accessories include augite, perovskite, magnetite and apatite. Much of the phlogopite is zoned; the zoning is variable and examples of normal, reversed and oscillatory types occur and are similar to the zoned phlogopites of the South African kimberlites described by Wagner (1914).

Phlogopite is a primary mineral in some leucite-rich rocks. In the West Kimberley area of Western Australia (Prider, 1939; Wade and Prider, 1940) it occurs in massive, vesicular and fragmental rocks consisting of varying proportions of leucite, kataphoritic amphibole and diopside. In some of the lavas phlogopite occurs both as phenocrysts and in the groundmass. The phlogopite (Table 10, anal. 7) has a low (OH,F) content, which Prider (1939) suggested may be due either to a loss of volatiles from the mineral during the period of intrusion or extrusion under low pressure conditions near or at the surface, or to its crystallization from an extremely "dry" magma. Other phlogopite and leucite-bearing rocks, wyomingite (leucite, phlogopite, pyroxene) and jumillite (leucite, phlogopite, pyroxene, olivine, sanidine) have been described respectively by Cross (1897) and Osann (1906). Phlogopite also occurs in the uncompahgrite, olivine pyroxenite and pyroxenite of Iron Hill, Colorado (Larsen, 1942). Phlogopite associated with apatite and calcite has been reported in veins in pyroxenite (Landes, 1938) where it is believed to have arisen from a liquid of granite pegmatite composition contaminated by dolomite or dolomitic limestone.

Other phlogopite occurrences include the dyke rocks (kersantite and minette) and the rhyolite of the San Juan region (the mica is described by Larsen, 1937, as biotite). Of the few well authenticated occurrences of manganophyllite most are associated, as at Långban, Sweden, with manganese deposits of metasomatic origin. Bilgrami (1956) has described manganophyllite (Table 10, anal. 12) from Chikla, India, in a pegmatite contaminated by manganese ore.

The relation between the experimentally determined stability curve of phlogopite and the melting curves of granites and basalts (Yoder and Eugster, 1954) is discussed in the section on biotite.

REFERENCES

Bilgrami, S. A., 1956. Manganese silicate minerals from Chikla, Bhandara district, India. *Min. Mag.*, vol. 31, p. 236.

Bloss, F. D., Shekarchi, E. and **Shell, H. R.**, 1959. Hardness of synthetic and natural micas. *Amer. Min.*, vol. 44, p. 33.

Caillère, S., Hénin, S. and **Guennelon, R.**, 1949. Transformation experimentale du mica en divers types de minéraux argileux par separation des feuillets. *Compt. Rend. Acad. Sci. Paris*, vol. 228, p. 1741.

Cross, W., 1897. The igneous rocks of the Leucite Hills and Pilot Butte, Wyoming. *Amer. Journ. Sci.*, ser. 4, vol. 4, p. 115.

DeVries, R. L. and **Roy, R.**, 1958. The influence of ionic substitution on the stability of micas and chlorites. *Econ. Geol.*, vol. 53, p. 958.

Drever, H. I., 1940. The geology of Ardgour, Argyllshire. *Trans. Roy. Soc. Edin.*, vol. 60, p. 141.

Eckermann, H. von., 1922. The rocks and contact minerals of the Mansjö Mountain. *Geol. För. Förh., Stockholm*, vol. 44, p. 205.

Eitel, W., Hatch, R. A. and **Denny, M. V.**, 1953. Synthetic mica investigations, II : The role of fluorides in mica batch reactions. *Journ. Amer. Ceram. Soc.*, vol. 36, p. 286.

Francis, G. H., 1958. Petrological studies in Glen Urquhart, Inverness-shire. *Bull. Brit. Mus. (Nat. Hist.), Min.*, vol. 1, p. 123.

Gower, J. A., 1957. X-ray measurement of the iron-magnesium ratio in biotites. *Amer. Journ. Sci.*, vol. 255, p. 142.

Grigoriev, D. P., 1934. The preparation of artificial magnesian mica. *Centr. Min. Geol.*, p. 219.

—— 1944. Synthesis and study of phlogopite. *Doklady Acad. Sci. USSR*, vol. 43, p. 63 (M.A. 9–93).

Hall, A. J., 1941a. The relation between colour and chemical composition in the biotites. *Amer. Min.*, vol. 26, p. 29.

—— 1941b. The relation between chemical composition and refractive index in the biotites. *Amer. Min.*, vol. 26, p. 34.

Hatch, R. A., Humphrey, R. A. and **Worden, E. C.**, 1956. Synthetic mica investigations VIII : The manufacture of fluorphlogopite by the internal electric-resistance melting process. *U.S. Bureau of Mines, Report of Investigations* 5283.

Heinrich, E. W., 1946. Studies in the mica group; the biotite–phlogopite series. *Amer. Journ. Sci.*, vol. 244, p. 836.

—— **Levinson, A. A., Levandowski, D. W.** and **Hewitt, C. H.**, 1953. *Studies in the natural history of micas.* University of Michigan Engineering Research Inst. Project M.978; final report.

Holmes, A., 1936. A contribution to the petrology of kimberlite and its inclusions. *Trans. Geol. Soc. S. Africa,* vol. 39, p. 379.

Hutton, C. O., 1947. Contributions to the mineralogy of New Zealand. Part 3. *Trans. Roy. Soc. New Zealand,* vol. 76, p. 481.

Jakob, J., 1925. Beiträge zur chemischen Konstitution der Glimmer. I. Mitteilung: Die schwedischen Manganophylle. *Zeit. Krist.,* vol. 61, p. 155.

—— and **Parga-Pondal, I.,** 1932. Beiträge zur chemischen Konstitution der Glimmer. X. Mitteilung: Über die Rolle des Titans in den Phlogopiten. *Zeit. Krist.,* vol. 82, p. 271.

Klingsberg, C. and **Roy, R.,** 1957. Synthesis, stability and polytypism of nickel and gallium phlogopite. *Amer. Min.,* vol. 42, p. 629.

Kohn, J. A. and **Hatch, R. A.,** 1955. Synthetic mica investigations, VI: X-ray and optical data on synthetic fluorphlogopite. *Amer. Min.,* vol. 40, p. 10.

Lacroix, A., 1940. Les transformations minéralogiques secondaires observés dans les gisements de phlogopite de l'extrême sud de Madagascar. *Compt. Rend. Acad. Sci. Paris,* vol. 210, p. 353.

Landes, K. K., 1938. Origin of the Quebec phlogopite-apatite deposits. *Amer. Min.,* vol. 33, p. 359.

Larsen, E. S., 1942. Alkalic rocks of Iron Hill, Gunnison County, Colorado. *U.S. Geol. Surv., Prof. Paper* 197-A.

—— **Gonyer, F. A.** and **Irving, J.,** 1937. Petrologic results of a study of the minerals from the tertiary volcanic rocks of the San Juan Region, Colorado—6. Biotite. *Amer. Min.,* vol. 22, p. 898.

Nagelschmidt, B., 1937. X-ray investigations on clays, Part 3. *Zeit. Krist.,* vol. 97. p. 514.

Noda, T. and **Roy, R.,** 1956. OH-F exchange in fluorine phlogopite. *Amer. Min.,* vol. 41, p. 929.

—— and **Sugiyama, S.,** 1943. Chemical compositions and optical properties of synthetic micas. *Journ. Soc. Chem. Ind. Japan,* vol. 46, p. 760.

Osann, A., 1906. Über einige Alkaligesteine aus Spanien. *Festschr. Rosenbusch, Stuttgart,* p. 262.

Osborne, G. D., 1932. The metamorphosed limestones and associated contaminated igneous rocks of the Carlingford district, Co. Louth. *Geol. Mag.,* vol. 69, p. 209.

Ostrovsky, I. A. and **Petrov, V. P.,** 1939. Dispersion of a phlogopite from "Sliadianka" deposit. *Bull. Acad. Sci. USSR, Sér. Géol.* No. 1, p. 105 (M.A. 7–556).

Pagliani, G., 1940. Flogopite e titanolivina di Monte Braccio (Val Malenco), *Atti Soc. Ital. Sci. Nat. Mus. Civ. Milano,* vol. 79, p. 20 (M.A. 7–106).

Pieruccini, R., 1950. La mica di un blocco pneumatolytico del Monte Somma ed i minerali che l'accompagnano. *Mem. (Atti) Soc. Toscana Sci. Nat., ser A.,* vol. 57 (M.A. 11–391).

Powell, R. W., Griffiths, E. and **Wood, W. A.,** 1937. The variation with temperature of the thermal conductivity and the X-ray structure of some micas. *Proc. Roy. Soc. Lond., A.,* vol. 163, p. 189.

Prider, R. T., 1939. Some minerals from the leucite-rich rocks of the West Kimberley area, Western Australia. *Min. Mag.,* vol. 25, p. 373.

Ramaseshan, S., 1945. Mahadevite—a new species of mica. *Proc. Ind. Acad. Sci., A.,* vol. 222, p. 177 (M.A. 9–189).

Ramberg, H., 1952. *The origin of metamorphic and metasomatic rocks.* Chicago.

Romo, L. A. and **Roy, R.,** 1957. Studies of the substitution of OH$^-$ by F$^-$ in various hydroxylic minerals. *Amer. Min.,* vol. 42, p. 165.

Roy, R., 1949. Decomposition and resynthesis of the micas. *Journ. Amer. Ceram. Soc.,* vol. 32, p. 202.

Roy, R. and **Mumpton, F. A.**, 1958. Weathering studies: 2. A note on the conversion of phlogopite to septechlorite. *Journ. Geol.*, vol. 66, p. 324.

Serdyuchenko, D. P., 1954. Asbestos-like phlogopite from southern Yakutia. *Doklady Acad. Sci. USSR*, vol. 97, p. 151 (M.A. 12–536).

Struwe, H., 1958. Data on the mineralogy and petrology of the dolomite-bearing northern contact zone of the Quérigut granite, French Pyrenees. *Leidse Geol. Mededel.*, vol. 22, p. 237.

Tolansky, S., 1948. *Multiple-beam interferometry of surfaces and films.* The Clarendon Press, Oxford.

Van Valkenburg, A. and **Pike, R. G.**, 1952. Synthesis of mica. *Journ. Research. Nat. Bur. Standards, U.S.A.*, vol. 48, p. 360.

Venkayya, E., 1949. A new occurrence of mahadevite. *Proc. Ind. Acad. Sci., A.*, vol. 30, p. 74 (M.A. 11–19).

Wade, A. and **Prider, R. T.**, 1940. The leucite-bearing rocks of the West Kimberley area, Western Australia. *Quart. Journ. Geol. Soc.*, vol. 96, p. 39.

Wagner, P. A., 1941. *The diamond fields of South Africa.* Johannesburg.

Walker, G. F., 1950. Trioctahedral minerals in the soil clays of north-east Scotland. *Min. Mag.*, vol. 29, p. 72.

Watson, K. D., 1955. Kimberlite at Bachelor Lake, Quebec. *Amer. Min.*, vol. 40, p. 565.

Williams, A. F., 1932. *The genesis of the diamond.* London. Chap. II, p. 381.

Winchell, A. N. and **Winchell, H.**, 1951. *Elements of optical mineralogy, Part II.* John Wiley and Sons, Inc., New York.

Yoder, H. S. and **Eugster, H. P.**, 1954. Phlogopite synthesis and stability range. *Geochim. et Cosmochim. Acta*, vol. 6, p. 157.

Biotite

$K_2(Mg,Fe^{+2})_{6-4}(Fe^{+3},Al,Ti)_{0-2}[Si_{6-5}Al_{2-3}O_{20}]O_{0-2}(OH,F)_{4-2}$

MONOCLINIC $(-)$

α	1·565–1·625
β	1·605–1·696
γ	1·605–1·696
δ	0·04–0·08
$2V_\alpha$	0°–25°

$\gamma : x = 0°$ to $9°$

$\beta = y$; O.A.P. (010)

Dispersion :   Weak:

    Fe-rich biotites $r < v$

    Mg-rich biotites $r \gtrless v$

D	2·7–3·3
H	$2\frac{1}{2}$–3

Cleavage :   {001} perfect.

Twinning :   Composition plane {001}, twin axis [310].

Colour :   Black, deep shades of brown, reddish brown or green; yellow,
brown or green in thin section.

Pleochroism :   Strong;

    α greyish yellow, brownish green or brown;

    $\beta = \gamma$ dark brown, dark green or dark reddish brown.

Unit cell : a 5·3, b 9·2, c 10·2 Å, β 100°.

    $Z = 1$.   Space group Cm (1M polymorph).

Bleached and attacked by sulphuric acid.

The term biotite is used here to denote an iron-rich tri-octahedral mica which is arbitrarily differentiated from phlogopite in having $Mg:Fe < 2:1$.   Biotite is named after the mineralogist J. B. Biot; many other names have been used to describe members of the biotite group, the more useful of which are annite, siderophyllite and lepidomelane; these are discussed in the section on chemistry. Since phlogopite and biotite are members of a continuous chemical and structural series, many characteristics described in the previous section for phlogopite are also possessed by biotite.

STRUCTURE

In biotite as in phlogopite the octahedral cation sites of the mica structure ideally are completely filled.   Hendricks and Jefferson (1939) gave the following cell parameters for biotite polymorphs:

1M	$a = 5·3$	$b = 9·2$	$c = 10·2$ Å	$\beta = 100°$	Space group Cm.
2M	$a = 5·3$	$b = 9·2$	$c = 20·2$ Å	$\beta = 95°$	Space group $C2/c$.
3T	$a = 5·3$		$c = 30·0$ Å		Space group $C3_112$ or $C3_212$.

Six-, eighteen- and twenty-four-layered triclinic cells have also been described but are of rare occurrence, and at least one of these (6-layered) has been shown in more recent work (Heinrich *et al.*, 1953) to be a simpler polymorph (1M).   An aluminium-free biotite, $K_2Fe_6^{+2}Fe_2^{+3}Si_6O_{20}(OH)_4$, synthesized by Wones (1958a) was found to have a three-layered cell with a 5·43, b 9·40, c 30·49 Å, and although the cell is dimensionally ortho-hexagonal, the true symmetry is given as monoclinic with $\beta = 90°$ (Donnay and Kingman, 1958).   The structure of this biotite may be similar to that of a three-layered monoclinic lepidolite referred to on p. 86.   X-ray diffraction photographs show that mixtures of polymorphs, and disordered structures, are not uncommon.   The polymorphs of biotite, in particular 3T and 1M, cannot be distinguished by their X-ray powder patterns as can those of muscovite.   Weissenberg photographs from single-crystals may be used but even these exhibit only minor differences and have to be interpreted with care.   The orientation of single-crystal flakes cannot be deduced optically because of their low 2V and low birefringence, but Laue photographs may be used to give an indication of special crystallographic directions which can then be checked by other X-ray methods.   Powder patterns are adequate, however, for distinguishing members of the phlogopite–biotite series from di-octahedral micas (Nagelschmidt, 1937).   No relationship has yet been established between

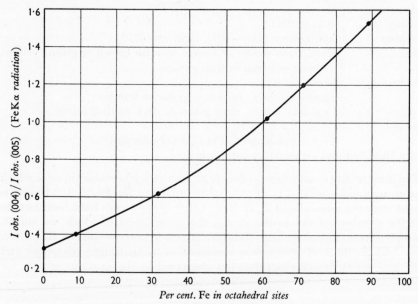

FIG. 12.   Change in ratio of observed X-ray intensities with iron content in the phlogopite–biotite series (after Gower, 1957).

polymorphic form and chemical composition, but there is some indication that biotites of a particular locality tend to have the same polymorphic structure. Thus biotites in nepheline-syenites from Bancroft, Canada, are mainly 1M, and those in quartz diorites from south-eastern U.S.A. are mainly 2M.   The effect of changing iron content on cell parameters has been discussed in the section on phlogopite.   Variation in cell size may accompany several types of chemical substitution involving Mn, Al and F as well as Fe so that it does not provide a reliable method for estimating the ratio Mg:Fe in a biotite. The method of measuring intensity ratios on powder patterns is applicable throughout the phlogopite–biotite series; Berkhin (1954) suggests the use of reflections 004 or 110, and the method of Gower (1957) in which the intensities of 004 and 005 are compared can, in favourable circumstances, be used to estimate the ratio Fe/(Fe+Mg) with an accuracy of ±5 per cent. (Fig. 12). The latter method appears to give better results if there is comparatively little substitution of Al in octahedral sites (Engel and Engel, 1960).

CHEMISTRY

Representative analyses of biotites from igneous rocks arranged in order of increasing Fe/Mg ratio are given in Table 12. Biotites from metamorphic rocks are listed in Table 13.

The general formula for biotite is

$$K_2(Fe^{+2},Mg)_{6-4}(Fe^{+3},Al,Ti)_{0-2}(Si_{6-5}Al_{2-3})O_{20-22}(OH,F)_{4-2}$$

Most specimens fall within a field outlined by four end-members, phlogopite, annite, eastonite and siderophyllite (Fig. 13). Thus in biotite as compared with phlogopite, magnesium is replaced by ferrous iron and also by trivalent ions (Fe^{+3},Al), and aluminium replaces silicon in tetrahedral sites usually beyond the ratio Al:Si=2:6. A subdivision of biotites themselves sometimes is made, those richest in iron ($Fe^{+2}+Fe^{+3}$) being called *lepidomelanes* (*e.g.* Table 12, anal. 10). Biotites which have little or no magnesium, high ferrous iron and low ferric iron have been described as *siderophyllites* although their compositions do not necessarily lie within the field of Fig. 13. Thus for anal. 13, Table 12, the formula approximates more closely to

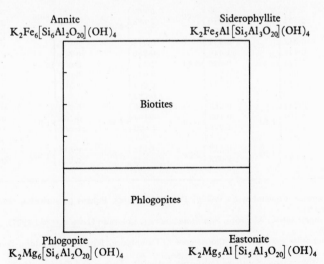

FIG. 13. Phlogopite–biotite compositional fields. Most phlogopites and biotites fall within these fields; the division between them is arbitrarily chosen to be where Mg:Fe=2:1.

Table 12. Biotite analyses (igneous rocks)

	1.	2.	3.	4.	5.
SiO_2	38·22	39·14	34·33	37·35	34·96
TiO_2	2·96	4·27	3·63	5·28	3·99
Al_2O_3	14·71	13·10	14·80	15·82	15·29
Fe_2O_3	3·83	12·94	2·48	4·42	2·90
FeO	13·44	5·05	19·07	15·43	18·30
MnO	0·52	0·14	0·35	0·02	0·39
MgO	13·45	12·75	11·62	10·25	10·42
CaO	1·46	1·64	1·56	1·30	1·11
Li_2O	—	—	0·36	—	0·33
Na_2O	0·50	0·70	0·65	0·52	0·41
K_2O	7·90	6·55	8·16	8·16	7·99
Rb_2O	—	—	—	—	—
F	—	1·11	2·38	1·25	1·17
H_2O^+	1·89	2·41	2·32	0·60	3·07
H_2O^-	0·60	0·58	0·18	—	0·41
	99·56	100·38	101·89	100·40	100·74
$O \equiv F$	—	0·46	1·01	0·53	0·49
Total	99·56	99·92	100·88	99·87	100·25
α	—	1·594	1·598	1·602	1·596
β	1·637	1·671	1·651	1·663	1·646
γ	1·637	1·672	1·652	1·664	1·650
$2V_\alpha$	0°	10°–25°	—	5°	—
D	2·997	2·862	—	—	—

Numbers of ions on the basis of 24(O,OH,F)

	1.	2.	3.	4.	5.
Si	5·859 ⎫8·00	5·790 ⎫8·00	5·262 ⎫	5·787 ⎫8·00	5·344 ⎫8·00
Al	2·141 ⎭	2·210 ⎭	2·688 ⎬8·00	2·213 ⎭	2·656 ⎭
Al	0·518 ⎫	0·074 ⎫	— ⎭	0·677 ⎫	0·102 ⎫
Ti	0·342	0·474	0·418 ⎫	0·615	0·460
Fe^{+3}	0·442	1·440	0·286	0·514	0·336
Fe^{+2}	1·724 ⎬6·17	0·625 ⎬5·44	2·454 ⎬6·04	2·000 ⎬6·18	2·346 ⎬5·88
Mn	0·067	0·017	0·046	0·002	0·050
Mg	3·073	2·811	2·664	2·367	2·382
Li	— ⎭	— ⎭	0·222 ⎭	— ⎭	0·202 ⎭
Ca	0·239 ⎫	0·260 ⎫	0·256 ⎫	0·216 ⎫	0·182 ⎫
Na	0·150 ⎬1·94	0·199 ⎬1·70	0·194 ⎬2·05	0·156 ⎬1·98	0·122 ⎬1·87
K	1·546 ⎭	1·236 ⎭	1·600 ⎭	1·612 ⎭	1·562 ⎭
Rb	—	—	—	—	—
F	— ⎫1·93	0·519 ⎫2·90	1·172 ⎫3·55	0·611 ⎫1·231	0·572 ⎫3·71
OH	1·932 ⎭	2·378 ⎭	2·382 ⎭	0·620 ⎭	3·140 ⎭

1. Biotite, diorite, Chocholowska valley, Tatra Mountains, Poland (Zastawniak, 1951) (Includes 0·08 P_2O_5).
2. Biotite, quartz latite, Alboroto, San Juan district, Colorado (Larsen *et al.*, 1937). Anal. F. A. Gonyer.
3. Biotite, tonalitic granodiorite, Cairnsmore of Carsphairn, Kirkcudbrightshire, Scotland (Deer, 1937). Anal. W. A. Deer.
4. Brown biotite, norite, Southern California batholith (Larsen and Draisin, 1948). Anal. F. A. Gonyer.
5. Biotite, hornblende hybrid (dioritic), Cairnsmore of Carsphairn, Kirkcudbrightshire, Scotland (Deer, 1937). Anal. W. A. Deer.

Table 12. BIOTITE ANALYSES (igneous rocks)—*continued*

	6.	7.	8.	9.	10.
SiO$_2$	36·67	38·30	37·88	34·64	33·42
TiO$_2$	3·39	3·60	0·62	3·48	3·14
Al$_2$O$_3$	17·10	13·99	12·87	16·30	12·22
Fe$_2$O$_3$	4·58	3·98	4·86	3·22	9·41
FeO	16·36	20·24	21·03	19·94	21·83
MnO	0·04	0·09	0·88	0·31	0·72
MgO	9·20	7·96	8·22	8·23	6·84
CaO	0·38	0·90	—	1·03	—
Li$_2$O	—	—	—	0·25	—
Na$_2$O	0·21	0·50	1·53	0·80	1·02
K$_2$O	9·17	8·31	8·65	7·90	7·86
Rb$_2$O	—	—	—	—	—
F	1·37	0·32	—	1·69	—
H$_2$O$^+$	1·98	1·63	3·51	2·88	4·32
H$_2$O$^-$	—	—	—	0·64	—
	100·45	99·84	100·15	101·31	100·78
O≡F	0·57	0·13	—	0·73	—
Total	99·88	99·71	"100·15"	100·58	100·78
α	1·604	1·608	—	1·595	—
β	1·656	1·666	—	1·652	—
γ	1·656	1·666	—	1·656	—
2V$_\alpha$	0°	2°	—	—	—
D	—	—	—	—	—

NUMBERS OF IONS ON THE BASIS OF 24(O,OH,F)

	6.		7.		8.		9.		10.	
Si	5·623	8·00	6·015	8·00	5·894	8·00	5·326	8·00	5·233	7·49
Al	2·377		1·985		2·106		2·674		2·256	
Al	0·713		0·605		0·254		0·282		—	
Ti	0·390		0·424		0·072		0·402		0·370	
Fe^{+3}	0·528		0·470		0·568		0·374		1·108	
Fe^{+2}	2·098	5·84	2·659	6·03	2·738	5·66	2·572	5·73	2·860	6·03
Mn	0·005		0·012		0·116		0·040		0·095	
Mg	2·103		1·863		1·907		1·892		1·596	
Li	—		—		—		0·166		—	
Ca	0·062		0·151		—		0·170		—	
Na	0·062	1·92	0·150	1·97	0·462	2·18	0·240	1·97	0·308	1·88
K	1·792		1·664		1·718		1·556		1·571	
Rb	—		—		—		—		—	
F	0·664	2·69	0·158	1·87	—	3·64	0·834	3·80	—	4·51
OH	2·024		1·708		3·644		2·966		4·512	

6. Biotite, tonalite, Lakeview, Southern California batholith (Larsen and Draisin, 1948). Anal. F. A. Gonyer.
7. Biotite, granodiorite, Woodson, Southern California batholith (Larsen and Draisin, 1948). Anal. F. A. Gonyer (Includes 0·02 BaO).
8. Lepidomelane, nepheline-syenite, Låven, Norway (Kunitz, 1929). Anal. W. Kunitz.
9. Biotite, adamellite, Cairnsmore of Carsphairn, Kirkcudbrightshire, Scotland (Deer, 1937). Anal. W. A. Deer.
10. Lepidomelane, nepheline-syenite pegmatite, Brevik, Norway (Kunitz, 1924). Anal. W. Kunitz.

Table 12.　Biotite analyses (igneous rocks)—*continued*

	11.	12.	13.	14.	15.	16.
SiO_2	37·17	35·40	39·60	37·38	37·01	42·24
TiO_2	3·14	2·14	0·21	1·84	0·02	0·18
Al_2O_3	14·60	11·82	22·80	11·89	15·89	19·62
Fe_2O_3	3·75	9·52	0·79	4·38	tr.	2·02
FeO	26·85	25·09	20·98	28·65	30·16	18·64
MnO	0·06	0·67	0·29	0·41	1·01	0·30
MgO	4·23	0·95	0·46	0·22	0·22	0·08
CaO	0·17	tr.	1·52	0·16	0·10	0·11
Li_2O	—	—	0·00	0·77	1·01	1·90
Na_2O	0·15	1·54	tr.	0·39	0·58	0·14
K_2O	8·25	9·02	8·95	8·78	9·02	8·84
Rb_2O	—	—	—	—	0·19	—
F	0·85	—	2·03	4·36	3·88	5·02
H_2O^+	1·35	3·64	2·93	1·84	1·92	2·35
H_2O^-	—	0·00	0·24	0·67	0·00	0·48
	100·57	'99·86'	100·80	101·94	101·37	102·01
$O \equiv F$	0·36	—	0·85	1·86	1·68	2·11
Total	100·21	'99·86'	99·95	100·08	99·69	99·90
α	1·610	—	1·582	1·600	1·590	—
β	1·676	1·653	1·625	—	1·640	1·602
γ	1·677	1·653	1·625	1·654	1·640	1·606
$2V_\alpha$	5°	0°	—	6°	—	—
D	—	—	3·04	—	3·121	—

Numbers of ions on the basis of 24(O,OH,F)

	11.		12.		13.		14.		15.		16.	
Si	5·972	\}8·00	5·739	\}8·00	5·932	\}8·00	6·025	\}8·00	5·952	\}8·00	6·213	\}8·00
Al	2·028		2·258		2·069		1·975		2·048		1·787	
Al	0·736		—		1·956		0·284		0·964		1·616	
Ti	0·379		0·261		0·024		0·223		—		0·019	
Fe^{+3}	0·454		1·160		0·088		0·530		—		0·222	
Fe^{+2}	3·608	\}6·20	3·403	\}5·14	2·626	\}4·83	3·863	\}5·51	4·056	\}5·87	2·293	\}5·33
Mn	0·007		0·091		0·036		0·056		0·138		0·037	
Mg	1·013		0·229		0·102		0·053		0·054		0·018	
Li	—		—		—		0·499		0·654		1·124	
Ca	0·029				0·244		0·028		0·018		0·018	
Na	0·046	\}1·77	0·482	\}2·35		\}1·95	0·122	\}1·96	0·182	\}2·08‡	0·040	\}1·72
K	1·691		1·866		1·710		1·806		1·850		1·660	
Rb	—		—		—		—		0·020		—	
F	0·431	\}1·88	—	\}3·94	0·960	\}3·89	2·223	\}4·23†	1·972	\}4·10§	2·335	\}4·64||
OH	1·446		3·936		2·926		1·978		2·058		2·296	

11. Biotite, fine-grained granite, Rubideaux, Southern California batholith (Larsen and Draisin, 1948).　Anal. F. A. Gonyer.
12. Biotite, granite, Mourne Mountains, Northern Ireland (Brown, 1956).　Anal. P. E. Brown.
13. Blue-green siderophyllite, greisen vein with topaz, Newcastle, Co. Down, Northern Ireland (Nockolds and Richey, 1939).　Anal. N. Sahlbom.
14. Biotite (lepidomelane), biotite granite, Liruei, Northern Nigeria (Jacobson *et al.*, 1958).　Anal. Min. Res. Div., Colonial Geol. Surv. (Includes Cl 0·09, CO_2 0·08, S 0·03 per cent.)
15. Green-grey siderophyllite, pegmatite sill in marble, Brooks Mountain, Alaska (Coats and Fahey, 1944).　Anal. J. J. Fahey (Includes 0·12 Cs_2O, 0·24 Cl).
16. Green mica (ferrophengite), greisen zone, Liruei lode, Northern Nigeria (Jacobson *et al.*, 1958).　Anal. Min. Res. Div., Colonial Geol. Surv. (Includes Cl 0·02, CO_2 0·05, S 0·02.)

† Includes Cl 0·024.
‡ Includes Cs 0·008.
§ Includes Cl 0·066.
\|\| Includes Cl 0·004.

$K_2(Fe_3^{+2}Al_2)(Si_6Al_2)O_{20}(OH,F)_4$, and it is noteworthy that the number of Y atoms is considerably less than six. Another "siderophyllite" (Table 12, anal. 15) approximates to $K_2(Fe^{+2},Li,Al)_6Si_6Al_2O_{20}(OH,F)_4$; it has considerable replacement of Al by Li and lies fairly close to the ideal tri-octahedral composition.

Other common substitutions are:

For K: Na, Ca, Ba, Rb, Cs (*e.g.* Table 13, anal. 15). Of these sodium is usually present in higher concentration than the others but rarely exceeds 0·5 atoms per formula unit.

For Fe^{+2}: Mn, rarely exceeding 0·2 atoms in biotites.

For Al: Li (Table 12, anal. 15: see also "zinnwaldite", p. 92).

Fluorine can replace hydroxyl ions and the total $(OH + F)$ is often lower than four, the number of available sites[1]: fluorine substitution occurs mostly when there is a rather large titanium content. Chlorine also can substitute for (OH) in micas and a biotite particularly rich in chlorine (Table 13, anal. 16) has been described by Lee (1958). The high chlorine content appears to have no effect on the optical properties of the biotite since its colour and refractive indices are those expected from its content of FeO, MgO and TiO_2. The role of titanium in the biotite structure remains in some respects uncertain. It substitutes mainly in octahedral sites, but according to some authors it also may replace silicon in small amounts. Some biotite analyses show insufficient silicon and aluminium to fill the tetrahedral sites (*e.g.* Table 12, anal. 10) and in such cases it is argued that titanium, when available, enters those which are vacant. Serdyuchenko (1948b) and others, have suggested that this occurs at high temperatures of crystallization and in more alkaline conditions, and moreover that small amounts of ferric iron also can substitute for silicon. The accepted dual role of aluminium in filling either or both octahedral and tetrahedral sites seems to be governed by similar conditions, in that those minerals formed at high temperatures tend to have more aluminium in fourfold coordination (Harry, 1950). Many authors allocate aluminium, titanium or iron atoms to tetrahedral positions leaving deficiencies in the number of octahedral cations, but it is by no means certain that vacant sites are less "tolerable" in the tetrahedral section of the structure than elsewhere.

The total number of ions in octahedral sites often falls short of the possible six per formula unit, but very rarely falls below five. To this extent, therefore, minerals exist which are intermediate between tri-octahedral and di-octahedral micas since these have six and four atoms in octahedral sites respectively. The field of composition phlogopite–eastonite–annite–siderophyllite is not adequate to describe all micas since within it only those of strictly tri-octahedral character can be plotted. Gower (1957) plots muscovites and phlogopite–biotites on a single triangular diagram showing the variation in Fe, Mg and $[Al]^6$. Replacement of (Fe,Mg) by $[Al]^6$ can proceed, however, in two ways, (a) with a balancing change in $[Si]^4 : [Al]^4$ ratio from Si_6Al_2 (phlogopite) to Si_5Al_3 (eastonite), or (b) with no change from Si_6Al_2 but a decrease in total $[Y]^6$ ions. Alternative (b) can lead towards the muscovite composition whereas (a) cannot. The true

---

[1] Some very low values of (OH,F) given for biotites may be a result of difficulties in chemical analysis, and not a true chemical feature, and in some cases they may be accounted for by failure to analyse for chlorine.

Table 13.　Biotite analyses (metamorphic rocks)

	1.	2.	3.	4.	5.
SiO$_2$	38·42	36·22	35·98	36·15	36·47
TiO$_2$	1·49	3·02	2·35	1·96	2·59
Al$_2$O$_3$	18·26	16·39	18·06	19·42	19·70
Fe$_2$O$_3$	9·69	3·92	1·47	2·00	1·44
FeO	6·93	14·41	21·56	17·41	15·37
MnO	0·36	0·16	0·13	0·10	0·07
MgO	9·46	11·11	7·40	9·70	11·44
CaO	0·59	0·00	0·15	0·00	0·17
Li$_2$O	—	—	—	—	—
Na$_2$O	2·67	0·37	0·42	0·18	0·16
K$_2$O	7·17	8·97	9·09	8·61	8·98
Rb$_2$O	—	—	—	—	—
F	—	0·08	0·09	—	0·08
H$_2$O$^+$	4·58	4·00	3·28	4·03	3·58
H$_2$O$^-$	0·64	0·75	0·23	0·23	0·15
	100·28	100·19	100·21	99·79	100·20
O ≡ F	—	0·03	—	—	—
Total	100·28	100·16	100·21	99·79	100·20
α	—	1·586	—	—	—
β	—	1·643	1·644	1·635	—
γ	1·649	1·643	—	—	1·642
2V$_\alpha$	≃0°	0°–8°	—	—	—
D	—	2·98	—	—	3·01

Numbers of ions on the basis of 24(O,OH,F)

	1.	2.	3.	4.	5.
Si	5·570 ⎫ 8·00	5·466 ⎫ 8·00	5·545 ⎫ 8·00	5·420 ⎫ 8·00	5·405 ⎫ 8·00
Al	2·430 ⎭	2·534 ⎭	2·455 ⎭	2·580 ⎭	2·595 ⎭
Al	0·691 ⎫	0·386 ⎫	0·827 ⎫	0·853 ⎫	0·847 ⎫
Ti	0·162	0·344	0·272	0·221	0·288
Fe^{+3}	1·056	0·452	0·170	0·225	0·160
Fe^{+2}	0·840 ⎬ 4·84	1·812 ⎬ 5·50	2·780 ⎬ 5·77	2·183 ⎬ 5·66	1·906 ⎬ 5·82
Mn	0·044	0·018	0·017	0·013	0·088
Mg	2·044	2·492	1·700	2·168	2·527
Li	— ⎭	— ⎭	— ⎭	— ⎭	— ⎭
Ca	0·091 ⎫	— ⎫	0·025 ⎫	— ⎫	0·027 ⎫
Na	0·751 ⎬ 2·17	0·108 ⎬ 1·88†	0·126 ⎬ 1·94	0·052 ⎬ 1·70	0·046 ⎬ 1·77
K	1·325	1·722	1·787	1·647	1·700
Rb	— ⎭	— ⎭	— ⎭	— ⎭	— ⎭
F	— ⎫ 4·43	0·036 ⎫ 4·06	0·043 ⎫ 3·42	— ⎫ 4·03	0·036 ⎫ 3·58
OH	4·428 ⎭	4·024 ⎭	3·373 ⎭	4·032 ⎭	3·540 ⎭

1. Green biotite, biotite schist, Seto, Ogawa-mati, Nakoso City, Fukusima Prefecture, Japan (Shidô, 1958).　Anal. H. Haramura (Includes P$_2$O$_5$ 0·02).
2. Dark brown biotite, pegmatite-like lens in oligoclase–quartz–biotite gneiss. Charles Sound, New Zealand (Hutton, 1947).　Anal. F. T. Seelye (Includes 0·05 V$_2$O$_3$, 0·74 BaO, P$_2$O$_5$ tr).
3. Biotite, low grade garnet–mica schist, Morar, Inverness-shire (Lambert, 1959).　Anal. R. St J. Lambert (Contains Ga 20, Cr 120, V 125, Li 65, Ni 70, Co 35, Zr 40, Sr 7, Ba 500, Rb 3000 p.p.m.).
4. Biotite, medium grade garnet–mica schist, Morar, Inverness-shire (Lambert, 1959).　Anal. R. St J. Lambert (Contains Ga 18, Cr 50, V 100, Li 185, Ni 30, Co 25, Zr 20, Ba 1000, Rb 1000 p.p.m.).
5. Biotite, regionally metamorphosed biotite–plagioclase hornfels, Carn Chuinneag–Inchbae region, Ross-shire, Scotland (Harker, 1954).　Anal. R. I. Harker.

† Includes Ba 0·046

Table 13. BIOTITE ANALYSES (metamorphic rocks)—*continued*

	6.	7.	8.	9.	10.
SiO_2	35·65	34·06	37·35	35·42	36·58
TiO_2	1·78	1·42	1·71	3·15	5·14
Al_2O_3	17·51	20·52	20·31	19·04	17·35
Fe_2O_3	3·48	0·58	2·80	2·70	1·13
FeO	18·15	19·90	12·29	16·11	13·93
MnO	0·34	0·02	0·04	0·25	0·00
MgO	8·53	9·55	13·21	9·56	13·08
CaO	0·69	0·47	0·06	0·24	0·18
Li_2O	—	—	—	—	—
Na_2O	0·48	0·41	1·25	0·40	0·07
K_2O	9·83	7·57	7·81	9·30	8·73
Rb_2O	—	—	—	—	—
F	—	—	0·06	0·37	0·52
H_2O^+	3·35	5·03	2·95	3·48	3·38
H_2O^-	0·14	0·21	0·31	—	—
	100·03	99·74	100·15	100·02	100·09
$O \equiv F$	—	—	0·02	0·16	0·22
Total	100·03	99·74	100·13	99·86	99·87
α	—	—	—	—	—
β	—	1·638	1·616	—	—
γ	1·641	1·638	—	1·646	1·641
$2V_\alpha$	—	—	—	—	—
D	—	—	—	3·147	3·152

NUMBERS OF IONS ON THE BASIS OF $24(O,OH,F)$

	6.	7.	8.	9.	10.
Si	5·495 ⎱ 8·00	5·089 ⎱ 8·00	5·513 ⎱ 8·00	5·347 ⎱ 8·00	5·422 ⎱ 8·00
Al	2·505 ⎰	2·911 ⎰	2·487 ⎰	2·653 ⎰	2·578 ⎰
Al	0·677	0·704	1·049	0·733	0·454
Ti	0·207	0·160	0·189	0·357	0·572
Fe^{+3}	0·402	0·064	0·310	0·306	0·124
Fe^{+2}	2·340 ⎬ 5·63	2·488 ⎬ 5·55	1·518 ⎬ 5·98	2·033 ⎬ 5·61	1·727 ⎬ 5·77
Mn	0·044	0·003	0·005	0·031	—
Mg	1·959	2·127	2·907	2·151	2·889
Li	—	—	—	—	—
Ca	0·114	0·075	0·009	0·039	0·028
Na	0·142 ⎬ 2·19	0·118 ⎬ 1·64	0·356 ⎬ 1·84	0·116 ⎬ 1·95	0·020 ⎬ 1·70
K	1·934	1·444	1·470	1·792	1·650
Rb	—	—	—	—	—
F	— ⎱ 3·45	— ⎱ 5·01	0·028 ⎱ 2·93	0·176 ⎱ 3·68	0·243 ⎱ 3·59
OH	3·446 ⎰	5·014 ⎰	2·904 ⎰	3·502 ⎰	3·342 ⎰

6. Biotite, muscovite–biotite–microcline–quartz schist, Kaiya, Tabilo-mura, Gosaisyo-Takanuki District, Japan (Miyashiro, 1958). Anal. H. Haramura (Includes P_2O_5 0·10).
7. Biotite, staurolite–garnet–mica schist, staurolite zone, Perthumie Bay, Stonehaven, Scotland (Snelling, 1957). Anal. N. J. Snelling.
8. Biotite, kyanite gneiss, Ross of Mull, Scotland (MacKenzie, 1953). Anal. W. S. MacKenzie.
9. Greenish black biotite, quartz–biotite gneiss, West Balmat, north-west Adirondack Mountains, New York (Engel and Engel, 1960). Anal. C. G. Engel (Contains 320 p.p.m. vanadium, 750 p.p.m. barium).
10. Deep reddish brown biotite, quartz–biotite gneiss, Colton, north-west Adirondack Mountains, New York (Engel and Engel, 1960). Anal. C. G. Engel (Contains 700 p.p.m. vanadium, 1800 p.p.m. barium).

Table 13.   Biotite analyses (metamorphic rocks)—*continued*

	11.	12.	13.	14.	15.	16.
SiO_2	35·59	35·03	35·21	34·87	42·02	33·09
TiO_2	1·66	2·56	2·65	5·12	1·35	1·30
Al_2O_3	19·83	20·38	20·27	19·79	18·75	17·65
Fe_2O_3	2·52	1·08	0·68	1·72	0·66	2·42
FeO	18·49	20·41	16·88	17·79	8·29	29·22
MnO	0·25	0·02	0·35	0·02	0·27	0·04
MgO	8·16	7·11	9·78	7·42	9·55	2·83
CaO	tr.	0·17	tr.	0·54	0·93	0·10
Li_2O	—	—	—	—	1·20	—
Na_2O	0·21	0·96	0·37	0·67	0·73	0·13
K_2O	9·72	8·62	8·94	8·18	8·54	9·04
Rb_2O	—	—	—	—	1·85	0·10
F	—	—	—	0·42	4·34	0·23
H_2O^+	3·69	3·60	3·80	2·89	2·44	2·92
H_2O^-	0·15	0·07	0·53	0·29	0·16	0·04
	100·32	100·01	"99·21"	99·72	101·55	100·31
$O \equiv F$	—	—	—	0·18	1·83	0·34
Total	100·32	100·01	"99·21"	99·54	99·72	99·97
α	—	—	—	1·603	1·555	1·605
β	—	1·640	—	1·660	1·589	1·668
γ	1·647	1·640	—	1·661	1·590	1·668
$2V_\alpha$	—	—	—	—	0°–5°	0°
D	—	—	—	—	—	3·21

Numbers of ions on the basis of 24(O,OH,F)

	11.	12.	13.	14.	15.	16.
Si	5·401 ⎫ 8·00	5·339 ⎫ 8·00	5·323 ⎫ 8·00	5·327 ⎫ 8·00	6·052 ⎫ 8·00	5·337 ⎫ 8·00
Al	2·599 ⎭	2·661 ⎭	2·677 ⎭	2·673 ⎭	1·948 ⎭	2·663 ⎭
Al	0·949 ⎫	1·001 ⎫	0·935 ⎫	0·891 ⎫	1·236 ⎫	0·693 ⎫
Ti	0·190 ⎪	0·293 ⎪	0·302 ⎪	0·589 ⎪	0·146 ⎪	0·158 ⎪
Fe^{+3}	0·288 ⎪	0·124 ⎪	0·076 ⎪	0·198 ⎪	0·070 ⎪	0·292 ⎪
Fe^{+2}	2·347 ⎬ 5·65	2·602 ⎬ 5·64	2·135 ⎬ 5·70	2·274 ⎬ 5·64	0·999 ⎬ 5·23	3·942 ⎬ 5·77
Mn	0·032 ⎪	0·003 ⎪	0·044 ⎪	0·003 ⎪	0·033 ⎪	0·005 ⎪
Mg	1·846 ⎭	1·615 ⎭	2·203 ⎭	1·689 ⎭	2·050 ⎪	0·680 ⎭
Li	—	—	—	—	0·696 ⎭	—
Ca	—	0·027 ⎫	—	0·088 ⎫	0·143 ⎫	0·017 ⎫
Na	0·062 ⎫ 1·94	0·282 ⎬ 1·99	0·109 ⎫ 1·83	0·198 ⎬ 1·88	0·204 ⎪ 2·12†	0·040 ⎬ 1·93‡
K	1·882 ⎭	1·676 ⎭	1·724 ⎭	1·596 ⎭	1·570 ⎬	1·860 ⎭
Rb	—	—	—	—	0·171 ⎭	0·010 ⎭
F	— ⎫ 3·74	— ⎫ 3·66	— ⎫ 3·83	0·202 ⎫ 3·15	1·977 ⎫ 4·32	0·117 ⎫ 3·56§
OH	3·736 ⎭	3·660 ⎭	3·832 ⎭	2·946 ⎭	2·344 ⎭	3·142 ⎭

11. Biotite, sillimanite-bearing pyralspite–biotite–oligoclase–quartz gneiss, Tinokubo Hurudono-mura, Gosaisyo–Takanuki District, Japan (Miyashiro, 1958). Anal. H. Haramura (Includes P_2O_5 0·05).

12. Biotite, garnet–sillimanite–mica schist, sillimanite zone, Glen Esk, Angus, Scotland (Snelling, 1957). Anal. N. J. Snelling.

13. Biotite, cordierite–biotite hornfels, Tenryôkyô, Simoina-gôri, Nagano Prefecture, Japan (Tsuboi, 1938). Anal. S. Tanaka.

14. Biotite, silica-poor hornfels, Sparcraigs, Belhelvie, Aberdeenshire (Stewart, 1942). Anal. F. H. Stewart.

15. Brown rare-alkali biotite, schist at contact of spodumene pegmatite, Kings Mountain, North Carolina, U.S.A. (Hess and Stevens, 1937). Anal. R. E. Stevens (Includes 0·47 Cs_2O).

16. Chlorine-rich biotite, garnet–muscovite–quartz schist, Lemhi Co., Idaho, U.S.A. (Lee, 1958). Anal. E. H. Oslund (Includes 0·09 BaO, 1·11 Cl).

† Includes Cs 0·028.
‡ Includes Ba 0·005.
§ Includes Cl 0·303.

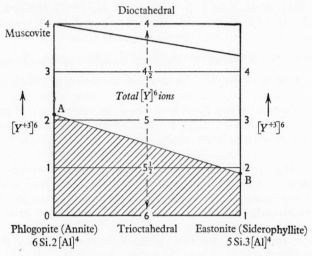

FIG. 14. Possible variations in the compositions of phlogopites and biotites, and their relation to the composition of
muscovite. Most phlogopites and biotites plot along the
base line but several are found elsewhere within the
shaded region.

relationship between muscovite, phlogopite and eastonite is shown in Fig. 14, where only two variables are plotted: as abcissa the number of Si ions and as ordinate the total number of Y ions. Along the sides of the diagram are shown the numbers of trivalent ions $(Al + Fe^{+3})$ in Y sites for each of the extremes (a) and (b). In this figure $Mg \rightleftharpoons Fe^{+2}$ substitution is not indicated, but a similar figure could be constructed with the annite–siderophyllite join as base line. Most compositions of phlogopite–biotites plot near to the base line, but two which deviate markedly (Table 12, anal. 13, and Table 10, anal. 11) are represented by the points A and B respectively, and many others are found to be within the shaded regions (see Tables 12, 13). Muscovites do not vary much from the ideal di-octahedral composition except when lithium substitution is appreciable (see p. 14).

It is generally agreed that there is not a complete solid solution series between biotite and muscovite, but opposite views have been stated. It has been suggested that biotites contain both di-octahedral (4Al) and tri-octahedral (6Mg) layers (Holzner, 1936; Serdyuchenko, 1948a): by combining these in varying proportions, any intermediate composition could in principle be achieved. No direct structural evidence is available, however, showing the existence of such mixtures, although they may occur in poorly crystalline, disordered micas.

The group of clay minerals known as illites were referred to in the previous section on muscovite. They differ from muscovite in having less Al replacing Si and having fewer inter-layer potassium ions; potassium may be partially replaced in illites by Ca^{2+}, Mg^{2+} and H^+ (or H_3O^+): particle size is very small and there is evidence of some randomness of layer stacking. Any or all of these features can be possessed by tri-octahedral micas, which can then be referred to as tri-octahedral illites or as clay biotites. A chemical analysis of a clay biotite (Walker, 1950) shows:

SiO_2 40·87, Al_2O_3 20·45, TiO_2 2·13, Fe_2O_3 12·81, MgO 6·86, MnO 0·25, CaO 0·89, K_2O 3·25, Na_2O 0·70, H_2O^+ 4·94, H_2O^- 6·90, total = 100·05, and, assuming (OH) = 4 and (O) = 20, this corresponds to the formula

$$(Ca_{0·15}K_{0·67}Na_{0·20})(Al_{2·48}Ti_{0·26}Fe^{+3}_{1·53}Mg_{1·63}Mn_{0·04})(Si_{6·6}Al_{1·4})(OH)_4O_{20}$$

in which $X = 1·02$ and $Y = 5·94$. In this case the deficit of inter-layer cations is compensated by a high trivalent ion content in Y sites. The term hydrobiotite could be used in cases where there is considerable substitution of potassium by H^+ (or perhaps by $(H_3O)^+$) as in hydromuscovite, but some specimens first described as hydrobiotite have later proved to be mixed-layer clay minerals (see p. 214).

Synthesis. High pressure hydrothermal investigation of systems containing oxidizable elements such as iron, until recently have not been undertaken, so that the iron-rich members of the phlogopite–biotite series have been synthesized mainly as fluorbiotites (*e.g.* Grigoriev, 1938; Michel Lèvy *et al.*, 1948). A purely ferruginous hydroxyl mica, however, has been synthesized (Veres *et al.*, 1955) (at 580°–590°C. and 750 bars) in the form of dark brown, flaky, almost uniaxial crystals with α 1·701, γ 1·733. The stability field of annite, $K_2Fe_6Al_2Si_6O_{20}(OH)_4$, has been investigated (Eugster, 1955) using a method in which the partial pressure of oxygen is controlled. In all there are five variables: temperature, composition, water vapour pressure, partial pressure of oxygen and total pressure. In practice $p_{H_2O} = P_{total}$, and in a given experiment a fixed composition and a constant total pressure were employed. The partial pressure of oxygen was defined by five buffers (mixtures of iron oxides, fayalite and quartz) surrounding a semipermeable sealed platinum tube in which the charge was contained. Hydrogen formed by the dissociation of water, and passing through the platinum tube, acted as a transfer agent, equalizing the partial pressure of oxygen p_{O_2} between buffer and sample. The partial pressures of hydrogen and oxygen are not independent variables since the dissociation constant of water is constant for a given T and P_{total}. With the composition of annite, p_{O_2} and T were varied for total pressures of 500, 1000 and 2000 bars, and the results are represented in Fig. 15. It is seen that in terms of T, P_{total} and p_{O_2}, annite occupies a volume within which it represents a stable phase; outside of this volume other assemblages, haematite + sanidine + vapour, magnetite + sanidine + vapour, fayalite + leucite + kalsilite + vapour, and iron + sanidine + vapour, are stable. Fig. 16 shows the section through this three dimensional figure at $P_{total} = 2000$ bars. For annite, the upper limit for p_{O_2} is that of the magnetite–haematite boundary. The $T–P_{total}$ diagram for the systems annite and annite + quartz is given in Fig. 17: for the composition annite + quartz, p_{O_2} and T were varied only for a constant P_{total} of 2000 bars (Fig. 18). This figure shows that the area $(p_{O_2}–T)$ of stability of annite is considerably reduced by the presence of quartz. From Eugster's work it is seen that for hydrous iron silicates, $P–T$ curves are inadequate for the description of stability and breakdown relations unless it is established that the Fe : O ratio is constant during the reaction.

Eugster and Wones (1958) report similar experiments for micas with various Fe:Mg ratios on the join phlogopite–annite. In these experiments compositions of the biotites synthesized at different temperatures are determined by measurement of refractive indices and the position of the 060

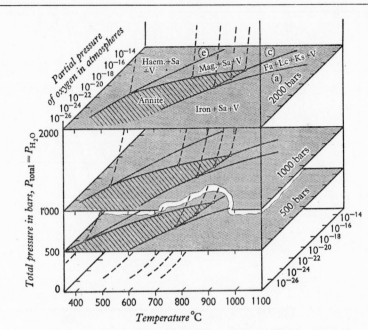

FIG. 15. P_{total}–p_{O_2}–T model of the stability volume of annite, presented in isobaric sections. The curved surfaces separating the five individual volumes are defined in this drawing by p_{O_2}–T and P_{total}–T curves (after Eugster, 1956).

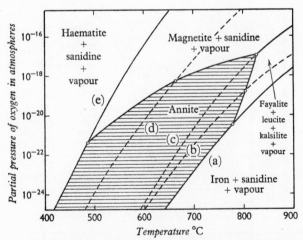

FIG. 16. Isobaric section of the stability field of annite for $P_{total} = p_{H_2O} = 2000$ bars. The curves are p_{O_2}–T curves for the following buffers: (a) iron+fayalite+silica; (b) iron+wüstite; (c) wüstite+magnetite; (d) fayalite+magnetite and silica, and (e) magnetite+haematite (after Eugster, 1956).

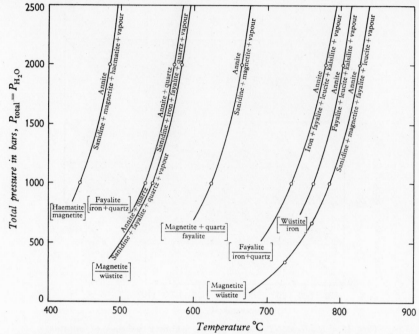

FIG. 17. Temperature—total pressure ($P_{\text{total}}=p_{\text{H2O}}$) diagram for systems annite and annite + quartz. For each of the selected univariant curves the partial pressure of oxygen is equal to that of the buffer used (brackets) and it changes with temperature accordingly (after Eugster, 1957).

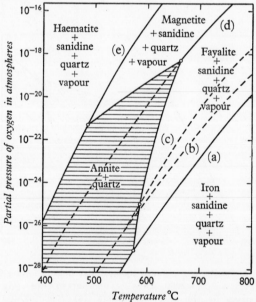

FIG. 18. Isobaric section of the stability field of annite + quartz for $P_{\text{total}} = P_{\text{H2O}} = 2000$ bars. (a), (b), (c), (d), (e) as in Fig. 16.

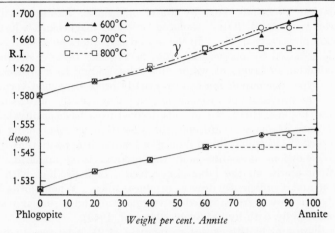

FIG. 19. Plot of refractive index and $d_{(060)}$ against composition for biotites on the join phlogopite–annite synthesized at several temperatures and oxygen pressures of a Ni–NiO buffer (after Eugster and Wones, 1958).

X-ray reflection (Fig. 19). Wones (1958a) has synthesized the pure iron, aluminium-free biotite $K_2Fe^{+2}_6Fe^{+3}_2Si_6O_{20}(OH)_4$ at 30,000 lb./in.[2] total pressure and at various temperatures and oxygen partial pressures (see also Veres *et al.*, 1955). This mica has been the subject of a crystal structure investigation by Donnay and Kingman (1958).

Alteration. The alteration of biotite by hydrothermal solutions at moderate temperatures and pressures is discussed by Schwartz (1958). Among the alteration products are green biotite, chlorite, muscovite and sericite; illite, kaolinite and other clay minerals; calcite, epidote–zoisite, leucoxene and rutile; pyrite and other sulphides. Mineralizing solutions commonly leach iron and magnesium, and substitute potassium, yielding secondary muscovite and sericite pseudomorphous after biotite. The fact that several alteration products are often found within a single small phenocryst is taken to indicate that equilibrium is rarely reached in the hydrothermal alteration of biotites. Although no single sequence of alteration is followed, Schwartz points out that recrystallized biotite is always earliest when present, and that this is commonly followed by chlorite. The elimination of titanium from biotite takes place at an early stage in alteration and results in fine- or coarse-grained rutile, the distribution of which is so uniform that it may be used to indicate the extent of former biotite areas. Of the clay minerals, kaolinite is the most common hydrothermal alteration product, but illites and smectites (probably earlier stages) have also been identified. The presence of ferrous iron in biotite facilitates the alteration by H_2S to yield pyrite and other sulphides. Schwartz (1958) draws the distinction between alteration which uses some of the elements originally present in the biotite (*e.g.* biotite→chlorite) and that in which the original material is completely removed and new elements are introduced (*e.g.* biotite→calcite). In either case there is a tendency for alteration to take place along zones parallel to the biotite cleavage.

The alteration of biotite by weathering produces either montmorillonite or vermiculite. According to Walker (1949) the first stage of weathering involves replacement of potassium ions by water molecules, forming hydrobiotite. Ferrous iron is oxidized, $(OH)^-$ replaces O^{-2}, and magnesium is lost, but the flakes remain physically stable.   In the second stage more potassium is removed and iron is replaced by magnesium from percolating waters; swelling occurs with introduction of layers of water molecules leading to a structure of the vermiculite type; decomposition can eventually proceed beyond vermiculite to kaolinite.   The procedure of weathering of a "clay biotite" was seen to follow similar lines (Walker, 1950), but in soils derived from basic or ultrabasic rocks, and under poor drainage conditions, the alteration by weathering of a clay biotite proceeded via a chlorite to montmorillonite: it appears that if either of these two conditions does not hold the product is vermiculite.   Artificial breakdown of biotite in the laboratory gives a final product with kaolinite composition, and if sufficiently drastic, produces silica.   When biotite is leached with $MgCl_2$ it is slowly transformed to vermiculite, and a similar result is obtained more rapidly with hydrobiotite (Barshad, 1948).

The weathering of biotite causes an increase of 2V, a decrease in density and refractive indices, and change of colour to yellow or white.   The rates of decomposition of muscovite and biotite in the soil are about the same, and compared with most other minerals, both are highly resistant to weathering. Biotite is readily bleached by sulphuric acid, and when strong sulphuric acid is passed over biotite flakes yellow amorphous silica is left (Mehmel, 1937).   The ferrous iron of biotite may be converted to ferric by prolonged grinding, and the transformation is accompanied by loss of hydrogen (Tzvetkov and Valyashikhina, 1956).

OPTICAL AND PHYSICAL PROPERTIES

The discussion of the relation between optical properties and chemical composition in the section on phlogopite is applicable to the whole of the phlogopite–biotite series.   Refractive indices generally show an increase with increasing iron content but are also affected appreciably by other substitutions (*e.g.* increase with Mn, Ti, decrease with F), so that an optical method of determining the Fe/Mg ratio is not reliable.   Wooster (1950) described an X-ray method for determining the iron content of members of the phlogopite–biotite series which involves measurement of the linear absorption coefficient of a mica plate, using crystal monochromatized copper $K\alpha$ radiation.   A straight line relationship is obtained when the absorption coefficient is plotted against $(2Fe_2O_3 + FeO)$.

The optic axial plane is parallel to (010) in most biotites but for some specimens it is perpendicular to (010), and these two types of biotite have been referred to by many writers as meroxene and anomite respectively.   It has now been established that meroxene and anomite are equivalent to 1M and $2M_1$ polymorphs respectively (Heinrich *et al.*, 1953), and in view of this the use of the above names would seem to be superfluous.   Throughout the mica group all $2M_1$ polymorphs have their optic axial plane perpendicular to (010) and in nearly all 1M polymorphs it is parallel to (010).   Among the very few biotites which have refractive indices outside of the ranges indicated above (p. 55) are those with an extremely high content of Fe^{+3}, which have γ and δ as high as 1·73 and 0·08 respectively: such minerals are sometimes called ferrian biotites.

The colours of biotites are generally deeper than those of phlogopite and are related to composition in a general way; colour zoning is uncommon. Hayama (1959) finds that the principal factors which influence colour are TiO_2 content and the ratio $Fe_2O_3/(Fe_2O_3 + FeO)$. High TiO_2 content gives a reddish brown colour while high ferric iron gives green. It is the balance of these two factors, however, rather than their absolute values which determines the colour. Thus a biotite with low TiO_2 will yet be brown provided that Fe_2O_3 is low, and one with low Fe_2O_3 can be green if there is very little TiO_2. Intermediate proportions of Ti and Fe^{+3} result in yellowish or greenish brown colourations. Biotite often exhibits pleochroic haloes which are attributed to the presence of inclusions of zircon or other minerals containing elements belonging to the radioactive series U–Ra and Th–Ac: Hutton (1947) found nuclei of monazite, xenotime and apatite. Pleochroism is generally more marked in biotites containing much iron, and the anisotropy of paramagnetic susceptibility follows a similar trend.

Biotite often occurs in large, well formed crystals with tabular {001} habit and pseudo-hexagonal outline. The test of percussion figures may be applied to determine crystallographic orientation (see p. 9), but as with other micas it is not always easy to interpret. Biotite cleaves perfectly on {001} yielding sheets of uniform thickness which have high elasticity.

DISTINGUISHING FEATURES

Biotite is generally darker in colour and more highly pleochroic than the other micas, and has higher refractive indices. It can be distinguished from muscovite by its low 2V. Vermiculite has lower refractive indices and birefringence, and chlorites have a much lower birefringence. Lepidolites can be distinguished by their paler colour and by the lithium flame test. X-ray powder patterns are distinctive from those of di-octahedral micas. Stilpnomelane may be mistaken for biotite (see p. 110).

PARAGENESIS

Biotite occurs in a greater variety of geological environments than any of the other micas. In metamorphic rocks it is formed under a wide range of temperature and pressure conditions, and it occurs abundantly in many contact and regionally metamorphosed sediments. Among the intrusive igneous rocks it occurs commonly in granites and granite pegmatites, granodiorites, tonalites, diorites, norites, quartz and nepheline-syenites and quartz monzonites. Biotite is particularly characteristic of the intermediate rocks of calc-alkali affinities and occurs in a wide range of rocks of hydrid origin. It is found less frequently in igneous extrusive rocks, but occurs in rhyolites, trachytes, dacites, latites, andesites and some basalts.

Thermal metamorphism. During the thermal metamorphism of many argillaceous rocks biotite, as small flakes interspersed in the chlorite–sericite groundmass, is generally the first new product of the recrystallization; it is only rarely absent from the succeeding higher grade hornfelses. The formation of biotite occurs at the expense of the chlorite, white mica, iron ore and rutile of the original sediment. At Comrie, Perthshire, Tilley (1924) noted that the biotite in the outer aureole of the Carn Chois diorite shows a tendency to crystallize in flakes parallel to the oriented wisps of chlorite and sericite. Closer to the contact the biotite increases in grain size and the well-defined orientation typical of the biotites in the outer aureole is less marked. Biotite is often associated with andalusite and cordierite in the low grade hornfelses but both minerals normally do not crystallize until after the initial formation of biotite. At higher grades of thermal metamorphism the amount of biotite diminishes, and it is ultimately replaced by potassium felspar, orthopyroxene and sillimanite, or by potassium felspar and cordierite. In the Comrie area biotite occurs in andalusite–cordierite–quartz hornfels (class I), cordierite–plagioclase–quartz hornfels (class III), quartz–cordierite–hypersthene–plagioclase–orthoclase hornfels (class IV), hypersthene–plagioclase hornfels (class V), and quartz–diopside–plagioclase–orthoclase hornfels (class VII).

The analysis of a biotite (Table 13, anal. 14) from a silica-poor argillaceous hornfels, consisting of garnet, spinel, cordierite, plagioclase, biotite, magnetite and pyrrohotite with a little sillimanite and potassium felspar, is given by Stewart (1942). The biotite has a high Al and Ti content and is one of the very few analysed biotites from thermally metamorphosed rocks (see also anal. 13, Table 13). Pitcher and Sinha (1957) have investigated the change in composition of the biotites in the aureole of the Ardara pluton of the Donegal granite complex. The country rocks consist of regionally metamorphosed pelitic sediments converted to fine-grained biotite–muscovite schists. Retrograde metamorphism subsequently caused a partial conversion of the biotite to chlorite. During the later thermal metamorphism, reconstruction of the biotite was effected largely at the expense of the chlorite, the white mica presumably being the source of the potassium. The biotites of the inner aureole have significantly higher contents of Fe^{+3} and Ti, and those of the outer aureole higher contents of Mg and K; sympathetic changes in the value of the γ refractive indices were also recorded. Tilley (1926) had earlier noted a progressive change in the colour of biotite during thermal metamorphism, those of the inner aureoles having a deeper red tint, and suggested that these biotites have a higher iron content than those in the less metamorphosed rocks of the outer parts of the aureoles.

The breakdown of biotite to sillimanite in the Dalradian schists of Barnesbeg, County Donegal, due to the contact action of the Donegal granite, has been described by Tozer (1955). In these rocks, as the ratio of sillimanite to biotite increases, the colour of the biotite becomes progressively paler. It has been suggested by Ramberg (1952) that in the highest part of the amphibolite facies the breakdown of biotite may take place by the following reactions:

$$\underset{\text{Fe-biotite}}{(OH)_2KFe_3AlSi_3O_{10}} + \underset{\text{muscovite}}{(OH)_2KAl_3Si_3O_{10}} + 3SiO_2 \rightleftharpoons$$

$$\underset{\text{orthoclase}}{2KAlSi_3O_8} + \underset{\text{almandine}}{Fe_3Al_2Si_3O_{12}} + 2H_2O$$

$$\underset{\text{phlogopite}}{(OH)_2KMg_3AlSi_3O_{10}} + \underset{\text{muscovite}}{(OH)_2KAl_3Si_3O_{10}} + 3SiO_2 \rightleftharpoons$$

$$\underset{\text{orthoclase}}{2KAlSi_3O_8} + \underset{\text{pyrope}}{Mg_3Al_2Si_3O_{12}} + 2H_2O$$

As iron-rich biotite is likely to react at lower PT conditions than iron-poor biotite, the more magnesium-rich biotite will remain stable under higher PT conditions, as indicated by the progressive decolorization of the Barnesbeg biotites. The sillimanitization reaction is expressed by Francis (1956) as follows:

$$(OH)_2KFe_3AlSi_3O_{10} + Al_2O_3 + SiO_2 \rightleftharpoons KAlSi_3O_8 + Al_2SiO_5 + 3FeO + H_2O$$

Fe-biotite   (from dissolved   orthoclase   sillimanite
              kyanite)

The formation of a more magnesium-rich biotite at this locality is in contrast with the development of a more iron-rich biotite in the inner aureole of the Ardara pluton. In the latter area, however, the biotite is stable at the *PT* conditions of the metamorphism, but at Barnesbeg the biotite is unstable and in the process of transformation to sillimanite.

Regional metamorphism. Compared with its formation in thermally metamorphosed rocks the crystallization of biotite occurs somewhat later in the recrystallization and reconstruction processes of regional metamorphism. The material for its formation is drawn, however, from the same minerals as in thermal metamorphism, *i.e.* from reaction between antigoritic chlorite, muscovite and iron ore (Tilley, 1924). The crystallization of biotite in rocks of argillaceous composition is taken to mark the onset of the *PT* conditions of the biotite zone, typical rocks of which include biotite schist, biotite–sericite schist, biotite–chlorite schist and albite–biotite schist. The textural relations in many pelitic and semi-pelitic sediments do not suggest that the biotite forms at the expense of any specific pre-existing material, but the increase in biotite in the biotite zone is coincident with a decrease in chlorite and especially in muscovite. Biotite is a stable mineral of the garnet zone of regional metamorphism, and is an important constituent of many garnet–mica schists. It has been suggested by Snelling (1957) that the formation of biotite in the garnet zone may lead to the development of a more magnesium-rich biotite than is formed in the biotite zone:

$$Fe^{+2}_{11}Mg_{10}Al_6Si_{13}O_{40}(OH)_{32} + 2KAl_3Si_3O_{10}(OH)_2 + 2SiO_2 \rightarrow$$

amesitic chlorite   muscovite

$$(Fe^{+2}_{11}Mg_4)Al_{10}Si_{15}O_{60} + 2KMg_3AlSi_3O_{10}(OH)_2 + 16H_2O$$

almandine garnet   phlogopite

Biotite is common also in many rocks of the succeeding zones of regional metamorphism, and its presence in the staurolite, kyanite and sillimanite zones is related in part to the limited substitution of Fe^{+2} by Mg in staurolite, and in the two highest zones to the absence of another ferromagnesian mineral. Although the most common rock type in the sillimanite zone rocks of the Abukuma Plateau (Miyashiro, 1958) is a biotite–potassium-felspar–plagioclase–quartz gneiss, usually with smaller amounts of muscovite and pyralspite garnet and sillimanite, some rocks also contain andalusite and cordierite; Miyashiro has suggested that at this grade of metamorphism biotite is no longer stable and reacts with muscovite to form some of the potassium felspar and cordierite:

$$6(OH)_2KAl_3Si_3O_{10} + 2(OH)_2K(Mg,Fe^{+2})_3AlSi_3O_{10} + 15SiO_2 \rightarrow$$

muscovite   biotite

$$8KAlSi_3O_8 + 3(Mg,Fe^{+2})_2Al_4Si_5O_{18} + 8H_2O$$

potassium   cordierite
felspar

From a study of the biotites in the Pre-Cambrian Grenville gneisses of southwestern Quebec, Kretz (1959) has shown that biotites which are associated with sillimanite contain less Ca than those not accompanied by sillimanite. This relationship is considered by Kretz to indicate that biotites with a Ca content above a particular concentration are not stable with sillimanite: the reaction may be:

$$Ca(Mg,Fe^{+2})_3Al_2Si_2O_{10}(OH)_2 + Al_2SiO_5 + 2SiO_2 \rightleftharpoons$$
Ca biotite mol. in K–Ca biotite   sillimanite   quartz

$$CaAl_2Si_2O_8 + (Mg,Fe^{+2})_3Al_2Si_3O_{12} + H_2O$$
(in plagioclase)   garnet

In a particular metamorphic PT environment the reaction will move to the left or right side of the equation until a specific Ca concentration of the biotite is obtained. Thus the Ca concentration of biotite which coexisted with sillimanite, anorthite, garnet, quartz and H_2O at the time of their crystallization may provide an indication of the temperature of formation and the metamorphic grade. Kretz (1959) has also shown that biotites which coexist with sillimanite tend to have a greater Al content (Al_2O_3 17·0 to 19·5 per cent.) than biotite not accompanied by sillimanite (Al_2O_3 12·7 to 17·6 per cent.).

The distribution of Fe, Mg, Mn, Ti, V, Cr, Zr, Y and Sc in the biotites, garnets and hornblendes of the Grenville gneisses of south-western Quebec has been investigated by Kretz (1959), and it has been shown that the distribution of some elements between coexisting minerals follows Nernst's distribution law very closely, *e.g.* the distribution of V between biotite and hornblende. The distribution diagram is interpreted by Kretz to express Nernst's distribution law graphically: the slope of the line is the distribution constant:

$$\frac{C_V^H}{C_V^B} = K_V^{H-B} = 1\cdot 2$$

where C_V^H is the concentration of V (or V_2O_3) in hornblende, C_V^B is the concentration of V in biotite, and K_V^{H-B} is the distribution constant. The distribution of some elements between coexisting minerals is completely irregular, *e.g.* the distribution of Ti between biotite and garnet. This may be due to contamination by small inclusions of simple oxides or silicates, or to the amount of the element in a mineral being less than the amount present at the time of crystallization because of exsolution beyond the crystal boundaries.

Variation in the composition of biotite with different grade of metamorphism has been demonstrated from a number of localities, thus Barth (1936) found that the biotite in the higher grade rocks of Dutchess County have a lower iron content than those in the lower grade rocks. From a detailed study of the biotites of the major Adirondack paragneiss Engel and Engel (1960) conclude that a decrease in Mn, Fe^{+2} and Fe^{+3}, and an increase in Ti, Mg, Ba, Cr and V, can be correlated with increasing grade of metamorphism. The most valuable indications of the degree of metamorphism are the ratios TiO_2:MnO and FeO (or $FeO+MnO$):MgO, the oxide pairs varying antipathetically. Examples of biotites from the lowest and highest grade rocks studied by Engel and Engel are given (Table 13) in anals. 9 and 10 respectively. Lambert (1959) from a study of fourteen biotites (*e.g.* Table 13, anals. 3, 4) from Moine rocks of the Morar district, Inverness-shire, likewise showed that the Mg content increases with increasing grade. Snelling's (1957) work on the biotites of the pelitic schists, ranging from the biotite to the sillimanite zones, of the Glen Esk,

Stonehaven and Aberdeen area, showed that in general the low grade biotites have a higher Si and lower Al content than the biotites of medium and higher grades. The biotites of this area, however, showed no systematic variation of the $Fe^{+2}:Mg$ ratio with metamorphic grade. An increase in the content of Fe^{+2} and Mn with increasing metamorphic grade in the biotite from a number of localities has been noted by DeVore (1955a), and in biotites of rocks in the amphibolite facies, Nagano Prefecture, Japan, by Miyashiro (1956). The latter has demonstrated that the biotites (Table 13, anals. 6, 11) in the pelitic rocks of the higher zones of the central Abukuma Plateau, Japan (Miyashiro, 1953, 1958) have a higher Ti and lower Mn content than those of the intermediate zone (intermediate zone biotites have MnO 0·47, 0·42 and 0·34 per cent., highest zone biotites have MnO 0·42, 0·33, 0·32, 0·25 and 0·05 per cent.).

The variation in biotite composition with metamorphic grade is clearly related in part to the nature of the other ferromagnesian minerals present. Thus DeVore's biotites are from garnet-free hornblende and pyroxene-bearing metamorphic rocks, whereas the biotites of Dutchess County (Barth, 1936) and from the Adirondacks (Engel and Engel, 1960) coexist with garnet. In the latter rocks Engel and Engel report that as the temperature of metamorphism increases garnet appears at the expense of biotite and quartz, and that fractionation of elements occurs, the biotite being enriched in Mg, Ba, Co, Cr, Cu, Ni, Ti and V, while the garnet takes Mn, Fe, Ca, Sr, Y and Yb (the ratios Co:Fe and Ni:Fe were thus also found to be useful indices of metamorphic grade). Snelling (1957) suggested that both almandine and staurolite take up Fe^{+2} in preference to Mg, and showed that the Mg content of biotites from staurolite schists is considerably higher than that of their parent rocks. In regionally metamorphosed rocks in which cordierite is present Mg preferentially enters the cordierite, and the biotites of such rocks have a lower Mg content than those of the parent rocks.

The biotites of the Adirondack paragneisses are intermediate in composition between those from granites and diorites. Increasing grade of metamorphism corresponds to a more basic environment of igneous crystallization, so that the compositions of biotites from lower grade rocks are more nearly comparable with those of granites. The increase in the barium content with increasing metamorphism is similar to that reported by Engelhart (1936) for igneous biotites in which barium increases with the temperature of crystallization.

A systematic change in colour from greenish brown through reddish brown to deep reddish black with increasing metamorphism was observed by Engel and Engel (1960) in the Adirondack biotites. The best correlation between chemistry and colour was obtained by considering the ratio $(TiO_2/MgO):$(total iron as FeO) rather than $(TiO_2):$(total iron), since the presence of magnesium in large amounts tends to dilute the colour effects of Fe and Ti (see Hall, 1941). In the central Abukuma Plateau rocks of Japan, Miyashiro (1958) found no systematic relationship between the γ refractive index of the biotite and metamorphic grade, but showed that the γ index of the biotites in the pelitic and psammitic rocks lies most frequently between 1·640 and 1·650, whereas the most common γ index of the biotites from the basic metamorphosed rocks lies between 1·630 and 1·640. The colour for γ in the biotites of the pelitic and psammitic rocks of the lower zone is greenish brown, brown or yellowish brown, and in the highest zones the colour for γ is brown.   From another area of the central Abukuma Plateau, Shidô (1958) noted that a green colour is characteristic of the biotite (*e.g.* Table 13, anal. 1) of the pelitic and psammitic schists belonging to the lowest metamorphic grades.   Similar variation in the colours of biotites with grade of metamorphism has been reported elsewhere (*e.g.* Tilley, 1925; Phillips, 1930; Ambrose, 1936).

Charnockites.   Biotite is neither a common nor an abundant mineral in charnockites but Howie (1955) has described an intermediate rock from Salem, Madras, containing 8 per cent. biotite.   Howie has shown that Ga, Li and V are more concentrated in the biotites from the more acid rocks, Sc, Y and Sr concentrated in biotite of the rocks of intermediate composition, while the highest content of Cr occurs in the more magnesium-rich biotites.   Parras (1958) has reported biotite as an abundant constituent in some of the rocks of charnockitic affinities from the West Uusimaa complex, south-western Finland.   In some of the pyroxene-bearing rocks of the West Uusimaa complex inclusions of biotite are present as small flakes outlining the prism faces of the host pyroxene, and are associated with minute amounts of secondary quartz.   The biotite flakes are interpreted by Parras as the result of exsolution, particularly of K, Al and Ti which entered the pyroxene during the high P,T conditions of its formation. The biotites of charnockites and related rocks characteristically are strongly pleochroic, with γ brown, dark brown or reddish brown.

Igneous rocks.   A large number of chemical analyses have been made of biotites from igneous rocks, and from these several close relationships between paragenesis and composition have been observed.   From a study of the biotites (Table 12, anals. 3, 5, 9) of the Carsphairn igneous complex, Deer (1937) concluded that those in the more acid parent rocks have higher $Fe^{+2}:Mg$ and $R^{+3}:R^{+2}$ ratios.   The octahedral sites are rarely completely filled and it appears that more vacancies occur as the trivalent ion content and the $Fe^{+2}:Mg$ ratio increase.   Similar relations are also shown by the biotites of the Garabal Hill–Glen Fyne complex (Nockolds, 1941).   These biotites show a decrease in Si, Ti and Mg, and an increase in Al, Fe^{+2} and Fe^{+3} on proceeding from the pyroxene–mica diorite to the porphyritic granodiorite.   Variation in the trace element content of these biotites shows a progressive increase in Ga, Mn and Rb, and a progressive decrease in Cr, V, Cu, Ni, Co and Sr from the early to the late-formed minerals.   A rapid increase in Li occurs in the early stages after which it remains more or less constant (Nockolds and Mitchell, 1948).   Although an increase in Fe^{+2} and $(Fe^{+2}+Fe^{+3})$ and a decrease in Mg is general for the late-formed biotites of any intrusion when compared with early formed biotites from any other intrusion, there is no simple relationship between the overall composition of a biotite and the silica content of the rock in which it occurs.

Analyses of eight biotites from rocks of the Southern California batholith (Larsen and Draisin, 1950) also show increasing Fe^{+2} content with the increasing acidity of the host rock, from Fe^{+2} 2·0 in norite, 2·1 in tonalite, 2·7 in granodiorite, to 3·6 in granite (Table 12, anals, 4, 6, 7, 11).   A similar relationship has also been reported by Larsen and Schmidt (1958) for the biotites of the quartz monzonite and tonalite of the Idaho batholith.   In the rocks of the Southern California batholith there is a general decrease in the Al content of the biotites in the granodiorite and granite compared with the norite and tonalite.   Low contents of Al in the biotite (Table 12, anal. 14) of the biotite granite of the Liruei ring complex, Northern Nigeria (Jacobson *et al.*, 1958), and in the biotite (Table 12, anal. 12) of the G.2 granite of the Mourne Mountains (Brown, 1956) have also been reported.   The latter rock is a highly siliceous granite, and it is interesting to note that the Mourne biotite contains just sufficient Al to fill the eight tetrahedral sites per formula unit.

A number of biotites from some Caledonian calc-alkali igneous rocks have been plotted by Nockolds and Mitchell (1948) on a FeO–MgO–Al_2O_3 diagram.   The biotite analyses plotted in this way, with the exception of a biotite from a muscovite–biotite adamellite, follow a well-defined trend, a trend which is continued by two biotites from the Dartmoor granites (Brammall and Harwood, 1932).   The behaviour of the trace elements with respect to the major elements of similar ionic radius in these biotites has also been investigated by Nockolds and Mitchell.   The ratios $Ga:Al$, $Li:Mg$, $Mn:Fe^{+2}$ and $Rb:K$ all show a strong tendency to increase, and the ratios $Ni:Mg$, $Co:Fe^{+2}$ and $Ba:K$ to decrease in the late formed biotites.   The ratios $Cr:Fe^{+3}$, $V:Fe^{+3}$ and $Sr:(K+Ca)$ are more variable, but show a general decrease in passing from early to late biotites in any particular intrusion.

Nockolds (1947) has examined the relation between the chemical composition and paragenesis of some seventy biotites of igneous rocks.   He concluded that in biotites from calc-alkali rocks the ratio $Al_2O_3:(MgO+\text{total Fe as }FeO)$ is determined by their paragenesis, but that in general the ratio $MgO:(\text{total Fe as }FeO)$ is dependent on the degree of differentiation of the magma from which the biotite crystallized, or the degree of contamination it has undergone.   Table 14 gives the average compositions of biotites of the above parageneses in calc-alkali igneous rocks, and in alkali igneous rocks.   In going

Table 14. AVERAGE COMPOSITIONS OF BIOTITES OF DIFFERENT PARAGENESES
(Nockolds, 1947)

	Calc-alkali igneous rocks					Alkali igneous rocks		
	a	b	c	d	e	f	g	h
Biotite associated with	Topaz etc.	Muscovite	Biotite alone	Hornblende	Pyroxene and/or olivine	Biotite alone	Alkali amphiboles	Aegirine
Si	5·89	5·30	5·49	5·53	5·74	5·48	5·63	5·52
[Al]^4	2·11	2·70	2·51	2·47	2·19	2·52	2·23	2·12
[Ti]^4	—	—	—	—	0·07	—	0·14	0·24
[Al]^6	1·42	0·78	0·38	0·15	0·09	0·44	0·19	0·10
Total octahedral atoms	5·08	5·45	5·66	5·85	5·81	5·75	5·44	5·67
(Total Fe as FeO) / MgO	43·7	3·20	3·05	1·75	0·62	—	—	—
Fe$_2$O$_3$ / FeO	0·23	0·22	0·14	0·22	0·17	0·23	0·28	0·33
MnO	—	0·46	0·53	0·34	0·13	0·49	0·82	1·46
Na$_2$O / K$_2$O	—	0·11	0·07	0·06	0·09	0·12	0·16	0·15

from column b, biotites associated with muscovite, to column e, biotites associated with pyroxene and/or olivine, the amount of Al in both tetrahedral and octahedral coordination decreases, the total number of ions in octahedral sites rises, and the ratio MgO : (total Fe as FeO) increases.   Biotites associated with topaz, spodumene, and beryl (column a) do not conform to these sequences. Data on biotites from alkali igneous rocks are more scanty but averages for these are shown in columns f, g and h.   More Ti enters into tetrahedral sites and the ratios $Fe^{+3} : Fe^{+2}$, Na : K, as well as the Mn content, are higher than for the biotites of the calc-alkali rocks (see anals. 8, 10, table 12).

The position of biotite in the sequence of crystallization of the ferromagnesian minerals in rocks of the calc-alkaline series has been investigated by Nockolds (1946).   In the Garabal Hill–Glen Fyne complex (Nockolds, 1947) biotite is confined to the groundmass of the chilled phase of the earliest rocks lying on the assumed liquid line of descent.   Likewise in the medium-grained rocks the crystallization of biotite generally begins after the cessation of olivine and pyroxene, and is only partially coincident with the formation of hornblende. The completion of biotite crystallization is believed to occur prior to that of the plagioclase, potassium felspar and quartz.   In the rocks of the Southern California batholith (Larsen and Draisin, 1950) the crystallization of biotite was in part coincident with the formation of pyroxene.   In this intrusion, however, there is little evidence of a reaction relation between hornblende and biotite, and for the most part the two minerals crystallized together.   The distribution of biotite is similar in both the plutonic and volcanic rocks of this region, and it is absent in the gabbros and basalts, crystallization beginning in both groups when the $(\frac{1}{3}SiO_2 + K_2O - CaO - FeO - MgO)$ value of the host rock is -2.   In the plutonic rocks biotite is the chief ferromagnesian mineral in host rocks in which the $(\frac{1}{3}SiO_2 + K_2O - CaO - FeO - MgO)$ value is > 5 (tonalites, granodiorites, granites) and in the volcanic rocks when this value is > 12 (quartz latite, rhyolite).

Biotite is a very common constituent of rocks of intermediate composition which have arisen by the assimilation of gabbroic, doleritic or noritic material in acid magmas.   The crystallization of biotite as the end product of a number of reaction series, *e.g.* monoclinic pyroxene→brown hornblende→green hornblende→biotite, and monoclinic pyroxene→orthorhombic pyroxene→biotite, has been emphasized by Nockolds (1934).   In particular the progressive alteration of hornblende to biotite with the increasing modification of basic xenoliths in rocks of both intermediate and acid composition has been noted by many workers.   Thus in the basic xenoliths in the tonalite of the Carsphairn Complex (Deer, 1935, 1937) the ratio biotite : hornblende changes from 1 : 4 in the least modified xenoliths to 1 : 0·5 in those most affected by the assimilation process. The convergence of the biotite : hornblende ratio in the xenoliths to that of the tonalite (biotite : hornblende ratio 1 : 0·4) is accompanied by the development of an almost equal amount of the two minerals in the most highly modified xenoliths and in the tonalite.

Although biotite occurs more commonly in the intermediate and acid plutonic rocks it is also an important constituent of some basic rocks.   Thus biotite is an abundant constituent in the quartz–biotite norites and cordierite norites of the Haddo House district (Read, 1935), where its crystallization may be due to the assimilation of andalusite–cordierite schists and cordierite–biotite gneisses in gabbroic magma.

Biotite occurs in most of the rocks of the amphibolite–gneissose quartz diorite series of the Gosaisyo–Takanuki district, Japan. The quartz diorite is considered by Ogura (1958) to have been derived from the amphibolite by a process of granitization due to soaking of the basic rock by quartzofelspathic components. With advancing granitization the content of total iron and Fe^{+3} in the biotites increases and that of Mg, Ti and Mn decreases. There is a tendency also for the γ refractive index of the biotite to increase as the anorthite content of the coexisting plagioclase decreases.

The partial chloritization of biotite during the hydrothermal stage of crystallization is common in many granites, and Chayes (1955) has suggested that the transformation, in terms of an iron-free and an iron mica, may be expressed:

$$(OH)_4K_2(Mg_5Al)(Al_3Si_5O_{20}) + 4SiO_2 + 2H_2O$$
eastonite

$$\rightarrow (OH)_8Mg_5Al_2Si_3O_{10} + 2KAlSi_3O_8$$
clinochlore   potassium felspar

$$2(OH)_2KFe_3^{+2}AlSi_3O_{10} + 2H_2O$$
iron mica

$$\rightarrow (OH)_8Fe_5^{+2}Fe^{+3}AlSi_3O_{10} + KAlSi_3O_8 + K$$
iron chlorite   potassium felspar

Biotite occurs much less frequently in extrusive than in plutonic rocks and when present it is usually partially altered to other minerals. An explanation of the different behaviour of biotite in plutonic and volcanic rocks, in terms of the experimentally determined stability curve of phlogopite and its relation to the minimum melting curves of granite and of basalt, has been given by Yoder and Eugster (1954). In Fig. 20 it is seen that the phlogopite stability curve lies above the granite melting curve for all but the lowest pressure, but it crosses the basalt melting curve at some intermediate pressure. Thus in a basic rock phlogopite would be stable at depth but would become unstable on extrusion. The validity of extending these conclusions to a mica of biotite composition is somewhat doubtful, since experimental work on annite has shown that the stability curve is much affected by the substitution of iron for magnesium (Eugster, 1956). Micas having a biotitic composition do, however, occur in extrusive rocks, and commonly are partially or completely resorbed, a feature which is most marked in the biotites of the least siliceous extrusives, *e.g.* in the volcanic rocks of the San Juan region, Colorado (Larsen *et al.*, 1937). Coronas of hornblende, with or

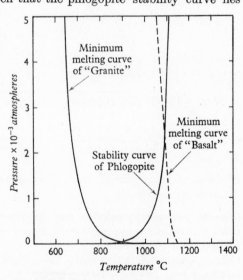

FIG. 20. Relation of upper stability curve of phlogopite to the determined minimum melting curve of granite (Bowen and Tuttle, 1953, p. 50) and the estimated minimum melting curve of basalt (after Yoder and Eugster, 1954).

without subordinate plagioclase laths, are common around the biotite in the volcanic rocks from Sambre, south-western Japan (Taneda, 1952). Except for basaltic biotite, the compositions of biotites of volcanic rocks do not fit the fields of their intrusive equivalents (see p. 78), and in general are poorer in Fe^{+2} and richer in Fe^{+3} and Ti (*e.g.* Table 12, anal. 2). In many volcanic rocks the biotites occur as phenocrysts, and their marginal and some-times complete oxidation is related to the crystallization of the groundmass material under surface conditions.

A general study of the relation between biotite composition and geological occurrence was made by Heinrich (1946). The results of this wide survey, which in general confirm those derived from more restricted fields, are sum-marized in Fig. 21. Here are plotted on a triangular diagram, $(Fe_2O_3 + TiO_2)$–$(FeO + MnO)$–(MgO), the main types of rocks in which biotites and phlogopites

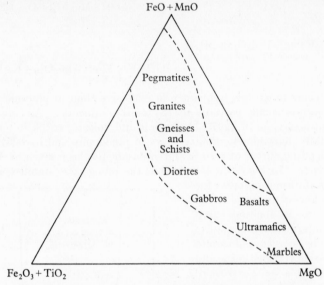

FIG. 21   Variation of chemical composition of phlogopites and
biotites with rock type (compiled from diagrams of Heinrich,
1946) (after Engel and Engel, 1960).

of different composition occur. The principal conclusions expressed in the diagram are as follows:

Granitic pegmatites: biotites are characterized mainly by a very high FeO content (maximum approximately 30 per cent.). Both MgO and $Fe_2O_3 + TiO_2$ are less than 10 per cent.

Granite, quartz monzonites and granodiorites: FeO content varies from about 12 to 25 per cent., $Fe_2O_3 + TiO_2$ generally less than 10 per cent., the MgO content may be as high as 12 per cent.

Tonalites, diorites: FeO content generally lower, $Fe_2O_3 + TiO_2$ approximately the same, MgO higher than in the previous group.

Gabbros: MgO content between 15 and 20 per cent., ratio of $(FeO + MnO):(Fe_2O_3 + TiO_2)$ close to unity. Maximum FeO and Fe_2O_3 are approximately

10 and 8 per cent. respectively, TiO_2 is high in minerals with a low content of Fe_2O_3.

Peridotites and other ultramafic rocks: mainly phlogopites, maximum FeO 5 per cent., Fe_2O_3 6 per cent. Maximum MgO approaches 30 per cent. Content of TiO_2 is generally small.

Syenites, nepheline-syenites and syenitic pegmatites: high content of FeO, maximum about 32 per cent., highest percentage of Fe_2O_3, MgO rarely greater than 7 per cent.

Gneisses and schists: limited range in composition, FeO maximum 20 per cent., FeO generally less than 10 per cent., and MgO usually less than 18 per cent.

Metamorphosed limestones: phlogopites—very rich in MgO with a maximum of approximately 30 per cent. Maximum content of $FeO + Fe_2O_3$ is less than 10 per cent.

The compositional relationships between coexisting biotite and pyroxene, and coexisting biotite and hornblende have been investigated by DeVore (1957). Biotites generally have a higher content of $[Al]^4$, $[Al]^6$, Fe^{+3} and Ti than the coexisting pyroxenes, and with few exceptions, a higher content of $[Al]^4$, Fe^{+3}, Ti and a lower $Mg:(Mg + Ti^{+2})$ ratio than the coexisting hornblende. The role of adsorption in the fractionation and distribution of the minor constituent elements in biotite and the variation of $Mg:(Mg + Fe^{+2})$ has been discussed by DeVore (1955a, b).

REFERENCES

Ambrose, J. W., 1936. Progressive kinetic-metamorphism of the Missi series near Flinflon, Manitoba. *Amer. Journ. Sci.*, ser. 5, vol. 32, p. 257.
Barshad, I., 1948. Vermiculite and its relation to biotite as revealed by base exchange reactions, X-ray analysis, differential thermal curves, and water content. *Amer. Min.*, vol. 33, p. 655.
Barth, T. F. W., 1936. Structural and petrological studies in Dutchess County, New York, Pt. II. *Bull. Geol. Soc. Amer.*, vol. 47, p. 775.
Berkhin, S. I., 1954. Rontgenograms of iron-magnesia micas. *Doklady Acad. Sci. USSR*, vol. 95, p. 145.
Bowen, N. L. and Tuttle, O. F., 1953. Beginning of melting of some natural granites. *Carnegie Inst. Washington, Ann. Rep. Dir. Geophys. Lab.*, 1952–1953, vol. 52, p. 50.
Brammall, A. and Harwood, H. F., 1932. The Dartmoor granites: their genetic relationships. *Quart. Journ. Geol. Soc.*, vol. 88, p. 171.
Brown, P. E., 1956. The Mourne Mountains granites—a further study. *Geol. Mag.*, vol. 93, p. 72.
Chayes, F., 1955. Potash feldspar as a by-product of the biotite-chlorite transformation. *Journ. Geol.*, vol. 63, p. 75.
Coats, R. R. and Fahey, J. J., 1944. Siderophyllite from Brooks Mountain, Alaska. *Amer. Min.*, vol. 29, p. 373.
Deer, W. A., 1935. The Cairnsmore of Carsphairn igneous complex. *Quart. Journ. Geol. Soc.*, vol. 91, p. 47.
—— 1937. The composition and paragenesis of the biotites of the Carsphairn igneous complex. *Min. Mag.*, vol. 24, p. 495.
DeVore, G. W., 1955a. The role of adsorption in the fractionation and distribution of elements. *Journ. Geol.*, vol. 63, p. 159.
—— 1955b. Crystal growth and the distribution of elements. *Journ. Geol.*, vol. 63, p. 471.

DeVore, G. W., 1957. The association of strongly polarizing cations with weakly polarizing cations as a major influence in element distribution, mineral composition, and crystal growth. *Journ. Geol.*, vol. 65, p. 178.

Donnay, G. and **Kingman, P.**, 1958. Synthetic mica of type 3M. *Carnegie Inst. Washington, Ann. Rep. Dir. Geophys. Lab.*, 1957–1958, vol. 57, p. 252.

Engel, A. E. J. and **Engel, C. G.**, 1960. Progressive metamorphism and granitization of the Major paragneiss, northwest Adirondack Mountains, New York. Part II, Mineralogy. *Bull. Geol. Soc. Amer.*, vol. 71, p. 1.

Engelhart, W. von, 1936. Die geochemie des Barium. *Chemie der Erde*, vol. 10, p. 187.

Eugster, H. P., 1956. Stability of hydrous iron silicates. *Carnegie Inst. Washington, Ann. Rep. Dir. Geophys. Lab.*, 1955–1956, vol. 55, p. 158.

—— 1957. Stability of annite. *Carnegie Inst. Washington, Ann. Rep. Dir. Geophys. Lab.*, 1956–1957, vol. 56, p. 161.

—— and **Wones, D. R.**, 1958. Phase relations of hydrous silicates with intermediate Mg/Fe ratios. *Carnegie Inst. Washington, Ann. Rep. Dir. Geophys. Lab.*, 1957–1958, vol. 57, p. 193.

Francis, G. H., 1956. Facies boundaries in pelites at the middle grades of regional metamorphism. *Geol. Mag.*, vol. 93, p. 353.

Gower, J. A., 1957. X-ray measurement of the iron-magnesium ratio in biotites. *Amer. Journ. Sci.*, vol. 255, p. 142.

Grigoriev, D. P., 1938. Synthesis and investigation of biotite. *Doklady Acad. Sci. USSR*, vol. 20, p. 391 (M.A. 7–284).

Hall, A. J., 1941. The relation between colour and chemical composition in the biotites. *Amer. Min.*, vol. 26, p. 29.

Harker, R. I., 1954. Further data on the petrology of the pelitic hornfelses of the Carn Chuinneag–Inchbae region, Ross-shire, with special reference to the status of almandine. *Geol. Mag.*, vol. 91, p. 445.

Harry, W. T., 1950. Aluminium replacing silicon in some silicate lattices. *Min. Mag.*, vol. 29, p. 142.

Hayama, Y., 1959. Some considerations on the colour of biotite and its relation to metamorphism. *Journ. Geol. Soc. Japan*, vol. 65, p. 21.

Heinrich, E. W., 1946. Studies in the mica group; the biotite–phlogopite series. *Amer. Journ. Sci.*, vol. 244, p. 836.

—— **Levinson, A. A., Levandowski, D. W.** and **Hewitt, C. H.**, 1953. *Studies in the natural history of micas.* University of Michigan Engineering Research Inst. Project M.978; final report.

Hendricks, S. B. and **Jefferson, M. E.**, 1939. Polymorphism of the micas. *Amer. Min.*, vol. 24, p. 729.

Hess, F. L. and **Stevens, R. E.**, 1937. A rare-alkali biotite from Kings Mountain, North Carolina. *Amer. Min.*, vol. 22, p. 1040.

Holzner, J., 1936. Über den anomalen Kristallbau der Biotite. *Zeit. Krist.*, vol. 95, p. 435.

Howie, R. A., 1955. The geochemistry of the charnockite series of Madras, India. *Trans. Roy. Soc. Edin.*, vol. 62, p. 725.

Hutton, C. O., 1947. The nuclei of pleochroic haloes. *Amer. Journ. Sci.*, vol. 245, p. 154.

—— 1947. Contributions to the mineralogy of New Zealand, Part 3. *Trans. Roy. Soc. New Zealand*, vol. 76, p. 481.

Jacobson, R. R. E., Macleod, W. N. and **Black, R.**, 1958. Ring-complexes in the younger granite province of Northern Nigeria. *Geol. Soc., Mem.* No. 1.

Jakob, J., 1937. Über das Auftreten von dreiwertigen Titan in Biotiten. *Schweiz. Min. Petr. Mitt.*, vol. 17, p. 149.

Kretz, R., 1959. Chemical study of garnet, biotite and hornblende from gneisses of southwestern Quebec, with emphasis on distribution of elements in co-existing minerals. *Journ. Geol.*, vol. 67, p. 371.

Kunitz, W., 1924. Die Beziehungen zwischen der chemischen Zusammensetzung und den physikalisch-optischen Eigenschaften innerhalb der Glimmergruppe. *Neues Jahrb.*, Bl-Bd. 50, p. 365.

—— 1929. Enthalten die Muskovite und Biotite Kalk. *Zeit. Krist.*, vol. 70, p. 508.

Lambert, R. St J., 1959. The mineralogy and metamorphism of the Moine schists of the Morar and Knoydart districts of Inverness-shire. *Trans. Roy. Soc. Edin.*, vol. 63, p. 553.

Larsen, E. S. Jr. and **Draisin, W.**, 1950. Composition of the minerals in the rocks of the Southern Californian Batholith. *Int. Geol. Congress, Report of 18th Session, Great Britain, 1948*, Part III, p. 66.

—— **Gonyer, F. A.** and **Irving, J.**, 1937. Petrologic results of a study of the minerals from the Tertiary volcanic rocks of San Juan Region, Colorado. 6. Biotite. *Amer. Min.*, vol. 22, p. 898.

—— and **Schmidt, R. G.**, 1958. A reconnaissance of the Idaho batholith and comparison with the Southern California batholith. *U.S. Geol. Surv. Bull.* 1070-A.

Lee, D. E., 1958. A chlorine-rich biotite from Lemhi County, Idaho. *Amer. Min.*, vol. 43, p. 107.

MacKenzie, W. S., 1953. *Metamorphism in the Ross of Mull.* Ph.D. Thesis, Cambridge.

Mehmel, M., 1937. Ab und Umbau am Biotit. *Chemie der Erde*, vol. 11, p. 307 (M.A. 7–28).

Michel-Lèvy, A., Wyart, J. and **Michel-Lèvy, M.**, 1947. Reproduction artificielle à haute pression de la biotite et de la hercynite. *Compt. Rend. Acad. Sci. Paris*, vol. 225, p. 85.

Miyashiro, A., 1953. Calcium-poor garnet in relation to metamorphism. *Geochim. et. Cosmochim. Acta*, vol. 4, p. 173.

—— 1956. Data on garnet–biotite equilibria in some metamorphic rocks of the Ryoke zone. *Journ. Geol. Soc. Japan*, vol. 62, p. 700.

—— 1958. Regional metamorphism of the Gosaisyo–Takanuki District in the Central Abukuma Plateau. *Journ. Fac. Sci., Univ. Tokyo*, sec. II, vol. 11, p. 219.

Nagelschmidt, G., 1937. X-ray investigations on clays, Part 3. *Zeit. Krist.*, vol. 97, p. 514.

Nockolds, S. R., 1934. The production of normal rock types by contamination and their bearing on petrogenesis. *Geol. Mag.*, vol. 71, p. 31.

—— 1941. The Garabal Hill—Glen Fyne igneous complex. *Quart. Journ. Geol. Soc.*, vol. 96, p. 451.

—— 1946. The order of crystallization of the minerals in some Caledonian plutonic and hypabyssal rocks. *Geol. Mag.*, vol. 83, p. 206.

—— 1947. The relation between chemical composition and paragenesis in the biotite micas of igneous rocks. *Amer. Journ. Sci.*, vol. 245, p. 401.

—— and **Mitchell, R. L.**, 1948. The geochemistry of some Caledonian plutonic rocks: a study in the relationship between the major and trace elements of igneous rocks and their minerals. *Trans. Roy. Soc. Edin.*, vol. 61, p. 533.

—— and **Richey, J. E.**, 1939. Replacement veins in the Mourne Mountain granites, N. Ireland. *Amer. Journ. Sci.*, vol. 237, p. 27.

Ogura, Y., 1958. On the granitization of some basic rocks of the Gosaisyo–Takanuki District, Southern Abukuma Plateau, Japan. *Jap. Journ. Geol. Geogr.*, vol. 29, p. 171.

Parras, K., 1958. On the charnockites in the light of a highly metamorphic rock complex in southwestern Finland. *Bull. Comm. géol. Finlande*, no. 181.

Phillips, F. C., 1930.   Some mineralogical and chemical changes induced by progressive metamorphism. *Min. Mag.*, vol. 22, p. 239.

Pitcher, W. S. and **Sinha, R. C.**, 1957.   The petrochemistry of the Ardara aureole. *Quart. Journ. Geol. Soc.*, vol. 113, p. 393.

Read, H. H., 1935.   The gabbros and associated xenolithic complexes of the Haddo House district, Aberdeenshire. *Quart. Journ. Geol. Soc.*, vol. 91, p. 591.

Schwartz, G. M., 1958.   Alteration of biotite under mesothermal conditions. *Econ. Geol.*, vol. 53, p. 164.

Serdyuchenko, D. P., 1948a.   On the chemical constitution and classification of micas. *Doklady Akad. Sci. USSR*, vol. 59, p. 545.

—— 1948b.   On the crystallochemical role of titanium in micas. *Doklady Akad. Sci. USSR*, vol. 59, p. 739.

Shidô, F., 1958.   Plutonic and metamorphic rocks of the Nakoso and Iritōno Districts in the Central Abukuma plateau. *Journ. Fac. Sci., Univ. Tokyo*, sec. II, vol. 11, p. 131.

Snelling, N. J., 1957.   Notes on the petrology and mineralogy of the Barrovian metamorphic zones. *Geol. Mag.*, vol. 94, p. 297.

Stewart, F. H., 1942.   Chemical data on a silica-poor argillaceous hornfels and its constituent minerals. *Min. Mag.*, vol. 26, p. 260.

Taneda, S., 1952.   Petrographic notes on the volcanic rocks from Sambre, southwestern Japan. *Jap. Journ. Geol. Geogr.*, vol. 22, p. 1.

Tilley, C. E., 1924.   Contact metamorphism in the Comrie area of the Perthshire Highlands. *Quart. Journ. Geol. Soc.*, vol. 80, p. 22.

—— 1925.   Metamorphic zones in the southern Highlands of Scotland. *Quart. Journ. Geol. Soc.*, vol. 81, p. 100.

—— 1926.   Some mineralogical transformations in crystalline schists. *Min. Mag.*, vol. 21, p. 34.

Tozer, C. F., 1955.   The mode of occurrence of sillimanite in the Glen District, Co. Donegal. *Geol. Mag.*, vol. 92, p. 310.

Tsuboi, S., 1938.   Petrological notes (19)–(32). *Jap. Journ. Geol. Geogr.*, vol. 15, p. 125.

Tzvetkov, A. I. and **Valyashikhina, E. P.**, 1956.   On the hydration and oxidation of micas. *Bull. Acad. Sci. URSS, Sér. Géol.*, No. 5, p. 74 (M.A. 13–396).

Veres, G. I., Merenkova, T. B. and **Ostrovsky, I. A.**, 1955.   An artificial purely ferruginous hydroxyl mica. *Doklady Acad Sci. USSR*, vol. 101, p. 147 (M.A. 13–110).

Wones, D. R., 1958a.   Ferrous-ferric biotites. *Carnegie Inst. Washington, Ann. Rep. Dir. Geophys. Lab.*, 1957–1958, p. 195.

—— 1958b.   The phlogopite-annite join. *Carnegie Inst. Washington, Ann. Rep. Dir. Geophys. Lab.*, 1957–1958, p. 194.

Wooster, W. A., 1950.   Mineralogical applications of a two-crystal Weissenberg X-ray goniometer. *Min. Mag.*, vol. 29, p. 427.

Yoder, H. S. and **Eugster, H. P.**, 1954.   Phlogopite synthesis and stability range. *Geochim. et Cosmochim. Acta*, vol. 6, p. 157.

Zastawniak, F., 1951.   Chemical composition of biotites in different rocks of the Tatra Mts. *Ann. Soc. Géol. Pologne*, vol. 20, p. 117 (M.A. 11–391).

Lepidolite

$K_2(Li,Al)_{5-6}[Si_{6-7}Al_{2-1}O_{20}](OH,F)_4$

MONOCLINIC (OR TRIGONAL) $(-)$

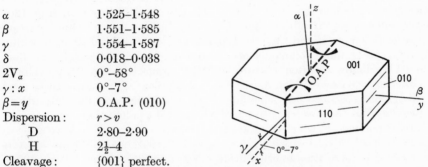

α	1·525–1·548
β	1·551–1·585
γ	1·554–1·587
δ	0·018–0·038
$2V_\alpha$	0°–58°
$\gamma : x$	0°–7°
$\beta = y$	O.A.P. (010)
Dispersion :	$r > v$
D	2·80–2·90
H	$2\frac{1}{2}$–4
Cleavage :	{001} perfect.
Twinning :	Rare : composition plane {001}, twin axis [310].
Colour :	Colourless, shades of pink, purple ; colourless in thin section.
Pleochroism :	Absorption greater for vibration directions in the plane of cleavage.
Unit cell :	a 5·3, b 9·2, c 10·2 Å, β 100°.

$Z=1$. Space group $C2/m$ or Cm (1M polymorph).

a 9·2, b 5·3, c 20 Å, β 98°.

$Z=2$. Space group $C2/c$ (2M$_2$ polymorph).

a 5·3 Å, c 30·0 Å.

$Z=3$.† Space group $P3_112$ or $P3_212$ (3T polymorph).

Attacked but not decomposed by acids.

Lepidolite is the most common lithium-bearing mineral, occurring almost entirely in pegmatites, sometimes as large tabular crystals but more often in aggregates of small flakes. To this scaly appearance it owes its name which is derived from the Greek *lepidos*, scale. It is mined not so much for its properties as a mica but rather as a source of lithium which, when added to glasses and enamels (often as lepidolite) lowers their coefficients of expansion and increases their strength : it can also serve as an opacifying agent.

STRUCTURE

The essential features of the lepidolite structure are those already described as typical of a mica (see p. 2), but the way in which the tetrahedral and octahedral sites are occupied, shows it to be intermediate between the di-octahedral and tri-octahedral types (see section on chemistry). Chemical analyses were made of a number of lepidolites by Stevens (1938) and the same specimens were investigated structurally by Hendricks and Jefferson (1939) and

† $3K(Li,Al)_{2\frac{1}{2}-3}(Si_{3-3\frac{1}{2}}Al_{1-\frac{1}{2}})O_{10}(OH,F)_2$.

again by Levinson (1953). The polymorphic unit cells recorded by the latter author were: single-layered monoclinic, six-layered monoclinic, and three-layered hexagonal. It has been noted that the six-layered monoclinic cell can also be described as two-layered monoclinic ($2M_2$) with $b = 5 \cdot 3$ Å, and the three-layered hexagonal is equivalent to the three-layered trigonal (3T) (Smith and Yoder, 1956). Thus the three polymorphs are 1M, $2M_2$ and 3T; lepidolites do not crystallize with the $2M_1$ structure adopted by muscovites. The 3T specimens are comparatively rare; they do not differ chemically from 1M lepidolites, but often occur mixed with other polymorphs. The 3T cell may be regarded as a "twinned" version of the 1M structure, successive layers being rotated by 120° in the same sense (Hendricks and Jefferson, 1939). Polymorphic variation (*e.g.* alternation of 1M and $2M_2$), both parallel to the z-axis and laterally within cleavage sheets, quite commonly occurs in a single crystal "book", and fine-grained lepidolites are often mixtures of $2M_2$ fractions with the $2M_1$ polymorph of either muscovite or lithian muscovite. X-ray powder patterns can be used to distinguish between 1M lepidolites, $2M_2$ lepidolites and the $2M_1$ lithian muscovites, but the powder patterns of 3T and 1M lepidolites are very similar. A further polymorph, which is of rare occurrence, was reported to have a three-layered monoclinic cell[1] with a 5·2, b 9·0, c 30·0 Å, β 90°, but little is known of its structure or of its relation to other lithium-bearing micas (Heinrich *et al.*, 1953).

The β angle of 1M lepidolites does not differ from the ideal value of 100°, as does that of 1M muscovite (101° 35'). This accords with the lesser distortion of the fundamental mica sheets, octahedral sites which are vacant in muscovite becoming increasingly filled in lepidolites as their lithium content rises.

CHEMISTRY

In addition to the substitutions indicated in the general formula for lepidolite considerable amounts of sodium, rubidium and caesium may substitute for potassium, and iron, manganese and magnesium may enter octahedral sites. Other ions often present in small quantities are: Ca, Ba, Sr, Ga, Nb, Th and Ti. Average content of some oxides and fluorine in 26 analysed lepidolites are given as: MnO 1·16, Li_2O 3·77, Rb_2O 0·54, Na_2O 0·41, F 5·41 per cent. (Heinrich *et al.*, 1953); Rb_2O and Cs_2O can be as high as 2 or 3 per cent. (as in the Varuträsk lepidolites) and MnO as high as 7·5 per cent. Lepidolite is one of the few minerals with appreciable Rb content and it has found considerable use in the radioactive method of age determination in which the $^{87}Rb : ^{87}Sr$ ratio is determined (Ahrens, 1956). Some typical lepidolite analyses are given in Table 16.

The problem of lepidolite chemistry has been considered by Stevens (1938) and Winchell (1942) making use of end-member concepts, but various workers differ as to whether or not there is a continuous chemical series between muscovite and lepidolite. If it is assumed that lithium-bearing micas are like muscovite in having at least six silicon atoms per formula unit and in having no divalent ions,[2] then their content of lithium sets rather narrow limits on the entire formula, as can be seen from Table 15.

In the section on muscovite chemistry (p. 13) it was seen that up to about 3·3 per cent. Li_2O can enter into muscovite without essentially changing its

---

[1] (*cf.* Al-free biotite, p. 56).

[2] Analyses show little or no divalent ion content and never as few as six silicon ions per formula unit.

Table 15.   COMPOSITIONS POSSIBLE FOR LITHIAN MUSCOVITES AND LEPIDOLITES
Numbers of ions on basis of 24(OH,F)

Approx. % Li₂O	[Li]⁶	[Al]⁶	[Al]⁴	[Si]⁴	Total [Y]⁶ ions
(a) ⎧ 0	0	4	2	6	4
2	1·0	3·0–3·7	0–2	8–6	4·0–4·7
3·3	1·8	2·7–3·4	0–2	8–6	4·5–5·2
4·5	2·5	2·5–3·2	0–2	8–6	5·0–5·7
5·5	3·0	2·3–3·0(b)	0–2(b)	8–6(b)	5·3–6·0(b)
6·3	3·5	2·2–2·5	0–1	8–7	5·7–6·0
7·0	4·0	2·0(c)	0(c)	8(c)	6·0(c)

structure.   Thus in Table 15 compositions (a) represent muscovite and lithian muscovites, with octahedral ions ranging between four and five, demonstrating solid solution to this extent from di-octahedral towards tri-octahedral composition. Composition (b) $K_2(Li_3Al_3)(Si_6Al_2)(OH,F)_4O_{20}$, is that which Stevens (1938) called "paucilithionite" and Winchell (1942) "lithium muscovite": composition (c) is polylithionite $K_2(Li_4Al_2)Si_8(OH,F)_4O_{20}$.   The relationships of Table 15 are shown graphically in Fig. 22 where lithium content is plotted against

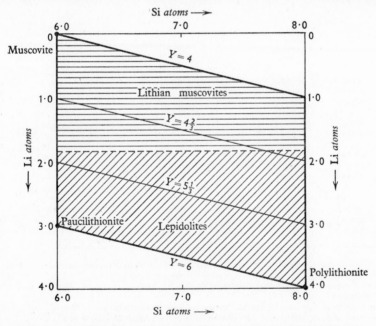

FIG. 22.   Possible compositions of lithian muscovites and lepidolites.

silicon (both in terms of atoms per formula unit).   It is seen that the end-members paucilithionite–polylithionite and their join represent only those lepidolites which are strictly tri-octahedral, and which have more than 3·0 atoms of Li (5·5 per cent. Li₂O).   Below this lithium content lepidolites necessarily have their Y sites incompletely filled (divalent ions could decrease the number of

Sheet Silicates

Table 16. LEPIDOLITE ANALYSES

	1.	2.	3.	4.	5.	6.	7.
SiO_2	48·58	50·00	53·45	48·94	50·83	51·25	49·80
TiO_2	tr.	0·00	tr.	0·00	tr.	0·01	0·00
Al_2O_3	28·93	24·96	22·15	22·21	23·70	23·71	25·56
Fe_2O_3	—	0·24	—	1·55	—	—	0·08
FeO	0·04†	0·00	0·16†	1·52	1·24	0·07†	0·00
MnO	0·92	0·16	0·52	0·75	0·97	0·61	0·38
MgO	0·00	0·01	0·14	0·03	0·46	0·08	0·22
CaO	tr.	0·20	0·00	0·10	0·24	tr.	0·00
Li_2O	3·70	4·35	5·04	4·99	5·51	5·78	5·95
Na_2O	0·87	0·67	0·74	0·53	1·06	0·65	0·40
K_2O	10·02	9·95	9·58	8·62	9·88	9·90	9·67
Rb_2O	0·91	2·70	1·56	3·80	1·64	2·00	1·97
Cs_2O	0·16	1·90	0·48	1·08		0·08	1·20
F	4·93	4·95	7·22	6·69	6·96	8·08	6·85
H_2O^+	2·56	1·30	1·28	1·46	0·90	0·90	0·38
H_2O^-	0·54	0·60	0·46	0·88	0·12	0·34	0·50
	102·16	101·99	102·78	103·15	103·51	103·46	102·96
$F \equiv 0$	2·08	2·08	3·04	2·62	2·93	3·40	2·89
Total	100·08	99·91	99·74	100·53	100·58	100·06	100·07
α	1·530	—	1·534	—	—	1·536	—
β	1·553	—	1·555	1·585	—	1·555	—
γ	1·559	—	1·559	1·587	—	1·559	—
$2V_\alpha$	33°	50°	33°	42°	—	—	36°
D	—	—	—	2·866	—	—	2·898

NUMBERS OF IONS ON THE BASIS OF 24(O,OH,F)

	1.	2.	3.	4.	5.	6.	7.
Si	6·460 } 8·00	6·897 } 8·00	7·122 } 8·00	6·754 } 8·00	6·804 } 8·00	6·822 } 8·00	6·750 } 8·00
Al	1·540	1·103	0·878	1·246	1·196	1·178	1·250
Al	2·996	2·857	2·602	2·368	2·504	2·543	2·834
Fe^{+3}	—	0·024	—	0·161	—	—	0·008
Fe^{+2}	0·005 } 5·08	— } 5·32	0·018 } 5·41	0·175 } 5·57	0·139 } 5·81	0·007 } 5·74‡	— } 6·17
Mn	0·104	0·019	0·058	0·088	0·110	0·069	0·044
Mg	—	0·002	0·028	0·006	0·092	0·016	0·044
Li	1·979	2·414	2·702	2·770	2·966	3·095	3·244
Ca	—	0·030	—	0·015	0·035	—	—
Na	0·224	0·178	0·191	0·140	0·276	0·168	0·106
K	1·700 } 2·01	1·752 } 2·31	1·629 } 1·98	1·518 } 2·07	1·688 } 2·13	1·681 } 2·02	1·674 } 2·02
Rb	0·078	0·238	0·133	0·336	} 0·132	0·171	0·172
Cs	0·010	0·110	0·027	0·064		0·004	0·070
F	2·074 } 4·34	2·158 } 3·36	3·043 } 4·18	2·920 } 4·26	2·946 } 3·75	3·402 } 4·20	2·936 } 3·28
OH	2·270	1·198	1·139	1·344	0·804	0·800	0·344

1. Fine compact purple lepidolite, Stewart mine, Pala, California (Stevens, 1938).   Anal. R. E. Stevens. $2M_2$ structure.
2. Colourless to pale rose lepidolite, Varuträsk pegmatite, Sweden (Berggren, 1941).   Anal. Th. Berggren. 1M structure.
3. Coarse pale blue talc-like lepidolite, Stewart mine, Pala, California (Stevens, 1938).   Anal. R. E. Stevens. $2M_2$ lepidolite and $2M_1$ lithian muscovite present (Heinrich *et al.*, 1953).
4. Lepidolite, pegmatite, Kimito, Finland (Pehrman, 1945).   Anal. Th. Berggren. Mainly uniaxial 3T but with small amount of lithian muscovite overgrowth (Heinrich *et al.*, 1953).
5. Lepidolite, pegmatite, Minagi, Okayama Prefecture, Japan (Ukai *et al.*, 1956).
6. Coarse purple lepidolite, Himalaya mine, Mesa Grande, California (Stevens, 1938).   Anal. R. E. Stevens. 1M structure.
7. Coarsely crystalline purple lepidolite, Varuträsk pegmatite, Sweden (Berggren, 1941).   Anal. Th. Berggren. 2M structure.

† Total iron expressed as FeO.
‡ Includes Ti 0·01.

vacancies but in fact do not usually occur in sufficient quantity). Only when Li_2O increases beyond 5·5 per cent. does the composition necessarily approach that of polylithionite. Analyses of lepidolites by Stevens and others show that there is a continuous range of Li content (between 3·3 and 7 per cent. Li_2O), and that between 5 and 6 Y sites are occupied (Si : Al is usually less than 7 : 1). It appears therefore that there is a continuous chemical series between di-octahedral muscovite and tri-octahedral lepidolite, with a structural transition at about 3·3 per cent. Li_2O from the $2M_1$ polymorph common for muscovite and lithian muscovites, to the 1M, $2M_2$ and 3T of lepidolites. Winchell (1942) rejected the conclusion of a continuous series, and interpreted the analyses as indicating a mixture of an end-member lepidolite with muscovite. Many specimens of lepidolite have indeed been shown by X-ray investigation to be mixtures of polymorphs sometimes including some lithian muscovite or muscovite, but in others with intermediate and low Li_2O content there has been no evidence of more than a single lepidolite phase. If the lithian muscovites (which have between four and five Y ions) were to be interpreted as mixtures there would have to be a large muscovite component: this would be discernible from X-ray powder patterns but is not in fact observed.

Polymorphism of lepidolites appears to be related to chemistry in the following manner (Levinson, 1953). Normal $2M_1$ muscovites can have as much as 3·3 per cent. Li_2O, but these are called lithian muscovites rather than lepidolites. Micas with 3·4 to 4 per cent. Li_2O are usually fine-grained, have anomalous optics and are combinations of more than one polymorph often including $2M_1$. Those with 4 to 5 per cent. Li_2O usually have the $2M_2$ structure, and those with more than 5 per cent. are usually 1M or 3T. Exceptions to these relations are not uncommon (Table 16, anals. 2 and 7).

A very rare mica, taeniolite (ideal formula $K_2Mg_4Li_2Si_8O_{20}F_4$), has no aluminium (Miser and Stevens, 1938). A synthetic taenolite crystallized at 1185°C. has a 5·27, b 9·13, c 10·25 Å, β 100° ± 15′ (Yamzin *et al.*, 1955). Since its octahedral positions are filled completely, and it has the 1M structure, it may be regarded as a magnesian lepidolite although it could be classed also as a lithian phlogopite. Entry of appreciable Fe^{+2} into octahedral sites gives compositions in the range for zinnwaldite, which itself could be regarded as an iron-lepidolite or as a lithian biotite (see p. 92).

OPTICAL AND PHYSICAL PROPERTIES

The optical properties of lepidolites show a wide range of variation depending upon the content of manganese and iron (particularly ferric) rather than on the amount of lithium present. The upper and lower limits of observed optical constants are listed above, but most lepidolites lie within the narrower ranges:

$$\alpha \quad 1·529–1·537$$
$$\beta \quad 1·552–1·565$$
$$\gamma \quad 1·555–1·568$$
$$2V_\alpha \quad 30°–50°$$

Generally the effect of increasing iron or manganese is to increase the refractive indices and to decrease 2V, so that the higher values for iron- and manganese-rich lepidolites approach the lower limits for muscovites. Lithian muscovites have lower refractive indices than true muscovites and fall in the lepidolite range. The polymorphs of lepidolite are not distinguishable by their optical properties although there is a tendency for 1M specimens to have a higher 2V (Heinrich *et al.*, 1953): for a particular uniaxial lepidolite Hendricks and Jefferson (1939) gave ϵ 1·525, ω 1·558. Optical properties may vary within a single sheet of lepidolite since more than one polymorph is often present; the interference figure given by a superposition of polymorphs is sometimes indistinct, and often appears to show a low 2V. The orientation of the indicatrix in lepidolite is described differently by different authors particularly with regard to the angle $\alpha : z$. It appears that sometimes z has been assumed to be perpendicular to (001), no account being taken of the β angle, but the extinction angle actually measured is $\gamma : x$ and this is usually less than 7°. Pleochroism is moderate in coloured specimens, the vibration direction normal to the cleavage plate corresponding to least absorption and having a paler colour. As with rose muscovites the colour of lepidolites is related, not to their lithium content, but to the dominance of Mn over Fe^{+3} ions in the absence of Fe^{+2}. Thus with higher Mn/Fe ratios colours deepen from colourless or grey through shades of pink and lilac to purple. If Fe is so high that it masks the effect of Mn the resulting colour is brown (Heinrich *et al.*, 1953).

The external morphology and physical characteristics of lepidolites are similar to those of muscovites. They have perfect {001} cleavage, and sometimes {110} faces are developed giving tabular pseudo-hexagonal crystals. Twinning is according to the "mica law" with composition plane {001} and twin axis [310].

Taeniolite has α 1·552, $\beta = \gamma$ 1·553, 2V very small.

DISTINGUISHING FEATURES

Lepidolite can usually be distinguished from muscovite by its lower refractive indices, its colour, and by the lithium flame test (see Hosking, 1957). It is easily confused, however, with rose muscovite and although it usually has a more purplish tinge, an X-ray powder photograph or an Li_2O determination may be necessary for differentiation. These methods are also necessary for distinguishing between lepidolite and lithian muscovite.

PARAGENESIS

Lepidolite occurs almost exclusively in granite pegmatites (Table 16, anals. 1–7) associated with other lithium minerals (amblygonite $LiAl(F,OH)PO_4$, spodumene, zinnwaldite), tourmaline, topaz, cassiterite, beryl and quartz. It has also been reported in granites and aplites and from high temperature veins which are often tin-bearing. In pegmatites, lepidolite is mainly derived by metasomatic replacement of biotite, or more commonly muscovite. Overgrowths of lepidolite on muscovite are usually fibrous or granular but sometimes are well crystallized in parallel growth with the core material. Heinrich *et al.* (1953) present evidence that rose muscovite is a later mineral than lepidolite, sometimes forming overgrowths upon it.

REFERENCES

Ahrens, L. H., 1956. Radioactive methods for determining geological age. *Physics and Chemistry of the Earth*, vol. 1, p. 44.

Berggren, T., 1941. Minerals of the Varuträsk pegmatite. XXV. Some new analyses of lithium-bearing mica minerals. *Geol. För. Förh.*, vol. 68, p. 262.

Heinrich, E. W., Levinson, A. A., Levandowski, D. W. and Hewitt, C. H., 1953. *Studies in the natural history of micas.* University of Michigan Engineering Research Inst. Project M.978; final report.

Hendricks, S. B. and Jefferson, M. E., 1939. Polymorphism of the micas. *Amer. Min.*, vol. 24, p. 729.

Hosking, K. F. G., 1957. Identification of lithium minerals. *Mining Mag.*, vol. 96, p. 271.

Levinson, A. A., 1953. Studies in the mica group: relationship between polymorphism and composition in the muscovite–lepidolite series. *Amer. Min.*, vol. 38, p. 88.

Miser, H. D. and Stevens, R. E., 1938. Taeniolite from Magnet Cove, Arkansas. *Amer. Min.*, vol. 23, p. 104.

Pehrman, G., 1945. Die Granitpegmatite von Kimito (S.W.-Finland) und ihre Minerale. *Acta Acad. Abo. Math. phys.*, vol. 15, (2), p. 57.

Smith, J. V. and Yoder, H. S., 1956. Experimental and theoretical studies of the mica polymorphs. *Min. Mag.*, vol. 31, p. 209.

Stevens, R. E., 1938. New analyses of lepidolites and their interpretation. *Amer. Min.*, vol. 23, p. 607.

Ukai, Y., Nishimura, S. and Hashimoto, Y., 1956. Chemical studies of lithium micas from the pegmatite of Minagi, Okayama Prefecture. *Min. Journ. (Japan)*, vol. 2, p. 27.

Winchell, A. N., 1942. Further studies of the lepidolite system. *Amer. Min.*, vol. 27, p. 114.

Yamzin, I. I., Timofeyeva, V. A., Shashkina, T. I., Belova, E. N. and Gliki, N. V., 1955. The structure and morphological characters of fluor-phlogopite and tainolite. *Mém. Soc. russe. Min.*, ser. 2, vol. 84, p. 415 (M.A. 13–419).

Zinnwaldite

$K_2(Fe^{+2}_{2-1},Li_{2-3}Al_2)[Si_{6-7}Al_{2-1}O_{20}](F_{3-2}(OH)_{1-2})$

MONOCLINIC $(-)$

α	1·535–1·558
β	1·570–1·589
γ	1·572–1·590
δ	$\simeq 0·35$
$2V_\alpha$	0° to 40°
$\beta = y$, $\gamma : x = 0°$ to 2°	
O.A.P. (010)	
Dispersion:	Weak $r > v$
D	2·90–3·02
H	$2\frac{1}{2}$–4
Cleavage:	{001} perfect.
Twinning:	Composition plane {001}, twin axis [310].
Colour:	Grey brown, yellowish brown, pale violet; colourless or light brown in thin section.
Pleochroism:	$\alpha < \beta < \gamma$.
	α = colourless to yellow brown.
	β = grey brown.
	γ = colourless to grey brown.
Unit cell :†	a 5·27, b 9·09, c 10·07 Å, β 100°.
	Z = 1. Space group Cm (1M polymorph).

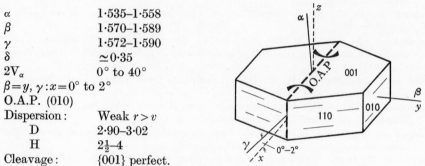

Zinnwaldite is one of the less common tri-octahedral micas and occurs mainly in granite pegmatites and in cassiterite-bearing veins. One of its localities is at Zinnwald, Germany, so named because of the tin (*Zinn*) veins found there. It is usually associated with other lithium-bearing minerals (lepidolite, spodumene), and often with topaz, cleavelandite, beryl, tourmaline, monazite and fluorite. Its properties are similar to those of the biotites and like them it can occur in any of three polymorphic forms (1M, 3T, 2M) of which 1M is the most common.

A large variety of chemical substitutions occur but since comparatively few specimens have been analysed the limits of many of the atomic replacements are not known. Thus Si may be replaced by Al (and possibly by Ti), and the Si : Al ratio is usually greater than 6 : 2. Ti, Fe^{+2}, Fe^{+3}, Mn and Mg may substitute for Al in Y positions, and potassium may be partially replaced by Na, Ba, Rb, Sr and small amounts of Ca. As with lepidolites, there is usually considerable replacement of (OH) by F, and the number of ions in Y sites is often considerably less than the theoretical value of six. Further evidence of this approach to di-octahedral character is provided by the presence on X-ray photographs from some specimens of 06l reflections with l odd. These should be absent for

† (Mauguin and Graber, 1928).

Table 17.   ZINNWALDITE ANALYSES

	1.	2.	3.	4.
SiO_2	43·70	38·83	46·74	51·88
TiO_2	0·32	0·12	0·00	0·21
Al_2O_3	22·96	22·27	21·78	20·65
Fe_2O_3	0·59	4·40	1·19	0·79
FeO	11·67	9·07	10·22	1·99
MnO	1·95	1·66	0·37	2·01
MgO	0·03	0·38	0·00	0·00
CaO	0·02	1·14	0·00	0·00
Li_2O	1·92	2·62	3·72	5·26
Na_2O	0·74	0·48	0·54	0·51
K_2O	9·58	9·53	10·37	10·55
Rb_2O	1·04	—	n.d.	n.d.
Cs_2O	0·10	—	n.d.	n.d.
F	5·52	3·82	7·54	7·65
H_2O^+	1·35	2·93	0·89	1·89
H_2O^-	0·08	3·74	n.d.	n.d.
	101·57	"100·80"	103·36	103·39
$O \equiv F$	2·32	1·39	3·17	3·22
Total	99·25	99·41	100·19	100·17
α	1·550–1·558	—	1·545	1·542
β	1·580–1·589	—	1·574	1·567
γ	1·580–1·590	—	1·576	1·570
$2V_\alpha$	0°–33°	—	30°	34°

NUMBERS OF IONS ON THE BASIS OF 24(O,OH,F)

	1.	2.	3.	4.
Si	6·369 ⎫ 8·00	5·802 ⎫ 8·00	6·518 ⎫ 8·00	6·877 ⎫ 8·00
Al	1·631 ⎭	2·198 ⎭	1·482 ⎭	1·123 ⎭
Al	2·314 ⎫	1·727 ⎫	2·099 ⎫	2·105 ⎫
Ti	0·018	0·014	—	0·020
Fe^{+3}	0·065	0·494	0·124	0·078
Fe^{+2}	1·422 ⎬ 5·19	1·134 ⎬ 5·24	1·192 ⎬ 5·58	0·221 ⎬ 5·46
Mn	0·241	0·210	0·077	0·225
Mg	0·006	0·084	—	—
Li	1·126 ⎭	1·576 ⎭	2·086 ⎭	2·806 ⎭
Ca	— ⎫	0·182 ⎫	— ⎫	— ⎫
Na	0·208	0·138	0·146	0·130
K	1·782 ⎬ 2·09	1·818 ⎬ 2·14	1·846 ⎬ 1·99	1·784 ⎬ 1·91
Rb	0·098	—	—	—
Cs	0·006 ⎭	⎭	⎭	⎭
F	2·544 ⎫ 3·86	1·805 ⎫ 4·73	3·326 ⎫ 4·15	3·208 ⎫ 4·88
(OH)	1·312 ⎭	2·920 ⎭	0·828 ⎭	1·672 ⎭

1. Bronze-coloured zinnwaldite, with topaz, Amelia pegmatite, Virginia (Glass, 1935) (Contains also B, Be, Sn, Zn).
2. Zinnwaldite, pegmatite, Naegitown, Ena county, Gihu, Japan (Harada, 1954).   Anal. H. Shibata.
3. Zinnwaldite, Zinnwald, Erzgebirge (Winchell, 1942).   Anal. F. A. Gonyer.   Description and previous analysis (Kunitz, 1924).
4. Grey-purple lepidolite, Wakefield, Quebec (Winchell, 1942).   Anal. F. A. Gonyer.

the ideal mica structure but are given strongly by the more distorted sheets of the di-octahedral micas (Heinrich *et al.*, 1953). Zinnwaldites resemble lepidolites also in their high Si : Al ratio as well as in their lithium content; they contain little or no magnesium. A wide variety of trace elements have been reported in zinnwaldite, among which are : B, Be, Sn, Zn, Pb, Cs and Ti (Glass, 1935) and P, He, Mg, Mn, Ga, Ba, Sc, Tl and Y (Rankama and Sahama, 1950). Very few complete analyses have been published, four of which are presented in Table 17 in order of increasing lithium content. It will be seen that only anal. 3 comes strictly within the limits of the formula set out above. Anal. 4 which is very low in iron, and anal. 1 which is low in lithium might better be termed "iron lepidolite" and "lithian biotite" respectively.

Zinnwaldite sometimes occurs as large well formed pseudohexagonal crystals which cleave readily into thin, highly elastic flakes. Colour zoning is sometimes observed and one case has been reported where 1M and 3T polymorphs occur in successive zones. In view of the relation between these two polymorphs discussed on page 4, this may well be a case of twinning rather than zoning.

REFERENCES

Glass, J. J., 1935. The pegmatite minerals from near Amelia, Virginia. *Amer. Min.*, vol. 20, p. 741.

Harada, Z., 1954. Chemical analyses of Japanese minerals (III). *Journ. Fac. Sci. Hokkaido University*, Ser. IV, vol. 8, p. 289.

Heinrich, E. W., Levinson, A. A., Levandowski, D. W. and Hewitt, C. H., 1953. *Studies in the natural history of micas.* University of Michigan, Engineering Research Inst. Project M 978; final report.

Kunitz, W., 1924. Die Beziehungen zwischen der chemischen Zusammensetzung und den physikalisch-optischen Eigenschaften innerhalb der Glimmergruppe. *Neues Jahrb. Min.*, Bl. Bd., 50, p. 365.

Mauguin, Ch. and Graber, L., 1928. Étude des micas fluorés au moyen des rayons X. *Compt. Rend. Acad. Sci. Paris*, vol. 186, p. 1131.

Rankama, K. and Sahama, T. G., 1950. *Geochemistry.* University of Chicago Press.

Winchell, A. N., 1942. Further studies of the lepidolite system. *Amer. Min.*, vol. 27, p. 114.

Margarite

$Ca_2Al_4[Si_4Al_4O_{20}](OH)_4$

MONOCLINIC ($-$)

α	1·630–1·638
β	1·642–1·648
γ	1·644–1·650
δ	0·012–0·014
$2V_\alpha$	40°–67°

$\beta:x=6°-8°$, $\gamma=y$.
O.A.P. $\perp$(010).

Dispersion:	$r<v$
D	3–3·1
H	$3\frac{1}{2}$–$4\frac{1}{2}$
Cleavage:	{001} perfect.
Twinning:	Composition plane {001}, twin axis [310].
Colour:	Greyish pink, pale yellow, pale green; colourless in thin section.
Pleochroism:	Very weak or absent.
Unit cell:†	a 5·13, b 8·92, c 19·50 Å, β 95°.
	$Z=2$. Space group $C2/c$.

Attacked by H_2SO_4.

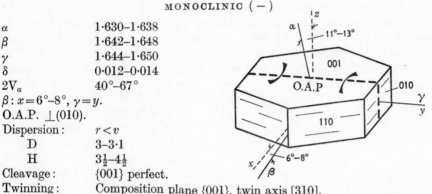

The common micas have potassium as the inter-layer cation and this is often replaced to a small degree by calcium and to a greater extent by sodium; in the distinct mineral species paragonite, nearly all of the X positions are occupied by sodium. More rarely, as in margarite and clintonite, calcium is the main inter-layer cation and this substitution is compensated by an increased $[Al]^4$:Si ratio. These minerals have the typical appearances of a mica but are harder and their cleavage sheets are less elastic, so that they are often called the "brittle micas". Margarite sometimes occurs in massive form but is more usually found in aggregates of lamellae with pearly lustre (the name margarite is from the Greek *margarites*, a pearl).

STRUCTURE

The layer polymorphism of margarite has not been investigated in detail. Although its c axis is given as 9·7 Å (Mauguin, 1928; Phillips, 1931–soda margarite), the true cell is probably of the two-layer type. This would be more consistent with margarite's di-octahedral character and with the orientation of its optic axial plane, normal to (010). Compared with that of muscovite, $[Si_6Al_2]^4$, the tetrahedral layer of margarite contains more Al atoms, $[Si_4Al_4]^4$, and might therefore be expected to have larger dimensions. In fact a and b are smaller than for muscovite, and moreover, smaller than for pyrophyllite, $[Si_8]^4$.

† See section on structure.

This anomaly is probably only partly explained by the presence of the smaller ion Ca instead of K between layers, and it seems likely that the $(Si,Al)_4O_{10}$ network is considerably distorted. Similar considerations are relevant to the tri-octahedral brittle micas clintonite and xanthophyllite.

CHEMISTRY

The available analyses of margarites show that most of them conform closely to the ideal formula of a di-octahedral brittle mica which has $[Si]:[Al]^4 = 4:4$ and a total of four ions in Y sites. Calcium ions may be replaced by small amounts of Ba, Sr, K, etc., and to a greater extent by sodium; when Ca is replaced by sodium it appears that charge balance is restored, at least in part,

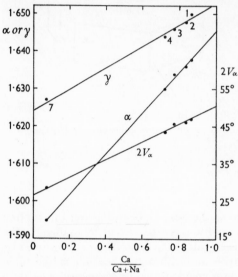

by replacement of $(O)^{-2}$ by $(OH)^-$ (*e.g.* anal. 5). Alternatively, increased sodium content may be accompanied by increased silica, and the composition then approaches that of paragonite (*e.g.* anal. 6, Table 18). For the material of anal. 7, originally described as soda-margarite, or ephesite (Phillips, 1931), a new analysis shows considerably more Li_2O than was first reported. For this specimen the high sodium content is accompanied by high lithium, there is no excess silica, and its charge balance is maintained by the total of 6 Y ions which confer on it tri-octahedral character. As with the lithian muscovites and lepidolites, the presence of lithium seems to be associated with tri-octahedral character. Y sites are

FIG. 23. α, γ and $2V$ plotted against ionic proportions $Ca/(Ca+Na)$ for five margarite specimens of Table 18.

occupied almost entirely by aluminium but small substitutions of Fe^{+3}, Fe^{+2}, Mn and Mg are evident. That the $(OH)^-$ ions often total more than four may be taken to indicate the replacement of some O^{-2} ions by $(OH)^-$, but the possibility that some of the water recorded as H_2O^+ is adsorbed and not "structural" cannot be discounted.

OPTICAL AND PHYSICAL PROPERTIES

Since the compositions of nearly all margarites listed in Table 18 are similar, and there are no major substitutions apart from Na–Ca, a plot of α, γ and $2V$ against $Ca/(Ca+Na)$ shows approximately a straight line relationship (Fig. 23). Specimen No. 6 (Table 18) is omitted because the $Si:[Al]^4$ ratio is approximately 5:3 not 4:4. Although specimen No. 7 has a greater number of atoms in Y sites, its optical data plot consistently with the others, since its high lithium content has little effect on refractive index. The relationships shown by Fig. 23

Table 18. MARGARITE ANALYSES

	1.	2.	3.	4.	5.	6.	7.
O$_2$	29·57	31·98	30·84	29·78	31·38	39·72	30·86
iO$_2$	—	—	—	—	0·10	—	0·03
l$_2$O$_3$	49·97	49·21	50·76	50·94	48·98	41·50	51·68
e$_2$O$_3$	2·94	—	0·12	1·13	1·55	0·75	0·47
eO	—	0·79	0·35	—	—	0·35	0·04
nO	0·22	—	0·11	—	0·02	—	0·12
gO	0·34	0·76	0·35	0·66	1·10	0·91	0·09
aO	10·89	10·64	10·52	10·21	8·00	3·28	0·02
aO	—	—	—	—	—	0·19	0·17
rO	—	—	—	—	—	0·62	—
a$_2$O	0·92	1·53	1·68	2·21	3·14	5·64	7·94
$_2$O	—	0·21	0·32	0·50	0·18	0·68	0·17
i$_2$O	0·39	—	0·23	—	—	—	3·80
$_2$O$^+$	4·81	4·95	4·97	4·77	5·71	5·60	4·92
$_2$O$^-$	—	—	—	—	0·11	1·01	0·06
otal	100·05	100·07	100·25	100·20	100·27	100·25	100·37
	1·638	1·636	1·634	1·630	—	1·586	1·595
	1·648	1·646	1·644	1·642	—	1·612	1·625
	1·650	1·648	1·646	1·644	—	1·613	1·627
V$_\alpha$	47°	46° 10′	45° 50′	43° 20′	—	50°	28° 32′ (calc)
	—	—	—	—	3·04	—	3·00

NUMBERS OF IONS ON THE BASIS OF 24(O,OH)†

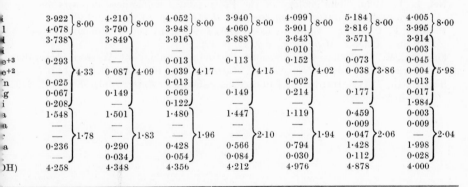

1. Margarite, Chester, Massachusetts.
2. Margarite, Unionville, Pennsylvania. }(Koch, 1935).
3. Margarite, Pennsylvania.
4. Margarite, Zillerthal.
5. Greyish white margarite, embedded in fine-grained corundum, Gibraltar, Western Australia (Simpson, 1932).
6. Sodium-margarite, Mt. Yatyrgvata, northern Caucasus, formed by intrusion of pegmatite into amphibolite (Afanasev and Aidinyan, 1952).
7. Pink crystals of sodium-margarite (ephesite), Postmasburg district, South Africa (Phillips, 1931; see also Nel, 1929). New analysis as above by M. K. Carron and W. W. Brannock, kindly supplied by M. Fleischer, U.S. Geol. Surv.

† Anal. 7 calculated on the basis of 22 oxygen equivalents.

7—R.F.M. 3

are of necessity only approximate since only five points have been used to determine each line and four of them are closely spaced.

The hardness of margarite is given in most texts as $3\frac{1}{2}$ to $4\frac{1}{2}$ compared with 2 to 3 for the common micas. These figures are relevant to the basal plane only, and for the direction perpendicular to (001) the hardness is approximately 6 for the brittle micas and 4 for the common micas (Switzer, 1941).

DISTINGUISHING FEATURES

Margarite may be distinguished from muscovite and talc by having higher refractive indices and lower birefringence, and from chlorites and chloritoid by the green colour of the latter minerals.

PARAGENESIS

The most common occurrence of margarite is in metamorphic emery deposits, along with diaspore and corundum from which it is probably derived. It also occurs in association with tourmaline and staurolite in chlorite and mica schists.

REFERENCES

Afanasev, G. D. and Aidinyan, N. Kh., 1952. On natron margarite from northern Caucasus. *Bull. Acad. Sci. USSR, Géol. Sér.*, No. 2, p. 138 (M.A. 12–140).

Koch, G., 1935. Chemische und physikalisch-optische Zusammenhänge innerhalb der Sprödglimmergruppe. *Chemie der Erde*, vol. 9, p. 453 (M.A. 6–238).

Mauguin, Ch., 1928. Étude des micas (non fluorés) au moyen des rayons X. *Comptes Rend. Acad. Sci. Paris*, vol. 186, p. 879.

Nel, L. T., 1929. The geology of the Postmasburg manganese deposits and the surrounding country. *Geol. Surv. South Africa*, p. 81 (M.A. 4–148).

Phillips, F. C., 1931. Ephesite (soda-margarite) from the Postmasburg district South Africa. *Min. Mag.*, vol. 22, p. 482.

Simpson, E. S., 1932. Contributions to the mineralogy of Western Australia, Series VII. *Journ. Roy. Soc. W. Australia*, vol. 18, p. 61 (M.A. 5–147).

Switzer, G., 1941. Hardness of micaceous minerals. *Amer. Journ. Sci.*, vol. 239, p. 316.

Clintonite and Xanthophyllite

$$Ca_2(Mg \text{ etc.}_{4\cdot6}Al_{1\cdot4})[Si_{2\cdot5}Al_{5\cdot5}O_{20}](OH)_4$$

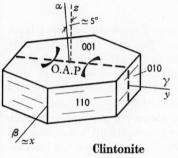

Clintonite

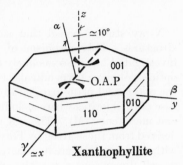

Xanthophyllite

α	$1\cdot643$–$1\cdot648$
β	$1\cdot655$–$1\cdot662$
γ	$1\cdot655$–$1\cdot663$
δ	$\simeq 0\cdot012$

$2V_\alpha \simeq 32°$ $2V_\alpha = 0°$–$23°$

$\beta \simeq x, \gamma = y, \alpha : z \simeq 5°$ $\gamma \simeq x, \beta = y, \alpha : z \simeq 10°$

O.A.P. $\perp(010)$ O.A.P. (010)

Dispersion: Weak $r < v$ D 3–3·1   H 3½ on (001), 6 $\perp$(001).

Cleavage: {001} perfect.

Twinning: Composition plane {001}, twin axis [310].

Colour: Colourless, yellow, green, reddish brown; colourless in thin
                 section.

Pleochroism: α colourless, yellow, orange or reddish brown; $\beta = \gamma$ green or
                 brown.

Unit cell:

  Clintonite: a 5·21, b 9·02, $c \sin \beta$ 19·24 Å†, $\beta \simeq 95°$.
                 Z=2. Space group $C2/c$.

  Xanthophyllite: a 5·21–5·25, b 9·00–9·04, c 9·81–9·97 Å, β 100° 05′.
                 Z=1. Space group Cm or $C2/m$.

  Insoluble in acids.

In the same way that margarite is related to muscovite by the substitution of
Ca for K, so the brittle micas clintonite and xanthophyllite may be regarded as
calcium analogues of phlogopite. It may be seen from Table 19 that they
conform very closely in composition to the ideal formula of a tri-octahedral
mica. Many other names have been used to describe minerals in this group,
among them seybertite, brandisite and valuevite. Chemical analyses show no
significant differences among them, but optical studies show that there are
essentially two sub-groups, clintonite and xanthophyllite, in which the optic

† Machatschki and Mussgnug, 1942.

axial plane is perpendicular and parallel to (010) respectively. For the most part it seems that specimens described as valuevite are xanothophyllites (Forman, 1951), and those described as brandisite or seybertite are clintonites. The two most commonly used names have been chosen here in preference to the others. Clintonite is named after De Witt Clinton, and xanthophyllite from the Greek *xanthos*, yellow, and *phullon*, leaf, in allusion to its foliated texture.

STRUCTURE

X-ray studies reveal that some specimens have 2-layer and some 1-layer structures. Polymorphism of the brittle micas has not been extensively investigated but it seems likely that clintonites have the $2M_1$ structure and the optic axial plane perpendicular to (010), while xanothophyllites are 1M and have the optic axial plane parallel to (010). This would form a strict parallel to the case of the biotites where a similar distinction was made between anomite ($2M_1$) and meroxene (1M). The cell parameters given above for xanthophyllite are derived from those given by Forman (1951) and by Sanero (1940). As compared with margarite the greater content of $[Al]^4$ and $[Mg]^6$ gives an expected increase in cell dimensions. In spite of the very high proportion of tetrahedral Al, however, the a and b parameters of clintonite are surprisingly smaller than those of phlogopite and talc. A similar feature was noted in comparing margarite with muscovite and pyrophyllite and in both brittle micas it seems likely that considerable distortion of the $(Si,Al)_4O_{10}$ network must occur.

CHEMISTRY

In Table 19, anals. 1–3 are of clintonites and 4–7 are of xanthophyllites. They all show a remarkably low content of silica, which results in a ratio $[Al]^4 : Si$ consistently as high as 2:1. Relating their formulae to that of phlogopite, this balances the substitutions of Ca for K and Al for Mg. Magnesium and octahedral aluminium are fairly constant at about 4·3 and 1·3 atoms per formula unit respectively, the remainder of the six sites being filled by iron and by other elements in very small or trace amounts. Small substitutions of sodium and potassium for calcium can occur but the totals in both X and Y sites vary very little from their ideal values, 2 and 6.

OPTICAL AND PHYSICAL PROPERTIES

The refractive indices of most clintonites and xanthophyllites are similar and lie within a rather narrow range, and 2V is small for both, but smaller for xanthophyllite. There is insufficient variation of chemical composition to provide any relationship between chemistry and optics beyond an indication that increasing iron content and decreasing substitution of calcium by sodium are associated with rise in refractive indices.

DISTINGUISHING FEATURES

Clintonite and xanthophyllite can be distinguished from other micas of similar colour since the latter have higher birefringence, lower hardness and are

Table 19.   CLINTONITE AND XANTHOPHYLLITE ANALYSES

	1.	2.	3.	4.	5.	6.	7.
O₂	17·02	18·34	18·29	17·6	16·74	17·11	16·28
iO₂	—	—	—	—	—	tr.	0·23
l₂O₃	43·02	40·69	40·42	39·6	42·70	41·71	40·95
e₂O₃	1·07	2·04	0·34	tr.	2·85	0·80	2·07
eO	0·60	1·12	2·56	—	0·41	0·94	0·72
nO	—	—	—	—	—	0·03	0·02
gO	20·64	20·53	20·81	21·6	20·03	21·03	20·44
aO	13·12	13·04	10·96	13·0	13·09	13·17	13·19
aO	—	—	—	—	—	tr.	tr.
a₂O	—	—	1·78	—	—	0·89	0·56
₂O	—	—	0·36	—	—	0·12	0·32
₂O⁺	4·81	4·71	4·62	}8·1	4·49	4·03	4·74
₂O⁻	—	—	—		—	—	0·22
otal	100·28	100·47	100·14	99·9	100·31	99·83	99·74
	1·648	1·648	1·582	—	—	1·646	1·647
	1·659	1·659	1·608	—	1·660	1·657	1·659
	1·660	1·660	1·610	1·638	1·660	1·658	1·660
V_α	32° 52′	32° 49′	31° 20′	2°–6°	12°–18°	7°–22°	12°–23°
	3·071	3·084	3·015	—	3·076	3·075	3·08

NUMBERS OF IONS†

	1.	2.	3.	4.	5.	6.	7.
i	2·365 }8·00	2·556 }8·00	2·571 }8·00	2·558 }8·00	2·34 }8·00	2·44 }8·00	2·311 }8·00
l	5·635	5·444	5·429	5·442	5·66	5·56	5·689
l	1·414	1·225	1·271	1·345	1·40	1·44	1·164
i	—	—	—	—	—	—	0·024
e⁺³	0·112 }5·87	0·215 }5·84	0·035 }5·97	— }6·02	0·30 }5·92	0·08 }6·10	0·220 }5·82
e⁺²	0·070	0·131	0·301	—	0·04	0·12	0·085
lg	4·275	4·265	4·360	4·679	4·18	4·46	4·324
a	1·953 }1·95	1·948 }1·95	1·651 }2·20	2·025 }2·02	1·96 }1·96	2·00 }2·26	2·006 }2·22
a	—	—	0·486	—	—	0·24	0·154
	—	—	0·064	—	—	0·02	0·058
OH)⁻	4·460	4·380	4·332	4·000	4·20	3·84	4·488
⁻²	19·540	19·620	19·668	20·000	19·84	20·32	19·512

1. Clintonite, Urals
2. Green clintonite, Monzoni   }(Koch, 1935).   Material dried at 110°C.
3. Red clintonite, Monzoni
4. Light green "clintonite", limestone, Parainen (Pargas) district, Finland (Laitakari, 1921).   Anal. A. Laitakari.
5. Green xanthophyllite, associated with blue calcite and monticellite, Crestmore, California (Eakle, 1916; Forman, 1951).   Anal: A. J. Eakle.
6. Green xanthophyllite, contact of dolomitic limestone with tonalitic diorite, Vacca lake, Adamello, Italy (Sanero, 1940).
7. Xanthophyllite, associated with pyroxene, garnet, etc., contact of diorite and dolomitic limestone, Monte Castone, Adamello, Italy (Bianchi and Hieke, 1946).

† For Nos. 1, 2, 3 and 7 formulae were calculated assuming 24(O + OH); No. 4 was calculated assuming 20 O's and 4(OH); Nos. 5 and 6 were derived directly from chemistry, cell volume and density, by Forman (1951).

not brittle.   Chlorites are also less hard and less brittle but most have lower birefringence than the brittle micas.   Chloritoid may be distinguished by its positive optic sign and larger 2V.

PARAGENESIS

The most common occurrences of clintonites and xanthophyllites are with talc in chlorite schist, and with spinel, grossular, calcite, vesuvianite, clinopyroxene (fassaite) and phlogopite in metasomatically altered limestones (Knopf, 1953; Knopf and Lee, 1957). Struwe (1958) reports xanthophyllite occurring with spinel in the silicate skarns between granite and dolomitic marbles in the granite massif of Quérigut, French Pyrenees, and notes that where clintonite occurs it is often accompanied by minerals of the humite group.

REFERENCES

Bianchi, A. and Hieke, O., 1946.   La xantofillite dell'Adamello meridionale. *Periodico Min. Roma*, vol. 15, p. 87 (M.A. 10–301).

Eakle, A. S., 1916.   Xanthophyllite in crystalline limestone. *Journ. Wash. Acad. Sci.*, vol. 6, p. 332.

Forman, S. A., 1951.   Xanthophyllite. *Amer. Min.*, vol. 36, p. 450.

Knopf, A., 1953.   Clintonite as a contact-metasomatic product of the Boulder bathylith, Montana. *Amer. Min.*, vol. 38, p. 1113.

—— and Lee, D. E., 1957.   Fassaite from near Helena, Montana. *Amer. Min.*, vol. 42, p. 73.

Koch, G., 1935.   Chemische und physikalisch-optische Zusammenhänge innerhalb der Sprödglimmergruppe. *Chem. der Erde*, vol. 9, p. 453 (M.A. 6–238).

Laitakari, A., 1921.   Über die Petrographie und Mineralogie der Kalksteinlagerstätten von Parainen (Pargas). *Bull. Comm. géol. Finlande*, No. 54, p. 87.

Machatschki, F. and Mussgnug, F., 1942.   Ueber die Kristall-struktur des Chloritoids. *Naturwiss.*, p. 106.

Sanero, E., 1940.   La struttura della xantofillite. *Periodico Min. Roma*, vol. 11, p. 53 (M.A. 8–15).

Struwe, H., 1958.   Data on the mineralogy and petrology of the dolomite-bearing northern contact zone of the Quérigut granite, French Pyrenees. *Leidse Geol. Mededel.*, vol. 22, p. 237.

Stilpnomelane

$(K,Na,Ca)_{0-1\cdot4}(Fe^{+3},Fe^{+2},Mg,Al,Mn)_{5\cdot9-8\cdot2}Si_8O_{20}(OH)_4(O,OH,H_2O)_{3\cdot6-8\cdot5}$

MONOCLINIC $(-)$

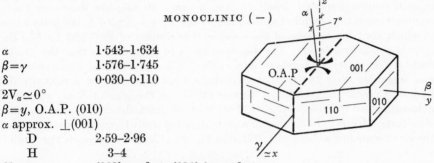

α	$1\cdot543-1\cdot634$
$\beta=\gamma$	$1\cdot576-1\cdot745$
δ	$0\cdot030-0\cdot110$

$2V_\alpha \simeq 0°$

$\beta=y$, O.A.P. (010)

α approx. $\perp$(001)

D	$2\cdot59-2\cdot96$
H	$3-4$

Cleavage: {001} perfect, {010} imperfect.

Colour: Stilpnomelane—golden brown, deep reddish brown or black; ferrostilpnomelane—dark green: pale yellow, dark brown or green in thin section.

Pleochroism:

	Stilpnomelane	Ferrostilpnomelane
α	bright golden yellow.	pale yellow.
$\beta=\gamma$	deep reddish brown, to nearly black.	deep green.

Cell size: $a\ 5\cdot40$, $b\ 9\cdot42$, $d_{001}\ 12\cdot14$ Å $\beta \simeq 93°$.

Z=1.   Space group   —

Soluble in warm $1:1\ H_2SO_4$ and HF.

The stilpnomelane minerals were earlier considered to occur only in iron- and manganese-rich low grade regionally metamorphosed sediments and associated veins. More recently, however, stilpnomelane has been described as a wide-spread and often abundant constituent of chlorite zone schists in New Zealand, and from rocks of the glaucophane metamorphic facies in Japan. Particularly in small flakes stilpnomelane may be confused with biotite, and it is probable that the stilpnomelane minerals occur more frequently than is evident from the literature. The stilpnomelane minerals vary in colour from dark green to reddish brown and black; their hardness is comparable with that of biotite and chlorite; plates of stilpnomelane are, however, neither as elastic as those of biotite nor as pliable as those of chlorite. The main compositional variation of the stilpnomelane minerals, excluding the manganese-rich variety parsettensite, is the wide range of the ferric and ferrous iron contents. The nomenclature of the stilpnomelane minerals has been considered by Hutton (1938) who proposed the restriction of the name stilpnomelane to the reddish brown to black ferric iron-rich varieties, and the use of the term ferrostilpnomelane to describe the dark green minerals rich in ferrous iron. Parsettensite, originally described (Jakob, 1923) as a separate mineral species, was shown by Fankuchen (Hutton, 1938) to be a manganese stilpnomelane, and it is proposed to retain this name to describe varieties rich in manganese. Stilpnomelane is derived from the Greek *stilpnos*, shining, and *melan*, black.

STRUCTURE

The structure of stilpnomelane has not been fully determined, but its physical and chemical characteristics, and cell parameters, are all consistent with a layered structure related closely to that of talc. Its talc-like sheets are based on an orthogonal (pseudohexagonal) cell with $a \simeq 5.4$ Å, $b \simeq 9.4$ Å, the parameters of which are large because of the considerable content of Fe^{+2} and Fe^{+3} in the central octahedral layer. The d_{001} spacing (12·1 Å) indicates that the "talc" units are separated by layers of ions unlike those of micas (d_{001} 10 Å), chlorites, and smectites (d_{001} 14–15 Å), and perhaps most like those of a partially dehydrated vermiculite (11·6 Å). Gruner (1937), on the basis of X-ray and other evidence, ruled out the possibility of mixed-layer mica-chlorite or mica-kaolinite structures (Holzner, 1936), and in a more detailed study Gruner (1944) suggested the layer sequence which is illustrated in Fig. 24. Midway between the "talc"

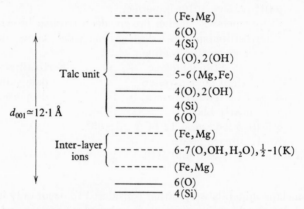

FIG. 24. Successive planes of atoms in structure of stilpnomelane proposed by Gruner (1944).

layers lie sheets of $(OH)^-$ ions, $(O)^{-2}$ ions and water molecules sandwiched between sheets containing iron and magnesium (and perhaps aluminium) ions. The distribution of these ions between inter- and intra-layer sites is not known but is assumed to be random. None of the three planes between the talc layers is fully occupied and it is assumed that potassium ions, which are readily exchangeable for thallium (Holzner, 1933), occupy particular sites in the central plane along what may be regarded as "zeolitic" channels. The numbers and relative proportions of inter-layer $(OH)^-$ ions, $(O)^{-2}$ ions, and H_2O molecules, are probably somewhat variable, and there seems to be only slight replacement of Si by Al (Hutton, 1956).

Single-crystal X-ray studies of stilpnomelanes by Fankuchen (*in* Hutton, 1938) revealed the presence of a super-lattice with fourfold a and b, and threefold c parameters. The super-lattice, which was observed also for ferro-stilpnomelane, probably has rhombohedral symmetry.

CHEMISTRY

The structure of stilpnomelane has not been determined in detail and the precise formula is still uncertain. On the basis of his X-ray investigation and a consideration of eight analyses of stilpnomelane Gruner (1937) computed the average formula as:

$$(OH)_{16}(K,Ca,Na)_2(Fe,Mg,Al)_{29}Si_{32}O_{92}\cdot 13H_2O$$

As a result of a later more accurate determination of the unit cell dimensions Gruner (1944) modified the earlier formula to:

$$(OH)_4(K,Ca,Na)_{0-1}(Fe,Mg,Al)_{7-8}Si_8O_{23-24}\cdot 2-4H_2O$$

Other suggested formulae have been discussed by Hutton (1938) who concluded that the compositional range shown by stilpnomelane can be represented as:

$$(OH)_{12}K(Al,Fe,Mg,Mn)_{10}Si_{12}O_{30}$$

The calculation by Hutton (1938) of a number of analyses on the basis of 42(O,OH) showed that in the majority of stilpnomelanes only a small amount of Al is required in tetrahedral positions to complete the ideal number of 12 silicon atoms per formula unit. The variation in the content of Al and Mg is small in relation to the magnitude of the differences in Fe^{+2} and Fe^{+3} contents, and Hutton (1938) suggested that in varieties in which Fe^{+3} is replaced by Fe^{+2} it is probable that hydroxyl replaces oxygen as in the ferric iron-rich amphiboles.

Thirteen analyses of stilpnomelane minerals, together with the numbers of ions on the basis of 8 silicons per formula unit are detailed in Table 20. In calculating the numbers of oxygen and hydrogen ions the H_2O^- has been ignored because it is not possible to distinguish between adsorbed water and that present as either inter-layer hydroxyls or H_2O molecules. Twenty oxygens and 4(OH) ions are assumed to be present in the talc-like layers, and the balance of oxygen and hydrogen ions are detailed separately because it is not possible to allocate them with certainty between the oxygen and hydroxyl ions and H_2O molecules in the inter-layer positions. The formula given at the head of p. 103 includes the range of ions shown by the analyses of Table 20, and in view of the wide variation in the compositions of the analyses selected it is unlikely that these ranges are appreciably exceeded.

Dehydration data are available for three stilpnomelanes; two curves (Fig. 25) determined *in vacuo* with a tensi-eudiometer by Armstrong (Gruner, 1937) show that the amount of H_2O lost on heating above 500°C. is less for a ferric iron-rich variety (curve C) than for a ferrous iron-rich mineral (curve B).

	B	C
Fe_2O_3	11·60	20·79 per cent.
FeO	20·00	12·83 per cent.
$H_2O > 500°C.$	≃3	≃2 per cent.

The dehydration curve (Fig. 25, curve A) of the Zuckmantel mineral (Table 20, anal. 4) although determined in air in an electric furnace (Hutton, 1938) is similar to the curves obtained by Armstrong. The Zuckmantel material lost 2 per cent. water between 350° and 425°C., oxidation being complete at the lower

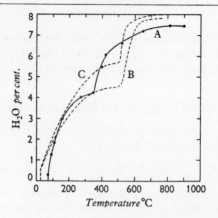

Fig. 25. Dehydration curves of stilpnomelanes (after Hutton, 1938).

temperature. Hutton also recorded a loss in weight of 3·04 per cent. by stilpnomelane kept for four months in a desiccator over concentrated H_2SO_4; the same weight of water was later regained on atmospheric exposure for eight hours.

OPTICAL AND PHYSICAL PROPERTIES

The great range in the ferric and ferrous iron contents of the stilpnomelane minerals is accompanied by a correspondingly large variation in their optical and physical properties (Fig. 26). Minerals with high contents of Fe^{+3} have

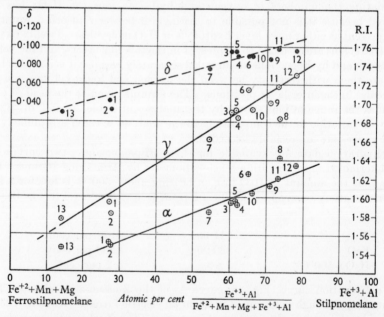

Fig. 26. Optical properties of the stilpnomelane series. Numbers refer to analyses in Table 20.

Table 20.   STILPNOMELANE ANALYSES

	1.	2.	3.	4.
SiO_2	48·03	46·00	44·45	44·67
TiO_2	0·23	tr.	0·00	tr.
Al_2O_3	6·48	7·34	7·26	6·83
Fe_2O_3	4·12	3·00	20·82	22·04
FeO	22·88	20·64	14·04	13·73
MnO	2·67	tr.	0·05	0·06
MgO	4·94	7·79	2·77	2·33
CaO	0·83	2·88	0·53	0·83
Na_2O	0·00	1·58	0·03	0·00
K_2O	0·83	1·54	2·06	1·36
H_2O^+	6·90	6·83	6·41	6·74
H_2O^-	2·64	2·58	1·35	1·57
Total	100·55	100·18	99·77	100·16
α	1·551	1·543–1·553	1·595	1·595
γ	1·594	1·576–1·586	1·690	1·685
$2V_\alpha$	0°	—	0°	0°
D	2·62	2·752	2·84	2·84

NUMBERS OF IONS ON THE BASIS OF 8 Si

	1.	2.	3.	4.
Si	8·00	8·00	8·00	8·00
Al	1·272⎫	1·505⎫	1·540⎫	1·442⎫
Ti	0·029	—	—	—
Fe^{+3}	0·516	0·392	2·818	2·970
Mg	1·226	2·019	0·743	0·622
Fe^{+2}	3·188 ⎬6·93	3·002 ⎬8·33	2·113 ⎬7·80	2·086 ⎬7·60
Mn	0·376	—	0·007	0·008
Na	—	0·532	0·010	—
Ca	0·148	0·536	0·101	0·159
K	0·176⎭	0·340⎭	0·472⎭	0·308⎭
(OH)	4·00	4·00	4·00	4·00
(O,OH,H_2O)	23·67	23·92	23·70	24·04

1. Ferrostilpnomelane, garnet–calcite–chlorite–ferrostilpnomelane schist, western Otago, New Zealand (Hutton, 1938).   Anal. C. O. Hutton.
2. Stilpnomelane, "3rd International mine," Urals (Lazarenko, 1954).
3. Stilpnomelane, vein, Zuckmantel, Silesia (Hutton, 1938).   Anal. C. O. Hutton.
4. Stilpnomelane, vein, Zuckmantel, Silesia (Hutton, 1938).   Anal. C. O. Hutton.

Table 20.   STILPNOMELANE ANALYSES—*continued*

	5.	6.	7.	8.
SiO$_2$	42·94	45·29	44·51	35·64
TiO$_2$	tr.	0·02	0·19	tr.
Al$_2$O$_3$	7·59	5·57	7·20	6·39
Fe$_2$O$_3$	21·64	23·95	19·42	27·80
FeO	13·23	8·99	8·94	5·32
MnO	0·11	1·14	2·93	3·08
MgO	2·80	3·30	6·24	2·12
CaO	0·91	4·28	0·47	3·11
Na$_2$O	0·10	—	0·37	0·11
K$_2$O	1·91	—	0·86	0·09
H$_2$O$^+$	6·95	6·12	6·92	7·85
H$_2$O$^-$	1·94	1·79	2·28	7·31
Total	100·12	100·45	100·33	"99·82"
α	1·597	1·626	1·584	1·643
γ	1·692	1·715	1·661	1·685
2V$_\alpha$	0°	—	—	—
D	2·85	—	2·80	2·89

NUMBERS OF IONS ON THE BASIS OF 8 Si

	5.	6.	7.	8.
Si	8·00	8·00	8·00	8·00
Al	1·664⎫	1·158⎫	1·524⎫	1·424⎫
Ti	—	0·002	0·026	—
Fe^{+3}	3·030	3·182	2·626	3·952
Mg	0·777	0·868	1·671	0·596
Fe^{+2}	2·062 ⎬8·22	1·327 ⎬7·52	1·343 ⎬8·05	0·840 ⎬8·00
Mn	0·017	0·170	0·446	0·493
Na	0·034	—	0·128	0·041
Ca	0·181	0·809	0·090	0·629
K	0·454⎭	—⎭	0·196⎭	0·023⎭
(OH)	4·00	4·00	4·00	4·00
(O,OH,H$_2$O)	24·64	23·21	24·30	25·75

5. Stilpnomelane, Anna mine, Baern, Moravia (Hutton, 1938).   Anal. C. O. Hutton.
6. Stilpnomelane, spherical vesicles in granophyre inclusion in olivine gabbro, Kangerdlugssuaq, east Greenland (Wager and Deer, 1939).   Anal. W. A. Deer.
7. Stilpnomelane, quartzose and albite–glaucophane schist, San Juan Bautista Mine,
   Santa Clara County, California (Hutton, 1956).   Anal. C. O. Hutton (2·80 density
   fraction, compare anal. 11).
8. Stilpnomelane, skarn-polymetallic deposit, Tetukhe, Far Eastern Province, USSR
   (Mozgova, 1957).

Table 20. STILPNOMELANE ANALYSES—*continued*

	9.	10.	11.	12.	13.
SiO_2	44·52	45·24	44·89	42·42	42·90
TiO_2	0·10	0·15	0·15	—	—
Al_2O_3	7·19	5·27	6·98	6·71	4·35
Fe_2O_3	27·32	26·87	28·80	33·24	0·35
FeO	3·31	2·96	1·02	0·85	—
MnO	0·42	2·74	2·74	2·27	34·43
MgO	5·63	5·97	5·23	5·20	2·70
CaO	0·23	0·85	0·65	—	tr.
Na_2O	0·32	0·75	0·42	—	0·20
K_2O	1·77	0·57	1·30	—	0·94
H_2O^+	6·70	7·11	6·59	8·33	9·66
H_2O^-	2·70	1·92	1·58	1·45	3·15
Total	100·21	100·40	100·35	100·47	99·27
α	1·612	1·605	1·620	1·634	1·546
γ	1·700	1·691–1·696	1·718	1·730	1·576
$2V_\alpha$	0°	—	—	—	0°
D	2·82	2·78	2·85	—	2·590

NUMBERS OF IONS ON THE BASIS OF 8 Si

	9.	10.	11.	12.	13.
Si	8·00	8·00	8·00	8·00	8·00
Al	1·522	1·098	1·467	1·490	0·956
Ti	0·012	0·020	0·020	—	—
Fe^{+3}	3·692	3·574	3·860	4·716	0·048
Mg	1·507	1·573	1·388	1·461	0·750
Fe^{+2}	0·497 (7·86)	0·437 (7·65)	0·152 (7·86)	0·133 (8·16)	(7·49)
Mn	0·063	0·410	0·413	0·362	5·440
Na	0·112	0·256	0·144	—	0·070
Ca	0·044	0·160	0·124	—	—
K	0·406	0·126	0·294	—	0·224
(OH)	4·00	4·00	4·00	4·00	4·00
(O,OH,H_2O)	24·03	24·39	23·83	26·48	28·02

9. Stilpnomelane, albite–epidote–stilpnomelane–chlorite schist, Cowcliff Hill, Otago, New Zealand (Hutton, 1945). Anal. F. T. Seelye.
10. Stilpnomelane, quartzose rock associated with albite–epidote–chlorite schist, Queenstown, western Otago, New Zealand (Hutton, 1956). Anal. R. Klemens.
11. Stilpnomelane, quartzose and albite–glaucophane schist, San Juan Bautista Mine, Santa Clara County, California (Hutton, 1956). Anal. C. O. Hutton (2·85 density fraction, compare anal. 7).
12. Stilpnomelane, ferruginous slate, Crystal Falls, Michigan (Ayres, 1940). Anal. V. L. Ayres and B. Park (Na, Li, Co, Ni, V, Ba and Zn occur in trace amounts).
13. Parsettensite, Alp Parsettens, Val d'Err, Graubünden (Jakob, 1923). Anal. J. Jakob (Includes HCl 0·02, CO_2 0·25, V_2O_5 0·32).

higher refractive indices, birefringence and density than those rich in ferrous iron, and Hutton (1938, 1945, 1956) has demonstrated that there is a relatively good correlation between the refractive indices and birefringence and the molecular proportions of (Fe,Mg,Mn)O and (Al,Fe)$_2$O$_3$. The refractive indices of artificially oxidized stilpnomelanes are also higher than those of natural ferrostilpnomelanes before oxidation (see Table 21, showing data for the Zuckmantel mineral before oxidation and after complete oxidation by heating at 350°C. for 24 hours). Basal plates of stilpnomelane, in thickness greater than 0·05 mm., are opaque but the γ refractive index can be readily obtained provided very thin plates are used for the determination. Due to the micaceous habit of the mineral considerable care is required to ensure that the minimum value for the α index is obtained. The great majority of stilpnomelanes show a negative uniaxial figure but minerals having a small optic axial angle have occasionally been noted. The maximum value observed by Turner and Hutton (1935) was approximately 40°.

Table 21. OPTICAL PROPERTIES OF A STILPNOMELANE BEFORE AND AFTER OXIDATION (Hutton, 1938)

Stilpnomelane Table 20 anal. 4.	Wt. per cent.		Refractive indices		Pleochroism	
	FeO	Fe$_2$O$_3$	α	γ	α	γ
Before heating	13·73	22·04	1·595	1·685	yellow	greenish brown
After heating	0·00	37·29	1·606	1·803	golden yellow	reddish brown

Stilpnomelane usually occurs in thin micaceous-like plates often showing a radiate or sheaf-like arrangement; basal sections invariably have irregular outlines. The perfect basal cleavage is not as regular nor as continuous as in mica, and stilpnomelane also has an imperfect cleavage perpendicular to {001}. The colour of the stilpnomelane minerals varies with the composition; the ferric iron-rich varieties are deep reddish brown to black, and the ferrostilpnomelane dark green in colour. Stilpnomelane is not infrequently zoned; the core consisting of ferrostilpnomelane is surrounded by a peripheral zone richer in ferric iron.

DISTINGUISHING FEATURES

Stilpnomelane may be mistaken for biotite; both minerals occur in green and brown pleochroic varieties, and have a very small optic axial angle (most stilpnomelanes are sensibly uniaxial) and similar pleochroism. The basal cleavage of stilpnomelane, however, is less perfect than that of biotite, and the former mineral has a second cleavage perpendicular to {001}. In the extinction position stilpnomelane does not show the characteristic mottling effect of biotite. Ferrostilpnomelanes are distinguished by their greater birefringence from chlorite, chloritoid and clintonite. In hand specimen stilpnomelane can be distinguished by its brittle character from both biotite and chlorite.

PARAGENESIS

Stilpnomelane is a widespread and often an abundant constituent of the semi-schists and schists of western Otago, New Zealand (Hutton and Turner, 1936; Hutton, 1940). In this area Hutton and Turner, from the degree of reconstitution of rocks of greywacke composition, recognized four texturally defined chlorite sub-zones, the rocks being progressively reconstituted from sub-zone 1 to 4. In the fine-grained greywackes of the first sub-zone stilpnomelane crystallized in small patches and radiating tufts and is often associated with relict hornblende. In the second sub-zone the grain size of the stilpnomelane and chlorite is larger and they are associated with albite, epidote and actinolite. The same mineral assemblages also occur in the third sub-zone and the stilpnomelane forms coarse flakes and foliae segregations; quartz–garnet(manganese-rich)–stilpnomelane schists also are found in this sub-zone. The stilpnomelane is a ferrostilpnomelane variety, but in some places shows brownish green peripheral zones; some of the stilpnomelane has originated by post-tectonic recrystallization, and its development is due to a process of segregation by solutions. In the rocks of the fourth sub-zone stilpnomelane is observed to have developed from chlorite, and is frequently zoned, the core consisting of ferrostilpnomelane, and the peripheral rims of a more ferric iron-rich variety. The production of a stilpnomelane (Table 20, anal. 1) from a chlorite having the composition $(OH)_{7.6}(Mg_{2.4}Fe^{+2}_{1.9}Fe^{+3}_{0.3}Al_{1.3})(Si_{2.7}Al_{1.3}O_{10})$ requires the addition of silicon and potassium and the subtraction of aluminium and magnesium:

$$chlorite + SiO_2 + K_2O \rightarrow stilpnomelane + MgO + Al_2O_3$$

In the western Otago schists, stilpnomelane, although most abundantly developed in iron- and to a lesser extent in manganese-rich bands, occurs also as an accessory mineral in rocks of more normal composition. Thus the initial constitution of the host rock is not the main factor on which the crystallization of stilpnomelane depends during regional metamorphism. Moreover Hutton (1938) has shown that stilpnomelane sometimes occurs in microfolds as well formed undistorted crystals, as sheaf-like aggregates lying across foliation planes, and in open fissure veins. Thus stilpnomelane may develop after the main phase of metamorphism during a period of post-tectonic recrystallization.

Stilpnomelane is a common mineral in the glaucophanitic metamorphic rocks of the Kanto Mountains, central Japan (Seki, 1958; Miyashiro and Seki, 1958), and occurs in metamorphosed pelitic and psammitic sediments as well as in metamorphosed rocks derived from mafic pyroclastic and igneous rocks. In this area stilpnomelane is found in rocks belonging to six zones of progressive metamorphism, and occurs sporadically even in the least metamorphosed types. In the rocks of zone II, which show very little schistosity, pelitic and psammitic rocks have been transformed to chlorite–stilpnomelane–sericite and chlorite–stilpnomelane schists, and the mafic pyroclastic and effusive rocks to actinolite–chlorite–stilpnomelane schists. In this zone stilpnomelane may also be associated with quartz, albite, calcite, graphite and haematite. In zone IV lawsonite–stilpnomelane–chlorite and lawsonite–stilpnomelane–sericite assemblages have developed from pelitic and psammitic sediments but in the metamorphosed mafic rocks stilpnomelane occurs only as an accessory mineral. In the highest metamorphic zone the following stilpnomelane-bearing assemblages occur: muscovite–chlorite–stilpnomelane, chlorite–epidote–garnet–stilpnomelane and chlorite–garnet–muscovite–stilpnomelane; other associated minerals include piemontite and magnesioriebeckite. The mineral assemblages in the metamorphic rocks of the Kanto Mountains are shown in the ACF diagram of Fig. 27; stilpnomelane is regarded by Miyashiro and Seki (1958) as a stable mineral of the lawsonite–pumpellyite–epidote–glaucophane sub-facies.

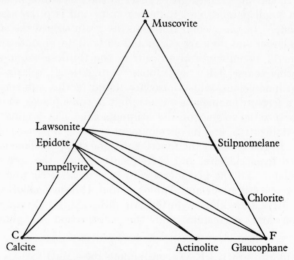

Fig. 27.   *ACF* diagram for rocks with quartz and albite in the lawsonite–pumpellyite–epidote–glaucophane sub-facies (after Miyashiro and Seki, 1958).

Grout and Thiel (1924) have described stilpnomelane in veins cutting carbonate and amphibole–magnetite slates of the Animikian iron formation, Minnesota. In most of the veins stilpnomelane is associated with quartz and carbonate, and in some of the larger veins with apatite and specular haematite. Stilpnomelane occurs in the slates also, and some bands in the magnetite slate consist almost entirely of quartz and radiating fibres and plates of stilpnomelane. Later work has shown that stilpnomelane, together with minnesotaite and greenalite, is a major constituent of the silicate-iron formations of the Lake Superior region. The iron-rich silicate layers, of variable mineralogical composition, occur in a banded formation and are often associated with magnetite bands interlayered with chert and carbonate; some bands consist almost entirely of stilpnomelane in extremely fine-grained crystals. Variations in the ferric and ferrous iron content, as indicated by refractive indices of the individual minerals of adjacent layers, are considered by James (1954) as evidence that the present composition of the layers is essentially the same as that of the original sediment. In this area stilpnomelane is present in some rocks which still have a clastic texture and which are considered to represent a fine-grained mechanical sediment which was enriched in iron during deposition. The formation of stilpnomelane is considered to have occurred during a period of low grade regional metamorphism associated with the development of the Huronian geosyncline.

Asbestiform veins consisting of stilpnomelane and chlorite in the meta-morphosed pisolitic ironstone of the Pen-y-rallt mine, Merionethshire, have been described by Hallimond (1924), and the replacement of tremolite by stilpnome-lane in copper-bearing veins cutting greenstone in the Karelia district of Finland has been noted by Eskola (1925).

An unusual occurrence of stilpnomelane (Table 20, anal. 6) in druses and in the groundmass of vesicular granophyre inclusions in the border group of the Skaergaard intrusion have been described by Wager and Deer (1939). Mozgova (1957) has reported the occurrence of stilpnomelane (Table 20, anal. 8), present in gel-like and recrystallized greenish brown masses, in cavities in a skarn-polymetallic deposit.

REFERENCES

Ayres, V. L., 1940. Mineral notes from the Michigan iron country. *Amer. Min.*, vol. 25, p. 432.

Eskola, P., 1925. The mineral development of basic rocks in the Karelian forma-tions. *Fennia*, vol. 45, p. 1.

Grout, E. F. and **Thiel, G. A.**, 1924. Notes on stilpnomelane. *Amer. Min.*, vol. 9, p. 228.

Gruner, J. W., 1937. Composition and structure of stilpnomelane. *Amer. Min.*, vol. 22, p. 912.

—— 1944. The structure of stilpnomelane re-examined. *Amer. Min.*, vol. 29, p. 291.

Gunderson, J. N. and **Schwartz, G. M.**, 1959. Metasomatic veins in the Biwabik iron formation. *Bull. Geol. Soc. Amer.*, vol. 70, p. 1613 (abstract).

Hallimond, A. F., 1924. On stilpnomelane in North Wales. *Min. Mag.*, vol. 20, p. 193.

Holzner, J., 1933. Beiträge zur Kenntnis der varistischen Gesteins- und Mineral-provinz im Lahn-Dillgebiet. 2. Über den Stilpnomelan von Grube Theodor (Lahngebiet) und einen beim Trennen mit Clericilösung auftretenden Basen-austausch. *Neues Jahrb. Min.*, Beil. Bd. 66, p. 213.

—— 1936. Über den anomalen Kristallbau der Biotite. *Zeit. Krist.*, vol. 95, p. 435.

Hutton, C. O., 1938. The stilpnomelane group of minerals. *Min. Mag.*, vol. 25, p. 172.

—— 1940. Metamorphism in the Lake Wakatipu region, western Otago, New Zealand. *Dept. Sci. Ind. Res. N.Z., Geol. Mem.*, No. 5.

—— 1945. Additional optical and chemical data on the stilpnomelane group of minerals. *Amer. Min.*, vol. 30, p. 714.

—— 1956. Further data on the stilpnomelane mineral group. *Amer. Min.*, vol. 41, p. 608.

—— and **Turner, F. J.**, 1936. Metamorphic zones in north-west Otago. *Trans. Roy. Soc. New Zealand*, vol. 65, p. 405.

Jakob, J., 1923. Vier Mangansilikate aus dem Val d'Err (Kt. Graubünden). *Schweiz. Min. Petr. Mitt.*, vol. 3, p. 227 (M.A. 2–251).

James, H. L., 1954. Sedimentary facies of iron-formation. *Econ. Geol.*, vol. 49, p. 235.

Lazarenko, E. K., 1954. On stilpnomelane. *Min. Sbornik, Lvov Geol. Soc.* no. 8, p. 119 (M.A. 13–61).

Miyashiro, A. and **Seki, Y.**, 1958. Mineral assemblages and subfacies of the glauco-phane-schist facies. *Jap. Journ. Geol. Geogr.*, vol. 29, p. 199.

Mozgova, N. N., 1957. On hisingerite and stilpnomelane from the skarn-polymetallic deposit of the upper mine of Tetukhe. *Min. Sbornik, Lvov Geol. Soc.* no. 11, p. 273 (M.A. 14–272).

Seki, Y., 1958. Glaucophanitic regional metamorphism in the Kanto Mountains, central Japan. *Jap. Journ. Geol. Geogr.*, vol. 29, p. 233.

Turner, F. J. and **Hutton, C. O.,** 1935. Stilpnomelane and related minerals as constituents of schists from western Otago, New Zealand. *Geol. Mag.*, vol. 72, p. 1.

Wager, L. R. and **Deer, W. A.,** 1939. The petrology of the Skaergaard intrusion, Kangerdlugssuaq, east Greenland. *Meddel. om Grøn,* Bd. 105, Nr. 4.

Pyrophyllite

$Al_4[Si_8O_{20}](OH)_4$

MONOCLINIC $(-)$

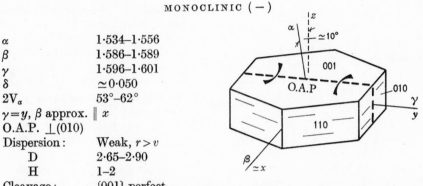

α	1·534–1·556
β	1·586–1·589
γ	1·596–1·601
δ	$\simeq 0\cdot050$
$2V_\alpha$	53°–62°

$\gamma = y$, β approx. $\parallel x$

O.A.P. $\perp(010)$

Dispersion:	Weak, $r > v$
D	2·65–2·90
H	1–2
Cleavage:	{001} perfect.
Colour:	White, yellow, pale blue, greyish or brownish green; pearly lustre; colourless in thin section.
Pleochroism:	Absorption greater for vibration directions in (001) plane.
Unit cell:	a 5·16, b 8·90, c 18·64 Å, β 99° 55′
	$Z=2$. Space group $C2/c$.

Soluble with difficulty in H_2SO_4.

Pyrophyllite is a soft mineral which occurs often with quartz and micas in hydrothermal veins, and in a massive form as the main constituent of some schistose rocks. The compact variety which resembles the form of talc called steatite is used for slate pencils, and also has good thermal and electrical insulating properties. Because of the similarity of the two minerals it is likely that some of the material marketed as talc is in fact pyrophyllite. Pyrophyllite, however, is slightly harder and does not flux when fired so that it is more useful for refractory purposes. Other uses of pyrophyllite are in lubricants, fillers for rubber and paper and as a carrier for insecticides. The name pyrophyllite, from the Greek *pur*, fire, and *phullon*, leaf, is descriptive of its thermal property and its common lamellar appearance.

STRUCTURE

Pyrophyllite is like the micas in that it has a layered structure in which a sheet of octahedrally coordinated Al ions is sandwiched between two sheets of linked SiO_4 tetrahedra.[1] The composition of the planar tetrahedral networks is Si_2O_5, and in pyrophyllite in contrast to muscovite, there is little or no substitution of Si by Al. The tetrahedra point inwards and their apical oxygen atoms form part of the di-octahedral central layer in which two thirds of the

[1] See structure of micas, p. 2.

available sites are occupied by Al, and one third are empty (Fig. 28). The resulting composite sheets are electrically neutral; thus no additional cations can be accommodated between them as are potassium ions and calcium ions in the common and brittle micas respectively. The superposition of successive layers follows the scheme described for the micas, "hexagonal" rings of SiO_4 tetrahedra lying directly above one another. The possibilities of rotating successive layers to build different regularly repeating sequences occur again as for the micas, leading to similar polymorphism. The principal polymorph of pyrophyllite has a two-layered cell ($2M_1$) which is commonest for muscovite, and in both cases the prevalence of the $2M_1$ structure is perhaps associated with distortions of the unit layers away from trigonal

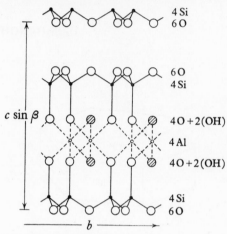

4 Si
6 O

6 O
4 Si

$c \sin \beta$ 4 O + 2(OH)

4 Al

4 O + 2(OH)

4 Si
6 O

b

F $_{\text{IG}}$. 28.   Illustration of structure of pyrophyllite as viewed along x axis (after Pauling, 1930).

symmetry as a consequence of incomplete filling of the octahedral Y sites (see p. 5). The general nature of the pyrophyllite structure was first predicted by Pauling (1930) and then confirmed using X-ray powder data by Gruner (1934), and by Hendricks (1938) using single-crystal X-ray methods. In a more recent study of the pyrophyllite cell by electron diffraction, Zvyagin and Pinsker (1949) found parameters similar to those given above.

X-ray diffraction patterns from flakes of pyrophyllite usually exhibit continuous scattering phenomena rather than sharp reflections, indicating a high degree of disorder in the crystal structure. This is not surprising in view of the weak "residual" forces bonding together neighbouring layers which therefore may easily be displaced from their ideal positions. It is quite probable that pyrophyllite layers sometimes occur intermixed with other sheet minerals: a regularly interstratified pyrophyllite-montmorillonite has been reported (Kodama, 1958).

The strong low angle basal reflection which characterizes the micas and illites at $d \simeq 10$ Å occurs for pyrophyllite at $d \simeq 9 \cdot 1$ or $9 \cdot 2$ Å. The position of this reflection is unchanged on heating to 500 °C. and is unaffected by treatment with glycerol. The position of the 060 reflection with $d = 1 \cdot 49$ Å is entirely consistent with the di-octahedral nature of the mineral.

CHEMISTRY

Pyrophyllites often occur in aggregates mixed with other minerals, but when separated they show little deviation from the ideal formula given above. Small replacements may occur, of silicon by aluminium, and of Al in Y sites by Mg, Fe^{+2}, Fe^{+3}, etc. Analyses usually show small amounts of Ca, Na and K, the location of which is unknown. These ions are unlikely to replace Al in Y sites, but they may exist between composite layers in the sites occupied by K in muscovite. In the latter case they would compensate electrically for small Si–Al replacements and would indicate some small degree of solid solution between pyrophyllite and the muscovite–paragonite micas. Some typical analyses of pyrophyllites are shown in Table 22. The fine-grained nature of many specimens causes the strong adsorption of water, so that there is often some uncertainty in the determination of constitutional water. For this reason formulae have been calculated on the basis of 22 oxygen equivalents (except anals. 6 and 7) without using the analytical figure for water content.

The d.t.a. curves for pyrophyllite show an endothermic peak at about 760°C. corresponding to loss of constitutional water, and a small exothermic peak at about 1200°C. where decomposition to mullite and cristobalite takes place. Bradley and Grim (1951) suggest that an intermediate "anhydride" occurs when pyrophyllite is heated to about 700°C. which involves the expulsion (in the form of water) of one sixth of the oxygens of the octahedral layer. Some confirmation of this is provided by X-ray structural studies of oriented aggregates (Kodama, 1958). The mullite formed at higher temperatures bears a simple crystallographic orientational relationship to the pyrophyllite in that the octahedral oxygen arrangement of the latter is more or less undisturbed by the thermal transformation (Bradley and Grim, 1951). The dehydration characteristics of pyrophyllite are given by Kiefer (1949) as 640°, 690°–780° and 850°C., the four figures corresponding to onset of dehydration, beginning and end of rapid dehydration, and end of dehydration. These show it to be the least stable of the sheet minerals which possess a $2:1$[1] type of structure. Kiefer (1950) also presents evidence that a less stable form of pyrophyllite (β) exists, produced from the α form in nature by erosion, or in the laboratory by grinding in aqueous conditions.

The synthesis of pyrophyllite from its constituent oxides is readily achieved. The system Al_2O_3–SiO_2–H_2O, at atmospheric pressure and at temperatures between 300° to 500°C., yields pyrophyllite with boehmite and kaolinite, and in the presence of CaO, MgO and alkalis at pressures between 87 and 300 atmospheres, pyrophyllite, boehmite and talc are produced above 400°C. (Noll, 1935; and other papers).

A systematic study of the system Al_2O_3–SiO_2–H_2O (Roy and Osborn, 1954) showed that pyrophyllite is a stable phase within the range 420° to 575°C. under varying water pressures in all alumina–silica mixtures high in silica. That the fine-grained pyrophyllite was formed with difficulty was attributed to the preference of Al for entering at least partly into tetrahedral as well as octahedral coordination. The experimental results indicate that pyrophyllite may also occur as a stable phase at temperatures below 420°C. if insufficient water is present to convert the mixture to higher hydrates, and the natural occurrence in some places of diaspore with pyrophyllite suggests a temperature of formation of 275° to 405°C.

Various experiments on the laboratory alteration of felspar (Norton, 1939; Gruner, 1944; Folk, 1947; and others) show that pyrophyllite is generally obtained at temperatures between 300° and 550°C. providing that there is insufficient Al to produce kaolinite. At moderate pressures and above 350°C.

[1] A composite sheet containing two tetrahedral parts and one inner octahedral component.

Table 22. PYROPHYLLITE ANALYSES

	1.	2.	3.	4.	5.	6.	7.
SiO_2	63·57	64·88	66·07	66·04	65·74	65·96	58·45
TiO_2	0·04	0·02	—	—	0·41	tr.	2·35
Al_2O_3	29·25	28·64	27·09	28·25	27·71	28·25	31·27
Fe_2O_3	0·10	0·48	0·53	0·64	0·21	0·18	0·84
FeO	0·12	—	—	—	—	—	—
MnO	0·00	0·02	—	—	0·00	—	—
MgO	0·37	0·08	0·07	}0·12	0·02	—	0·12
CaO	0·38	0·03	0·36		0·12	—	0·05
Na_2O	0·02	0·03	0·60	}0·06	0·60	—	0·30
K_2O	tr.	0·04	0·10		0·18	—	0·16
P_2O_5	tr.	—	—	—	—	—	—
H_2O^+	5·66	5·47	5·43	5·02	4·90	5·27	4·88
H_2O^-	0·66	0·09	—	—	0·29	0·14	0·23
Total	100·17	99·78	100·25	100·13	100·18	99·80	100·08
α	—	1·556	—	—	—	—	1·534
β	—	1·589	—	—	—	—	1·586
γ	—	1·601	—	—	—	—	1·596
$2V_\alpha$	—	62°	—	—	—	—	60±5°
D	—	—	—	—	—	—	2·84

NUMBERS OF IONS†

	1.		2.		3.		4.		5.		6.		7.	
Si	7·764	}8·00	7·877	}8·00	7·995	}8·00	7·940	}8·00	7·938	}8·00	7·929	}8·00	7·380	}8·00
Al	0·236		0·123		0·005		0·060		0·062		0·071		0·620	
Al	3·976		3·978		3·861		3·940		3·883		3·933		4·036	
Ti	—		0·001		—		—		0·037				—	
Fe^{+3}	0·009	}4·07	0·044	}4·04	0·048	}3·92	0·058	}4·02	0·019	}3·94	0·016	}3·95	0·080	}4·14
Fe^{+2}	0·012		—		—		—		—				—	
Mg	0·068		0·020		0·012		0·021		0·004		—		0·023	
Ca	0·04		0·004		0·047		—		0·015		—		0·007	
Na	—	}0·04	0·008	}0·02	0·140	}0·20	—	}0·01	0·140	}0·18	—		0·072	}0·11
K	—		0·006		0·016		0·008		0·028		—		0·026	
(OH)	4·000		4·000		4·000		4·000		4·000		4·226		4·112	

1. Pale blue pyrophyllite, Honami Mine, Nagama Prefecture, Japan (Kodama, 1958).
2. Pyrophyllite, Vastana area, Nasum parish, Kristianstad County, Sweden (Henriques, 1957). Anal. A. Aaremäe.
3. Pyrophyllite, Vando, South Korea (Johnstone, 1954).
4. Pyrophyllite, Moore County, North Carolina (Hendricks, 1938). Anal. C. S. Rist.
5. White flaky pyrophyllite, North Carolina (Bosazza, 1941). Anal. V. L. Bosazza.
6. Radiating needles of yellow pyrophyllite, Tres Cerritos, Mariposa Co., California (Gruner, 1934, and Doelter, 1917).
7. Blue-grey compact cryptocrystalline pyrophyllite, "wonderstone", containing rutile and carbo impurities, Gestoptefontein, S.E. Transvaal (Bosazza, 1940). (Includes 0·10 SO_3 and 1·33 CO_2).

† Anals. 6 and 7 were calculated on the basis of 24(O,OH), the remainder on the basis of 20(O) and 4(OH).

pyrophyllite forms rather than kaolinite, since in these conditions excess Al_2O_3 forms boehmite. When Al_2O_3, SiO_2 and KCl are added to a felspar, hydrothermal treatment yields both muscovite and pyrophyllite. At higher temperatures kaolinite and pyrophyllite can develop even in the presence of excess K_2O.

OPTICAL AND PHYSICAL PROPERTIES

The comparatively rare occurrence of pyrophyllite, and its fine-grained nature have allowed the collection of only scanty optical data. Since chemical analyses of separated pyrophyllites show very little variation in their compositions, the range of physical properties is not wide and the optical constants listed above are probably valid for most specimens. The orientation of the optic axial plane, perpendicular to (010), is consistent with that found for micas with a two-layer cell. Pyrophyllite is found mainly in three forms, fine-grained foliated lamellae with platy cleavage, radiating granular larger crystals and needles, and massive compact spherulitic aggregates of smaller crystals. The larger platy crystals show perfect {001} cleavage, yielding flexible but inelastic lamellae: all the forms have a greasy feel. The low electrical conductivity of pyrophyllite makes it a useful component material for insulators, and the high fusion point of its decomposition products makes it a useful constituent of various ceramic bodies.

DISTINGUISHING FEATURES

Talc and muscovite have a higher 2V than pyrophyllite, and kaolinite has lower birefringence. Distinction from talc may also be made by the chemical test for aluminium in which a deep blue coloration is produced by heating a specimen after moistening with a cobalt solution. A field test of the abrasion pH (Stevens and Carron, 1948), can be applied to pyrophyllite or talc by rubbing in a drop of water on a streak plate for one minute: pyrophyllite gives pH 6 and talc pH 9. Pyrophyllites do not exhibit swelling characteristics with organic liquids, or ion exchange properties, so that they would not be expected to take up dyes. This property is said to distinguish them from illites and montmorillonites which are stained by *malachite green* and *safranine yellow*, but the staining of a pyrophyllite by *malachite green* has been reported (Bosazza, 1941).

PARAGENESIS

Pyrophyllite generally occurs in layered deposits usually in areas which have been subjected to metamorphism. It is a comparatively uncommon mineral which occurs largely through the hydrothermal alteration of felspars, and is often accompanied by quartz. It is also found with kyanite, and in quartz veins from reef mines (Frankel, 1944) as needles, flakes and rosettes. It can be pseudomorphous after kyanite, felspar and pyroxene.

REFERENCES

Bosazza, V. L., 1940. Wonderstone—a unique refractory material. *Trans. Brit. Ceram. Soc.*, vol. 39, p. 369.

—— 1941. Further notes on the absorption of malachite green by some clay minerals. *Amer. Min.*, vol. 26, p. 396.

Bradley, W. F. and **Grim, R. E.**, 1951. High temperature thermal effects of clay and related minerals. *Amer. Min.*, vol. 36, p. 182.

Doelter, C., 1917. *Handbuch der Mineralchemie.* Vol. 2, p. 121.

Folk, R. L., 1947. The alteration of feldspar and its products as studied in the laboratory. *Amer. Journ. Sci.*, vol. 245, p. 388.

Frankel, J. J., 1944. On silicates and dusts from the Witwatersrand gold mines. *Journ. Chem. Metall. Mining Soc. South Africa*, vol. 44, p. 169.

Gruner, J. W., 1934. The crystal structures of talc and pyrophyllite. *Zeit. Krist.* vol. 88, p. 412.

—— 1944. The hydrothermal alteration of feldspars in acid solutions between 300 and 400°C. *Econ. Geol.*, vol. 39, p. 578.

Hendricks, S. B., 1938. On the crystal structure of talc and pyrophyllite. *Zeit. Krist.*, vol. 99, p. 264.

Henriques, Å., 1957. Swedish pyrophyllite deposits and the optical properties of pyrophyllite. *Arkiv. Min. Geol. Stockholm*, vol. 2, p. 279.

Johnstone, S. J., 1954. *Minerals for the chemical and allied industries.* Chapman and Hall, Ltd., London.

Kiefer, C., 1949. Déshydration thermique des minéraux phylliteux. *Compt. Rend. Acad. Sci. Paris*, vol. 229, p. 1021.

—— 1950. Note sur les minéraux phylliteux et leurs altérations. *Compt. Rend. Acad. Sci. Paris*, vol. 230, p. 977.

Kodama, H., 1958. Mineralogical study on some pyrophyllites in Japan. *Min. Journ. Japan*, vol. 2, p. 236.

Noll, W., 1935. Hydrothermalsynthetische Untersuchungen in System Al_2O_3–SiO_2–H_2O. *Fortschr. Min. Krist. Petr.*, vol. 19, p. 46 (M.A. 7–96).

Norton, F. H., 1939. Hydrothermal formation of clay minerals in the laboratory. *Amer. Min.*, vol. 24, p. 1

Pauling, L., 1930. The structure of micas and related minerals. *Proc. Nat. Acad. Sci. U.S.A.*, vol. 16, p. 123 (M.A. 4–368).

Roy, R. and **Osborn, E. F.**, 1954. The system Al_2O_3–SiO_2–H_2O. *Amer. Min.*, vol. 39, p. 853.

Stevens, R. E. and **Carron, M. K.**, 1948. Simple field test for distinguishing minerals by abrasion pH. *Amer. Min.*, vol. 33, p. 31.

Zvyagin, B. B. and **Pinsker, Z. G.**, 1949. Electronographic determination of the elementary cells of pyrophyllite and talc and structural relation of these minerals to montmorillonite. *Doklady Acad. Sci. USSR*, vol. 68, p. 505 (M.A. 11–105).

Talc

$Mg_6[Si_8O_{20}](OH)_4$

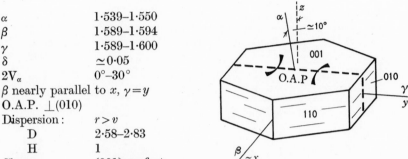

α	1·539–1·550
β	1·589–1·594
γ	1·589–1·600
δ	$\simeq 0·05$
$2V_\alpha$	0°–30°

β nearly parallel to x, $\gamma = y$
O.A.P. $\perp(010)$
Dispersion: $r > v$

D	2·58–2·83
H	1
Cleavage:	{001} perfect.
Colour:	Colourless, white, pale green, dark green, brown; colourless in thin section.
Unit cell:	a 5·28, b 9·15, c 18·9 Å, β 100° 15′.
	$Z = 2$. Space group $C2/c$.†

Insoluble in acids.

Talc is the major constituent of rocks known as soapstone or steatite, blocks of which can be useful for thermal and electrical insulating purposes. When fired in ceramic bodies talc has the advantage of a very low shrinkage coefficient. Other uses of talc (sometimes known as French chalk) are as a filler for paints, paper and rubber, in soaps, cosmetics and other toilet preparations, and as a lubricant. The name "talc" is probably of Arabic derivation.

STRUCTURE

The structure of talc is like that of pyrophyllite except that octahedral sites in the composite layers are occupied by magnesium instead of aluminium, and none are vacant: talc is thus a tri-octahedral layered mineral. Its structure was first determined by Gruner (1934) and later investigated by Hendricks (1938) who found, as for pyrophyllite, that the stacking of successive layers is not regular. Thus single-crystal X-ray reflections show considerable streakiness, and no structure which is strictly compatible with any space group ($C2/c$ and Cc are the principal alternatives) gives complete agreement between observed and calculated intensities. Best agreement is given with the $2M_1$ stacking (see p. 4) and space group $C2/c$, meaning that nearest neighbouring layers are most likely to be found with the $2M_1$ stacking sequence. Cell parameters, as

† X-ray data are those obtained by Hendricks (1938) who gave $C2/c$ as the space group best describing the structural relation between neighbouring layers (see above).

Table 23. TALC ANALYSES

	1.	2.	3.	4.	5.
SiO_2	62·61	62·67	62·47	62·16	60·06
TiO_2	—	—	0·00	—	—
Al_2O_3	tr.	0·38	0·47	0·88	1·60
Fe_2O_3	—	0·68	—	—	—
FeO	2·46	0·65	0·79	1·41	1·74
MnO	0·01	—	0·00	—	—
MgO	30·22	29·95	31·76	30·86	30·83
CaO	—	1·35	0·00	—	0·40
Na_2O	—	—	—	—	—
K_2O	—	—	—	—	—
H_2O^+	4·72	5·05	4·70	4·92	5·02
H_2O^-	—	—	0·06	—	—
Total	100·02	100·73	100·25	100·23	99·65
α	1·550	—	—	—	—
β	—	—	1·572	—	—
γ	1·596	—	(1·580)	—	—
$2V_\alpha$	—	6°	30°	—	—
D	2·791	2·58	—	—	2·616

NUMBERS OF IONS†

	1.	2.	3.	4.	5.
Si	7·989 ⎫ 7·99	7·905 ⎫ 7·96	7·914 ⎫ 7·98	7·874 ⎫ 8·01	7·686 ⎫ 7·93
Al	— ⎭	0·056 ⎭	0·070 ⎭	0·131 ⎭	0·241 ⎭
Al	—	—	—	—	—
Fe^{+3}	—	0·065	—	—	—
Fe^{+2}	0·261 ⎫ 6·01	0·068 ⎫ 5·76	0·084 ⎫ 6·08	0·149 ⎫ 5·98	0·186 ⎫ 6·07
Mn	0·007 ⎬	— ⎬	— ⎬	— ⎬	— ⎬
Mg	5·743 ⎭	5·631 ⎭	5·996 ⎭	5·826 ⎭	5·881 ⎭
Ca	—	0·183	—	—	0·055
Na	—	—	—	—	—
K	—	—	—	—	—
(OH)	4·018	4·250	3·972	4·158	4·288

1. Talc, altered peridotite, Muruhatten, northern Sweden (Du Rietz, 1935). Anal. R. Blix and N. Sahlbom.
2. Talc, Shabrov, Urals (Dromashko, 1953).
3. Talc, Murphy, North Carolina (Bennington, 1956). Anal. H. B. Wiik.
4. Light green talc, Malangen, Norway (Haraldsen, 1930).
5. Green talc, altered serpentine, Parma district, Appenines, Italy (Repossi, 1942).

Table 23. TALC ANALYSES—*continued*

6.	7.	8.	9.	
60·02	60·88	61·07	51·29	SiO_2
—	0·10	—	0·04	TiO_2
1·88	1·98	2·42	0·61	Al_2O_3
—	0·83	1·49	2·00	Fe_2O_3
1·51	—	0·00	33·66	FeO
—	—	—	0·12	MnO
30·39	31·18	29·13	6·26	MgO
1·00	0·14	0·75	0·00	CaO
—	—	—	0·08	Na_2O
—	—	—	0·03	K_2O
5·37	4·98	4·82	5·54	H_2O^+
0·32	—	—	0·24	H_2O^-
100·49	100·09	99·68	99·87	Total
—	—	—	1·580	α
—	—	—	—	β
—	—	—	1·615	γ
—	—	—	small	$2V_\alpha$
2·769	—	2·717	3·01	D

NUMBERS OF IONS†

6.	7.	8.	9.	
7·722 } 8·00	7·707 } 8·00	7·780 } 8·00	7·874 } 7·95	Si
0·282	0·293	0·220	0·074	Al
—	0·002	0·143	—	Al
—	0·079	0·143	0·231	Fe^{+3}
0·162 } 5·99	— } 5·97‡	— } 5·82	4·323 } 6·00	Fe^{+2}
—	—	—	0·016	Mn
5·828	5·884	5·531	1·432	Mg
0·138	0·019	0·103	—	Ca
—	—	—	0·024	Na
—	—	—	0·006	K
4·000	4·206	4·098	4·000	(OH)

6. Black talc, with carbonaceous material derived from a bluish grey rock, Parma, Apeninnes, Italy (Repossi, 1942).
7. Talc, Mount Fitton, South Australia (Alderman, 1952).
8. Talc, altered tremolite, Yellandu Warangal district, Hyderabad, India (Jayaraman, 1940).
9. Greenish grey iron-talc (minnesotaite), East Mesabi range, Minnesota, U.S.A. (Gruner, 1944). Anal. R. B. Ellestad.

† Nos. 6 and 9 were calculated on the basis of 20(O) and 4(OH), and the remainder on the basis of 24(O,OH).
‡ Includes 0·01 Ti.

determined by X-ray methods by several workers are in close agreement with those quoted above, and an electron diffraction determination (Zvyagin and Pinsker, 1949) gave a $5 \cdot 27 \pm 0 \cdot 02$, b $9 \cdot 13 \pm 0 \cdot 02$, c $18 \cdot 94 \pm 0 \cdot 14$ Å, β $100° 40' \pm 50'$. Minnesotaite, an iron-talc, has a $5 \cdot 4$, b $9 \cdot 42$, $c \sin \beta$ $19 \cdot 14$ Å. The structural changes accompanying thermal decomposition (Avgustinik *et al.*, 1949) do not begin until 700°C., below which adsorbed water is driven off. There is evidence from X-ray and other experiments that between 700° and 900°C. amphibole-like double chains, and between 1000° and 1200°C. pyroxene-like chains, are formed; between 1250° and 1350°C. clinoenstatite is formed and free silica crystallizes as cristobalite. The X-ray powder patterns of talc and pyrophyllite are similar, corresponding planes having a larger d value for talc, *e.g.* for talc $d_{006} \simeq 3 \cdot 10$ Å and for pyrophyllite $d_{006} \simeq 3 \cdot 06$ Å. Basal spacings are not affected by organic liquids nor by heating to 700°C. since there are no interchangeable cations and no water molecules between the structural layers. The strong 060 reflection is at $d \simeq 1 \cdot 52$ Å for talc as compared with $1 \cdot 495$ Å for pyrophyllite. Both talc and pyrophyllite probably occur interstratified with various clay minerals but their presence often may not be recognized.

CHEMISTRY

There appears to be little variation in the chemical composition of talc; sometimes small amounts of Al or Ti substitute for Si, and small amounts of iron, manganese or aluminium may substitute for magnesium. The relatively minor contents of Ca and alkalis also may substitute for magnesium, but are more likely to be present as interlayer ions or in impurities. These features are evident in the selection of analyses presented in Table 23. Generally the H_2O^+ content is approximately $4 \cdot 7$–5 per cent. which is sufficient for the requirements of the chemical formula, *i.e.* for 4(OH). The fine-grained nature of talc makes it not unlikely, however, that some adsorbed water remains beyond 110°C. causing values for H_2O^+ to be high. Analysis 6 (Table 23) when calculated without regard to the H_2O^+ figure yields a better approximation to the ideal formula. Although apparently uncommon elsewhere, a talc with almost complete substitution of iron for magnesium (minnesotaite) is abundant in the iron formations of Minnesota (Gruner, 1944). Using the analysis (Table 23, anal. 9) and the measured cell parameters and density, the following formula was derived:

$$\underbrace{Si_{7 \cdot 6}(Al,Fe^{+3})_{0 \cdot 35}}_{7 \cdot 95}(Mg,Fe^{+2},Mn)_{5 \cdot 58}O_{18 \cdot 5}(OH)_{5 \cdot 5}$$

This resembles the formula for talc but has excess (OH) and a deficiency of oxygen, and is low in silicon. Distribution of the remaining ions, Fe^{+2}, Mg, Fe^{+3} and Al, leaves vacancies in either or both Y and Z sites. In this case, too, if the H_2O^+ determination is disregarded and a formula is calculated on the basis of 20(O) plus 4(OH) a far better approximation to the ideal formula results (Table 23, anal. 9).

Several studies of the thermal decomposition of talc have been made (Haraldsen, 1930; and others) and all have shown that the end products are clinoenstatite and cristobalite, but the formation of an intermediate phase before clinoenstatite also has been reported. Thus Thilo (1937) calls the intermediate produced at 950°C. meta-talc, and states that it has composition $MgSiO_3$, and a crystal structure different from enstatite, whereas Eitel and Kedesdy (1943) describe the product of heating at 700°–1000°C. as protoenstatite. Both enstatite and protoenstatite are forms of $MgSiO_3$ with stability fields different from that of clinoenstatite (Foster, 1951; Atlas, 1952). X-ray investigation of the thermal decomposition of talc shows intermediates with features first of amphibole chains and, at higher temperature, of pyroxene chains (Avgustinik et al., 1944). Bennington (1956) gives the heat of solution of talc (Table 23, anal. 3) as $\Delta H = -201{,}987$ cal./mole. and the heat of formation as $\Delta H = -35{,}530$ cal./mole.

The stability field of talc in the system $MgO–SiO_2–H_2O$ has been investigated by Jander and Fett (1939), Bowen and Tuttle (1949) and Noll (1950), and as part of the system $MgO–SiO_2–Al_2O_3–H_2O$ by Yoder (1952): the stability curve

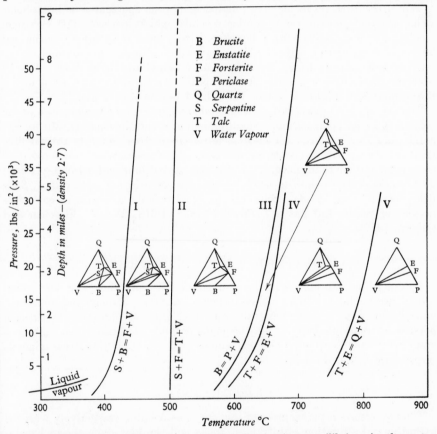

Fig. 29. Pressure–temperature curves (I–V) of univariant equilibrium in the system $MgO–SiO_2–H_2O$. Equation on each curve indicates the reaction to which the curve refers. Triangular diagram on each divariant region between curves indicates, for all compositions, the stable phase assemblages under the range of P,T-conditions represented by the region. Lower left – vapour pressure curve of water ending at the critical temperature and pressure. This figure is from Bowen and Tuttle (1949) but has been modified to take account of the redetermined $B = P + V$ curve (Roy and Roy, 1957).

for talc is illustrated in Fig. 29.[1] Talc can be prepared at all temperatures below 800°C. from mixtures of 3MgO and 3SiO$_2$ at water vapour pressure between 6000 and 30,000 lb./in.[2]. Hydrothermal syntheses attempted with different compositions yielded a pure talc plus silica or forsterite, thus confirming the indications of reliable analyses that little variation in the ratios of X to Z ions in talc is possible. Hydrothermal syntheses of serpentines and related layer silicates (Roy and Roy, 1954) have shown that complete substitution of magnesium by nickel can be effected, yielding nickel talc, and that both Mg and Ni talcs can be prepared in which Ge substitutes for Si. Ferrous iron talc, $Fe_6Si_8O_{20}(OH)_4$, has been synthesized, using ferrosilicon alloy as starting material, below 480°C. (Flaschen and Osborn, 1957).

OPTICAL AND PHYSICAL PROPERTIES

Talc usually occurs in massive foliated or fibrous aggregates or in globular stellar groups, but the rarer tabular crystals exhibit perfect {001} cleavage, yielding flexible slightly elastic lamellae. Its atomic structure of uncharged layers makes talc physically more like a molecular substance whose "molecules" (in this case infinite sheets) are only weakly bound to one another. Talc in nearly all its forms has a greasy feel and pearly lustre, and it is taken as one of the standards of hardness, having the value 1 on the Mohs scale.

The variation of optical properties recorded for talc is surprising in view of the constancy of its composition. Small amounts of certain ions (Ti, Mn for example) may have a large influence on refractive indices, but it is also possible that adsorbed water is a contributory factor. Minnesotaite is fibrous (positive elongation) rather than platy, has a greenish grey colour and α 1·580, γ 1·615; 2V is small, and pleochroism when present is α colourless or pale yellow, $\beta = \gamma$ pale green (Gruner, 1944). Synthetic ferrous iron talc is formed as colourless needles or plates and has α 1·586, β 1·618, γ 1·618, 2V$\simeq$5° (Flaschen and Osborn, 1957).

DISTINGUISHING FEATURES

Pyrophyllite and muscovite have a larger 2V than talc, and the "high silica" mica, phengite, has higher refractive indices. Brucite has refractive indices similar to β and γ for talc, but it is uniaxial positive. Distinction between pyrophyllite and talc may be made by the "pH abrasion test" (Stevens and Carron, 1948), which yields pH values of 6 and 9 for these two minerals respectively (see p. 119).

PARAGENESIS

The two common parageneses of talc are in association respectively with the hydrothermal alteration of ultrabasic rocks and the low grade thermal metamorphism of siliceous dolomites. In ultrabasic rocks talc commonly occurs as lenticular veins and along faults and shear planes (see Wilson *et al.*, 1946).

---

[1] Univariant equilibrium curves appreciably different from those shown in Fig. 29, were obtained for the system MgO–SiO$_2$–H$_2$O by Bennington (1956) using thermodynamic data.

The formation of talc-rich schists by the hydrothermal alteration of ultrabasic rocks is generally described as steatitization. The source of the hydrothermal solutions in many instances is not obvious, but in some cases there is little doubt that they have been derived from the original ultrabasic body; in other examples an external source from adjacent intrusions is indicated. Steatitization is commonly, but not always, associated with serpentinization, and some talc schists have formed directly from unserpentinized ultrabasic rocks. Intermediate and transitory stages in the development of such talc-rich rocks are characterized by actinolite–chlorite assemblages.

At many localities it has been shown that the steatitization occurred subsequent to the serpentinization during a period of greenschist facies metamorphism (Hess, 1933a,b; Du Rietz, 1935; Haapala, 1936; Wiik, 1953, and others). Although Bowen and Tuttle (1949) and Bennington (1956) have shown that talc is stable at higher temperatures and pressures than serpentine there is a considerable overlap of the stability fields of the two minerals and such factors as the greater ease of crystallization of serpentine, and its greater ease of acceptance of replacement ions compared with talc, are no doubt important factors which influence the crystallization of these two minerals. Bennington has also suggested that the presence of carbonate solutions may be a critical factor in the formation of talc, and may act as a transportation medium through which ions not acceptable by the talc structure are removed and used in the crystallization of chlorite.

The processes of steatitization have been considered by Turner (1948) who has shown that the formation of talc-rich bodies may arise by silicification, carbonation, or by the addition of CaO. The conversion of serpentine to talc by the addition of silica and the removal of magnesia without change in volume may be illustrated (Turner, 1948) by the following equation:

$$(OH)_4Mg_3Si_2O_5 + 1\cdot16\ SiO_2 \rightarrow 0\cdot79(OH)_2Mg_3Si_4O_{10} + 0\cdot63MgO + 1\cdot21H_2O$$

serpentine (276 gm.; 110 cc.)   (70 gm.)   talc (299 gm.; 110 cc.)   (25 gm.)   (22 gm.)

(removed in solution)

The conversion of serpentine to talc and magnesite by the addition of CO_2 also occurs without any essential volume change:

$$2(OH)_4Mg_3Si_2O_5 + 3CO_2 \rightarrow (OH)_2Mg_3Si_4O_{10} + 3MgCO_3 + 3H_2O$$

serpentine (220 cc.)   talc (140 cc.)   magnesite (84 cc.)

The hydrothermal alteration of more calcium-rich ultrabasic rocks, as well as the effects of calcium-rich solutions on normal ultrabasic rocks, results in the formation of tremolitic amphibole, and of chlorite if sufficient aluminium is available. At lower temperatures in the greenschist facies both tremolite and chlorite may be converted to talc by CO_2 metasomatism and the equations (Turner, 1948) of the constant volume reactions are:

$$(OH)_2Ca_2Mg_5Si_8O_{22} + CO_2 \rightarrow 2CaMg(CO_3)_2 + (OH)_2Mg_3Si_4O_{10} + 4SiO_2$$

tremolite (810 gm.; 270 cc.)   dolomite (368 gm.; 130 cc.   talc (378 gm.; 140 cc.)

(removed in solution

$$4(OH)_4Mg_2Al_2SiO_5 + 6(OH)_4Mg_3Si_2O_5 + 13\cdot2SiO_2$$

penninite (2768 gm.; 1025 cc.)

$$\rightarrow 7\cdot3(OH)_2Mg_3Si_4O_{10} + 4\cdot1MgO + 4Al_2O_3 + 12\cdot7H_2O$$

talc (2759 gm.; 1022 cc.)

(removed in solution)

At lower temperatures talc is unstable in the presence of excess CaO and CO_2, and is replaced by magnesite.   The talc–magnesite and quartz–magnesite rocks of the Cobb–Takaka district, New Zealand, investigated by Wellman (1942) have been derived from dunitic and pyroxenitic rocks by the action of CO_2. The alteration of the serpentine rock to a talc–magnesite and finally to a magnesite–quartz assemblage due to progressive carbonation and dehydration occurred with only a slight decrease in volume, and the reaction may be expressed :

$$\underset{\text{serpentine}}{(OH)_8Mg_6Si_4O_{10}} + 6CO_2 \rightarrow \underset{\text{magnesite}}{3MgCO_3} + \underset{\text{talc}}{(OH)_2Mg_3Si_4O_{10}} + 3CO_2 + 3H_2O$$

$$\rightarrow \underset{\text{magnesite}}{6MgCO_3} + \underset{\text{quartz}}{4SiO_2} + 4H_2O$$

In the magnesite–quartz rock, quartz is present in amounts less than that indicated in the above equation; the remainder, however, is probably located in numerous quartz veins which become increasingly abundant as the amount of magnesite in the metasomatized rocks rises.

The occurrence of talc-rich zones around nodules of serpentine in schist has been described by Pabst (1942) ; the talc, which is the most abundant constituent of the zones, is associated with vermiculite, chlorite, anthophyllite and tremolite. Similar zoned hydrothermally altered bodies in serpentine have been described by Francis (1955).   Details of many talc–serpentine localities in Canada are given by Wilson (1926) and Spence (1940), and in the United States by Ladoo (1923).   British occurrences of talc associated with serpentine are detailed by Wilson *et al.* (1946), and those of northern Sweden by Du Rietz (1935).

Talc is the first new mineral to form as the result of thermal metamorphism of siliceous dolomites.   In the Broadford–Kilchrist area, Skye (Tilley, 1948), talc occurs at the contact of chert nodules with the dolomite, and its formation can be ascribed to a reaction between dolomite and silica :

$$\underset{\text{dolomite}}{3CaMg(CO_3)_2} + \underset{\text{quartz}}{4SiO_2} + H_2O \rightleftharpoons \underset{\text{talc}}{(OH)_2Mg_3Si_4O_{10}} + \underset{\text{calcite}}{3CaCO_3} + 3CO_2$$

Talc also occurs within some of the chert nodules where, with calcite, it may form pseudomorphs after idioblastic rhombohedra of dolomite.   At this stage of the metamorphism the common assemblages are talc–calcite–dolomite and talc–calcite–quartz.   At a higher grade of metamorphism talc is replaced by tremolite, and the formation of talc and tremolite can be ascribed to a series of reactions involving progressive decarbonation.   The formation of tremolite from talc and calcite may be expressed :

$$\underset{\text{talc}}{5(OH)_2Mg_3Si_4O_{10}} + \underset{\text{calcite}}{6CaCO_3} + 4SiO_2 \rightleftharpoons \underset{\text{tremolite}}{3(OH)_2Ca_2Mg_5Si_8O_{22}} + 6CO_2 + 2H_2O$$

A more recent example of the early formation of talc during the thermal metamorphism of siliceous dolomite has been described by Cooper (1957). Pebbles, estimated to have consisted of dolomite 85 per cent., calcite 7 per cent. and quartz 6 per cent. in the Glance conglomerate, have been transformed in the outer aureole of a quartz monzonite stock at Johnson Camp, Cochise County, Arizona, to a mixture of fine-grained calcite and talc in almost equal proportions.   Here the talc–calcite assemblage cannot have arisen through simple isochemical metamorphism as the quartz originally present was below the stoichiometric proportion for the reaction:

$$\text{dolomite} + \text{quartz} \rightleftharpoons \text{talc} + \text{calcite} + CO_2$$

Cooper has suggested that the silica may have been introduced either from the quartzose matrix of the conglomerate or from solutions which gave rise to the associated quartz–galena vein mineralization.

REFERENCES

Alderman, A. R., 1952.   Mount Fitton talc as a possible source of forsterite refractories. *Sir Douglas Mawson anniversary volume, University of Adelaide,* pp. 1–6 (M.A. 12–81).
Atlas, L., 1952.   The polymorphism of $MgSiO_3$ and solid state equilibria in the system $MgSiO_3–CaMgSi_2O_6$. *Journ. Geol.,* vol. 60, p. 125.
Avgustinik, A. I., Tandura, P. Z. and Sverckava, L. I., 1949.   Mechanism of reactions in talc during heating. *Zhur. Prikl. Khim. Leningr.,* vol. 22, p. 1150 (*Structure Reports,* vol. 13, p. 374).
Bennington, K. O., 1956.   Role of shearing stress and pressure in differentiation as illustrated by some mineral reactions in the system $MgO–SiO_2–H_2O$. *Journ. Geol.,* vol. 64, p. 558.
Bowen, N. L. and Tuttle, O. F., 1949.   The system $MgO–SiO_2–H_2O$. *Bull. Geol. Soc. Amer.,* vol. 60, p. 439.
Cooper, J. R., 1957.   Metamorphism and volume losses in carbonate rocks near Johnson Camp, Cochise County, Arizona. *Bull. Geol. Soc. Amer.,* vol. 68, p. 577.
Dromashko, S. G., 1953.   Comparative characteristics of palygorskite, talc and pyrophyllite. *Min. Sbornik, Lvov. Geol. Soc.,* No. 7, p. 191 (M.A. 13–60).
Du Rietz, T., 1935.   Peridotites, serpentines and soapstones of northern Sweden with special reference to some occurrences in northern Jämtland. *Geol. För. Förh. Stockholm,* vol. 57, p. 133.
Eitel, W. and Kedesdy, H., 1943.   Die Metaphase der Entwasserung des Talks. *Abh. Preuss. Akad. Wiss.* No. 5, p. 21 (Structure Reports, vol. 9, p. 268).
Flaschen, S. S. and Osborn, E. F., 1957.   Studies of the system iron oxide–silica–water at low oxygen partial pressures. *Econ. Geol.,* vol. 52, p. 923.
Foster, W. R., 1951.   High temperature X-ray diffraction study of the polymorphism of $MgSiO_3$. *Journ. Amer. Ceramic Soc.,* vol. 34, p. 255 (M.A. 11–470).
Francis, G. H., 1955.   Zoned hydrothermal bodies in the serpentinite mass of Glen Urquhart (Inverness-shire). *Geol. Mag.,* vol. 92, p. 433.
Gruner, J. W., 1934.   The crystal structure of talc and pyrophyllite. *Zeit. Krist.,* vol. 88, p. 412.
—— 1944.   The composition and structure of minnesotaite, a common iron silicate in iron formations. *Amer. Min.,* vol. 29, p. 363.
Haapala, P., 1936.   On the serpentine rocks in Northern Karelia. *Bull. Comm. géol. Finlande,* No. 114.
Haraldsen, H., 1930.   Beiträge zur Kenntnis der thermischen Umbildung des Talks. *Neues Jahrb. Min., Abt. A.,* vol. 61, p. 145.
Hendricks, S. B., 1938.   On the crystal structure of talc and pyrophyllite. *Zeit. Krist.,* vol. 99, p. 264.
Hess, H. H., 1933a.   The problem of serpentinization and the origin of certain chrysotile asbestos, talc and soapstone deposits. *Econ. Geol.,* vol. 28, p. 634.
—— 1933b.   Hydrothermal metamorphism of an ultrabasic intrusive at Schuyler, Virginia. *Amer. Journ. Sci.,* 5th ser., vol. 26, p. 377.

Jander, W. and **Fett, R.,** 1939.   Hydrothermalen Reaktionen.   II.   Mitteilung. Magnesiumhydrosilikate.   *Zeits. anorg. Chem.,* vol. 242, p. 145 (M.A. 8–258).

Jayaraman, N., 1940.   Alteration of tremolite to talc in the dolomitic marbles of Yellandu Warangal district (Hyderabad, Dn).   *Proc. Ind. Acad. Sci., A.,* vol. 12, p. 65 (M.A. 8–161).

Ladoo, R. B., 1923.   Talc and soapstone, their mining, milling and uses.   *U.S. Bureau of Mines Bull.,* No. 213.

Noll, W., 1950.   Synthesen in System $MgO/SiO_2/H_2O$.   *Zeits. anorg. Chem..* vol. 261, p. 1 (M.A. 11–315).

Pabst, A., 1942.   The mineralogy of metamorphosed serpentine at Humphreys, Fresno County, California.   *Amer. Min.,* vol. 27, p. 570.

Repossi, E., 1942.   Il talco dell'Appennino parmense.   *Rend. Soc. Min. Ital.,* vol. 2, p. 47 (M.A. 10–422).

Roy, D. M. and **Roy, R.,** 1954.   An experimental study of the formation and properties of synthetic serpentines and related layer silicate minerals.   *Amer. Min.,* vol. 39, p. 957.

—— —— 1957.   A re-determination of equilibria in the system $MgO–H_2O$ and comments on earlier work.   *Amer. Journ. Sci.,* vol. 255, p. 574.

Spence, H. S., 1940.   *Talc, steatite and soapstone; pyrophyllite.*   Dept. Mines and Mineral Resources, Canada.

Stevens, R. E. and **Carron, M. K.,** 1948.   Simple field test for distinguishing minerals by abrasion pH.   *Amer. Min.,* vol. 33, p. 31.

Thilo, E., 1937.   Chemische Untersuchungen von Silikaten, VII.   Über das bei der thermischen Zersetzung von Talk entstehende Magnesium-metasilikat. *Ber. deutsch. Chem. Gesell.,* Abt. B., vol. 70, p. 2373.

Tilley, C. E., 1948.   Earlier stages in the metamorphism of siliceous dolomites. *Min. Mag.,* vol. 28, p. 272.

Turner, F. J., 1948.   Mineralogical and structural evolution of the metamorphic rocks.   *Geol. Soc. Amer.,* Mem. 30, p. 132.

Wellman, H. W., 1942.   Talc-magnesite and quartz-magnesite rock, Cobb–Takaka District.   *Journ. Sci. Tech. New Zealand,* vol. 24, p. 103B.

Wiik, H. B., 1953.   Composition and origin of soapstone.   *Bull. Comm. géol. Finlande,* no. 165.

Wilson, G. V., Phemister, J. and **Anderson, J. G. C.,** 1946.   Talc, other magnesium minerals and chromite associated with British serpentines.   *Geol. Surv. Gt. Britain, War-time Pamphlet* No. 9.

Wilson, M. E., 1926.   Talc deposits of Canada.   *Dept. Mines, Geol. Surv., Econ. Geol. Series,* No. 2.

Yoder, H. S., Jr., 1952.   The $MgO–Al_2O_3–SiO_2–H_2O$ system and the related metamorphic facies.   *Amer. Journ. Sci.,* Bowen vol., p. 569.

Zvyagin, B. B. and **Pinsker, Z. G.,** 1949.   Electronographic determination of the elementary cells of pyrophyllite and talc and structural relation of these minerals to montmorillonite.   *Doklady Acad. Sci. USSR,* vol. 68, p. 505 (M.A. 11–105).

Chlorite

$(Mg,Al,Fe)_{12}[(Si,Al)_8O_{20}](OH)_{16}$

MONOCLINIC, $(+)$ OR $(-)$

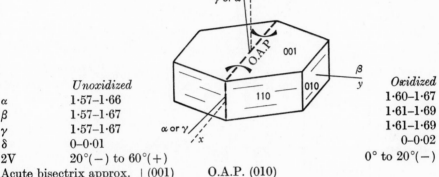

	Unoxidized		Oxidized
α	1·57–1·66		1·60–1·67
β	1·57–1·67		1·61–1·69
γ	1·57–1·67		1·61–1·69
δ	0–0·01		0–0·02
2V	20°(−) to 60°(+)		0° to 20°(−)

Acute bisectrix approx. $\perp(001)$ O.A.P. (010)

Dispersion :	Strong $r<v$. D 2·6–3·3 H 2–3
Cleavage :	{001} perfect.
Twinning :	(a) Twin plane {001}. (b) Twin axis [310], composition plane {001}.
Colour :	Green, white, yellow, pink, red, brown; mostly colourless or green in thin section.
Pleochroism :	Weak to moderate with either $\alpha<\beta=\gamma$ or $\alpha=\beta>\gamma$; strong absorption colours are usually dark or olive green.
Unit cell :	a 5·3, b 9·2, c 14·3 Å, $\beta\simeq97°$.
	$Z=1$. Space group: $C2/m$. (Other cells less common.)

Readily attacked by strong acids.

The chlorites are a group of minerals with layered structure, which in many respects resemble the micas. Their principal occurrences are as products of hydrothermal alteration in igneous rocks, in chlorite schists in metamorphic rocks and, together with clay minerals, in argillaceous sediments. They often occur in large crystalline blocks with perfect cleavage yielding flexible but inelastic (*cf.* micas) basal laminae, but are also widespread as fine-grained scaly or massive aggregates.

The name chlorite is from the Greek *chloros*, green, and is descriptive of the colour of most specimens. Optical properties are variable but most have small 2V and many appear to be uniaxial.

STRUCTURE

The cell parameters of a number of chlorite specimens were first determined by Mauguin (1928, 1930) and the basic features of the atomic structure of chlorites were described by Pauling (1930). More detailed investigation of chlorites by the X-ray powder method (McMurchy, 1934; Engelhardt, 1942; and others) established more firmly that the structure is one of regularly alternating talc-like $Y_6Z_8O_{20}(OH)_4$ and brucite-like $Y_6(OH)_{12}$ sheets. The pseudo-hexagonal networks of these components all have an a parameter of

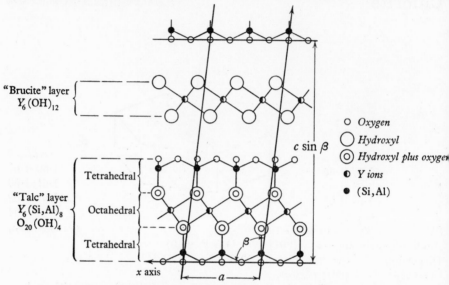

"Brucite" layer
$Y_6(OH)_{12}$

$c \sin \beta$

○ Oxygen
◯ Hydroxyl
◎ Hydroxyl plus oxygen
◑ Y ions
● (Si, Al)

Tetrahedral

"Talc" layer
$Y_6(Si,Al)_8$
$O_{20}(OH)_4$

Octahedral

Tetrahedral

x axis

a

FIG. 30. Projection of the chlorite structure on (010) (after McMurchy, 1934).

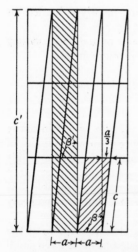

FIG. 31. Projection on (010) to show the relation between chlorite monoclinic (a, c, β) and ortho-hexagonal (a, c', β') cells.

approximately 5·3 Å, and the cell which results from their superposition has:

$$a\ 5\cdot3, \quad b\ 9\cdot2, \quad c\ 14\cdot3\ \text{Å}, \quad \beta\ 97°$$

The height of the cell ($c \sin \beta$) is the thickness of one chlorite layer, and the β angle results from a layer displacement of $a/3$ in successive cells (see Fig. 30). An alternative choice of unit cell for the same structure is the three-layered ortho-hexagonal cell with a 5·3, b 9·2 ($\simeq \sqrt{3}a$), $c \sin \beta = 3 \times 14\cdot3$ Å, β 90° (Fig. 31). The mode of stacking which leads to a one-layered cell is only one of several possibilities which have been investigated by single-crystal X-ray methods (Brindley *et al.*, 1950). All chlorites give diffraction patterns which are similar except for weak reflections of the class where $k \neq 3n$ and it is the latter which have different intensities for different stacking sequences and are diffuse if the stacking is irregular. Paying particular attention to these reflections from well-ordered crystals it has proved possible to recognize the different polymorphs of chlorites. The various stacking methods possible (and exhibited) are best described in terms of displacements either in

Table 24. SOME CHLORITE POLYMORPHS (after Brindley *et al.*, 1950).

	1	2	3	4
a Å	5·3	5·3	5·3	9·2
b Å	9·2	9·2	9·2	5·3
c Å	14·3	14·3	28·6	42·6
β	97° 6′	97° 6′	97° 6′	86°
No. of layers per cell	1	1	2	3
No. of layers in ortho-hexagonal cell	3	3	6	9
Symmetry	$C1$	$C2/m$	$C1$	$C1$
System	triclinic	monoclinic	triclinic	triclinic

the direction of the x axis or in directions at 120° to it in the xy plane, which may or may not be accompanied by layer rotations of 120°. Four ordered structures which have been observed in natural specimens have the parameters set out in Table 24.

An additional chlorite polymorph has been reported (Shirozu, 1958) which has a one-layered ortho-hexagonal cell (see Table 25, anal. 27). Many specimens are partially or wholly disordered, and these may be distinguished readily from ordered crystals by rotation photographs about the y axis. For an ordered crystal all spots are sharp, but for the disordered crystal those on the first and second layer lines are replaced by streaks characteristic of the two dimensional order of individual chlorite sheets. In powder patterns these reflections are often too weak to be visible. The structures of two chlorite specimens have been studied in still greater detail by Steinfink (1958a,b). One has a monoclinic one-layered cell with space group $C2$, and the other has a triclinic one-layered cell with space group $C1$.[1] Structure analysis by Fourier methods confirms that the polymorphism of these chlorites is due to different arrangements of the two Si–O networks relative to each other within the "talc" component, but also shows several divergences from the ideal atomic coordinates previously assumed (Fig. 32). In both cases there are rotations of the Si–O tetrahedra about an axis perpendicular to the layers which aids in "fitting" the tetrahedral and octahedral parts of the "talc" layer. In the monoclinic case, which also has a higher iron content, the amount of mis-match between tetrahedral and octahedral layer dimensions is greater and is accompanied by greater rotations. The occupation of tetrahedral sites by (Si, Al) in the monoclinic example is non-random (judged by bond distances) and occupation of the octahedral sites by Fe, Mg and Al is also non-random, one site in the talc layer being almost wholly occupied by iron. It is suggested that substitution of aluminium ions for magnesium takes place in the brucite layer and not in the octahedral part of the talc layer. In the triclinic chlorites the allocation of magnesium, aluminium, and the smaller amount of iron appears to take place

[1] A C-centred rather than Primitive cell is preferred for the description of these triclinic structures.

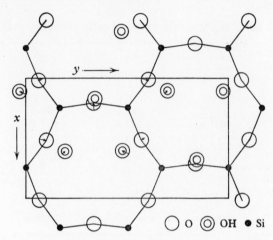

Fig. 32. The Si–O net and the brucite (OH) positions in chlorite projected on the basal plane. The arrows indicate the amount of shift of the atoms away from the "ideal" position to their true location (after Steinfink, 1958a).

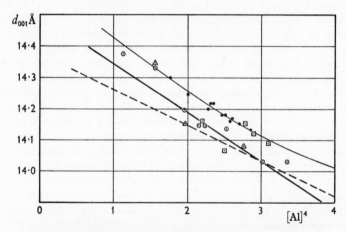

⊙ Bannister and Whittard, 1945.   • Shirozu, 1958.   ⊡ McMurchy, 1934.
△ Brindley and Ali (See Brindley and Robinson, 1951)
—— Shirozu, 1958.   – – Hey, 1954.   —— Brindley and Gillery, 1956.

Fig. 33. Plot of d_{001} against number of $[Al^4]$ ions per formula unit $(Si+[Al]^4=8)$.

randomly among all available octahedral sites. Further distortions from the ideal structure revealed by the above analyses result in stronger hydrogen bonding between (OH) ions of the brucite and oxygens of the talc layers.

In the chlorites a wide range of replacements (Al for Si, and Fe^{+2}, Mn^{+2}, Fe^{+3}, Al, for Mg) occur, some of which affect the positions and intensities of X-ray reflections, and these to some extent can be used to estimate chemical composition. The basal spacing d_{001} is influenced principally by the substitution of Al for Si and quantitative relationships have been examined by Hey (1954), Brindley and Gillery (1956), and Shirozu (1958) (see Fig. 33). Extrapolation of the curve given by Shirozu to the compositions of serpentine and amesite ($[Al]^4$ = zero and 4 respectively) yields values approximately equal to $2d_{001}$ of these 7 Å minerals. A study of the variation of inter-layer distance with composition in synthetic normal 14 Å chlorites and 7 Å septechlorites (see p. 164) shows that $2d_{001}$ for a septechlorite is slightly smaller than d_{001} for the normal chlorite of the same composition (Nelson and Roy, 1958). The value of the b cell parameter (as indicated by the position of the 060 reflection) is relatively uninfluenced by Al content but it can be a useful guide to Fe content (Fig. 34). Regression equations derived by Hey (1954) from the measured cell parameters of twenty analysed chlorites are:

$$a = 5\cdot320 + 0\cdot008(Fe^{+3} + Fe^{+2}) + 0\cdot0165Mn \quad (\sigma = 0\cdot059)$$
$$b = 9\cdot202 + 0\cdot014(Fe^{+3} + Fe^{+2}) + 0\cdot0235Mn \quad (\sigma = 0\cdot015)$$
$$d_{001} = 13\cdot925 + 0\cdot115(Si - 4) - 0\cdot025Fe^{+3} + 0\cdot025Mn.$$

Si, Fe^{+2}, Fe^{+3}, Mn are the numbers of these ions per formula unit as given on p. 131, and σ is the mean standard deviation of the observed data. These equations indicate that a and b increase with increasing substitution of iron or manganese for magnesium, but that d_{001} is independent of Fe^{+2} and decreases slightly with increase of Fe^{+3}. The terms for the effect of manganese were derived from measurements for pennantite (Table 25, anal. 38) which has a 5·43, b 9.4, $c \sin \beta$ 28·5 Å.

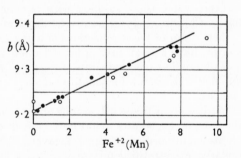

Fig. 34. Relation between b and (Fe^{+2} + Mn) content in chlorite (max. value of Fe^{+2} + Mn = 12) (after Shirozu, 1958). • Shirozu, 1958; ○ Engelhardt, 1942.

Brindley and Gillery (1956) prefer to use intensity relationships rather than cell parameters for the determination of iron content. Intensities of the first five or six orders of the basal reflection may be used to derive scattering amplitudes, the ratios of which indicate (a) the total number of Fe atoms substituting for Mg, (b) the manner in which these are distributed between the "talc" and "brucite" components (see also Brown, 1955). For tri-octahedral chlorites, as for other tri-octahedral layered silicates, d_{060} is rarely less than 1·53 Å; a di-octahedral chlorite should exhibit a lower value. The relation between the chromium content of chlorites (if greater than 1 per cent. Cr_2O_3) and the intensity of different X-ray reflections is found in most cases to depend upon whether the chromium occupies tetrahedral or octahedral sites in the structure (Lapham, 1958). The difference in intensity of 003 and 001 reflections, however, is not so influenced, and when (I_{003} - I_{001}) is plotted against Cr_2O_3 percentage a smooth curve is obtained.

X-ray methods have been used to study the structural mechanism of thermal transformations in the magnesian chlorites, penninite, clinochlore and sheridanite (Brindley and Ali, 1950). The first stage of dehydration involves the loss of about half of the structural water and is accompanied by a migration of Mg ions towards the hydroxyl sheets of the brucite layer. During the second stage of dehydration, olivine increasingly forms at the expense of the chlorite, and single-crystal studies show that the orientation of olivine produced is related simply to the original chlorite structure. It is seen that the transformation to olivine can be effected with but little disturbance of the approximately close-packed oxygen layers of the talc and "dehydrated brucite" components, and by movements of magnesium ions only in the direction normal to the basal plane. In the course of the transformation, silica and water are expelled from the structure, but the role of aluminium is not understood; for clinochlore and penninite, where the Al_2O_3 content is greater, the formation of olivine is impeded. The X-ray oscillating-heating method of following thermal decomposition (Weiss and Rowland, 1956) shows how differences in iron content in chlorites affect the first stage dehydration process. Both vermiculites and montmorillonites have basal reflections at about 14 Å but can be distinguished from chlorites by heating to about 600°C., when for chlorites the 001 reflection is enhanced, and also by the swelling characteristics of the former minerals, not generally possessed by chlorites. Certain chlorites have been described, however, which show swelling with organic liquids (Stephen and MacEwan, 1951). Chlorites may generally be distinguished from other layered minerals by their series of basal reflections starting at $d_{001} \simeq 14 \cdot 3$ Å, but since iron-rich chlorites have a weak first order reflection their patterns can be mistaken for those of kandites (clay minerals of the kaolinite group). In this case heating to 550°–600°C. is useful, for kandites are decomposed and their powder patterns disappear.

Chlorites occur frequently as one of the two or more components in randomly mixed layer aggregates (chlorite-vermiculite, chlorite-montmorillonite, illite-chlorite-montmorillonite, etc.; Weaver, 1956). Chlorite layers also occur in regularly interstratified mixtures giving a large basal spacing (*e.g.* 29 Å from montmorillonite-chlorite, Early *et al.*, 1956; and chlorite-vermiculite,[1] Bradley and Weaver, 1956).

Some layered minerals (the septechlorites, see p. 164) which are chemically similar to chlorites and which have been described as "chamosite" (Brindley, 1951) are structurally more closely related to the kandites or serpentines, and therefore give powder patterns characteristic of the latter minerals. They have a strong basal reflection at about 7 Å, none at 14 Å, and are decomposed on heating to 500°–600°C.

CHEMISTRY

The chemistry of the chlorite minerals, as well as their structure, can be described in relation to a chlorite with hypothetical composition $Mg_6Si_8O_{20}(OH)_4 + Mg_6(OH)_{12}$ which has equal numbers of talc and brucite layers. In chlorites a wide range of substitutions occur in both layers, silicon being replaced by aluminium within the range $[Si_7Al]^4 - [Si_4Al_4]^4$. Magnesium in both the talc and brucite components is replaceable principally by aluminium within the range $Mg_{11}Al$ to Mg_8Al_4. Replacement of Si by Al causes charge

---

[1] The name "corrensite" has been suggested (Lippmann, 1956).

unbalance in the "talc" sheet and it has not been established to what extent this is compensated by substitution of Al for Mg within the same component, or in the brucite layer, or in both. While the range of these replacements is restricted, any degree of substitution of Fe^{+2} for Mg can occur also, so that the ratio $Fe^{+2}:(Fe^{+2}+Mg)$ can lie between zero and unity. One other important aspect of chlorite composition is the role of ferric iron. The variations in chlorite chemistry can be classified in a number of ways employing boundaries which are to a great extent arbitrary. The method adopted here is that recommended by Hey (1954) which in many respects is consistent with prior attempts

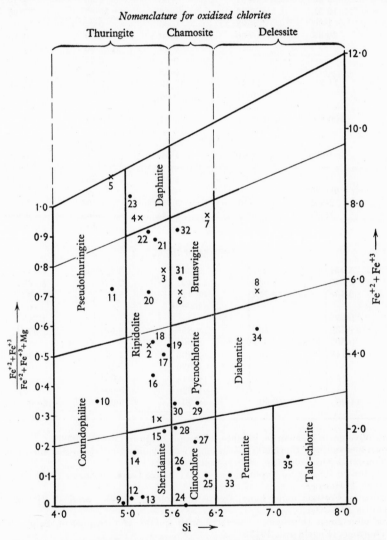

FIG. 35. Nomenclature of ortho-chlorites and oxidized chlorites (after Hey, 1954). Specimens for which analyses are given in Table 25 are plotted thus:

● ortho-chlorite   × oxidized chlorite

Table 25. CHLORITE ANALYSES
(Anals. 1–8, oxidized chlorites)

	1.	2.	3.	4.	5.
SiO_2	27·56	25·35	25·09	22·18	20·82
TiO_2	—	tr.	0·05	0·04	—
Al_2O_3	24·47	22·06	18·94	20·04	17·64
Fe_2O_3	3·85	18·97	9·60	7·35	8·70
FeO	10·51	8·36	25·66	35·23	37·96
MnO	1·80	0·08	0·02	0·02	—
MgO	20·86	15·06	9·80	3·79	4·15
CaO	—	tr.	0·30	0·40	—
Na_2O	—	—	0·11	0·07	—
K_2O	—	—	0·08	0·02	—
H_2O^+	11·35	11·34	10·40	9·11	10·31
H_2O^-	—	0·07	0·08	0·13	—
Total	100·40	101·29	100·13	99·84	99·58
α	1·606	1·670	1·641	—	—
β	—	—	—	—	1·662
γ	1·615	1·685	1·643	1·664	1·662
2V	$(+)0°–20°$	—	$(-)$	$(-)0°$	$(-)0°$
D	2·832	2·960	3·063	3·206	3·31
ω calc.	1·604	1·631	1·644	1·663	1·680

NUMBERS OF IONS†

	1.	2.	3.	4.	5.
Si	5·451 ⎫8·00	5·317 ⎫8·00	5·509 ⎫8·00	5·272 ⎫8·00	4·834 ⎫8·00
Al	2·549 ⎭	2·683 ⎭	2·491 ⎭	2·728 ⎭	3·166 ⎭
Al	3·158 ⎫	2·773 ⎫	2·412 ⎫	2·890 ⎫	1·662 ⎫
Ti	—	—	0·008	—	—
Fe^{+3}	0·573	—	—	—	1·518
Fe^{+2}	1·739	4·460	6·298	8·321	7·374
Mn	0·302 ⎬11·92	0·014 ⎬11·96‡	0·004 ⎬12·06‡	— ⎬12·69‡	— ⎬11·99
Mg	6·149	4·708	3·206	1·343	1·436
Ca	—	—	0·070	0·101	—
Na	—	—	0·044	0·031	—
K	— ⎭	— ⎭	0·020 ⎭	0·004 ⎭	— ⎭
(OH)	14·98	16·00	16·00	15·92	16·00

1. Dark olive-green klementite, phyllite, Vielsalm, Belgium (Mélon, 1938).
2. Brown klementite, "thuringite", associated with hyaline quartz, Messina-sur-Limpopo, Transvaal (Orcel, 1927, p. 262). Anal. J. Orcel.
3. Green-brown thuringite, "aphrosiderite", Weilburg, Lahn, Germany (Holzner, 1938). Anal. J. Holzner.
4. Thuringite, Fortuna mine, Lahn, Germany (Holzner, 1938). Anal. J. Holzner (Includes 1·46 CO_2).
5. Dark olive-green thuringite, associated with quartz and magnetite, Schmiedefeld, Thuringia (Engelhardt, 1942).

† Where (OH) is given as 16·00, formula has been calculated on the basis of 28 oxygen equivalents, ignoring H_2O^+; in other cases 36(O,OH) has been assumed.
‡ All iron has been expressed as ferrous for the purpose of this calculation.

Table 25. CHLORITE ANALYSES—*continued*

	6.	7.	8.	9.	10.
SiO$_2$	26·40	26·65	29·94	24·40	23·20
TiO$_2$	—	—	0·16	—	
Al$_2$O$_3$	18·23	16·14	13·77	22·77	24·42
Fe$_2$O$_3$	5·70	6·69	10·46	0·45	3·48
FeO	25·87	34·43	20·96	—	13·40
MnO	0·04	—	0·18	0·09	—
MgO	11·35	4·47	10·71	32·70	22·76
CaO	0·42	—	1·10	0·10	1·04
Na$_2$O	0·17	—	0·17	}0·30	—
K$_2$O	0·17	—	0·07		—
H$_2$O$^+$	10·60	11·42	10·00	}19·63	12·00
H$_2$O$^-$	1·05	0·08	2·48		—
Total	100·00‡	99·88	100·00‡	100·44	100·30
α	—	—	< 1·63	1·570	1·600
β	—	1·658	—	—	1·603
γ	1·620	1·658	> 1·650	—	1·610
2V	—	(−)0°	(−)small	(+)	(+)60°
D	3·034	—	2·73	—	2·85
ω calc.	1·633	1·651	1·623	1·584	1·617

NUMBERS OF IONS†

	6.	7.	8.	9.	10.
Si	5·747 ⎱8·00	6·099 ⎱8·00	6·706 ⎱8·00	4·933 ⎱8·00	4·645 ⎱8·00
Al	2·253 ⎰	1·901 ⎰	1·294 ⎰	3·067 ⎰	3·355 ⎰
Al	2·425	2·454	2·340	2·359	2·410
Ti	—	—	0·027	—	—
Fe^{+3}	—	—	—	0·068	0·522
Fe^{+2}	5·645	7·744	5·690	—	2·245
Mn	0·007 ⎰11·97	— ⎰11·72§	0·033 ⎰12·02§	0·014 ⎰12·32	— ⎰12·19
Mg	3·681	1·524	3·575	9·855	6·793
Ca	0·097	—	0·263	0·020	0·223
Na	0·071	—	0·072	—	—
K	0·047	—	0·018	—	—
(OH)	16·00	16·00	14·94	16·00	16·03

6. Green oolitic chamosite, siltstone, Wickwar, Gloucestershire (Bannister and Whittard, 1945). Anal. Geochemical Laboratories.
7. Yellow-green chamosite, associated with siderite, quartz and magnetite, Schmiedefeld, Thuringia (Engelhardt, 1942).
8. Black delessite, diabase, Somerville, Massachusetts (Frondel, 1955). Anal. E. H. Oslund.
9. Corundophilite, Quebec (Poitevin and Graham, 1918).
10. Dark green corundophilite, emery deposit, Chester County, Massachusetts (Shannon and Wherry, 1922).

‡ Recalculated to 100 per cent. after deducting impurities.
† Where (OH) is given as 16·00, formula has been calculated on the basis of 28 oxygen equivalents, ignoring H$_2$O$^+$; in other cases 36(O,OH) has been assumed.
§ All iron has been expressed as ferrous for the purpose of this calculation.

Table 25. CHLORITE ANALYSES—*continued*

	11.	12.	13.	14.	15.
SiO_2	22·47	27·12	27·78	26·68	27·64
TiO_2	—	—	—	tr.	0·22
Al_2O_3	23·57	27·68	24·30	25·20	22·48
Fe_2O_3	4·01	0·20	1·43	—	0·06
FeO	29·27	1·24	0·35	8·70	12·06
MnO	—	0·54	—	—	0·02
MgO	9·81	30·96	32·71	26·96	24·32
CaO	—	—	tr.	0·28	0·00
Na_2O	—	—	—	—	0·17
K_2O	—	—	—	—	0·06
H_2O^+	11·06	12·82	13·01	11·70	11·45
H_2O^-	—	0·01	—	—	1·80
Total	100·19	100·57	99·58	99·52	100·34
α	—	1·578	1·580	—	1·600
β	1·661	1·580	1·581	—	1·600
γ	—	1·586	1·589	—	1·606
2V	—	(+)12°	(+)21°	—	(+)0°–8°
D	—	2·680	2·668	2·797	2·80
ω calc.	1·647	1·585	1·582	1·595	1·596

NUMBERS OF IONS†

	11.		12.		13.		14.		15.	
Si	4·839	8·00	5·037	8·00	5·214	8·00	5·127	8·00	5·523	8·00
Al	3·161		2·963		2·786		2·873		2·477	
Al	2·824		3·098		2·590		2·837		2·819	
Ti	—		—		—		—		0·032	
Fe^{+3}	0·650		0·029		0·200		—		—	
Fe^{+2}	5·273		0·193		0·054		1·398		2·015	
Mn	—	11·90	0·085	11·98	—	12·00	—	12·01	—	12·11
Mg	3·149		8·570		9·151		7·722		7·243	
Ca	—		—		—		0·057		—	
Na	—		—		—		—		—	
K	—		—		—		—		—	
(OH)	15·89		15·89		16·00		16·00		15·27	

11. Pseudo-thuringite, Granitzer, Weiz, Styria, Austria (Hödl, 1941).
12. Greenish white spherulitic sheridanite, talc–serpentine schist, Camberousse, Savoy, France (Orcel, 1927, No. 31). Anal. J. Orcel.
13. Yellow-green sheridanite, Miles City, Montana (Shannon and Wherry, 1922). Anal. E. V. Shannon.
14. Sheridanite (grochauite), Burra Burra, Ducktown, Tennessee (McMurchy, 1934). Anal. E. V. Shannon.
15. Sheridanite, dravite–chlorite rock, Aorere, Nelson, New Zealand (Hutton and Seelye, 1945). Anal. F. T. Seelye (Includes Ni tr., V 0·06).

† Where (OH) is given as 16·00, formula has been calculated on the basis of 28 oxygen equivalents, ignoring H_2O^+; in other cases 36(O,OH) has been assumed.

Table 25. CHLORITE ANALYSES —*continued*

	16.	17.	18.	19.	20.
SiO_2	26·50	26·45	25·62	26·69	24·60
TiO_2	0·03	tr.	0·88	0·30	0·00
Al_2O_3	20·85	20·88	21·19	19·57	19·10
Fe_2O_3	1·90	2·82	3·88	3·49	3·12
FeO	18·73	21·06	21·55	21·80	29·04
MnO	0·52	0·44	0·35	0·30	—
MgO	19·85	16·84	15·28	16·23	13·10
CaO	—	0·16	0·16	0·17	tr.
Na_2O	—	0·12	0·00	tr.	—
K_2O	—	0·19	0·00	tr.	—
H_2O^+	11·65	10·98	10·87	11·19	10·60
H_2O^-	0·12	0·11	0·19	0·12	—
Total	100·15	100·05	99·97	99·99	99·56
α	1·618	1·619	1·622	—	1·637
β	1·618	—	1·622	—	—
γ	1·621	1·623	1·626	1·625	1·642
2V	$(+)0°$	small	$0°$	$(+)0°$	$(-)22°$
D	2·883	2·980	2·96	2·96	—
ω calc.	1·615	1·620	1·625	1·621	1·639

NUMBERS OF IONS[†]

	16.		17.		18.		19.		20.	
Si	5·387	}8·00	5·500	}8·00	5·364	}8·00	5·565	}8·00	5·286	}8·00
Al	2·613		2·500		2·636		2·435		2·714	
Al	2·383		2·618		2·595		2·375		2·123	
Ti	0·003		—		0·138		0·046		—	
Fe^{+3}	0·288		0·439		0·611		0·546		0·504	
Fe^{+2}	3·185		3·663		3·775		3·802		5·220	
Mn	0·089	}11·96	0·077	}12·15	0·062	}11·98	0·052	}11·89[‡]	—	}12·04
Mg	6·014		5·219		4·767		5·044		4·195	
Ca	—		0·035		0·035		—		—	
Na	—		0·047		—		—		—	
K	—		0·050		—		—		—	
(OH)	16·00		15·23		15·18		15·57		16·00	

16. Dark green ripidolite, felspathic amphibolite schist, Androta, Madagascar (Orcel, 1927).
17. Ripidolite, albite–chlorite schist, Springburn, western Otago, New Zealand (Hutton, 1940). Anal. C. O. Hutton.
18. Ripidolite, chlorite–epidote–albite schist, Limebury Point, Salcombe Estuary, South Devon (Tilley, 1938). Anal. H. C. G. Vincent.
19. Ripidolite, albite–epidote–chlorite–actinolite–calcite schist, Coronet Peak, Wakatipu region, western Otago, New Zealand (Hutton, 1938). Anal. C. O. Hutton (Includes NiO 0·13).
20. Grey-green ripidolite, Ore Knob, southern Appalachians, U.S.A. (Ross, 1935). Anal. E. V. Shannon.

† Where (OH) is given as 16·00, formula has been calculated on the basis of 28 oxygen equivalents, ignoring H_2O^+; in other cases 36(O,OH) has been assumed.

‡ Includes Ni 0·021.

Table 25. Chlorite analyses—*continued*

	21.	22.	23.	24.	25.
SiO_2	24·35	23·62	22·27	31·44	31·87
TiO_2	0·04	—	0·08	—	0·17
Al_2O_3	20·21	22·26	21·40	17·62	14·51
Fe_2O_3	2·13	—	0·67	—	1·86
FeO	36·27	38·97	43·01	tr.	3·57
MnO	0·48	0·98	0·05	tr.	tr.
MgO	5·57	1·09	2·35	37·64	32·76
CaO	0·10	0·29	0·15	tr.	—
Na_2O	n.d.	1·10	} 0·35	—	0·04
K_2O	n.d.	0·28		—	0·02
H_2O^+	10·46	11·16	10·10	13·19	13·05
H_2O^-	0·35	—	0·11	—	0·90
Total	99·96	99·75	100·54	99·89	100·13
α	1·646	—	1·658	1·572	1·581
β	1·646	—	—	1·572	1·581
γ	1·655	—	1·667	1·575	1·586
2V	(−)	—	(−)small	(+)6°–14°	(+)0°–20°
D	3·08	—	3·20	3·02	2·60
ω calc.	1·572	1·654	1·667	1·572	1·579

Numbers of ions†

	21.	22.	23.	24.	25.
Si	5·409 } 8·00	5·300 } 8·00	5·058 } 8·00	5·830 } 8·00	6·084 } 8·00
Al	2·591	2·700	2·942	2·170	1·916
Al	2·702	3·188	2·788	1·682	1·338
Ti	0·007	—	0·014	—	0·022
Fe^{+3}	0·355	—	0·115	—	0·252
Fe^{+2}	6·740	7·314	8·172	—	0·560
Mn	0·089 } 11·76	0·186 } 11·68	0·009 } 12·08	— } 12·09	— } 11·75‡
Mg	1·844	0·364	0·796	10·403	9·384
Ca	0·023	0·069	0·037	—	—
Na	—	0·080	0·152	—	—
K	—	0·478	—	—	—
(OH)	16·00	16·71	16·00	16·32	16·62

21. Dark green ripidolite (aphrosiderite), coating on quartz, Tolgus mine, Cornwall (Hallimond, 1939). Anal. C. O. Harvey.
22. Ripidolite, coating arsenopyrite and quartz, Penzance, Cornwall (Tschermak, 1891).
23. Green daphnite (bavalite), Bas Vallon, Forêt de Lorges, Quintin, Côtes-du-Nord, France (Orcel, 1927, no. 128).
24. Colourless to pale green clinochlore, metamorphosed limestone, Philipsburg, Montana (McMurchy, 1934). Anal. E. V. Shannon.
25. Silvery white to pale green chromiferous clinochlore, serpentinite, Kaukapakapa, north Auckland, New Zealand (Hutton and Seelye, 1947). Anal. F. T. Seelye (Includes NiO 0·28, Cr_2O_3 1·10).

† Where (OH) is given as 16·00, formula has been calculated on the basis of 28 oxygen equivalents, ignoring H_2O^+; in other cases 36(O,OH) has been assumed.
‡ Includes Cr 0·160, Ni 0·034.

Table 25. CHLORITE ANALYSES—*continued*

	26.	27.	28.	29.	30.
SiO_2	30·30	29·73	28·73	29·84	28·32
TiO_2	—	—	0·41	0·15	0·09
Al_2O_3	18·25	17·95	19·16	20·20	19·03
Fe_2O_3	2·64	0·68	1·97	0·80	1·19
FeO	3·98	10·05	10·99	15·00	14·85
MnO	—	8·24	0·15	0·13	0·09
MgO	32·66	21·84	26·37	21·83	23·72
CaO	tr.	0·00	0·06	0·68	0·62
Na_2O	0·03	—	0·01	0·10	0·01
K_2O	0·38	—	0·03	0·02	0·00
H_2O^+	12·26	11·90	12·17	11·19	11·95
H_2O^-	—	0·42	0·07	0·21	0·06
Total	100·50	100·81	100·12	100·18	99·93
α	—	—	—	—	1·620
β	n1·576	—	1·595	1·607	1·621
γ	—	—	—	—	1·625
2V	(+)	—	(+)10°	(−)	(+)14°
D	2·65	—	—	2·847	2·82
ω calc.	1·585	1·601	1·596	1·597	1·605

NUMBERS OF IONS†

	26.		27.		28.		29.		30.	
Si	5·727	8·00	5·951	8·00	5·630	8·00	5·972	8·00	5·654	8·00
Al	2·273		2·049		2·370		2·028		2·346	
Al	1·795		2·185		2·056		2·736		2·130	
Ti	—		0·100		0·060		0·023		0·012	
Fe^{+3}	0·375		—		0·290		0·120		0·180	
Fe^{+2}	0·629		1·683		1·802		2·511		2·480	
Mn	—	12·10	1·396	11·88	0·024	11·96	0·022	12·11	0·014	12·01
Mg	9·202		6·515		7·702		6·512		7·058	
Ca	—		—		0·011		0·145		0·132	
Na	0·008		—		0·002		0·038		—	
K	0·090		—		0·008		0·004		—	
(OH)	16·00		16·00		16·00		14·94		15·94	

26. Clinochlore, West Town, Pennsylvania (Dschang, 1931).
27. Chlorite (manganese clinochlore), veinlet in manganese ore, Kumanohata mine, Shiga Prefecture, Japan (Shirozu, 1958). Anal. H. Shirozu.
28. Clinochlore, chlorite schist, Chester, Vermont (Stone and Weiss, 1955).
29. Clinochlore, actinolite–chlorite schist, Prieska District, Cape Province (Mathias, 1952). Anal. P. L. le Roux (Includes P_2O_5 0·03).
30. Pycnochlorite, rodingite, Pastoki dyke, Hindubagh, Pakistan (Bilgrami and Howie, 1960). Anal. R. A. Howie.

† Where (OH) is given as 16·00, formula has been calculated on the basis of 28 oxygen equivalents, ignoring H_2O^+; in other cases 36(O,OH) has been assumed.

Table 25. CHLORITE ANALYSES—*continued*

	31.	32.	33.	34.	35.
SiO$_2$	27·11	25·07	33·83	33·46	36·43
TiO$_2$	0·35	0·12	—	—	tr.
Al$_2$O$_3$	17·42	19·78	12·95	10·96	12·24
Fe$_2$O$_3$	2·91	3·50	2·25	2·56	0·94
FeO	30·98	35·80	3·02	24·72	6·87
MnO	—	0·50	—	0·40	0·11
MgO	9·75	1·11	34·94	16·52	30·94
CaO	0·21	1·04	—	0·92	0·33
Na$_2$O	—	0·18	—	0·29	tr.
K$_2$O	—	0·93	—	—	0·00
H$_2$O$^+$	11·07	10·82	13·11	9·96	11·42
H$_2$O$^-$	0·51	1·13	—	—	0·13
Total	100·31	99·98	100·10	99·79	100·04
α	—	1·663	—	—	—
β	1·638	1·669	—	1·612	—
γ	—	1·669	—	—	—
2V	—	$(-)0°$	—	—	—
D	2·988	3·08	—	2·79	2·738
ω calc.	1·635	1·651	1·573	1·613	1·567

NUMBERS OF IONS[†]

	31.		32.		33.		34.		35.	
Si	5·864	}8·00	5·667	}8·00	6·413	}8·00	6·884	}8·00	7·027	}8·00
Al	2·136		2·333		1·587		1·116		0·973	
Al	2·307		2·939		1·307		1·544		1·809	
Ti	0·057		0·020		—		—		—	
Fe^{+3}	0·473		0·594		0·321		0·396		0·134	
Fe^{+2}	5·605		6·770		0·479		4·255		1·108	
Mn	—	}11·63	0·095	}11·39	—	}11·98	0·069	}11·64	0·017	}12·12‡
Mg	3·143		0·373		9·872		5·066		8·895	
Ca	0·048		0·251		—		0·202		0·067	
Na	—		0·270		—		0·112		—	
K	—		0·080		—		—		—	
(OH)	15·98		16·32		16·00		16·00		14·69	

31. Brunsvigite, spilite, Great Island, Three Kings Group, New Zealand (Battey, 1956). Anal. M. H. Battey.

32. Brunsvigite, vein in granite, Silent Valley quarry, east Mourne Mountains, Northern Ireland (Nockolds and Richey, 1939). Anal. N. Sahlbom.

33. Penninite, Zillerthal, Tyrol, Austria (Tschermak, 1891). Anal. Ludwig.

34. Diabantite, Farmington Hills, Connecticut (Hawes, 1875; Bannister and Whittard, 1945).

35. Chromian talc-chlorite, Ogushi, Hizen, Japan (Lapham, 1958). Anal. W. H. Herdsman (Includes Cr$_2$O$_3$ 0·54, NiO 0·09).

† Where (OH) is given as 16·00, formula has been calculated on the basis of 28 oxygen equivalents, ignoring H$_2$O$^+$; in other cases 36(O,OH) has been assumed.
‡ Includes Cr 0·080, Ni 0·014.

Table 25. CHLORITE ANALYSES—*continued*

	36.	37.	38.	39.
SiO_2	32·12	33·06	22·64	33·40
TiO_2	—	—	—	—
Al_2O_3	9·50	0·58	18·60	47·47
Fe_2O_3	—	9·42	4·43	0·00
FeO	1·98	—	—	0·71
MnO	—	33·83	38·93	tr.
MgO	35·36	11·55	1·48	0·20
CaO	1·24	0·07	—	0·45
Na_2O	—	—	—	} 0·09
K_2O	—	—	—	
H_2O^+	10·25	10·31	9·40	14·98
H_2O^-	2·04	0·02	—	0·23
Total	100·37	99·82	96·81	100·65
α	1·587	1·646	1·646	—
β	1·590	—	1·661	—
γ	1·590	1·664	1·661	—
2V	$(-)0°$	$(-)0°$	$(-)0°$	—
D	—	3·01	3·06	—
ω calc.	1·597	1·630	1·661	—

NUMBERS OF IONS†

	36.	37.	38.	39.
Si	6·156 } 8·00	7·676 } 7·84	5·333 } 8·00	5·898 } 8·00
Al	1·844	0·159	2·667	2·102
Al	0·303	—	2·497	7·782
Ti	—	—	—	—
Fe^{+3}	0·303	—	0·784	—
Fe^{+2}	0·318 } 12·47‡	1·645* } 12·42§	— } 11·69‖	0·105 } 10·30¶
Mn	—	6·656	7·770	—
Mg	10·100	3·997	0·520	0·053
Ca	0·255	0·017	—	0·085
Na	—	—	—	0·032
K	—	—	—	0·022
(OH)	16·00	15·97	16·00	16·00

36. Kämmererite, Deer Park, Wyoming (Shannon, 1921). Anal. E. V. Shannon (Includes Cr_2O_3 7·88).

37. Deep brown gonyerite, with barytes and bementite in hydrothermal veinlets, Långban, Sweden (Frondel, 1955). Anal. F. A. Gonyer (Includes PbO 0·56, ZnO 0·42).

38. Orange-brown pennantite, manganese ore, Benallt mine, Rhiw, Caernarvonshire (Smith, *et al.*, 1946). Anal. M. H. Hey (Includes BaO 1·33).

39. Cookeite, Kalbinsky range, Urals (Ginzburg, 1953) (Includes Li_2O 3·12).

† Where (OH) is given as 16·00, formula has been calculated on basis of 28 oxygen equivalents, ignoring H_2O^+; in other cases 36(O,OH) has been assumed.
‡ Includes Cr 1·195.
* All iron has been expressed as ferrous for the purpose of this calculation.
§ Includes Pb 0·035, Zn 0·073.
‖ Includes Ba 0·122.
¶ Includes Li 2·216.

at classification (Tschermak, 1890, 1891; Orcel, 1926; Orcel *et al.*, 1950) and with accepted nomenclature. A first subdivision is made between chlorites with more than 4 per cent. Fe_2O_3 and those with less, and these are termed oxidized and unoxidized respectively. The unoxidized chlorites are the most common and for these divisions are drawn according to Si content, where the numbers of silicon atoms per formula unit are 5, 5·6, 6·2 and 7 out of a maximum of 8. At these compositions there will thus be 3, 2·4, 1·8 and 1·0 atoms of Al in tetrahedral sites, and an equal number of Al (or $Al+Fe^{+3}$) in octahedral sites. The oxidized chlorites are divided only at silicon contents 5·6 and 6·2. Both main groups are further subdivided according to their content of total iron and the resulting "areas" of composition, with their associated names, are shown in Fig. 35 (p. 137). In this way chlorites are described by three suitable parameters: ferric iron, silicon, and total iron. Many names other than those shown in Fig. 35 have been used for chlorite specimens, *e.g.* leuchtenbergite in the clinochlore area, grochauite (a sheridanite), aphrosiderite (a ripidolite), and bavalite (a daphnite). Chlorites with the compositions of the end-members of Fig. 35, $Mg_{12}Si_8O_{20}(OH)_{16}$ and $(Mg_8Al_4)(Si_4Al_4)O_{20}(OH)_{16}$, have not been reported but these are the ideal formulae of the minerals serpentine and amesite respectively, both of which are structurally related to the kaolinite group. In fact very few specimens with the chlorite structure have compositions outside of the range Si 4·5 to 7·0. In addition to the major substitutions described above, many chlorites contain small amounts of Mn, Cr, Ni, Ti, etc. Two unusual chlorites with very high manganese content are gonyerite (*e.g.* Table 25, anal. 37) which has very little aluminium, and pennantite (anal. 38) which is extremely low in magnesium. Gonyerite has thus an almost serpentinic composition with (Mn,Fe^{+2}) replacing Mg but it nevertheless has the chlorite structure, and pennantite may be regarded as a manganese klementite. Another chlorite which is particularly rich in manganese is given in Table 25, anal. 27.

Chromium also occurs in chlorites, often in small amounts, but for some specimens as much as 8, 11 and 13·5 per cent. has been reported. From a study of chromium-bearing chlorites, Lapham (1958) concluded that chromium may substitute in either tetrahedral or octahedral sites and that in the latter case it is located in the brucite rather than the talc component. Hey (1954) suggested that no special name need be given to chromium-bearing chlorites with less than 4 per cent. Cr_2O_3 (*e.g.* Table 25, anal. 25, can be called chrome clinochlore) and that those richer in Cr_2O_3 may be called kochubeite (kotschubeite). The figure of 4 per cent. is arbitrary, and Lapham suggested a different nomenclature based upon observable crystallo-chemical characteristics which appear with Cr_2O_3 content greater than 2 per cent. Above this value those with Cr in tetrahedral sites should be called kochubeite, and those with Cr in octahedral sites should be called kämmererite. (An earlier definition distinguished kochubeite and kämmererite by their Si:Al ratio, in which respect they resembled clinochlore and penninite respectively.) If structural detail is unknown the prefix "chromium" can be used together with the nomenclature based on Si:Al and Fe:Mg ratios. Most analyses of chlorites show a small content of calcium or alkali ions, and since these do not significantly affect the calculated formulae they have been regarded in Table 25, as structural ions. It is quite likely, however, that they occur in impurities, or possibly as adsorbed surface or inter-layer cations.

The compositions of oxidized chlorites are capable of two different interpretations. In many of them a high content of Fe_2O_3 is associated with a low figure for H_2O^+, and when a formula is calculated on the basis of 28 oxygen equivalents (see Table 25, footnote †) the total of octahedral ions falls somewhat short of the ideal twelve. Many writers have suggested that these "oxidized chlorites" are truly chlorites which have been oxidized (Holzner, 1938; Winchell, 1946; etc.) effecting the reaction $Fe^{+2} \rightarrow Fe^{+3}$ with loss o hydrogen; the possibility of such a reaction has been verified experimentally (Orcel and Renaud, 1941). In these cases a better fit to the ideal chlorite formula is obtained if Fe_2O_3 is first expressed as its equivalent of FeO. Some chlorites, however, which have a high content of Fe_2O_3, nevertheless have normal water content and give a normal chlorite formula when ferric iron is treated as such. Thus when ferric iron is primary, its occurrence in the structure is compensated by the replacement of Al for Si, but when it is the product of oxidation the associated substitution is $(O)^{-2}$ for $(OH)^-$. A rather different approach to chlorite classification is made by Serdyuchenko (1953), particularly in relation to the treatment of total iron and ferric iron content. In deriving formulae from over two hundred analyses, Fe_2O_3 is not re-calculated to its FeO equivalent, and total iron content is disregarded for the purpose of classification. The resulting chemical formulae show that many chlorites have approximately the ideal number of octahedral ions (twelve) and so are members of the serpentine $Mg_{12}Si_8O_{20}(OH)_{16}$ – amesite$(Mg_8Al_4)(Si_4Al_4)O_{20}(OH)_{12}$ series. Many others, however, have Y less than twelve, and the number of Y ions is used by Serdyuchenko to divide chlorites into types α, β, γ and δ. Further division of the compositional field according to Si content, drawn where $Si = 4 \cdot 6$, $5 \cdot 2$, $5 \cdot 8$, $6 \cdot 4$, $7 \cdot 2$ and $8 \cdot 0$, serves for a chlorite nomenclature which is essentially similar to that adopted by Hey (1954). Although many of the analyses presented by Serdyuchenko could be made to yield formulae nearer the ideal by expressing Fe_2O_3 as its FeO equivalent, some of them do not have the low H_2O^+ expected for an internally oxidized chlorite, and moreover some have low Y values despite having little or no ferric iron. Providing that the materials analysed did not contain non-chlorite minerals there thus appears to be ample evidence for the existence of partially di-octahedral chlorites. These may be regarded as chlorites in which the constituent talc and brucite components are partially replaced by their well known di-octahedral analogues pyrophyllite and gibbsite respectively, and in which there is considerable replacement of Al by Fe^{+3}. Among the analyses in Table 25, the lithium-bearing cookeite (anal. 39) illustrates a tendency in this direction (see also Quensel, 1937, and Serdyuchenko, 1953, Table 101). It is perhaps significant that many examples of the rare intermediates between di- and tri-octahedral micas (and montmorillonites) also contain appreciable lithium.

A selection of analyses of chlorites is presented in Table 25 and their compositions are plotted in Fig. 35. Determination of the approximate composition of a chlorite can sometimes be achieved by X-ray methods (Brown, 1955; Brindley and Gillery, 1956). Weight loss curves of clinochlores show inflections at 600° and 850°C. (total loss 12·5 per cent.) and the d.t.a. curves have endothermic peaks at roughly corresponding temperatures. It is assumed that these two stages correspond to dehydration of first the "brucite" and then the "talc" layers of the chlorite structure (Brindley and Ali, 1950; Caillère and

Hénin, 1957). Thermal data are, however, considerably influenced by the state of subdivision of the specimen (Sabatier, 1950), and by the precise chemical composition, particularly the iron content. Thus fine-grained chlorites often show a low temperature endothermic peak related to expulsion of adsorbed water, ripidolites and certain other chlorites show one instead of two major endothermic peaks, and for some specimens each of the main endothermic peaks is a doublet. That positions of peaks are also affected by composition is demonstrated by curves from clinochlore and sheridanite, which have endothermic peaks at 800° and 710°C. respectively. The temperature of decomposition of chromium chlorites decreases with increasing chromium content (Lapham, 1958). The exothermic peaks at about 900°C. are similarly variable with composition as are the products of decomposition to which these relate. The most common among the decomposition products are olivine and spinel (Orcel and Caillère, 1938; Brindley and Ali, 1950).

Using natural minerals, mixtures of oxides, glasses, or co-precipitated gels, detailed studies of stability in the system $MgO-Al_2O_3-SiO_2-H_2O$ have been made (Yoder, 1952; Roy and Roy, 1955; Nelson and Roy, 1958). With

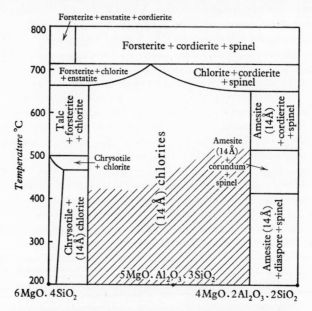

FIG. 36(a). Preferred version of a composition–temperature diagram drawn for a pressure of 1000 atmospheres, for the join chrysotile–amesite extended. The lower part of the diagram is a true binary join, above this, however, the equilibrium is quarternary and the diagram shows only the stable solid phases at various compositions as a function of temperature. The preferred version shows as a shaded area the *PT* range in which septechlorites form and persist metastably for long periods. Note also the 2-phase region chrysotile + chlorite showing a discontinuity in solid solubility along the chlorite join (after Nelson and Roy, 1958).

decreasing temperature, the first hydrated mineral, talc, is formed at 780°C., and below 710°C. at 20,000 lb./in.[2] the first quaternary compound to be synthesized is the chlorite clinochlore, $(Mg_{10}Al_2)(Si_6Al_2)O_{20}(OH)_{16}$. The range of compositions yielding solid solutions in the chlorite structure is from penninite $(Mg_{11}Al)(Si_7Al)O_{20}(OH)_{16}$ to amesite $(Mg_8Al_4)(Si_4Al_4)O_{20}(OH)_{16}$. If more Al is present a three phase assembly is produced containing a chlorite of the amesite composition; if less Al is present than in the penninite composition, a three phase assemblage including penninite is produced. In the same compositional range (and beyond it in one direction to the serpentine composition $Mg_{12}Si_8O_{20}(OH)_{16}$) a second isomorphous series can be synthesized the members of which have a "tri-octahedral kaolinite" structure. These have a 7 Å instead of a 14 Å inter-layer spacing and are called septechlorites (see p. 164): the precise stability relationships between the two polymorphic forms have not been established. Higher pressures and temperatures yield the normal chlorite (14 Å), the lowest temperature for chlorite synthesis being 450°C. for clinochlore. It may be that the septechlorites exist only metastably, as indicated in the pressure–temperature diagram of Fig. 36(a). In Fig. 36(b), however, it is assumed that septe-chlorites undergo a polymorphic transformation to normal chlorites at about

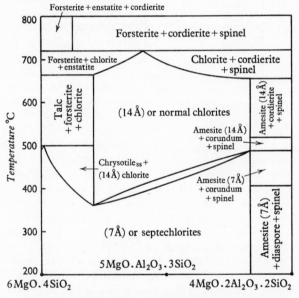

Fig. 36(b). Possible alternative to Fig. 36(a) with septechlor-ites now shown as stable low temperature polymorphic forms of chlorites (after Nelson and Roy, 1958).

400°–500°C. The upper limit of stability of clinochlore is surprisingly high, as can be seen from the pressure–temperature curve of the transformation clino-chlore→forsterite + cordierite + spinel + vapour (Fig. 37). Non-equilibrium decomposition of clinochlore yields forsterite, spinel, and possibly enstatite (Brindley and Ali, 1950).

Maximum charge occurs on the "brucite" component of the normal chlorite structure when Al–Si substitution is compensated entirely by Al substitution for

Mg in the "brucite", rather than in the "talc", sheet. By analogy with the micas, the stability of the normal chlorite structure may require a minimum charge, the brucite sheet equivalent to say $\frac{1}{2}K^+$ (per formula unit) between the layers in mica. This may explain why a chlorite with less Al than penninite (brucite layer charge $= \frac{1}{2}^+$) does not exist (Nelson and Roy, 1958).

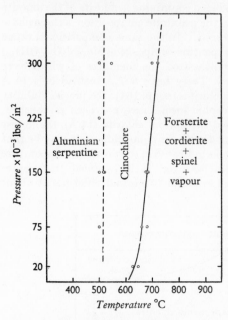

The iron-rich analogue of amesite is the mineral chamosite, and this can also exist in either the septe-chlorite[1] or normal chlorite form. Since the type locality material from Chamoson has the normal chlorite structure the name has been retained for a subdivision of the oxidized chlorites (Fig. 35); Nelson and Roy suggest that 7 Å chamosites be called septechamosites. Further difficulty arises in the case of a specimen with the composition of a magnesian chamosite (*e.g.* anal. 6) since this could be interpreted either as a normal chlorite or as a mixture of a 14 Å ferrous chamosite with serpentine (Bannister and Whittard, 1945). In poorly crystalline material recognition of serpentine in the presence of chlorite may prove difficult by any method.

Fig. 37. Pressure–temperature curve of the transformation aluminian serpentine→ clinochlore and of the reaction clinochlore ⇌ forsterite + cordierite + spinel + vapour (after Yoder, 1952).

Turnock and Eugster (1958) have studied equilibrium conditions for the composition of the chlorite, daphnite $Fe_{10}Al_2Si_6Al_2O_{20}(OH)_{16}$, using a controlled oxygen partial pressure. A 7 Å daphnite was synthesized at temperatures as low as 400°C., and even with pressures as high as 5000 bars it was not possible to convert this wholly to the 14 Å polymorph.

Chlorite-like substances have been produced from montmorillonite (Orcel *et al.*, 1950) by the action of solutions of $Mg(OH)_2$ and $Fe(OH)_2$: these have a basal spacing of approximately 14 Å and sometimes (like true chlorites) are stable when heated to 550°C., but (like montmorillonites) they show swelling characteristics with glycerol. These substances, which may be called swelling chlorites, have also been synthesized from sodium silicate and iron and magnesium salts (Caillère *et al.*, 1953), and have been found to occur naturally (*e.g.* Honeyborne, 1951).

Chlorites are readily attacked by acids, which extract magnesium and iron, sometimes leaving behind a skeletal plate of silica. In the case of a magnesian chlorite, extraction of alumina by acid proceeds in two stages, suggesting that aluminium ions in tetrahedral coordination are less readily removed than those in octahedral sites (Brindley and Youell, 1951).

---

[1] The name "berthierine" has sometimes been used for this form of chamosite.

OPTICAL AND PHYSICAL PROPERTIES

The two variables, Si and total Fe, chosen to represent the chemical compositions of unoxidized chlorites are also the principal factors influencing optical properties. Refractive indices increase with increasing iron and with decreasing silicon content. Chlorites are monoclinic or triclinic and are therefore biaxial, but often refractive indices for the two vibration directions in the (001) plane are so close that 2V is too small to discern. In Fig. 38 the chlorites are regarded as uniaxial and it is seen that birefringence ($\epsilon - \omega$) decreases from positive through zero to negative values as iron or silicon increase. Division of the main types of chlorite according to optic sign puts penninite, clinochlore, ripidolite,

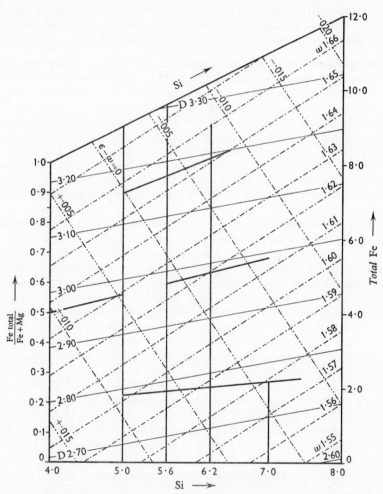

FIG. 38. Refractive index (ω) (see above), birefringence (ϵ–ω), and specific gravity (D) of ortho-chlorites in relation to composition. For oxidized chlorites ω and D are higher and (ϵ–ω) is lower in proportion to percentage of the Fe_2O_3. The boundaries of the ortho-chlorite species and varieties are shown (*cf.* Fig. 35) (after Hey, 1954).

sheridanite, corundophilite and klementite as positive, and diabantite, brunsvigite, thuringite, chamosite and delessite as negative. Chromium chlorites are generally optically positive, but those with more than about 6 per cent. Cr_2O_3 are negative. In addition to ω and $(\epsilon-\omega)$, Fig. 38 shows how density increases with iron and decreases with silicon content. Using data from nearly a hundred analysed specimens, Hey (1954) derived a number of linear regression equations relating various physical properties to composition, and used the relevant parts of these in Fig. 38. The latter figure does not take account of the influence of ferric iron, manganese and chromium, each of which increases refringence and decreases birefringence. The full equations are given below:

1. $\omega = 1{\cdot}5954 - 0{\cdot}01315(Si-4) + 0{\cdot}0104Fe^t + 0{\cdot}00175Fe^{+3} + 0{\cdot}0095Mn + 0{\cdot}015Cr$.
2. $\epsilon - \omega = 0{\cdot}0170 - 0{\cdot}0048(Si-4) - 0{\cdot}001675Fe^t - 0{\cdot}0024Fe^{+3} - 0{\cdot}003Mn$.
3. $D = 2{\cdot}694 - 0{\cdot}0305(Si-4) + 0{\cdot}068Fe^t + 0{\cdot}005Fe^{+3} + 0{\cdot}055Mn$.

In these equations Fe^t is the total number of iron atoms, and all numbers of atoms refer to the formula unit given on p. 131. Mean standard deviations of the observed values for the specimens examined are given as 0·0100, 0·003 and 0·016 for equations 1, 2 and 3 respectively. The density relationships were calculated from cell parameter measurements for which regression equations have been given on p. 135. The equations show that in their effects upon refractive index, manganese and chromium are like ferrous and ferric iron respectively. The value of ω calculated from the above equation is given at the foot of each column in Table 25 and, with a few exceptions where ω (calc.) is low, agreement with observed values is good. Pleochroism is generally exhibited more strongly by chlorites with higher iron content, the pleochroic scheme being either $\alpha < \beta = \gamma$ or $\alpha = \beta > \gamma$. For the direction of least absorption chlorites are almost colourless, pale yellow, or green, and the higher absorption colours are usually dark green or olive-green. Chromium chlorites are strongly pleochroic and often pink or violet; pennantite is orange-red. Pleochroic haloes similar to those found in micas sometimes occur in chlorite plates, and in some cases at least are associated with inclusions of zircon at their centres (Corin, 1942): the optic sign may change from positive to negative in passing into the area within the halo. Some chlorites, in particular those which are more iron-rich, show anomalous interference colours (Hödl, 1941); those iron-chlorites which have one-layered ortho-hexagonal cells, however, show normal interference colours (Shirozu, 1958).

The hardness of well formed chlorite crystals is similar to that of the common micas, and the more rarely measured hardness in the direction perpendicular to (001) is about 4 as compared with 2 to 3 parallel to (001). Cleavage flakes from large crystals generally have a pearly lustre and are brittle, but many chlorites (usually "oxidized chlorites") occurring in clay particle sizes are relatively soft.

DISTINGUISHING FEATURES

Chlorites are usually green and pleochroic and some show anomalous interference colours. Birefringence is much lower than that of the micas, illites, montmorillonites and vermiculite, and refractive indices are higher than those of kaolinite. Some serpentines have a similar flaky morphology but have lower refractive indices than chlorites and show little or no pleochroism. Those "chamosite" specimens which do not have the structure of a chlorite may yet have similar optical properties, and distinction is best made by X-ray powder patterns of heated and unheated samples.

PARAGENESIS

Chlorite is widely distributed in low grade metamorphic rocks, and is the most characteristic mineral of the greenschist facies. Chlorites are common constituents of igneous rock in which they have generally been derived by the hydrothermal alteration of primary ferromagnesian minerals. Chlorite is also a common product of weathering and occurs in many argillaceous rocks as well as in some iron-rich sediments.

Metamorphic rocks. The status of chlorite in regionally metamorphosed basic igneous rocks was investigated by Carstens (1924) who first showed that the chlorite in such rocks have a high content of aluminium. The chlorite–albite schists of the Sulitjelma region, southern Norway, were shown by Vogt (1927) to have formed as the end-product of the retrograde metamorphism of a series of basic igneous rocks. Here the earlier formed chlorite was due to the instability of aluminium-rich hornblende and its transformation, without a change in the bulk composition of the rock, to chlorite, clinozoisite, actinolite and quartz; the later formation of the chlorite–albite schists involved a loss in Ca and Si. The development of hornblende–epidote–albite and chlorite–epidote–albite assemblages from basic igneous rocks has been described by Tilley (1938) from the Start area, south Devon. Here there is clear evidence that the chlorite, an Al-rich ripidolte (Table 25, anal. 18), formed largely at the expense of actinolite, and that epidote was the most likely source of the aluminium in the chlorite, the formation of which was due to a reaction of the type:

$$\text{actinolitic hornblende} + \text{epidote} \rightarrow \text{chlorite} + SiO_2 + CaO$$

Thus Tilley considered that the chlorite-rich assemblage involved a change in the bulk composition of the rock, the most notable change being a loss of Ca.

Wiseman's (1934) study of the progressive metamorphism of the epidiorites of the southwest Highlands also showed that the chlorite of the low grade chlorite–albite schists of this area is rich in aluminium (the calculated composition of the chlorite is SiO_2 28·2, Al_2O_3 24·9, Fe_2O_3 0·2, FeO 26·8, MgO 10·9, H_2O 9·0). Chlorite is present in all the low grade epidiorites of the southwest Highlands, and in rocks also containing hornblende, the chlorite β refractive index ranges from 1·605 to 1·635, and varies sympathetically with the β index of the coexisting hornblende (Fig. 39). Chlorites with higher indices are found unaccompanied by hornblende, and in rocks containing little or no epidote, *e.g.* β 1·650 for chlorite in a calcite–chlorite–biotite schist, β 1·653 for chlorite in a calcite–chlorite–albite schist.

In the greenstones of northern Michigan derived from basic intrusions, 95 per cent. of the original igneous assemblage has been converted during the chlorite zone metamorphism, to chlorite, pale green hornblende, clinozoisite–epidote, and albite (James, 1955). In these rocks chlorite is the most widespread secondary mineral and occurs within original pyroxene and felspar as well as in

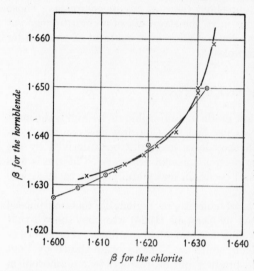

FIG. 39.   Relation between the refractive index of the primary chlorite and coexisting hornblende: × in low grade epidiorites (Wiseman, 1934), ⊙ greenschists of the Start area, Devon (Tilley, 1938).

the groundmass alteration.   Similar greenschists have been described from western Otago by Hutton (1940), and have been derived by the low grade regional metamorphism not only of basic igneous rocks but also of tuffs containing argillaceous and arenaceous impurities.   Chlorite is extensively developed in the regionally metamorphosed basic rocks of the Gosaisyo–Takanuki (Miyashiro, 1958) and the Nakoso and Iritōno (Shidô, 1958) districts of the central Abukuma Plateau, Japan.   In the lowest grade the common assemblage is actinolite–epidote–chlorite–albite but in some rocks local concentration of H_2O and/or CO_2 pressure has promoted the breakdown of actinolite to chlorite and calcite with the development of calcite–chlorite–epidote–albite rocks.   At higher grades of metamorphism chlorite decreases in amount and, together with epidote and/or actinolite, is involved in the formation of an aluminium-rich amphibole and plagioclase:

$$3(OH)_8Mg_5Al_2Si_3O_{10} + 6(OH)Ca_2Al_3Si_3O_{12} + 7SiO_2$$
$$\text{chlorite} \qquad\qquad \text{epidote}$$
$$\rightarrow 5(OH)_2Ca_2Mg_3Al_4Si_6O_{22} + 2CaAl_2Si_2O_8 + 10H_2O$$
$$\text{tschermakite} \qquad\qquad \text{anorthite}$$

$$14(OH)_8Mg_5Al_2Si_3O_{10} + 24(OH)Ca_2Al_3Si_3O_{12} + (OH)_2Ca_2(Mg,Fe)_5Si_8O_{22}$$
$$\text{chlorite} \qquad\qquad \text{epidote} \qquad\qquad \text{actinolite}$$
$$+ 28SiO_2 \rightarrow 25(OH)_2Ca_2(Mg,Fe)_3Al_4Si_6O_{22} + 44H_2O$$
$$\text{iron-bearing tschermakite}$$

The optical properties of the chlorites in the low grade schists of the Gosaisyo–Takanuki district, Japan, are similar to those of the epidiorites of the southwest Highlands of Scotland.   Miyashiro (1957) has also shown that the refractive indices of both minerals are related to the $Fe^{+2} : (Mg + Fe^{+2})$ ratio of the host rock.

The formation of chlorite during the regional metamorphism of ultrabasic rocks is not common, but has been described from a number of localities (Hess, 1933; Hödl, 1941; Avias, 1956).   Albite–chlorite schists, calcite–albite–chlorite schists, and epidote–albite–chlorite schists are typical products of the Dalradian green beds, the bulk composition of which is directly derived from the waste of basic igneous rocks (Phillips, 1930).

In pelitic sediments chlorite is generally stable until the onset of the *PT* conditions of the biotite zone.   The transformation of chlorite to biotite, however, is possible only by reaction with a potassium-rich mineral.   The formation of biotite from chlorite and muscovite cannot be a simple reaction, and the production of an aluminium-rich chlorite, in addition to biotite, has been postulated by Ramberg (1952):

$$6(OH)_2KAl_3Si_3O_{10} + 5(OH)_8(Mg,Fe)_6Si_4O_{10} \rightleftharpoons$$
muscovite   talc-chlorite

$$6(OH)_2K(Mg,Fe)_3AlSi_3O_{10} + 3(OH)_8(Mg,Fe)_4Al_4Si_2O_{10} + 14SiO_2 + 8H_2O$$
biotite   corundophilite

In some low grade metamorphic schists chlorite is associated with a manganese-rich garnet (Goldschmidt, 1921; Tilley, 1923). From the pelitic schist of the chlorite zone at Oyahana, Japan, Miyashiro (1957) has described a quartz–albite–chlorite–sericite–garnet ($Mn:Fe^{+2}:Mg = 62·8:37·2:0·0$) assemblage, and has shown that the garnet has considerably higher $Fe^{+2}:Mg$ and $Mn:(Mg+Fe^{+2})$ ratios than the associated chlorite. Seitsaari (1954) has also presented compositional data for an Mn-rich garnet and chlorite in a garnet–bytownite schist from Kangasala, Finland. The latter rocks are of higher grade than those of the Japanese locality, and although the $Fe^{+2}:Mg$ and $Mn:(Mg+Fe^{+2})$ ratios are higher in the garnet than in the chlorite, the Kangasala garnet, in conformity with its higher grade paragenesis, is less manganese-rich than the Oyahana mineral.

Fractionation ratios of some elements including Mg, Fe^{+2}, Mn, Ti and Cr between coexisting chlorite and garnet, as well as chlorite and biotite, and chlorite and hornblende in metamorphic rocks, are given by DeVore (1955a, b).

Hutton and Turner (1936) and Hutton (1940) recognized four subzones of the chlorite zone, based on the degree of reconstitution of rocks of greywacke composition in the regionally metamorphosed area of western Otago. The original sediments contain abundant relics of green and brown hornblende, calcic plagioclase, quartz and some augite. With the onset of regional metamorphism the hornblende is converted to actinolite and chlorite, or to chlorite both with and without calcite. Two chlorite analyses (Table 25, anals. 17, 19) confirm that the chlorites, one from an albite–chlorite schist and the other from a calcite–albite–epidote–chlorite–actinolite schist have a high aluminium content, and Hutton considered that the original plagioclase takes part in the formation of the chlorite and actinolite:

hornblende + anorthite → chlorite + actinolite.
hornblende + anorthite → chlorite + SiO_2 + CaO.

With increasing metamorphism the chlorite increases in grain size and in some rocks of this area it is associated with stilpnomelane which in the highest grade (chlorite subzone 4) is partially derived from chlorite.

In the Pre-Cambrian greywackes of northern Michigan (James, 1955) the clastic grains of felspars are irregularly embayed by chlorite, sericite and carbonate, and James has suggested that the alteration and reconstruction of the sediment may have started, and may even have been completed, during diagenesis and lithification. The presence of a thuringitic chlorite in the silicate iron formation of northern Michigan has also been reported by James. In these rocks the chlorite is not considered to be a primary clastic constituent, but a low grade metamorphic product of the iron-rich clay fraction of the original sediment. Thuringite is also present in some rocks of the garnet and staurolite zones but here it is retrograde in origin.

Chlorite–albite–glaucophane–epidote schists showing all gradations to chlorite–albite–actinolite–epidote schists have been described by Banno (1958) from the Omi district, Japan. The mineral associations in the epidote-glaucophane subfacies have been discussed by Miyashiro and Seki (1958), who suggest that the assemblages of this subfacies may be derived from those of the greenschist facies by reactions of the type:

$$(OH)_4Mg_3Si_2O_5 + 2NaAlSi_3O_8 \rightarrow (OH)_2Na_2Mg_3Al_2Si_8O_{22} + H_2O$$

antigorite mol.   albite   glaucophane
of chlorite

$$9(OH)_8Mg_5Al_2Si_3O_{10} + 6(OH)_2Ca_2Mg_5Si_8O_{22} + 50NaAlSi_3O_8$$

chlorite   actinolite   albite

$$\rightarrow 25(OH)_2Na_2Mg_3Al_2Si_8O_{22} + 6(OH)Ca_2Al_3Si_3O_{12} + 7SiO_2 + 14H_2O$$

glaucophane   epidote

Miyashiro and Seki (1958) and Seki (1958) have also described chlorite associated with stilpnomelane and lawsonite, and with lawsonite, pumpellyite and glaucophane, from the regional metamorphic terrain of the Kanto Mountains, Japan.

Igneous rocks. Chlorite is a common product of the hydrothermal alteration of pyroxenes, amphiboles and biotite in igneous rocks. The composition of the chlorite is often related to that of the original igneous mineral, and the more iron-rich chlorites, thuringite, delessite and daphnite, are commonly found as replacements of the iron-rich ferromagnesian minerals. Partial and complete chloritization of biotite is particularly common in granites and in most cases the transformation is markedly pseudomorphous. The question as to whether some of the chlorite in granite is of primary crystallization has been considered by Chayes (1955), who has shown that in many cases the transformation of biotite to chlorite is accompanied by the development of minute granules of potassium felspar, some of which remain enclosed within the chlorite. There is no direct evidence that quartz is involved in the transformation reaction but, unless a magnesium-free biotite composition is assumed, silica must be added, and Chayes suggests that this is derived from the quartz already present. Thus it is evident that below some particular PT curve the reaction (see p. 79) will be biotite + quartz→chlorite + orthoclase, and the stable assemblages will be chlorite + orthoclase + quartz and chlorite + orthoclase + biotite. Above this curve the reaction direction changes and the stable assemblages are biotite + quartz + orthoclase and biotite + quartz + chlorite.

Chlorite is commonly found filling amygdales in lavas, and together with epidote, alkali felspar, quartz, sericite, zeolites, carbonates and pyrite, it is an important product of the intense hydrothermal alteration (propylitization) of andesites and to a lesser extent of basalts. Chlorite also occurs as dense slickensided lamellar coatings along joint planes and fissures particularly in basalts. Chlorite (Table 25, anal. 31) is an abundant constituent of the spilites of northern New Zealand, and here occurs in angular interstitial areas, in small rounded pools, in fine veinlets, and in amygdales. The chlorite is associated with unaltered albite and pyroxene ($Ca_{41}Mg_{38}Fe_{21}$ to $Ca_{36}Mg_{35}Fe_{29}$) and is considered by Battey (1956) to have crystallized as a primary mineral from a residual liquid rich in iron. Green and brown coloured chlorite, together with sphene and calcite, is common as pseudomorphs after ferromagnesian minerals in the spilites of the Builth Volcanic Series (Nicholls, 1958). In the less strongly metasomatized spilites of the area some amygdales are completely filled with chlorite while others are lined by chlorite which surrounds cores of calcite. In these lavas the crystallization of the brown chlorite preceded that of the green variety indicating that the composition of the later formed chlorite changed in the direction of either a lower $Fe^{+2}:Mg$ or lower $Fe^{+3}:Fe^{+2}$ ratio. In the more strongly metasomatized spilites the chlorite pseudomorphs of the original ferromagnesian phenocrysts are replaced by albite with or without quartz, and the brown coloured chlorite in the groundmass by albite or quartz; the pale green chlorite in the groundmass does not appear to have suffered replacement. The amygdaloidal chlorite is also replaced by quartz.

The association of chlorite with albite and quartz is an essential characteristic of adinoles. Chlorite–quartz pseudomorphs after andalusite in the adinoles developed in Devonian slates metasomatized by albite dolerite at Dinas Head, Cornwall, have been described by Agrell (1939). The corundophilite (Table 25, anal. 10) in the chlorite-bearing schists of the emery deposits of Chester County, Massachusetts (Shannon and Wherry, 1922) is also of metasomatic origin and at this locality is associated with margarite and white mica.

The formation of chlorite by the alteration of rhyolite porphyry wall rock along a vertical fissure has been described by Vitaliano (1957). Here the earlier deuteric chloritization of primary hornblende and biotite has been followed by later and more extensive hydrothermal action: the hydrothermally formed chlorite differs from the deuteric chlorite in being finer-grained and colourless. The chlorite is the last mineral of the hydrothermal alteration sequence, and in the most advanced stage of the alteration almost completely replaced the earlier formed talc and pyrophyllite and gave rise to a chlorite–talc assemblage. Chlorite also occurs in fissure veins in some massive igneous rocks, and an example of an iron-rich daphnite has been described by Nockolds and Richey (1939). Many low temperature hydrothermal veins of alpine type in low grade metamorphosed sediments carry chlorite in addition to adularia and quartz.

Manganese-rich chlorites are generally associated with manganese deposits. The pennantite (Table 25, anal. 38) in the manganese ores of the Benallt mine, Caernarvonshire (Smith *et al.*, 1946) is present in the ore matrix, and patches of the mineral frequently enclose minute garnets which are probably of spessartine composition. The pennantite also occurs in the walls of thin veins which traverse the ore, and here the chlorite is associated with paragonite, analcite, banalsite and ganophyllite. Another manganese-rich chlorite, gonyerite (Table 25, anal. 37) occurs as radial aggregates with barytes and bementite in hydrothermal veinlets at Långban (Frondel, 1955). A chromium-rich chlorite (Cr_2O_3 3·7 per cent., formula $Mg_{4·90}Al_{0·52}Fe^{+2}_{0·14}Cr_{0·21}Fe^{+3}_{0·03}Ti_{0·06}Na_{0·03}Si_{2·71}Al_{1·29}O_{9·85}OH_{8·15}$) associated with chromite has been described by Dunham *et al.* (1958) in some ultrabasic rocks of eastern Sierra Leone.

Recently Coombs *et al.* (1959) have established the identity of a facies bridging the *PT* environment of diagenesis and the lower limit of the greenschist facies. In this zeolitic facies chlorite and white mica develop from the celadonite and clay minerals of the sediments. The formation of chlorite by the replacement of celadonite (see p. 37) in an andesite–dacite volcanic agglomerate and rhyolitic welded tuff has been reported by Ross (1958). Some of the cavities between the volcanic fragments in the agglomerate are occupied by celadonite, some of which is surrounded by a narrow rim of saponite; many of the cavities originally filled by celadonite are now, however, occupied by chlorite. The latter mineral also occurs in the pore spaces of the originally glassy pumice, and also as a replacement material in some of the fine-grained fragments of andesite. Other alteration products in these rocks associated with the chlorite are epidote, laumontite and quartz.

Sedimentary rocks. Chlorite group minerals are common constituents of argillaceous sediments, in which they occur both as detrital and as authigenic crystals. Due to their usual fine-grained nature their characterization is often difficult, and in many sediments the chlorite is present in mixed-layer structures, *e.g.* in regular interstratification with vermiculite. The chlorites are derived by the aggradation of less organized sheet minerals such as celadonite, by the degradation of pre-existing ferromagnesian minerals, and by crystallization from dilute solutions of their components.

Chamosite is an important constituent of some sedimentary iron formations, *e.g.* the chamosite–kaolinite and the oolitic ironstone groups of the Northampton ironstone field (Wilson, 1952). The chamosite occurs as ooliths and as fine-grained flaky and fibrous forms in the groundmass of the ironstone. Better crystalline material occurs less commonly in the nuclei of ooliths and in rolled fragments dispersed through the groundmass. The cores of the ooliths are frequently occupied by relatively large flakes, up to 0·3 mm. in diameter, and often show cleavage. The cores are surrounded by concentric and sometimes discontinuous layers which consist of very minute fibrous crystals. Chamosite ooliths may show a considerable range in colour; this variation is not confined to the concentric layers but is also shown by the relatively large central flakes, and it is clear that these chamosite crystals have a variable chemical composition. It is, however, not known whether the variation represents a continuous range from an iron-rich chamosite to an iron-free kaolinite. Specimens with chamosite composition can occur with either chlorite- or kaolinite-type structure (septe-chlorites, see p. 164), and in some reports of chamosite occurrence the structure type is not recorded. The chamosites in the Northampton Sand ironstones are of the septechlorite type and show a continuous variation between ordered and disordered structures; this variation can be correlated with the iron content of the chamosite and also with the type of environment represented by the iron-stone in which it occurs. Thus the chamosite of the main oolitic ironstone is relatively rich in iron and shows a relatively well-ordered structure while the chamosite in the chamosite–kaolinite ironstone groups has a lower iron content and a highly disordered structure (Youell, 1958). A full description and dis-cussion of the petrography and chemistry of the chamosite in the Northampton Sand ironstone formation has been given by Taylor (1949) who concluded that in these rocks the chamosite formed as a primary chemical precipitate, and not as a replacement mineral. The chamosite ooliths are sometimes replaced by calcite, and Taylor has suggested that some of the rocks containing chamosite ooliths in a chamosite–siderite groundmass are partially sideritized oolitic chamosite mudstones (see also Cohen, 1952). Chamosite is readily converted by oxidation to yellow, yellow-brown and red-brown alteration products con-sisting essentially of kaolinite and goethite. A magnesian chamosite (chlorite-type; Table 25, anal. 6) from a chamositic siltstone in the Wenlock Limestone at Wickwar, Gloucestershire, has been described by Bannister and Whittard (1945). The high magnesium content of this chamosite is probably related to the action of the saline solutions which were responsible for the dolomitization of the associated limestones.

REFERENCES

Agrell, S. O., 1939. The adinoles of Dinas Head, Cornwall. *Min. Mag.,* vol. 25, p. 305.

Avias, J., 1956. Des phénomènes de chloritisation, de serpentinisation et de feldspathisation en Nouvelle Calédonie. *Compt. Rend. Soc. Géol. France,* vol. 6, p. 307.

Bannister, F. A. and **Whittard, W. F.,** 1945. A magnesian chamosite from the Wenlock Limestone of Wickwar, Gloucestershire. *Min. Mag.,* vol. 27, p. 99.

Banno, S., 1958. Glaucophane schists and associated rocks in the Omi District, Japan. *Jap. Journ. Geol. Geogr.,* vol. 29, p. 29.

Battey, M. H., 1956. The petrogenesis of a spilitic rock series from New Zealand. *Geol. Mag.,* vol. 93, p. 89.

Bilgrami, S. A. and **Howie, R. A.,** 1960. The mineralogy and petrology of a rodingite dike, Hindubagh, Pakistan. *Amer. Min.,* vol. 45, p. 791.

Bradley, W. F. and **Weaver, C. E.,** 1956. A regularly interstratified chlorite-vermiculite clay mineral. *Amer. Min.,* vol. 41, p. 497.

Brindley, G. W., 1951. The crystal structure of some chamosite minerals. *Min. Mag.,* vol. 29, p. 502.

—— and **Ali, S. Z.,** 1950. X-ray study of thermal transformations in some magnesian chlorite minerals. *Acta Cryst.,* vol. 3, p. 25.

—— and **Gillery, F. H.,** 1956. X-ray identification of chlorite species. *Amer. Min.,* vol. 41, p. 169.

—— **Oughton, B. M.** and **Robinson, K.,** 1950. Polymorphism of the chlorites. I. Ordered structures. *Acta Cryst.,* vol. 3, p. 408.

—— and **Robinson, K.,** 1951. The chlorite minerals, in *X-ray identification and crystal structure of the clay minerals.* Min. Soc., London.

—— and **Youell, R. F.,** 1951. A chemical determination of tetrahedral and octahedral aluminium ions in a silicate. *Acta Cryst.,* vol. 4, p. 495.

—— —— 1953. Ferrous chamosite and ferric chamosite. *Min. Mag.,* vol. 30, p. 57.

Brown, G., 1955. The effect of isomorphous substitutions on the intensities of (001) reflections of mica- and chlorite-type structures. *Min. Mag.,* vol. 30, p. 657.

Caillère, S. and **Hénin, S.,** 1957. The chlorite and serpentine minerals, in *The differential thermal investigation of clays.* Min. Soc., London.

—— —— and **Esquevin, J.,** 1953. Synthèse à basse temperature de phyllites ferrifères. *Compt. Rend. Acad. Sci. Paris,* vol. 237, p. 1724.

Carstens, C. W., 1924. Der Unterdoricische Vulkanhorizont in dem Trondhjemgebiet, mit besonderer Berüchsichtigung der in ihm auftretenden Kiesvorkommen. *Norsk. Geol. Tidsskr.,* vol. 7, p. 185.

Chayes, F., 1955. Potash feldspar as a by-product of the biotite-chlorite transformation. *Journ. Geol.,* vol. 63, p. 75.

Cohen, E., 1952. The nature of silicates and carbonates of iron in the Northampton Sand Ironstone of central England. *XIX Inter. Geol. Congress, Algiers; Symposium sur les gisements de fer du monde,* vol. 2, p. 466.

Coombs, D. S., Ellis, A. J., Fyfe, W. S. and **Taylor, A. M.,** 1959. The zeolite facies, with comments on the interpretation of hydrothermal syntheses. *Geochim. Cosmochim. Acta,* vol. 17, p. 53.

Corin, F., 1942. Observations nouvelles sur les inclusions à halos pleochroiques. *Bull. Soc. Belge Géol.,* vol. 50, p. 48.

DeVore, G. W., 1955a. The role of adsorption in the fractionation and distribution of elements. *Journ. Geol.,* vol. 63, p. 159.

DeVore, G. W., 1955b. Crystal growth and the distribution of elements. *Journ. Geol.*, vol. 63, p. 471.

Dschang, G. L., 1931. Die Beziehungen zwischen chemischer Zusammensetzung und den physikalisch optischen Eigenschaften in der Chloritgruppe. *Chemie der Erde*, vol. 6, p. 416 (M.A. 5–39).

Dunham, K. C., Phillips, R., Chalmers, R. A. and Jones, D. A., 1958. The chromiferous ultrabasic rocks of eastern Sierra Leone. *Overseas Geol. Min. Res. London, Bull. Supp.* No. 3.

Earley, J. W., Brindley, G. W., McVeagh, W. J. and Vanden Heuvel, R. C., 1956. A regularly interstratified montmorillonite-chlorite. *Amer. Min.*, vol. 41, p. 258.

Engelhardt, W. von, 1942. Die Strukturen von Thuringit, Bavalit und Chamosit und ihre Stellung in der Chloritgruppe. *Zeit. Krist.*, vol. 104, p. 142.

Frondel, C., 1955. Two chlorites: gonyerite and melanolite. *Amer. Min.*, vol. 40, p. 1090.

Gillery, F. H., 1959. X-ray studies of synthetic Mg–Al serpentines and chlorites. *Amer. Min.*, vol. 44, p. 143.

Ginzburg, A. I., 1953. On lithium chlorites–cookeite. *Doklady Acad. Sci. USSR*, vol. 90, p. 871 (M.A. 12–451).

Goldschmidt, V. M., 1921. Die Injektionsmetamorphose im Stavanger-Gebiete. *Vidensk. Skrifter. I. Mat.-naturv. Kl.*, Oslo.

Hallimond, A. F., 1939. On the relation of chamosite and daphnite to the chlorite group. *Min. Mag.*, vol. 25, p. 441.

Hawes, G. W., 1875. On diabantite, a chlorite occurring in the trap of the Connecticut Valley. *Amer. Journ. Sci.*, ser. 3, vol. 9, p. 454.

Hess, H. H., 1933. Hydrothermal metamorphism of an ultrabasic intrusive at Schuyler, Virginia. *Amer. Journ. Sci.*, ser. 5, vol. 26, p. 377.

Hey, M. H., 1954. A new review of the chlorites. *Min. Mag.*, vol. 30, p. 277.

Hödl, A., 1941. Über Chlorite der Ostalpen. *Neues Jahrb. Min.*, Bl. Bd. 77, p. 1 (M.A. 8–304).

Holzner, J., 1938. Beiträge zur Kentnnis der varistischen Gesteins- und Mineralprovinz im Lahn-Dillgebiet. 7. Eisenchlorite aus dem Lahngebiet. *Neues, Jahrb. Min.*, Bl. Bd. 73, p. 389.

Honeyborne, D. B., 1951. Clay minerals in the Keuper Marl. *Clay Minerals Bull.*. vol. 1, p. 150.

Hutton, C. O., 1938. The stilpnomelane group of minerals. *Min. Mag.*, vol. 25, p. 172.

—— 1940. Metamorphism in the Lake Wakatipu region, western Otago, New Zealand. *Dept. Sci. Ind. Res. New Zealand, Geol. Mem.* No. 5.

—— and **Seelye, F. T.**, 1945. Contributions to the mineralogy of New Zealand— Part I. *Trans. Roy. Soc. New Zealand*, vol. 75, p. 160.

—— —— 1947. Contributions to the mineralogy of New Zealand—Part 3. *Trans. Roy. Soc. New Zealand*, vol. 76, p. 581.

—— and **Turner, F. J.**, 1936. Metamorphic zones in north-west Otago. *Trans. Roy. Soc. New Zealand*, vol. 65, p. 405.

James, H. L., 1955. Zones of regional metamorphism in the Pre-Cambrian of northern Michigan. *Bull. Geol. Soc. Amer.*, vol. 66, p. 1455.

Lapham, D. M., 1958. Structural and chemical variation in chromium chlorite. *Amer. Min.*, vol. 43, p. 921.

Lippmann, F., 1956. Clay minerals from the Rot member of the Triassic near Gottingen, Germany. *Journ. Sed. Petr.*, vol. 26, p. 125.

Lyons, J. B., 1955. Geology of the Hanover quadrangle, New Hampshire–Vermont. *Bull. Geol. Soc. Amer.*, vol. 66, p. 105.

Mathias, M., 1952. A note on two actinolites and a chlorite from the Prieska district, Cape Province. *Trans. Geol. Soc. South Africa*, vol. 55, p. 13.

Mauguin, G., 1928. Étude des chlorites au moyen des rayons X. *Comptes Rend. Acad. Sci. Paris*, vol. 186, p. 1852.

—— 1930. La maille crystalline des chlorites. *Bull. Soc. franç. Min.*, vol. 53, p. 297.

McMurchy, R. C., 1934. The crystal structure of the chlorite minerals. *Zeit. Krist.*, vol. 88, p. 420.

Mélon, J., 1938. Description des chlorites et clintonites belges. *Mém. Acad. Roy. Belgique, Cl. Sci.*, vol. 17, No. 4 (M.A. 7–360).

Miyashiro, A., 1957. Chlorite of crystalline schists. *Journ. Geol. Soc. Japan*, vol. 63, p. 1.

—— 1958. Regional metamorphism of the Gosaisyo–Takanuki District in the central Abukuma Plateau. *Journ. Fac. Sci., Univ. Tokyo*, vol. 11, p. 219.

—— and **Seki, Y.**, 1958. Mineral assemblages and subfacies of the glaucophane-schist facies. *Jap. Journ. Geol. Geogr.*, vol. 29, p. 199.

Nelson, B. W. and **Roy, R.**, 1958. Synthesis of the chlorites and their structural and chemical constitution. *Amer. Min.*, vol. 43, p. 707.

Nicholls, G. D., 1958. Autometasomatism in the Lower Spilites of the Builth Volcanic Series. *Quart. Journ. Geol. Soc.*, vol. 114, p. 137.

Nockolds, S. R. and **Richey, J. E.**, 1939. Replacement veins in the Mourne Mountain granites, N. Ireland. *Amer. Journ. Sci.*, vol. 237, p. 27.

Orcel, J., 1927. Recherches sur la composition chimique des chlorites. *Bull. Soc. Franç. Min.*, vol. 50, p. 75.

—— and **Caillère, S.**, 1938. Nouvelles observations sur les transformations des prochlorites magnesiénnes sous l'action de la chaleur. *Compt. Rend. Acad. Sci. Paris*, vol. 207, p. 788.

—— —— and **Hénin, S.**, 1950. Nouvel essai de classification des chlorites. *Min. Mag.*, vol. 29, p. 329.

—— and **Renaud, P.**, 1941. Étude du dégagement d'hydrogène associé au départ de l'eau de constitution des chlorites ferromagnésiennes. *Compt. Rend. Acad. Sci. Paris*, vol. 212, p. 918.

Pauling, L., 1930. The structure of the chlorites. *Proc. Nat. Acad. Sci. Wash.*, vol. 16, p. 578.

Phillips, F. C., 1930. Some mineralogical and chemical changes induced by progressive metamorphism in the Green Bed Group of the Scottish Dalradian. *Min. Mag.*, vol. 20, p. 230.

Poitevin, E. and **Graham, R.**, 1918. Contributions to the mineralogy of the Black Lake area, Quebec. *Geol. Surv. Canada, Mus. Bull.* No. 27.

Quensel, P., 1937. Minerals of the Varuträsk pegmatite. VI. On the occurrence of cookeite. *Geol. För. Förh.*, vol. 59, p. 262.

Ramberg, H., 1952. *The origin of metamorphic and metasomatic rocks.* Chicago.

Ross, C. S., 1935. Origin of the copper deposits of the Ducktown type in the southern Appalachian region. *U.S. Geol. Surv., Prof. Paper*, 179, p. 66.

—— 1958. Welded tuff from deep-well cores of Clinch County, Georgia. *Amer. Min.*, vol. 43, p. 537.

Roy, D. M. and **Roy, R.**, 1954. An experimental study of the formation and properties of synthetic serpentines and related layer silicate minerals. *Amer. Min.*, vol. 39, p. 957.

—— —— 1955. Synthesis and stability of minerals in the system $MgO–Al_2O_3–SiO_2–H_2O$. *Amer. Min.*, vol. 40, p. 147.

Sabatier, G., 1950. Sur l'influence de la dimension des cristaux de chlorites sur leur courbes d'analyse thermique differentielle. *Bull. Soc. franç. Min. Crist.*, vol. 73, p. 43.

Seitsaari, J., 1954. Paragenesis of bytownite, chlorite and manganoan garnet from Kangasala, Finland. *Bull. Comm. géol. Finlande,* no. 166, p. 75.

Seki, Y., 1958. Glaucophanitic regional metamorphism in the Kanto Mountains, central Japan. *Jap. Journ. Geol. Geogr.,* vol. 29, p. 233.

Serdyuchenko, D. P., 1953. *Chlorite, its chemical constitution and classification.* Trans. Inst. Geol. Sci. Acad. Sci. USSR.

Shannon, E. V., 1921. Analyses and optical properties of amesite and corundophilite from Chester, Mass., and of chromium bearing chlorites from California and Wyoming. *Proc. U.S. Nat. Mus.,* vol. 58, p. 371.

—— 1923. Note on leuchtenbergite from Philipsburg, Montana. *Amer. Min.,* vol. 8, p. 8.

—— and **Wherry,** 1922. Notes on white chlorites. *Journ. Wash. Acad. Sci.,* vol. 12, p. 239 (M.A. 2–189).

Shidô, F., 1958. Plutonic and metamorphic rocks of the Nakoso and Iritōno districts in the Central Abukuma Plateau. *Journ. Fac. Sci., Univ. Tokyo,* vol. 11, p. 131.

Shirozu, H., 1958. X-ray powder patterns and cell dimensions of some chlorites in Japan, with a note on their interference colours. *Min. Journ. Japan,* vol. 2, p. 209.

Smith, W. C., Bannister, F. A. and **Hey, M. H.,** 1946. Pennantite, a new manganese-rich chlorite from Benallt mine, Rhiw, Caernarvonshire. *Min. Mag.,* vol. 27, p. 217.

Steinfink, H., 1958a. The crystal structure of chlorites. I. A monoclinic polymorph. *Acta Cryst.,* vol. 11, p. 191.

—— 1958b. The crystal structure of chlorites. II. A triclinic polymorph. *Acta Cryst.,* vol. 11, p. 195.

Stephen, I. and **MacEwan, D. M. C.,** 1951. Some chlorite clay minerals of unusual type. *Clay Min. Bull.,* vol. 1, p. 157.

Stone, R. L. and **Weiss, E. J.,** 1955. Examination of four coarsely crystalline chlorites by X-ray and high-pressure d.t.a. techniques. *Clay Min. Bull.,* vol. 2, p. 214.

Taylor, J. H., 1949. *Petrology of the Northampton Sand Ironstone Formation.* Mem. Geol. Surv., Great Britain.

Tilley, C. E., 1923. The petrology of the metamorphosed rocks of the Start Area (South Devon). *Quart. Journ. Geol. Soc.,* vol. 79, p. 172.

—— 1938. The status of hornblende in low-grade metamorphic zones of green schists. *Geol. Mag.,* vol. 75, p. 497.

Tschermak, G., 1890. Die Chloritgruppe. *Sitzber. Akad. Wiss. Wien,* vol. 99, p. 174.

—— 1891. Die Chloritgruppe. *Sitzber. Akad. Wiss. Wien,* vol. 100, p. 29.

Turnock, A. C. and **Eugster, H. P.,** 1958. Iron-rich chlorites. *Carnegie Inst. Washington, Ann. Rep. Dir. Geophys. Lab.,* (1957–1958), vol. 57, p. 191.

Vitaliano, C. J., 1957. Wall-rock alteration in the Broken Hills Range, Nevada. *Journ. Geol.,* vol. 65, p. 167.

Vogt, T., 1927. Geology and petrology of the Sulitjelma district. *Norges Geol. Undersôk.,* No. 121.

Weaver, C. E., 1956. The distribution and identification of mixed-layer clays in sedimentary rocks. *Amer. Min.,* vol. 41, p. 202.

Weiss, E. J. and **Rowland, R. A.,** 1956. Oscillating-heating X-ray diffractometer studies of clay mineral dehydroxylation. *Amer. Min.,* vol. 41, p. 117.

Wilson, V., 1952. The Jurassic ironstone fields of the East Midlands of England. *XIX Inter. Géol. Congrès, Algiers; Symposium sur les gisements de fer du monde,* vol. 2, p. 441.

Winchell, A. N., 1946. Mineral oxidation. *Amer. Min.,* vol. 31, p. 288.

Wiseman, J. D. H., 1934. The central and southwest Highland epidiorites : a study in progressive metamorphism. *Quart. Journ. Geol. Soc.,* vol. 90, p. 354.

Yoder, H. S., 1952. The $MgO-Al_2O_3-SiO_2-H_2O$ system and the related metamorphic facies. *Amer. Journ. Sci.,* Bowen vol., p. 569.

Youell, R. F., 1958. A clay mineralogical study of the ironstone at Easton Neston, Northamptonshire. *Clay Min. Bull.,* vol. 3, p. 264.

Septechlorites

$Y_6[Z_4O_{10}](OH)_8$

The four minerals amesite, chamosite, greenalite and cronstedtite are closely related chemically to the chlorites and structurally to the serpentine and kandite minerals. In general, all four minerals are extremely fine-grained so that only X-ray powder data are available for the elucidation of their structures. This has been sufficient, however, to show that their previous designation as true chlorites was erroneous. The name septechlorite has been proposed for them (Nelson and Roy, 1958) as they are structurally characterized by serpentine-like layers with $d_{001} \simeq 7$ Å. All septechlorites possess a layered structure, each layer having a tetrahedral $(Si,Al)_2O_5$ component, and linked to it a tri-octahedral ("brucite-type") component. This, which may be called a two component structure, is quite different from chlorite which has four components, three forming a "talc" and one a "brucite" layer. The problem of misfitting of tetrahedral and octahedral parts encountered in serpentine structures is alleviated in the case of amesite and chamosite since Al ions substitute both for the smaller Si ions and for the larger Mg (or Fe^{+2}) ions, thus making the two components more nearly equi-dimensional. For greenalite, however, as in serpentine, tubular, curved or otherwise irregular structures might be expected but have not been reported. As with serpentines and kandites, various arrangements of layer stacking are possible, leading to different unit cells. Cell parameters of some septechlorites are presented in Table 26.

Compositional relationships between chlorites, septechlorites and serpentines are illustrated in Fig. 40. For compositions along the serpentine–amesite join a chlorite and a septechlorite polymorph can exist except at the magnesium-rich end, where only the septechlorite is found. Under appropriate conditions one form can undergo transformation into the other, higher temperatures favouring the 14 Å polymorph (see p. 149). Amesite, for example, in natural occurrences so far reported, has a septechlorite structure, but Nelson and Roy (1958) have synthesized a true chlorite with this composition and suggest the name septeamesite for the former. With ferrous iron replacing magnesium in the amesite formula the polymorphic pair chamosite and septechamosite result.

Chamosite

The specimen to which the name chamosite (from Chamoson) was first given has the 14 Å chlorite structure (Orcel et al., 1949) but some specimens which have since been described as chamosite (or sometimes as berthierine) are in fact septechlorites. The composition of natural septechamosites is variable but a typical ferrous chamosite has $Fe^{+2}_{3\cdot6}Al_{1\cdot6}(Mg,Fe^{+3}, etc.)_{0\cdot8}(Si_{2\cdot6}Al_{1\cdot4})O_{10}(OH)_8$, and in ferric chamosite the numbers of Fe^{+2} and Fe^{+3} ions are reversed. Powder data of a number of lateritic septechamosites examined by Brindley (1951) show that these specimens exhibit two kinds of stacking of kaolinite-type layers, which result in single-layer ortho-hexagonal and monoclinic cells. Varying

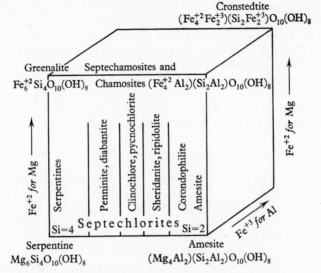

FIG. 40. Compositional relationships between chlorites, septechlorites and serpentines (after Nelson and Roy, 1958). The septechlorites can occur as the low-temperature polymorph at any composition which forms a chlorite. Chlorite nomenclature is that used by Hey (1954).

proportions of the two were found in different specimens, and varying degrees of disorder in the form of y axis displacements. Ironstone septechamosites gave reflections of varying diffuseness corresponding to random displacements in the x direction, and these can be regarded as disordered intermixing of monoclinic and ortho-hexagonal stacking (Youell, 1955). The degree of order apparently increases with the iron content, and is decreased by oxidation of ferrous to ferric iron: the oxidation product, ferric chamosite, has smaller cell parameters. Most septechamosites give d.t.a. patterns similar to those of kaolinite with a marked endothermic peak at about 550°C., at which temperature they decompose to an amorphous state. At a lower temperature, however, the structure undergoes a modification when heated in air to about 400°C., corresponding to the conversion of ferrous to ferric septechamosite (see Table 27, anals. 2 and 3). Not only are lattice parameters affected in the change (Table 26), but chemical analysis and X-ray pattern intensities show that some outer (OH)$^-$ ions of the octahedral layer are converted to (O)$^{-2}$, and some are driven off completely. The oxidation and dehydration reactions, which are to some extent reversible, are represented (Brindley and Youell, 1953) as follows:

$$Fe^{+2} + (OH)^- \rightleftharpoons (Fe)^{+3} + (O)^{-2} + H$$
$$(OH)^- \rightleftharpoons \tfrac{1}{2}H_2O + \tfrac{1}{2}(O)^{-2}$$

On heating septechamosite in air beyond 550°C. crystallization of haematite commences and continues until 1000°C. Spinel appears at 800°C. but has disappeared by 1100°C., while α-cristobalite appears at about 900°C. and beyond this temperature mullite and enstatite probably form. When ferrous chamosite is heated in steam or *in vacuo*, ferric chamosite is not formed; in steam, ferrous aluminate appears at 675°C. and spinels at 800°C. Brindley and Youell (1953) noted that chemical variation and state of oxidation can result in a wide range of chamosite X-ray patterns, and that dehydrated forms may still possess the kaolinite structure, although they do not give the characteristic endothermic peak on differential thermal analysis.

Chamosites often occur in fine-grained yellow, greenish grey or greenish brown aggregates, associated with other clay minerals and iron oxides, in lateritic clay deposits. They are also found as ooliths and in the groundmass, together with siderite and kaolinite, in sedimentary ironstones.

Amesite

The mineral amesite was for many years regarded exclusively as a chlorite, but X-ray powder studies have shown that natural specimens have the septe-chlorite structure (Gruner, 1944). Later work using partially disordered single-crystals (Brindley *et al.*, 1951), demonstrated that the structure contains two kaolinite-type (but tri-octahedral) layers in an ortho-hexagonal cell. X-ray photographs showed evidence of considerable disorder due to random displacements of layers by multiples of $b/3$ parallel to the y axis. Steinfink and Brunton (1956) have determined the structure using a well-ordered single-crystal and have shown that this septeamesite is hexagonal with a 5·31, c 14·04 Å[1] and space group $P6$. The two layers in the unit cell are directly superimposed but are related by a 60° rotation about the sixfold axis passing through the two

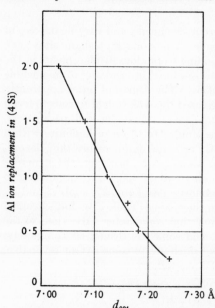

equivalent silicon atoms, and neighbouring layers are held together by hydrogen bonds. Oughton (1957) shows that other modes of regular stacking, such as that resulting in the space group $P6_3cm$, can occur. The effect of substitution of Al for Si and Mg in the synthetic amesite–serpentine septechlorite series is shown by Fig. 41. The basal spacing d_{001} of septechlorites is approximately 0·08 Å smaller than $\frac{1}{2}d_{001}$ of the corresponding 14 Å chlorite (Nelson and Roy, 1958).

The amesite crystals studied by Steinfink and Brunton are twinned and are biaxial, with α 1·597, β 1·600, γ 1·615, $2V_\gamma$ 10°–14°, $\gamma = z$ and $\alpha : x = 20°$: these optical properties are attributed to strain biaxiality. In common with serpentine and kandite minerals, decomposition of amesite occurs at about 600°C. Heating to this temperature increases the randomness of stacking and produces a strong 14 Å

FIG. 41. Variation in d_{001} for the (7 Å) septechlorite solid solution to amesite (Si₂Al₂) (after Nelson and Roy, 1958).

---

[1] The c parameter of 14 Å results from the superposition of two 7 Å layers and so is not an indication of a chlorite rather than a septechlorite structure.

reflection (002 at 7 Å is the first basal reflection for unheated septeamesite) (Steinfink and Brunton, 1956). At about 800°C. a transitory phase is formed the nature of which is uncertain, and at 900°C., a spinel. Attempts to synthesize amesite from oxides (2MgO,Al$_2$O$_3$, SiO$_2$) were unsuccessful (Yoder, 1952), but the possibility of forming serpentine structures with compositions slightly poorer in Al$_2$O$_3$ has been suggested (Roy and Roy, 1954).

Amesite occurs as pale green crystals at Chester, Massachussetts, U.S.A., associated with diaspore, magnetite and corundophilite. The specimen studied by Steinfink and Brunton was from the Saranovskoye chromite deposit, north Urals, U.S.S.R.

Greenalite and Cronstedtite

The formulae given for these minerals in Fig. 40 are for idealized end-members. A typical greenalite composition is Fe$^{+2}_{4.5}$Fe$^{+3}_{1.0}$Si$_4$O$_{10}$(OH)$_8$ and that of cronstedtite is (Fe^{+2},Fe^{+3},Al)$_{4.6}$(Fe$^{+3}_{2.0}$Si$_{2.0}$)O$_{10}$(OH)$_8$. In greenalite, nearly all the octahedral layer is occupied by iron (mainly ferrous) and there is no significant replacement of Si by Al or by Fe^{+3} in the tetrahedral component. In both greenalite and cronstedtite a little magnesium can occupy octahedral sites but the total of octahedral ions is less than six per formula unit, and a similar feature is observed in formulae derived for certain septeamesites and septechamosites. It seems therefore that intermediates between the di- and

Table 26. CELL PARAMETERS OF AMESITE, CHAMOSITE, GREENALITE AND CRONSTEDTITE

	a Å	b Å	$c \sin \beta$Å	$\beta°$	Reference
Amesite	5·31	9·19	14·01	90	Brindley *et al.*, 1951.
Lateritic ferrous chamosite	5·39	9·333	7·040	90	Brindley, 1951.
Ironstone ferrous chamosite	5·415	9·38	7·11	90	Brindley and Youell, 1953.
Ironstone ferric chamosite	5·255	9·10	7·062	90	Brindley and Youell, 1953.
Monoclinic ferrous chamosite	5·41	9·333	7·040	104·5	Brindley, 1951.
Greenalite	5·555	9·61	7·20	90	Steadman and Youell, 1958.
Cronstedtite	5·49	9·52	7·08 ×1, 2 or 6)	90 or 104·5	Steadman and Youell, 1958.
Oxidized cronstedtite	5·25	9·10	7·06		Steadman and Youell, 1957.

Table 27.   SEPTECHLORITE ANALYSES

	1.	2.	3.	4.	5.
SiO$_2$	20·95	23·81	24·69	33·58	16·42
Al$_2$O$_3$	35·21	23·12	23·61	—	0·90
Fe$_2$O$_3$	—	0·23	45·61	11·16	29·72
FeO	8·28	39·45	0·47	45·19	41·86
MnO	tr.	—	—	—	—
MgO	22·88	2·72	2·74	—	—
CaO	0·58	—	—	—	1·32
H$_2$O$^+$	13·02	10·67	2·88	10·07	10·17
H$_2$O$^-$	0·23	—	—	—	—
Total	101·15	100·00	100·00	100·00	100·39
α	1·597	—	—	—	—
β	1·597	1·60–1·67	—	1·67	—
γ	1·612	—	—	—	—
2V$_\gamma$	v.small	—	—	—	—
D	2·77	3·3	—	$\simeq$3·2	3·45

NUMBERS OF IONS†

	1.	2.	3.	4.	5.
Si	1·006 ⎫	1·327 ⎫	1·32 ⎫	2·176 ⎫	1·068 ⎫
Al	0·994 ⎬ 2·00	0·673 ⎬ 2·00	0·68 ⎬ 2·00	— ⎬ 2·18	0·068 ⎬ 2·00
Fe^{+3}	— ⎭	— ⎭	— ⎭	— ⎭	0·864 ⎭
Al	0·999 ⎫	0·847 ⎫	0·81 ⎫	— ⎫	— ⎫
Fe^{+3}	—	0·008	1·83	0·446	0·590
Fe^{+2}	0·330 ⎬ 2·97	1·840 ⎬ 2·92	0·02 ⎬ 2·88	2·339 ⎬ 2·79	2·278 ⎬ 2·96
Mg	1·637	0·225	0·22	—	—
Ca	— ⎭	— ⎭	— ⎭	— ⎭	0·091 ⎭
OH	4·00	3·968	1·02	3·278	4·414

1. Amesite, pale bluish green crystals, Chester, Massachussetts (Gruner, 1944).   Anal. F. V. Shannon.
2. Ferrous chamosite, in matrix of siderite, Stanion Lane pit, Corby, Northamptonshire (Brindley & Youell, 1953).   Anal. R. F. Youell (Analysis recast to 100 per cent. after subtraction of carbonate and sulphate impurities).
3. Ferric chamosite, prepared by heating above sample (anal. 2) in air at 400°C. for two hours (Brindley & Youell, 1953) (Analysis recast to 100 per cent. after subtraction of carbonate and sulphate impurities).
4. Greenalite, Mesabi Range, Minnesota (Gruner, 1936) (Re-calculated from anal. by Jolliffe (1935) after subtracting insol. SiO$_2$ and other impurities).
5. Cronstedtite, Kisbanya, Hungary (Hendricks, 1939).   Anal. B. Gossner.

† The formula for anal. 1 is calculated on the basis of 5(O) and 4(OH); the formula for anal. 3 is that derived by Brindley and Youell in such a way that the total of octahedral ions is approximately the same as that in anal. 2; anals. 2, 4 and 5 are calculated on the basis of 9(O,OH).

tri-octahedral kaolinite-type minerals are not uncommon, although they may be restricted to the range $5·0 < Y < 6·0$ (Youell, 1958).

The X-ray powder pattern of greenalite resembles that of ortho-hexagonal chamosite (and of serpentine) and shows little or no "x" disorder.   Cronstedtite exhibits considerable polymorphism, showing one-layer, two-layer and six-layer orthorhombic cells, and a one-layer monoclinic cell, all with varying degrees of disorder.   Those with one-layer cells are similar to the two polymorphs of chamosite, while those with a two-layer orthorhombic cell are similar to amesite.

Greenalite, like chamosite, changes on heating (by oxidation and dehydration) to a completely ferric form. For cronstedtite oxidation of ferrous iron takes place at 275°C., and continued heating causes considerable reduction in the a and b cell parameters and an increase in c. At 700°C. an unusual spinel is formed in which Si ions occupy what are normally sites for ferric iron. Above 750°C. haematite appears, and at a still higher temperature cristobalite is formed (Steadman and Youell, 1957). Crystals of greenalite with a refractive index of about 1·67 have been synthesized at temperatures below 470°C. using ferrosilicon alloys and water as starting materials. The known occurrence of greenalite is restricted to the iron formation of the Mesabi Range, Minnesota, but cronstedtite, in the form of brown or black plates of varying size and perfection, is more common.

REFERENCES

Brindley, G. W., 1951. The crystal structure of some chamosite minerals. *Min. Mag.*, vol. 29, p. 502.

—— Oughton, B. M. and Youell, R. F., 1951. The crystal structure of amesite and its thermal decomposition. *Acta. Cryst.*, vol. 4, p. 552.

—— and Youell, R. F., 1953. Ferrous chamosite and ferric chamosite. *Min. Mag.*, vol. 30, p. 57.

Flaschen, S. S. and Osborn, E. F., 1957. Studies of the system iron oxide–silica–water at low oxygen partial pressures. *Econ. Geol.*, vol. 52, p. 923.

Gruner, J. W., 1936. The structure and chemical composition of greenalite. *Amer. Min.*, vol. 21, p. 449.

—— 1944. The kaolinite structure of amesite, and additional data on chlorites. *Amer. Min.*, vol. 29, p. 422.

Hendricks, S. B., 1939. Random structures of layer minerals as illustrated by cronstedtite. Possible iron content of kaolin. *Amer. Min.*, vol. 24, p. 529.

Hey, M. H., 1954. A new review of the chlorites. *Min. Mag.*, vol. 30, p. 277.

Jolliffe, F., 1935. A study of greenalite. *Amer. Min.*, vol. 20, p. 405.

Nelson, B. W. and Roy, R., 1958. Synthesis of the chlorites and their structural and chemical constitution. *Amer. Min.*, vol. 43, p. 707.

Orcel, J., Hénin, S. and Caillère, S., 1949. Sur les silicates phylliteux des minerais de fer oolithiques. *Comptes Rend. Acad. Sci. Paris*, vol. 229, p. 134.

Oughton, B. M., 1957. Order–disorder structures in amesite. *Acta Cryst.*, vol. 10, p. 692.

Roy, D. M. and Roy, R., 1954. An experimental study of the formation and properties of synthetic serpentines and related layer silicate minerals. *Amer. Min.*, vol. 39, p. 957.

Steadman, R. and Youell, R. F., 1957. Crystallography and thermal transformations of cronstedtite. *Nature*, vol. 180, p. 1066.

—— —— 1958. Mineralogy and crystal structure of greenalite. *Nature*, vol. 181, p. 45.

Steinfink, H. and Brunton, G., 1956. The crystal structure of amesite. *Acta Cryst.*, vol. 9, p. 487.

Yoder, H. S., 1952. The $MgO–Al_2O_3–SiO_2–H_2O$ system and the related metamorphic facies. *Amer. Journ. Sci.*, Bowen vol., p. 569.

Youell, R. F., 1955. Mineralogy and crystal structure of chamosite. *Nature*, vol. 176, p. 560.

—— 1958. Isomorphous replacement in the kaolin group of minerals. *Nature*, vol. 181, p. 557.

Serpentines

$Mg_3[Si_2O_5](OH)_4$

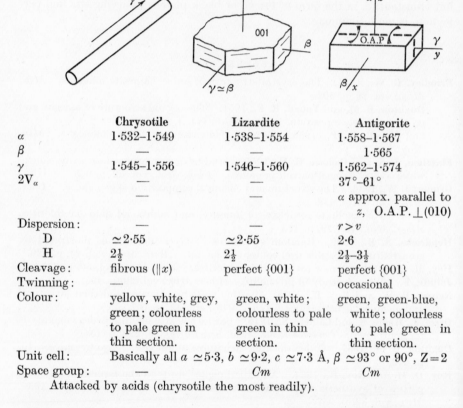

	Chrysotile	Lizardite	Antigorite
α	1·532–1·549	1·538–1·554	1·558–1·567
β	—	—	1·565
γ	1·545–1·556	1·546–1·560	1·562–1·574
$2V_\alpha$	—	—	37°–61°
	—	—	α approx. parallel to z, O.A.P. $\perp$(010)
Dispersion:	—	—	$r > v$
D	$\simeq$2·55	$\simeq$2·55	2·6
H	$2\frac{1}{2}$	$2\frac{1}{2}$	$2\frac{1}{2}$–$3\frac{1}{2}$
Cleavage:	fibrous ($\parallel x$)	perfect {001}	perfect {001}
Twinning:	—	—	occasional
Colour:	yellow, white, grey, green; colourless to pale green in thin section.	green, white; colourless to pale green in thin section.	green, green-blue, white; colourless to pale green in thin section.
Unit cell:	Basically all $a \simeq 5\cdot3$, $b \simeq 9\cdot2$, $c \simeq 7\cdot3$ Å, $\beta \simeq 93°$ or 90°, Z=2		
Space group:	—	Cm	Cm

Attacked by acids (chrysotile the most readily).

The principal minerals of the serpentine group all have the approximate composition $H_4Mg_3Si_2O_9$, and comparatively little substitution of other ions is found to occur in natural specimens. The most well-known serpentine mineral, chrysotile, often occurs in veins of silky fibres and is the most important source of commercial asbestos. The tensile strength of chrysotile asbestos may be greater than that of amphibole fibres, but where acid as well as heat resistant properties are required the fibres of the latter mineral are generally more suitable. Chrysotile fibres are usually aligned approximately across the veins (although slip fibres also occur) and their length, though generally less than half an inch, can reach as much as six inches. The structure of all serpentines is essentially a tri-octahedral analogue of the kaolinite structure, but there are three principal polymorphic forms: chrysotile, antigorite and lizardite. The name serpentine alludes to the appearance of many impure serpentinite rocks, the surface pattern of which recalls the skin of a serpent. Chrysotile is from the Greek *chrusos*, golden, and *tilos*, fibre; antigorite and lizardite are respectively named after the type localities, Antigorio in Italy, and The Lizard in Cornwall. *Serpentine* is used to describe the group of similar minerals, and *serpentinite* to describe a rock which consists mainly of serpentine.

STRUCTURE

There is now ample evidence that although some of the serpentine minerals are fibrous the structures of all of them are nevertheless of a layered type similar to that found in the kaolinite group[1] (Warren and Hering, 1941; Aruja, 1943; Whittaker, 1953). One part of the layer is a pseudo-hexagonal network of linked SiO_4 tetrahedra, with approximate parameters a 5·3, b 9·2 Å. All tetrahedra in the sheet point one way, and joined to it is a brucite layer in which, on one side only, two out of every three hydroxyls are replaced by apical oxygens of SiO_4 tetrahedra (Fig. 42). The perpendicular distance between composite sheets of this type is approximately 7·3 Å. Consideration of the dimensions of a brucite layer and of a tridymite layer[2] shows that the joining of the two components will probably involve appreciable mis-matching. (When referred to an ortho-hexagonal cell, corresponding parameters are approximately $5·4 \times 9·3$ Å for brucite and $5·0 \times 8·7$ Å for tridymite.) The several ways in which the two components can nevertheless accommodate one another are probably responsible for many of the unusual crystallographic and morphological features of the serpentine minerals. Moreover, as with other layered minerals, various regular and disordered stacking methods may occur, giving rise to additional polymorphs. There are three ways in which better matching of the layer components can be achieved, (a) by substitution of larger ions for Si in the tetrahedral layer and/or smaller ions for Mg in the octahedral layer; (b) by distortion of the ideal octahedral and/or tetrahedral networks, probably resulting in a strained configuration which could perhaps be stabilized by strong inter-layer bonding; (c) by curvature of the composite sheet with its tetrahedral component on the inside of the curve. Combinations of the above methods may occur.

Many experimental results point to the existence of serpentine minerals with curved sheet structures. Chrysotile fibres when seen under an electron microscope often have a tube-like appearance (Plate 1), and their X-ray diffraction photographs contain unusual features which are, however, completely explicable in terms of sheet curvature. Most chrysotiles appear to have their fundamental layers curved about the x axis only, forming either concentric hollow cylinders or rolls elongated parallel to x. In these cases the mis-match in the direction of the fibre axis may be partly relieved by distortions involved in the bending. Although the y direction follows a curve, Whittaker (1953) has derived from

---

[1] Serpentines differ from kandites, however, in being tri-octahedral, and in the mode of stacking of their fundamental layers.

[2] The tetrahedra in a tridymite layer, unlike those in serpentine, point alternately in opposite directions, but the tridymite structure is nevertheless assumed to provide a "norm" for the parameters of a strain-free tetrahedral network.

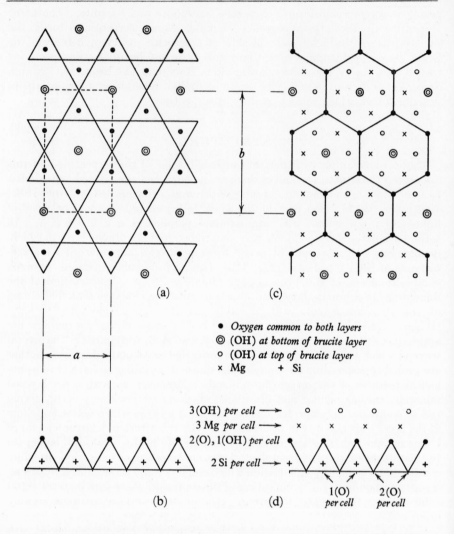

FIG. 42.　Structure of serpentine layer:
(a) Tetrahedral Si_2O_5 network in plan.
(b) Tetrahedral network as viewed along y axis.
(c) Tri-octahedral component of serpentine layer (plan).
(d) Serpentine layer as viewed along y axis (after Zussman, 1954).

X-ray fibre diagram data a projection of the chrysotile structure on to a radial plane which corresponds to an (010) projection in a flat-layered case: the electron density projection confirms the kaolinite-type layer. The fibre photographs show that the chrysotile cell is two-layered and that two alternative stacking methods occur, with $\beta \simeq 93°$ or $\beta = 90°$ for clino- or ortho-chrysotile respectively. Ortho-chrysotile is orthorhombic (if the sheet curvature is disregarded) and its cell is two-layered through the occupation of alternative sites for Mg and (OH) ions in successive sheets, and through the off-setting of alternate layers in the

$+x$ and $-x$ direction.   In clino-chrysotile successive sheets are off-set in the same direction and have the same Mg–OH configuration, but alternate sheets are off-set by different amounts and there are minor differences in atomic positions within alternate layers resulting again in a two-layered cell.   Although stacking is ordered with respect to translations in the x direction there is complete translational disorder between sheets in the y direction so that in effect atoms at the bases of layers are restricted, not to precisely located depressions in layers below, but to circumferential grooves.

In addition to ortho- and clino-chrysotile a third variety called para-chrysotile exists, in which the axis of curvature is y instead of x (Whittaker, 1956c).

Much of the matrix material containing veins of chrysotile is the variety of serpentine called lizardite.   This is extremely fine-grained but is seen under the electron microscope to have platy morphology.   It may be that in this variety the strains resulting from mis-matching of the layer components place a severe limitation on crystal growth.   In lizardite the unit cell is single-layered and ortho-hexagonal (*i.e.* $\beta = 90°$) as determined from powder patterns, but structural details have not been established.   The structure may be only effectively single-layered through a random mixing of layers with two alternative (Mg,OH) configurations.   Some fibrous and massive serpentine specimens have a 6-layered ortho-hexagonal cell (Zussman and Brindley, 1957) and it seems likely that other stacking arrangements exist.   A synthetic serpentine in which all silica is replaced by germanium has platy morphology and a 6-layered ortho-hexagonal cell: this is an extreme example of the reduction of mis-match by ionic substitution.   In both examples of 6-layered cells mentioned above the structure approximates to a 2-layered cell, but Gillery (1959) reports a 6-layered cell for some synthetic serpentines and septechlorites which approximates to a 3-layered cell.

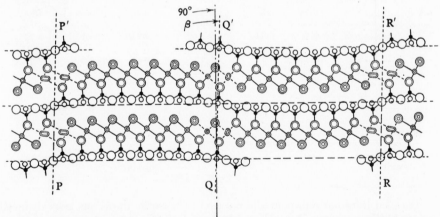

FIG. 43.   Structure of antigorite as viewed along y axis.   The curved layers (radius of curvature 75 Å) reverse polarity at PP′, RR′ and near QQ′ (after Kunze, 1956).

Antigorite is another serpentine mineral which is structurally distinct. Antigorite specimens have b dimensions and (001) spacings similar to those of chrysotile and lizardite, but the a dimension of the unit cell is large and in most cases is in the region of 40 Å.   X-ray investigation of single-crystals of one specimen (Aruja, 1945), gave a 43·5 Å, β 91·4°, and a one-layered cell. It is clear from the diffraction patterns that a pseudo-cell has $a \simeq 5\cdot3$ Å, so that the antigorite structure involves a regularly distorted form of the ideal serpentine layers. An explanation of the large a parameter has been sought in terms of curvature of serpentine layers about y in such a way as to form corrugations parallel to y, the periodicity of corrugation being a. X-ray diffraction studies (Kunze, 1956, 1958) indicate a structure in which the serpentine sheet is undulating and reverses polarity at each line of inflection (Fig. 43). Electron diffraction patterns from single-crystals of antigorite show that a variety of a parameters can be adopted, values of $a \simeq 33, 35, 38, 40, 43$ Å having been recorded (Zussman *et al.*, 1957). Furthermore one variety called Yu Yen stone has $a \simeq 100$ Å and another, a fibrous specimen, has $a \simeq 18\cdot5$ Å. It may be that the a parameter adopts values which are spaced approximately at intervals of multiples of 5·3/2 Å. The fibrous antigorites are sometimes called picrolite, and in these y is consistently parallel to the fibre axis as compared with x in most chrysotiles. The characteristic features of the various serpentine structures are summarized in Table 28. Analogous nickel serpentines have similar parameters ($d_{001} = 7\cdot35$ Å for Ni–Si, 7·49 Å for Ni–Ge) and an aluminian serpentine has $d_{001} \simeq 7\cdot1$ Å.

Table 28.   CELL PARAMETERS OF SERPENTINE MINERALS

	Chrysotile (Whittaker, 1956a, b, c)			Lizardite (Whittaker and Zussman, 1956)	6-layered ortho-hexagonal (Zussman and Brindley, 1957)		Antigorite (Kunze, 1956)
	clino-	ortho-	para-		Mg–Si	Mg–Ge	
aÅ	5·34	5·34	5·3	5·31	5·322	5·436	43·3
b Å	9·25	9·2	9·24	9·20	9·219	9·415	9·23
c Å	14·65	14·63	14·7	7·31	43·59	44·66	7·27
β	93° 16′	90°	90°	90°	90°	90°	91·6°
No. of layers per cell	2	2	2	1	6	6	1
Fibre axis	x	x	y	—	x when fibrous	—	y when fibrous

Detailed information about the nature of chrysotile fibres has been deduced from evidence contained in low and high angle X-ray diffraction patterns, from electron diffraction patterns, and from numerous electron micrographs. The fundamental fibrils have various diameters but the most frequently occurring fibril has an inner diameter 110 Å, outer diameter 260 Å and ten layers in the wall. The strain-free layer has a radius of curvature of about 88 Å. These estimates are from wide angle X-ray evidence (Whittaker, 1957), and are compatible with those deduced from low angle scattering experiments (Fankuchen and Schneider,

1944; Jagodzinski and Kunze, 1954), and with electron microscope observations (Noll *et al.*, 1958, and others). Various possible cylindrical lattices have been defined and described (Whittaker, 1955) some of which involve concentric closed cylinders, some continuous spirals, and some continuous helical arrangements, of similar atoms. The diffraction data from natural chrysotiles in some cases indicate concentric cylinders, sometimes a helical arrangement, and in some cases may be compatible with longitudinally split fragments: it is probable that many different configurations occur.

The structural relationship between serpentine and the product of its thermal decomposition, olivine, has been investigated by several workers. Olivine produced from chrysotile by heating is largely oriented with [010] or [013] of the olivine cell[1] parallel to the fibre axis [100] of the chrysotile (Epprecht and Brandenburger, 1946; Hey and Bannister, 1948), and other orientations have been reported (Aruja, 1943; Wondratschek, 1956). In heating experiments on lizardite and fibrous antigorite, it has been shown that the relationship is more than unidimensional, since in addition to the above, [001] or [011] of olivine was seen to be parallel to [010] of serpentine, and [100] of olivine parallel to z of serpentine (Brindley and Zussman, 1957). Dimensional as well as directional relationships also exist, $2a_{serp.} \simeq b_{olivine}$ and $2b_{serp.} \simeq 3c_{olivine}$, so that a relatively simple transition mechanism may be involved similar to that described for the chlorites (Brindley and Ali, 1950). X-ray study of the transition at various intermediate stages shows that two different processes are involved according to whether the initial serpentine has a one-layered or two-layered cell. The two-layered serpentines behave similarly to the two-layered aluminium silicate dickite, giving an intermediate structure with 14·5 Å spacing which changes very little with heating, while the one-layered serpentines give an intermediate with a spacing which diminishes from 14 to about 10 Å. There is also some evidence, during the transition, of a large cell which is the least common multiple of the serpentine and olivine cells. This might be called a "transformation cell", to which the whole reorganization process could be referred in much the same way that a whole crystal is described in terms of its unit cell.

Oriented intergrowths of chrysotile with other serpentines, with calcite (Wondratschek, 1957), and with brucite, have been reported.

CHEMISTRY

The chemistry of the serpentine group as a whole is relatively simple in that most natural specimens deviate little from the ideal composition $H_4Mg_3Si_2O_9$. The principal replacements which do occur are of silicon by aluminium, and of magnesium by aluminium, ferrous iron and ferric iron. That nickel may adopt the role of magnesium is shown by the synthesis of a pure nickel serpentine and by the existence of garnierite, a naturally occurring nickel serpentine, but most magnesium serpentines contain little nickel (on average about 0·25 per cent.). Other elements such as chromium, copper and platinum, occur in very small amounts. Minerals with a tri-octahedral kaolinite-type sheet structure which have a very high iron content are known to occur (*e.g.* greenalite and the non-chloritic variety of chamosite, see p. 164), yet little substitution of iron for

[1] The olivine forsterite is orthorhombic with a 4·755, b 10·21, c 5·985 Å.

Table 29. SERPENTINE ANALYSES

	Chrysotiles				Lizardites		
	1.	2.	3.	4.	5.	6.	7.
SiO_2	41·80	41·97	41·83	42·02	41·80	41·25	44·29
TiO_2	0·05	—	0·02	0·00	0·10	0·02	0·03
Al_2O_3	0·11	0·10	0·30	0·52	0·19	0·54	2·18
Fe_2O_3	0·68	0·38	1·29	0·19	0·93	1·32	0·50
Cr_2O_3	0·003	—	—	—	0·003	—	—
FeO	0·05	1·57	0·08	0·11	0·06	0·09	—
NiO	0·00	—	—	—	0·00	—	—
MnO	0·04	—	0·04	0·03	0·04	0·07	—
MgO	42·82	42·50	41·39	41·44	42·67	41·84	40·43
CaO	0·10	—	tr.	0·00	0·19	0·02	0·03
Na_2O	0·03	—	—	—	0·02	—	—
K_2O	0·01	0·08	—	—	0·01	—	—
SO_3	0·09	—	—	—	0·08	—	—
CO_2	0·01	—	—	—	0·04	—	—
H_2O^+	14·04	13·56	13·66	14·04	13·88	13·68	12·42
H_2O^-	0·28	—	1·57	1·64	0·24	0·97	—
Total	100·11	100·26	100·18	99·99	100·25	99·80	99·88
α	—	1·549	—	—	—	—	1·545
β	—	—	—	—	—	—	1·545
γ	—	1·556	—	1·540	—	—	1·555
$2V_\alpha$	—	—	—	—	—	—	2°
D	—	2·56	—	—	—	—	2·55

NUMBERS OF IONS ON THE BASIS OF 9(O,OH)

	1.		2.		3.		4.		5.		6.		7.	
Si	1·921		1·943		1·950		1·954		1·926		1·924		2·004	
Al	—	1·92	0·001	1·96	—	1·95	0·026	1·98	0·010	1·97	0·030	1·95	—	2·00
Fe^{+3}	—		0·014		—		0·001		0·032		—		—	
Al	0·006		—		0·016		—		—		—		0·117	
Fe^{+3}	0·024		—		0·045		—		—		0·046		0·018	
Cr	—		—		—		—		—		—		—	
Fe^{+2}	0·001		0·061		0·003		0·004		0·002		0·004		—	
Mn	0·001	2·98†	—	3·00	0·001	2·94	0·001	2·88	0·002	2·95‡	0·002	2·96	—	2·88§
Mg	2·937		2·932		2·877		2·871		2·930		2·904		2·738	
Ca	0·005		—		—		—		0·008		0·001		0·002	
Na	0·001		—		—		—		0·002		—		—	
K	—		0·004		—		—		—		—		—	
(OH)	4·00		4·188		4·248		4·352		4·00		4·250		3·87	
(H_4)	0·079		—		—		—		0·066		—		—	

1. Chrysotile, cross-fibre vein, Aboutville, New York (Kalousek and Muttart, 1957). Anal. W. E. Smith.
2. Chrysotile fibre, Danville area of Quebec, Canada (Pundsack, 1955a). Anal. T. Sopoci and R. Wiley (Includes 0·10 other oxides).
3. Chrysotile, cross-fibre vein (metamorphosed limestone occurrence), Transvaal (Brindley and Zussman, 1957). Anal. W. A. Deer.
4. Chrysotile, asbestos deposits, Gila County, Arizona (Nagy and Faust, 1956). Anal. J. J. Fahey.
5. Lizardite, matrix containing chrysotile vein of analysis no. 1, Aboutville, New York (Kalousek and Muttart, 1957). Anal. W. E. Smith.
6. Lizardite, matrix containing chrysotile vein of analysis no. 3, Transvaal (Unpublished). Anal. W. A. Deer.
7. Lizardite, white serpentine mineral, Kennack Cove, Lizard, Cornwall (Midgley, 1951; Whittaker and Zussman, 1956). Anal. L. J. Larner. 2nd analysis by W. A. Deer (Mean of two analyses given: formula calculated using cell volume and density).

† Includes 0·003 Ti.
‡ Includes 0·004 Ti.
§ Includes 0·001 Ti.

Table 29.   SERPENTINE ANALYSES—*continued*

	Antigorites				Al-Serpentine	Ni-Serpentine
	8.	**9.**	**10.**	**11.**	**12.**	**13.**
SiO_2	43·60	43·45	44·70	44·50	42·54	41·00
TiO_2	0·01	0·02	0·00	0·00	—	—
Al_2O_3	1·03	0·81	0·50	1·41	5·68	0·22
Fe_2O_3	0·90	0·88	0·07	0·00	1·06	3·28
Cr_2O_3	0·02	n.d.	—	0·06	—	—
FeO	0·81	0·69	0·29	0·35	0·74	0·40
NiO	0·16	n.d.	—	0·095	—	15·56
MnO	0·04	0·00	—	0·00	—	—
MgO	41·00	41·90	42·05	41·56	35·57	22·86
CaO	0·05	0·04	0·12	0·02	0·13	0·30
Na_2O	0·01	0·05	—	0·00	—	—
K_2O	0·03	0·02	—	0·00	—	—
SO_3	—	—	—	—	—	—
CO_2	—	—	—	—	—	—
H_2O^+	12·18	12·29	12·43	12·36	13·26	9·74
H_2O^-	0·08	0·04	0·06	0·00	0·38	6·22
Total	99·92	100·19	100·22	100·36	99·36	99·58
α	1·5615	1·560	—	—	—	—
β	1·5660	1·563	—	—	—	—
γ	1·5670	1·564†	1·564	1·568	—	—
$2V_\alpha$	47½°	55°	—	—	—	—
D	2·607	2·60	—	—	—	—

NUMBERS OF IONS ON THE BASIS OF 9(O,OH)

	8.		**9.**		**10.**		**11.**		**12.**		**13.**	
Si	2·028		2·022		2·060		2·055		1·970		2·225	
Al	—	2·03	—	2·02	—	2·06	—	2·06	0·030	2·00	—	2·23
Fe^{+3}	—		—		—		—		—		—	
Al	0·057		0·044		0·024		0·069		0·280		0·013	
Fe^{+3}	0·032		0·030		0·024		—		0·037		0·134	
Cr	—		—		—		0·001		—		—	
Fe^{+2}	0·032		0·027		0·011		0·014		0·029		0·018	
Ni	0·006	3·00	—	3·01	—	2·95	0·003	2·95	—	2·60	0·678	2·71
Mn	0·002		—		—		—		—		—	
Mg	2·863		2·905		2·886		2·859		2·246		1·849	
Ca	0·003		0·002		—		0·001		0·006		0·017	
Na	0·001		0·004		—		—		—		—	
K	0·001		—		—		—		—		—	
(OH)	3·807		3·814		3·818		3·806		4·098		3·528	

8. Antigorite, vicinity of Caracas, Venezuela (Hess *et al.*, 1952).   Anal. L. C. Peck.
9. Antigorite, Cropp river, Mikonnui, New Zealand (Zussman, 1954).   Anal. R. A. Howie.
10. Antigorite, "Yu-Yen Shi Stone", Pei-wa-ku and Lao-yeh-ling, Hsiu-yen-Hsien, Liaoning Province, Manchuria (Nagy and Faust, 1956).   Anal. J. J. Fahey.
11. Antigorite, State Line pits, Lowes Mine, Rock Springs, Cecil County, Maryland, U.S.A. (Nagy and Faust, 1956).   Anal. J. J. Fahey.
12. Aluminous chrysotile, Contact ravine, Markopidj river basin, North Caucasus (Serdyuchenko, 1945).
13. Ni-serpentine, hydrothermal vein in dunite, Webster, North Carolina, U.S.A. (Ross *et al.*, 1928).   Anal. F. A. Gonyer.

† Kunze (1956) gives γ 1·568, $2V_\alpha = 37°$.

magnesium occurs in serpentines.   Where serpentines are formed in peridotitic rocks, most of the iron present in the original olivine or pyroxene is incorporated in magnetite or haematite impurity and does not enter the serpentine structure.

The chemical relationships between the different serpentine varieties, chrysotile, lizardite and antigorite, are not fully understood.   It is conceivable that these are purely polymorphic forms with identical chemical composition so that their existence would be attributed to the different physical stability fields of the three structures.   As yet the products of serpentine synthesis have been either extremely small chrysotile fibres or have not been identified except as members of the serpentine group, so that stability fields of the three varieties are not known.   If the three varieties have no essential chemical difference it could also be inferred that the formation of each polymorph in nature is favoured by particular environmental conditions: for example, chrysotile fibres may form readily under conditions of lateral compression or longitudinal tension.   It seems probable, however, that small chemical differences are associated with each of the three varieties, and in this context it has been suggested that platy serpentines have a higher trivalent ion (particularly Al) content than chrysotile, since this substitution reduces the mis-match between layer components.   This thesis has been supported experimentally by the synthesis of substituted serpentines and by the demonstration that those with appreciable replacement of Si and Mg by Al, or of Si by Ge, have platy morphology whereas others form as fibres.   The application of this idea (and its converse) to natural specimens must be made with caution, however, since antigorites, although they form platy crystals, nevertheless according to X-ray evidence possess a curved sheet structure, and therefore need not necessarily have high Al content. Chemical analyses in fact do not show a consistently higher Al content in anti-gorites, and indeed certain specimens of antigorite (*e.g.* anal. 10, Table 29) have less Al than some chrysotiles and lizardites.   In lizardites, however, there is no evidence of either a tubular or corrugated structure, so that these might be expected to have high Al content.   Again chemical analyses do not consistently support this expectation, some lizardites (usually matrix material bearing chrysotile veins) having almost as little Al as chrysotile itself (*cf.* anals. 5 and 1, also 6 and 3, Table 29).   In these examples the grain size is extremely small and it may be that strains due to mis-match can be tolerated over small areas of the structure.   It is perhaps significant that in the one example where lizardite has developed as relatively large platy crystals (Table 29, anal. 7) the Al content is appreciably higher than in other chrysotiles and lizardites.   Detection of small systematic differences in the chemistry of serpentines is, however, rendered difficult by the presence of impurities in what is often very fine-grained material, and the higher trivalent ion content in matrix materials may well be associated with a greater abundance of inseparable impurity.

A specific chemical feature of antigorites appears to be a slightly higher Si:Mg ratio than that of the ideal serpentine composition.   This would be expected on the basis of the structure models involving corrugated sheets.   By contrast a number of analyses of chrysotile (Kalousek and Muttart, 1957), when calculated on the basis of 9(O,OH), show a deficit of Si ions below the ideal of 2 per formula unit, together with an excess of hydrogen ions (beyond that required for 4 hydroxyls) which closely balances the silicon deficit. (The ions have been distributed in this manner for analysis 1 in Table 29.)   This suggests a replacement of (OH) for some oxygens of the tetrahedral network, perhaps of the type described by McConnell (1954) for a serpentine and various other minerals. A similar deficit of Si ions is shown for massive matrix material but the balance with excess hydrogens is not so precisely achieved (see Table 29, anal. 5): nor is a close balance shown for several other chrysotile specimens. When the formulae of pure chrysotiles are calculated on the basis of 9(O,OH) it is notice-able that the numbers of tetrahedral and octahedral ions fall below their ideal values of 2 and 3 respectively. The same feature is observed for lizardites except in the case of the coarsely grained specimen (Table 29, anal. 7) where only the octahedral total is low. This is in marked contrast to the antigorites where similar calculations yield a high total of tetrahedral cations. For anti-gorites a recalculation based on two tetrahedral cations per cell is more fruitful in showing a deficit of octahedral cations and a deficit of anions both of which are compatible with known features of the crystal structure : the result agrees with that found by direct evaluation of the cell contents (Zussman, 1954). A similar calculation of chrysotile and lizardite formulae on the basis of two tetrahedral cations per cell shows an excess of anions. This, together with the excess hydrogens, suggests an alternative interpretation of the chemical composition which again is compatible with knowledge of the atomic structure. Extra (OH) ions and substitutions of (OH) for (O) might be expected to occur at the edges of serpentine sheets, and if the particle size is small enough these additional anions can appreciably affect the chemical composition. Thus for infinite ribbons the excess anions found experimentally would be accommodated at edges if the average width of ribbon was of the order of 100 Å. The existence of many such ribbons has been suggested elsewhere as the only way to account for X-ray, electron microscope and density observations on certain chrysotile specimens (see page 183). In the case of lizardites the idea is not so well supported. The excess anions found experimentally would be accommodated at the edges of small rafts of which the average dimension is about 150 Å. The particle size of massive lizardites is known to be very small but although some particles of the above magnitude are seen under the electron microscope, the average size of particle is probably about five times as great. It is perhaps significant, however, that the coarse-grained lizardite does not show excess anions or hydrogen (Table 29, anal. 7). Table 29 gives analyses and ionic proportions for several serpentine minerals of each structural variety. The absolute numbers of ions per cell can only be checked where cell volume and density are known, and even then the allocation of ions to different structural sites is in many cases somewhat arbitrary. The merits of different possibilities can only be evaluated in the light of additional structural, chemical and physical information. Extra hydrogen (in some cases) could reasonably be explained as being bound with oxygen in the form of strongly adsorbed water. Bates (1959), after study of a number of reliable chemical analyses of different serpentine minerals, considers that "the amount of hydrogen provides the most important distinction between platy and tubular varieties." Bates also develops for the serpentine, septechlorite, and kaolinite groups of minerals, a quantitative measure of the amount of misfit between layer components which is derived from the cationic substitutions which they exhibit.

Analysis 12 is for an aluminous serpentine, and the low octahedral total would seem to indicate that this specimen is intermediate between di- and tri-octahedral in character. Many specimens described as garnierite, nickel gymnite or genthite are mixtures of serpentine with other hydrosilicates (Pecora *et al.*, 1949). Anal. 13 is of a nickel silicate the formula of which approximates to that of a serpentine with Ni substituting for Mg.

Experimental. On heating serpentines in air, olivine is formed at about 600 °C. In most cases olivine begins to appear before the disruption of the serpentine structure is complete, and the temperature of breakdown is slightly higher for antigorites than for other varieties. The reaction which occurs is most probably:

$$2Mg_3Si_2O_5(OH)_4 \rightarrow 3Mg_2SiO_4 + SiO_2 + 4H_2O$$
$$\text{serpentine} \qquad\qquad \text{forsterite}$$

SiO_2 being present in the decomposition product as amorphous silica (Vermaas, 1953): crystallographic relationships involved in the transformation have been discussed in the previous section. Early experiments on thermal decomposition reported enstatite formation at comparatively low temperatures (Caillère, 1936) but this has not been observed subsequently (Hargreaves and Taylor, 1946). The d.t.a. curves have been obtained for many serpentine specimens and although these are variable according to the grain size of specimen and other experimental conditions, they are consistent in showing that antigorite gives an endothermic peak at about 750°–780°C. while for chrysotile and lizardite the peak occurs between 680° and 750°C. This endothermic peak corresponds to the expulsion from the serpentine of "structural" water, and it is followed closely by an exothermic peak related to the formation of olivine. The latter occurs at about 800°–820°C. but appears with widely varying intensity and sometimes is not present at all. It is possible that the dehydration process is followed so closely by the formation of olivine that in some cases the exothermic peak is overlapped and reduced by the endothermic one. A weak, broad, low temperature endothermic peak is shown by some serpentines, corresponding to the expulsion of water which is held on the surface of fine-grained material. In chemical analyses of chrysotile some water of this kind may be registered erroneously as H_2O^+ since prolonged heating at 110°C. is required to dislodge it completely.

A colloid and surface chemistry study of chrysotile (Pundsack, 1955a) showed that it behaves like layers of brucite on substrata of silica: the pH of a 0·5 per cent. suspension in water is 10·33 as compared with 10·37 for brucite. In acid solution chrysotile particles become positively charged, while in alkaline solution, or in CO_2-free distilled water, they acquire a negative charge. It is clear that dissociation of the "brucite" layer which occurs, is increased in acid and repressed in alkaline solution. While chrysotile is readily decomposed by acids, antigorite is more stable. Thus after treatment for one hour with 1N HCl at 100°C. the basal X-ray reflections from a chrysotile specimen are no longer visible but those of an antigorite subjected to similar treatment are unaffected (Nagy and Bates, 1952). The structure of lizardite is also not disrupted by the above treatment, but is affected by somewhat stronger acid while antigorite is still unchanged. Indications, by X-ray patterns, of stability to acid can be used as a quantitative method of estimating proportions of antigorite and chrysotile in a mixture (Nagy and Faust, 1956), provided that no lizardite is present (Whittaker and Zussman, 1958). Experimental studies of the system MgO–

SiO_2–H_2O (Bowen and Tuttle, 1949) have shown that serpentine can be prepared at temperatures below 500°C. and at pressures from 2000 to 40,000 lb./in.².† Under hydrothermal conditions above 500°C. serpentine breaks down into forsterite, talc and vapour (see Fig. 29, p. 125). Without the introduction of reagents other than water, serpentinization of olivine has been achieved only at temperatures below 400°C. (serpentine + brucite ⇌ forsterite + vapour), and for iron-bearing olivines serpentinization requires still lower temperatures, and is accompanied by the formation of either magnetite or haematite. Synthesis of serpentine in the above and in other experiments (*e.g.* Noll, 1944), always yields small fibres of chrysotile and attempts to grow larger ones have had only very limited success. Although in some cases small flaky grains of serpentine have been produced (*e.g.* Brandenburger *et al.*, 1947, using Na_2SiO_3 and $MgCl_2$) no positive identification of a synthetic lizardite or antigorite has been made. With the agency of $NiCl_2$, fibres of the nickel serpentine garnierite have been prepared (Noll and Kircher, 1952). With Al_2O_3 added to the system MgO–SiO_2–H_2O (Yoder, 1952), it was found that the composition $5MgO·Al_2O_3·3SiO_2$ yielded a platy aluminous serpentine mineral which was stable up to 520°C. Beyond this temperature it transformed to clinochlore under equilibrium conditions.

In a series of hydrothermal experiments to determine the effect of chemical substitution on morphology of serpentines, Roy and Roy (1954) synthesized many phases possessing the "tri-octahedral kaolinite" structure. Nelson and Roy (1958) have suggested that substances with this structure should be called "septechlorites", see p. 164. The term would include serpentines, substituted serpentines and amesite; "septechamosite" would cover analogous iron-rich minerals. These terms are considered appropriate since the substances are chemically more closely related to the chlorite group than to the kandites, and can be considered as polymorphic variations possessing a "7 Å" as compared with the chlorites' "14 Å" structure. Starting with a mixture of oxides $3MgO·2SiO_2$ tubular chrysotile fibres resulted, with an upper stability limit of 490°C. With $3MgO·2GeO_2$ as starting material, hexagonal plates were produced which were subsequently shown to have the 6-layered ortho-hexagonal cell (Zussman and Brindley, 1957). Substitution of nickel for magnesium ($3NiO·2SiO_2$) gave platy or tubular particles, the additional presence of NaCl favouring the formation of tubes. Synthetic Ni–Ge serpentine was platy and did not adopt tubular morphology even in the presence of NaCl, so that although impurity ions have some influence, the principal factor is evidently ionic size. Temperature of crystallization had no great influence on morphology, but slower crystallization appeared to favour plate rather than tube formation when NaCl was present: manganese, zinc or cobalt in place of magnesium did not yield a serpentine. The substitution of aluminium for magnesium yielded platy crystals of aluminian serpentine in which Al occurs in both octahedral and tetrahedral layers (Roy, 1952). The composition $5MgO·Al_2O_3·3SiO_2$, gave well-developed plates at 600°C., but even as little as 1 mol. per cent. of alumina caused a tendency toward platiness. The further substitution of aluminium up to the composition of amesite, $4MgO·2Al_2O_3·2SiO_2$, was achieved resulting in a

† Univariant equilibrium curves appreciably different from those shown in Fig. 29, p. 125, were obtained for the system MgO–SiO_2–H_2O, by Bennington (1956) using thermodynamic data.

decreasing basal spacing : Mn–Ge, Ga–Ge, Ga–Si, Cr–Si, and Fe^{+3}–Si serpentine compositions were also investigated but yielded no serpentine. The upper stability limits derived by Roy and Roy for some synthetic serpentines are :

$$\text{Mg–Si } 490°C., \quad \text{Mg–Ge } 520°C., \quad \text{Ni–Si } 530°C., \quad \text{Ni–Ge } 360°C.$$

The results of a more recent study of synthetic Mg–Al serpentines and chlorites prepared from gels (Gillery, 1959), are summarized below. Chlorites were produced from compositions with more than 0·50 Al per formula unit $(0·25[Al]^6$ and $0·25[Al]^4)$ at temperatures above 500°C. Septechlorites were produced for all compositions from $Mg_3Si_2O_5(OH)_4$ (serpentine) up to $(Mg_2Al)(SiAl)O_5(OH)_4$ at temperatures below 500°C. The serpentine–septechlorite structures were seen to display three polymorphic forms. Those with very little Al are fibrous and are similar to natural chrysotile. With high aluminium content platy crystals result, some of which have a 1-layered and some a 6-layered ortho-hexagonal cell, and the highest proportion of 6-layered septechlorite occurs for compositions with highest Al content.

OPTICAL AND PHYSICAL PROPERTIES

The fine-grained nature of most serpentine specimens makes a complete optical description impossible except for certain specimens. Thus antigorite crystals allow the observation of all three refractive indices, optic axial angle, and optical orientation. All grains are plate-like parallel to (001), and many have rectangular outline due to (010) and (100) cleavages. Elongation is sometimes parallel to y and sometimes to x, the optic axial plane is perpendicular to (010), and the acute bisectrix is approximately perpendicular to (001). The optic axial angle is between 37° and 61° and the crystals are optically negative. Antigorites sometimes show twofold or threefold twins, related by rotations of 60° about the normal to the plate.

The specimen of lizardite from Kennack Cove, Lizard, Cornwall, is coarse-grained and has α 1·545, $\beta = \gamma$ 1·555 (Midgley, 1951), 2V very small, sign negative. Other lizardites usually give only a mean refractive index, and this varies between 1·54 and 1·55. As can be seen on page 170, the ranges of refractive index for antigorites and lizardites are barely separated, so that distinction between them cannot reliably be made by optics alone. Chrysotile fibres yield different values of refractive index for the directions parallel and perpendicular to their length, and most have positive elongation. A true interpretation of the optical properties of chrysotile may be complicated by the rolling (or at least curvature) of the fundamental serpentine layers, by the random orientation of fibrils about the fibre axis, and also by the phenomenon of form birefringence consequent upon the extremely small particle size. An exceptional phenomenon is that of serpentine mesh structure displayed by many massive serpentine specimens when viewed in thin section between crossed polarizers (Selfridge, 1936; Francis, 1956; and others). In a typical serpentine mesh structure a lattice-work of longitudinally divided cross-fibre veins encloses areas of isotropic or nearly isotropic material (Fig. 44a). The fibres of the rims appear to have positive elongation whereas the cores appear to consist of negatively elongated fibres sometimes parallel to one direction only, but sometimes adopting an "hour-glass" configuration (Fig. 44b). The positive and negative fibres are known as γ- and α-serpentine respectively, and occasionally mesh structures are

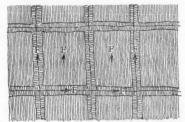 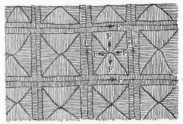

FIG. 44(a).   Illustration of serpentine "mesh" structure.
   (b).   Illustration of serpentine "hour-glass" structure.
F denotes fast vibration direction.

observed in which cores are α- and rims are γ-serpentine.   Other configurations of apparently fibrous material are found, such as parallel sets of cross-fibre veins the boundaries of which are defined by lines of magnetite, and magnetite or haematite sometimes occurs as a partial or complete filling of mesh structure cores.   Although the various textures have been often observed and described, the precise nature of their components, and their mode of formation, are not known.   The assumption that fibres within the mesh structure are similar to the fibres of large scale chrysotile veins may be too facile.   Francis (1956) observed that the birefringence of mesh γ-serpentine is lower than that of vein chrysotile.   In fact the evidence of a "sweeping extinction" is hardly sufficient for the assumption that the material has a fibrous character.   It is difficult to understand why fibrous material should sometimes appear isotropic (except if seen end-on), and it is perhaps significant that "α-serpentine" has not been observed as large scale fibres: the distinction between α- and γ-serpentine and the isotropic components, may be purely one of different orientations of a single material.   Alternatively the isotropic cores of mesh structure (sometimes referred to as serpophite) could be amorphous material of serpentine, olivine or enstatite composition.

   The physical nature of chrysotile has for some time been enigmatic.   To explain its fibrous nature in terms of atomic structure, analogy was drawn with the amphibole asbestos fibres, where good prismatic cleavages result from a chain-like atomic structure.   (Even for the amphiboles, the reason why some specimens are fibrous and others are not, is unknown.)   For chrysotile, however, the sheet-like structure has been proved and an explanation of fibrosity is offered in terms of curled and rolled sheets.   Considerable evidence for such configurations is provided by X-ray and electron-diffraction patterns, and electron microscopy (Plate 1) reveals many particles as hollow tubes (*e.g.* Noll and Kircher, 1952; Bates *et al.*, 1950; Bates and Comer, 1959).   The evidence for hollow tubes is contradicated, however, by measurements of the density of compact sealed bundles of some specimens of fibres (Pundsack, 1956b).   For a chrysotile from Danville (Table 29, anal. 2) it was found that the density of a sealed block is compatible with the solid stacking of flat serpentine layers (2·56 gm./cm.^{3}), whereas hollow tubes of appropriate dimensions, packed as closely as possible, would, by virtue of their intra- and inter-tubular spaces, have an effective density of about 1·9 gm./cm^3.   Even the packing of solid cylinders would lead to a density about 10 per cent. lower than that of a specimen with no voids. In view of these results Pundsack suggests that the tubes seen under the electron microscope are not present as such in the specimen before its preparation and examination, and that chrysotile in its natural state consists of closely packed ribbon-like particles, which may be distorted by curvature about the fibre axis.

Against the thesis that tubes are produced by grinding or by exposure to the electron beam, is the evidence of replicas taken from side and end surfaces of blocks of chrysotile: when examined under the electron microscope these too show features most reasonably ascribed to a tubular morphology.[1] Density measurements made on other specimens (Kalousek and Muttart, 1957) show that some are like that from Danville, with no voids, whereas a specimen from Globe, Arizona, has about 12 per cent. voids. Whittaker (1957) suggests that both density and other evidence are compatible with the existence of tubes, a high proportion of which are filled with curved ribbons; such fragments of cylinders may also fill most of the channels between tubes. When a suspension of particles is prepared for electron microscope examination the "stuffed" tubes would tend to sink and a high proportion of hollow tubes therefore may be withdrawn and placed on the specimen grid. The relative abundance of tubes and ribbons probably varies in different specimens. Some support for the existence of extremely narrow ribbons may be found in the interpretation of chemical analyses of chrysotiles suggested on p. 179. The density experiments by Pundsack on chrysotile from Danville show that the only void spaces observed are those associated with absorbed water which causes swelling of the fibre bundles. The adsorbed water may be removed and subsequently replaced at temperatures between 175°C. and 200°C., but above 200°C. some water is lost and cannot be replaced. At 100 per cent. relative humidity and at 25°C., 2·5 per cent. of water is adsorbed causing a 6·7 per cent. increase in volume. Gas adsorption measurements (Young and Healey, 1954) show that nitrogen, argon and carbon dioxide are adsorbed no more than on a non-fibrous material, whereas the values for water and ammonia are anomalously high. Young and Healey suggest that "plugs" of water at the ends of chrysotile tubes prevent the entry of most gases. The results of these experiments do not necessarily favour the presence of hollow tubes, since the spaces inside them cannot be distinguished from those between fibres. Furthermore nitrogen adsorption is found to vary (from 4 m.^{2}/gm. to 50 m.^{2}/gm.) according to the state of specimen dispersion (Pundsack, 1956a). Adsorption measurements have been made also by Noll *et al.* (1958). The infra-red absorption spectra for the principal structurally distinct varieties of serpentine have been recorded (Brindley and Zussman, 1959), and can be used to distinguish antigorite from the others.

Chrysotile asbestos is often in the form of silky fibres which are excellent for commercial use, but it is sometimes greasy, sometimes harsh, and sometimes brittle. No definite correlation of texture with structure has been found, but certain splintery specimens show evidence in electron diffraction patterns of possessing a structure which has greater three-dimensional order. Water content may have an influence on the harshness. Antigorite, which has a density of about 2·61 gm./cm.^{3} usually occurs in very small crystals, but is sometimes less well ordered, as in the fibrous varieties called picrolite. Lizardite

---

[1] Cross-sections of bundles of fibres of chrysotile have been prepared, and examined by electron microscopy (Maser *et al.*, 1960). The micrographs show many end-on views of concentric tubes.

ate 1. (a) Electron micrograph showing tubular fibres of chrysotile from Globe, Arizona. Magnification × 40,000 (after Nagy and Faust, 1956).

ate 1. (b) Electron micrograph showing tubular fibres of synthetic chrysotile. Magnification × 21,400 (after Noll *et al.*, 1958).

(density 2·55 gm./cm.³) occurs mostly in extremely fine-grained green massive aggregates, but also in small white scales. The massive green serpentine often contains a mixture of lizardite and chrysotile, and other mixtures of varieties can also occur.

DISTINGUISHING FEATURES

Antigorites may be distinguished from micas since the latter have higher birefringence. The chlorite delessite has higher refractive indices, and ripidolite is noticeably pleochroic. Chrysotile is less birefringent than chlorite. Serpentine asbestos fibres have γ less than 1·58, while fibres of amphibole asbestos have γ greater than 1·58. When ground in a mortar, amphibole fibres rub to a powder, but chrysotile fibres form a matted aggregate which can only be powdered with great difficulty.

PARAGENESIS

The principal occurrences of serpentine minerals are those in which they are derived from ultrabasic rocks. The processes by which serpentinization takes place in such rocks as dunites, pyroxenites and peridotites have been the subject of much discussion (*e.g.* Du Rietz, 1935; Hess, 1938; Sosman, 1938; Hess, 1955). Experimental studies on the system $MgO-SiO_2-H_2O$ (Bowen and Tuttle, 1949) have indicated that serpentines cannot be formed at temperatures above 500°C., and that formation of serpentine by the action of water on forsterite can occur only below 400°C. Since they found no liquid phase in the system at temperatures of up to 1000°C. and pressures of 15,000 lb./in.², Bowen and Tuttle deduced that serpentines cannot be formed by the intrusion, at comparatively low temperatures, of a magma of serpentine composition. They also concluded that serpentines are unlikely to occur through the transformation of a mixture of olivine and pyroxene crystals by their aqueous mother liquor:

$$\underset{\text{forsterite}}{Mg_2SiO_4} + \underset{\text{enstatite}}{MgSiO_3} + 2H_2O \rightarrow \underset{\text{serpentine}}{Mg_3Si_2O_5(OH)_4}$$

Bowen and Tuttle suggest that the olivine and pyroxene are intruded in the crystalline state without water, and are subsequently serpentinized below 500°C. by water vapour acquired through contact with wet rocks. If the rocks contain only olivine then water vapour will yield serpentine and brucite, below 400°C.:

$$\underset{\text{forsterite}}{2Mg_2SiO_4} + 3H_2O \rightarrow \underset{\text{serpentine}}{Mg_3Si_2O_5(OH)_4} + \underset{\text{brucite}}{Mg(OH)_2}$$

If CO_2 were present to remove excess magnesia as soluble carbonate the serpentine could still be formed up to 500°C. Another reaction by which serpentinization of olivine could occur involves the addition of silica:

$$3Mg_2SiO_4 + SiO_2 + 2H_2O \rightarrow 2Mg_3Si_2O_5(OH)_4$$

but this would involve a considerable increase in volume for which there is no substantial field evidence. In some circumstances peridotite, reheated by extraneous solutions, may be serpentinized during the cooling cycle, as for example when talc occurs as a pseudomorph after enstatite.

$$\underset{\text{enstatite}}{6MgSiO_3} + 3H_2O \rightarrow \underset{\text{serpentine}}{Mg_3Si_2O_5(OH)_4} + \underset{\text{talc}}{Mg_3Si_4O_{10}(OH)_2}$$

An example of the serpentinization of an ultrabasic rock is provided at Glen Urquhart (Francis, 1956). Here the field evidence supports the thesis of a solid intrusion, but also favours subsequent autometasomatism by water which accompanied the emplacement of the ultrabasic rock. In conflict with experimental results on the $MgO-SiO_2-H_2O$ system, field evidence in certain cases suggests a magmatic origin for peridotites and serpentine emplacements (*e.g.* Bailey and McCallien, 1953; Wilkinson, 1953).

Another problem of serpentine paragenesis concerns the conditions favourable for the formation of each of the structural varieties, in particular antigorite. It should be remembered that in much early discussion of this kind the term antigorite has been used without precise crystallo-chemical definition and may have been applied to any of the serpentine varieties. In most cases it appears that antigorite is derived from chrysotile, but according to Hess *et al.* (1952), pure thermal metamorphism is not a sufficient agency, and chrysotile transforms to antigorite sluggishly at low temperatures with the assistance of shearing stress. The grade of metamorphism required for antigorite formation is placed between the chlorite–biotite greenschist facies and the albite–epidote amphibolite facies. Wilkinson (1953) describes the generation of antigorite from chrysotile by thermal metamorphism by nearby granites. Francis (1956) states that antigorite can replace either olivine or enstatite directly but is more usually found replacing mesh serpentine, and it seems that at Glen Urquhart shearing stress generally accompanied antigorite formation; sometimes, however, antigorite is found where there is no evidence of shearing stress, and it is by no means always found where shearing has taken place. It is possible that chemical environment has an important influence on the formation of chrysotile or antigorite, and it has been suggested that in general olivine yields chrysotile and enstatite yields antigorite (Hess *et al.*, 1952). Support for this has been claimed in the presence of "bastite" pseudomorphs after enstatite, the platy character of which makes them resemble antigorite: it has been shown, however, for several specimens that bastite crystals are not antigoritic. Antigorite may nevertheless be preferentially derived from enstatite, since the latter mineral generally has a higher Al and Si content than olivine. Each of these features has been claimed as characteristic of antigorite chemistry, as compared with that of chrysotile.

When serpentines are derived by any of the methods outlined above it is not surprising that they often contain many accessory minerals, among them olivine (unchanged or regenerated), pyroxene, tremolite, actinolite, chlorite, talc, brucite, calcite, magnesite, magnetite, chromite and chalcedony. A detailed description of the serpentine masses of the Thetford area, Quebec, and in particular of the chrysotile veins within them is given by Cooke (1937) who concluded from his study that the three factors required for the formation of the asbestos deposits are: faulting to break up the peridotite rock and allow access of solutions, an adequate supply of dilute aqueous solutions, and the proximity of acid dykes which served to heat the serpentine and solutions. Cooke argues against the formation of asbestos veins by replacement of massive serpentine rock proceeding from the walls of narrow cracks, and against their formation by the filling of pre-existing fissures. He concludes that fibres began to grow in narrow fissures from solutions which permeated the rock, and that the fibre growth was able to push apart the fissure walls. Riodon (1955) suggests that both wall replacement and fissure filling have been involved and that one or other may predominate in any particular vein. He presents some evidence that the serpentine within fissures was once in a colloidal state, and that coarse and silky chrysotile fibres were formed in two successive stages of crystallization.

In South Africa much of the chrysotile occurs in basic igneous rocks as veins bordered by magnetite grains; in some cases the agency of granitic vapours is evident, but in others granitic masses are not present. Certain serpentines of the Transvaal (Carolina, Pilgrimsrest, Pietersburg districts) are examples, however, of a different paragenesis. Here and elsewhere serpentines are found in metamorphic rocks and in metamorphosed limestones or dolomites. In the Transvaal, serpentinized dolomitic rocks are associated with diabase sills, and in these circumstances veins of chrysotile, parallel to the contact, are free from magnetite and other impurities except for small amounts of talc. The siliceous dolomite is transformed to forsterite which is subsequently serpentinized:

$$2CaMg(CO_3)_2 + 2SiO_2 \rightarrow 2CaCO_3 + Mg_2SiO_4 + 2CO_2$$
$$\underset{\text{dolomite}}{\qquad} \underset{\text{silica}}{\qquad} \underset{\text{calcite}}{\qquad} \underset{\text{forsterite}}{\qquad}$$

Poldervaart (1950) discusses the formation of serpentine by dolerite intrusion in dolomite in the Bechuanaland Protectorate. He suggests that a rise in temperature in the dolomite resulted in concentration, along bedding planes, of vadose water which dissolved material from the dolomite and gave rise to saturated aqueous solutions of calcium and magnesium carbonate and silica. Subsequent cooling of Mg-rich fluids resulted in the crystallization of chrysotile. If enstatite and forsterite were also formed they were probably serpentinized at lower temperatures, and where Mg concentrations were lower, talc and calcite were formed. Fibre growth, in these circumstances, is thought to proceed by slow replacement of massive serpentine material, and Hall (1930) made the general observation that the length of fibre diminishes with depth below the surface. Serpentines may also occur in contact metamorphic deposits and in hydrothermal veins.

REFERENCES

Aruja, E., 1943. An X-ray study of silicates. Chrysotile, antigorite, gümbelite. *Ph.D. Thesis*, Cambridge.
—— 1945. An X-ray study of the crystal structure of antigorite. *Min. Mag.*, vol. 27, p. 65.
Bailey, E. B. and **McCallien, W. J.**, 1953. Serpentine lavas, the Ankara melange and the Anatolian thrust. *Trans. Roy. Soc. Edin.*, vol. 62, p. 403.
Bates, T. F., 1959. Morphology and crystal chemistry of 1:1 layer lattice silicates. *Amer. Min.*, vol. 44, p. 78.
—— and **Comer, J. J.**, 1959. Further observations on the morphology of chrysotile and halloysite. *Proc. 6th Natnl. Clay Conf. Clays and clay minerals. Monograph No. 2. Earth Science series.* Pergamon Press.
—— **Sand, L. B.** and **Mink, J. F.**, 1950. Tubular crystals of chrysotile asbestos. *Science*, vol. 111, p. 512.
Bennington, K. O., 1956. Role of shearing stress and pressure in differentiation as illustrated by some mineral reactions in the system $MgO-SiO_2-H_2O$. *Journ. Geol.*, vol. 64, p. 558.
Bowen, N. L. and **Tuttle, O. F.**, 1949. The system $MgO-SiO_2-H_2O$. *Bull. Geol. Soc. Amer.*, vol. 60, p. 439.

Brandenburger, E., Epprecht, W. and Niggli, P., 1947.   Die Serpentin-Mineralen und ihre Synthese.   *Helv. Chim. Acta.,* vol. 30, p. 9 (M.A. 10–265).

Brindley, G. W. and Ali, S. Z., 1950.   X-ray study of thermal transformation in some magnesian chlorite minerals.   *Acta Cryst.,* vol. 3, p. 25.

—— and **von Knorring, O.,** 1954.   A new variety of antigorite (ortho-antigorite) from Unst, Shetland Islands.   *Amer. Min.,* vol. 39, p. 794.

—— and **Zussman, J.,** 1957.   A structural study of the thermal transformation of serpentine minerals to forsterite.   *Amer. Min.,* vol. 42, p. 461.

—— —— 1959.   Infra-red absorption data for serpentine minerals.   *Amer. Min.,* vol. 44, p. 185.

Caillère, S., 1936.   Contribution a l'étude des minéraux de serpentines.   *Bull. Soc. Franç. Min.,* vol. 59, p. 163.

Cooke, H. C., 1937.   *Thetford, Disraeli and eastern half of Warwick map areas, Quebec.*   Canadian Geol. Surv., Mem. 211.

Du Rietz, T., 1935.   Peridotites, serpentines and soapstones, of northern Sweden.   *Geol. För. Förh. Stockholm,* vol. 57, p. 135.

Epprecht, W. and Brandenburger, E., 1946.   Die Entwasserung von Chrysotil und Antigorit.   *Schweiz. Min. Petr. Mitt.,* vol. 26, p. 229.

Fankuchen, J. and Schneider, W., 1944.   Low angle X-ray scattering from chrysotiles.   *Journ. Amer. Chem. Soc.,* vol. 66, p. 500.

Francis, G. H., 1956.   The serpentinite mass in Glen Urquhart, Inverness-shire, Scotland.   *Amer. Journ. Sci.,* vol. 254, p. 201.

Gillery, G. H., 1959.   X-ray study of synthetic Mg–Al serpentines and chlorites.   *Amer. Min.,* vol. 44, p. 143.

Hall, A. L., 1930.   *Asbestos in the Union of South Africa.*   Union of S. Africa Geol. Surv., Mem. 12.

Hargreaves, A. and Taylor, W. H., 1946.   An X-ray examination of decomposition products of chrysotile (asbestos) and serpentine.   *Min. Mag.,* vol. 27, p. 204.

Hess, H. H., 1938.   A primary peridotite magma.   *Amer. Journ. Sci.,* 5th ser., vol. 35, p. 321.

—— 1955.   Serpentines, orogeny, epeirogeny.   *Crust of the earth (a symposium).*   *Geol. Soc. Amer., Special Paper* 62, p. 391.

—— **Smith, R. J. and Dengo, G.,** 1952.   Antigorite from the vicinity of Caracas, Venezuela.   *Amer. Min.,* vol. 37, p. 68.

Hey, M. H. and Bannister, F. A., 1948.   A note on the thermal decomposition of chrysotile.   *Min. Mag.,* vol. 28, p. 333.

Jagodzinski, H. and Kunze, G., 1954.   Die Röllchenstruktur des Chrysotils.   I, II and III.   *Neues Jahrb. Min., Monat.,* p. 95, p. 113 and p. 137.

Kalousek, G. L. and Muttart, L. E., 1957.   Studies on the chrysotile and antigorite components of serpentine.   *Amer. Min.,* vol. 42, p. 1.

Kunze, G., 1956.   Die gewellte Struktur des Antigorits, I.   *Zeit. Krist.,* vol. 108, p. 82.

—— 1957.   Die gewellte Struktur des Antigorits.   *Fortsch. Min.,* vol. 35, p. 46.

—— 1958.   Die gewellte Struktur des Antigorits, II.   *Zeit. Krist.,* vol. 110, p. 282.

McConnell, D., 1954.   Ortho-antigorite and the tetrahedral configuration of hydroxyl ions.   *Amer. Min.,* vol. 39, p. 830.

Maser, M., Rice, R. V. and Klug, H. P., 1960.   Chrysotile morphology.   *Amer. Min.,* vol. 45, p. 680.

Midgley, H. G., 1951.   A serpentine mineral from Kennack Cove, Lizard, Cornwall.   *Min. Mag.,* vol. 29, p. 526.

Nagy, B. and Bates, T. F., 1952.   Stability of chrysotile asbestos.   *Amer. Min.,* vol. 37, p. 1055.

Nagy, B. and **Faust, G. T.**, 1956.   Serpentines : natural mixtures of chrysotile and antigorite. *Amer. Min.*, vol. 41, p. 817.

Nelson, B. W. and **Roy, R.**, 1958.   Synthesis of the chlorites and their structural and chemical constitution. *Amer. Min.*, vol. 43, p. 707.

Noll, W., 1944.   Anwendung der Elektronmikroskopie beim studium hydrothermaler Silikatreaktionen. *Kolloid. Zeits.*, vol. 107, p. 181.

—— 1950.   Synthesen im System $MgO/SiO_2/H_2O$. *Zeits. anorg. Chem.*, vol. 261, p. 1.

—— and **Kircher, H.**, 1952.   Synthesen von Garnierites. *Naturwiss.*, vol. 39, p. 233.

—— **Kircher, H.** and **Sybertz**, 1958.   Adsorptionsvermögen und specifische Oberfläche von Silikaten mit röhrenformig gebauten Primärkristallen. *Koll. Zeit.*, vol. 157, p. 1.

Pecora, W. T., Hobbs, S. W. and **Murata, K. J.**, 1949.   Variations in garnierite from the nickel deposit near Riddle, Oregon. *Econ. Geol.*, vol. 44, p. 13.

Poldervaart, A., 1950.   Chrysotile asbestos produced by dolerite intrusions in dolomite. *Colonial Geol. Min. Resources*, vol. 1, p. 239.

Pundsack, F. L., 1955a.   The properties of asbestos.   I.   The colloidal and surface chemistry of chrysotile. *Journ. Phys. Chem.*, vol. 59, p. 892.

—— 1955b.   The properties of asbestos.   II.   The density and structure of chrysotile. *Journ. Phys. Chem.*, vol. 60, p. 361.

Riodon, P. H., 1955.   The genesis of asbestos in ultrabasic rocks. *Econ. Geol.*, vol. 50, p. 67.

Ross, C. S., Shannon, E. V. and **Gonyer, F. A.**, 1928.   Origin of nickel silicates at Webster, North Carolina. *Econ. Geol.*, vol. 23, p. 528.

Roy, D. M., 1952.   Phase equilibria in the system $MgO–Al_2O_3–H_2O$ and in quaternary systems derived by the addition of SiO_2, CO_2 and N_2O_5. *Ph.D. thesis*, The Pennsylvania State University, 1952.

—— and **Roy, R.**, 1954.   An experimental study of the formation and properties of synthetic serpentines and related layer silicate minerals. *Amer. Min.*, vol. 39, p. 957.

Selfridge, G. C., 1936.   An X-ray and optical investigation of the serpentine minerals. *Amer. Min.*, vol. 21, p. 463.

Serdyuchenko, P. P., 1945.   Alumino-chrysotile, a member of the isomorphous series serpentine–parakaolinite. *Doklady Acad. Sci. USSR*, vol. 46, p. 117.

Sosman, R. B., 1938.   Evidence on the intrusion-temperature of peridotites. *Amer. Journ. Sci.*, 5th ser., vol. 35A, p. 353.

Vermaas, F. H. S., 1953.   The thermal characteristics of some Transvaal serpentines and the production of forsterite. *Journ. Chem. & Mining Soc. of South Africa*, vol. 53, p. 191.

Warren, B. E. and **Hering, K. W.**, 1941.   The random structure of chrysotile asbestos. *Phys. Rev.*, vol. 59, p. 925 (abstract).

Whittaker, E. J. W., 1953.   The structure of chrysotile. *Acta Cryst.*, vol. 6, p. 747.

—— 1955.   A classification of cylindrical lattices. *Acta Cryst.*, vol. 8, p. 571.

—— 1956a.   The structure of chrysotile.   II.   Clinochrysotile. *Acta Cryst.*, vol. 9, p. 855.

—— 1956b.   The structure of chrysotile.   III.   Orthochrysotile. *Acta Cryst.*, vol. 9, p. 862.

—— 1956c.   The structure of chrysotile.   IV.   Parachrysotile. *Acta. Cryst.*, vol. 9, p. 865.

—— 1957.   The structure of chrysotile.   V.   Diffuse reflexions and fibre texture. *Acta Cryst.*, vol. 10, p. 149.

—— and **Zussman, J.**, 1956.   The characterisation of serpentine minerals by X-ray diffraction. *Min. Mag.*, vol. 31, p. 107.

Whittaker, E. J. W. and **Zussman, J.**, 1958.   The characterization of serpentine minerals.   *Amer. Min.*, vol. 43, p. 917.

Wilkinson, J. F. G., 1953.   Some aspects of the alpine-type serpentinites of Queensland.   *Geol. Mag.*, vol. 90, p. 305.

Wondratschek, H., 1956.   Über die Voränge bei der Entwässerung des Chrysotils. *Tercera Reunion Internacional sobre reactividad de los Sólidos.*   Madrid.

—— 1957.   Orientierte Verwachsungen von Chrysotils mit Mineralen der Serpentin-Gruppe und mit Kalzit.   *Neues. Jahrb. Min., Monat.*, p. 135.

Yoder, H. S., Jr., 1952.   The MgO–Al$_2$O$_3$–SiO$_2$–H$_2$O system and the related metamorphic facies.   *Amer. Journ. Sci.*, Bowen vol., p. 569.

Young, G. J. and **Healey, F. H.**, 1954.   The physical structure of asbestos.   *Journ. Phys. Chem.*, vol. 58, p. 881.

Zussman, J., 1954.   Investigation of the crystal structure of antigorite.   *Min. Mag.*, vol. 30, p. 498.

—— and **Brindley, G. W.**, 1957.   Serpentines with 6-layer orthohexagonal cells. *Amer. Min.*, vol. 42, p. 666.

—— —— and **Comer, J. J.**, 1957.   Electron diffraction studies of serpentine minerals.   *Amer. Min.*, vol. 42, p. 133.

CLAY MINERALS

The constituents of clays may be assigned to one of two groups, those called clay minerals, which by their nature give to the clay its plastic properties, and the others which are accessory "non-clay minerals". The clay minerals have a number of characteristics in common. Their structures are, with a few minor exceptions, based on composite layers built from components with tetrahedrally and octahedrally coordinated cations. Most of them occur as platy particles in fine-grained aggregates which when mixed with water yield materials which have varying degrees of plasticity. Chemically, all are hydrous silicates (principally of aluminium or magnesium) which, on heating, lose adsorbed and constitutional water, and at high temperatures yield refractory materials. Important differences among the clay minerals, however, lead to their subdivision into several main groups. The four important layered clay mineral groups are: kandites, illites, smectites and vermiculites. These have characteristic basal spacings of approximately 7 Å, 10 Å, 15 Å and 14·5 Å respectively, but for some categories (the kandite mineral halloysite, smectites and vermiculites) the layer separation is variable since swelling may occur through the intercalation of water or organic liquids, and shrinkage may result from dehydration. The clay minerals attapulgite and sepiolite have chain-like crystal structures and are less common than the layered clay minerals. The particles of clay minerals may be crystalline or amorphous, platy or fibrous, and, though nearly always small, may vary from colloid dimensions to those above the limit of resolution of an ordinary microscope. Chemical composition may vary according to the extent of replacement of Si, Al and Mg by other cations, the nature and quantity of inter-layer cations, and the water content. The clay minerals vary in their dehydration and breakdown characteristics and in their decomposition products, and they also differ in their cation exchange properties according to the nature of their inter-layer cations and residual surface charges. Their uses are many, some being particularly suitable as components of drilling muds, some for catalysts in petroleum processing, others for fillers in paper manufacture, and for ceramic and refractory ware. The clay minerals are the main constituents of one class of sediments (consequently called argillaceous) which on accumulation and compaction yield shales or mudstones. Whether in sedimentary deposits or not the clays are usually products of weathering or hydrothermal alteration, different clays resulting according to physico-chemical conditions and the nature of parent materials, *e.g.* felspars, micas, volcanic glasses, or ferromagnesian minerals. The principal clay mineral groups are as follows:

1. Kandite group, including kaolinite, dickite and nacrite, anauxite, halloysite, meta-halloysite and allophane.
2. Illite group, including illite, hydro-micas, phengite, brammallite, glauconite and celadonite.

Table 30.   SUMMARY OF THE PRINCIPAL CHARACTERISTICS OF THE CLAY MINERAL GROUPS

	Kandites	Illites	Smectites	Vermiculites
Structure type:	1:1 tetrahedral and octahedral components (di-phormic)	2:1 (triphormic)	2:1 (triphormic)	2:1 (triphormic)
Octahedral component:	di-octahedral	mostly di-octahedral	di- or tri-octahedral	mostly tri-octahedral
Principal inter-layer cations:	nil	K	Ca,Na	Mg
Inter-layer water:	only in halloysite (one layer water mols.)	some in hydromuscovite	Ca, two layers; Na, one layer water mols.	two layers
Basal spacing:	7·1 Å (10 Å in halloysite)	10 Å	variable; most $\simeq$ 15 Å (for Ca)	variable; 14·4 Å when fully hydrated
Glycol:	taken up by halloysite only	no effect	takes two layers glycol, 17 Å	takes one layer glycol, 14 Å
Chem. formula:	$Al_4Si_4O_{10}(OH)_8$, little variation	$K_{1.0-1.5}Al_4(Si,Al)_8O_{20}(OH)_4$	$M^+_{0.66}(Y^{+3},Y^{+2})_{4-6}(Si,Al)_8O_{20}$ $(OH)_4 nH_2O$	$M^{+2}_{0.66}(Y^{+2},Y^{+3})_6(Si,Al)_8O_{20}$ $(OH)_4 8H_2O$
Acids:	kaolinite scarcely soluble in dil. acids	readily attacked	attacked	readily attacked
Heating 200°C.	halloysite collapsed to 7·4 Å, others unchanged	no marked change	collapse to approx. 10 Å	exfoliation; shrinkage of layer spacing
Heating 650°C.	kaolinite→meta-kaolinite 7 Å dickite→meta-dickite strong 14 Å	10 Å	9·6–10 Å	collapse to 9 Å of talc
Optics α	1·55–1·56	1·54–1·57	1·48–1·51	1·52–1·57
γ	1·56–1·57	1·57–1·61	1·50–1·53	1·54–1·58
δ	$\simeq$ 0·006	$\simeq$ 0·03	0·01–0·02	0·02–0·03
2V	24°–50°	<10°	variable	<10°
Paragenesis:	alteration of acid rocks, felspars, etc. Acidic conditions	alteration of micas, felspars, etc. Alkaline conditions. High Al and K concentrations favourable	alteration of basic rocks, volcanic material. Alkaline conditions. Availability of Mg and Ca, deficiency of K	alteration of biotite flakes or of volcanic material, chlorites, hornblende, etc.

3. Smectite group, including montmorillonite, nontronite, hectorite, saponite and sauconite.

4. Vermiculite.

5. Palygorskite group, including palygorskite, attapulgite and sepiolite.

All except the fifth group are discussed in the following pages.   Table 30 lists very briefly some of the important characteristics of the various clay mineral groups.

Kaolinite Group (Kandites)

$Al_4[Si_4O_{10}](OH)_8$

TRICLINIC OR MONOCLINIC $(-)$

α 1·553–1·565†
β 1·559–1·569
γ 1·560–1·570
δ $\simeq 0\cdot006$
$2V_\alpha$ 24°–50°
$\beta : x = 1°–3\frac{1}{2}°$
$\gamma = y$
Dispersion :   Weak, $r > v$.
$\quad$ D   2·61–2·68
$\quad$ H   2–2$\frac{1}{2}$

O.A.P. $\perp$ (010).

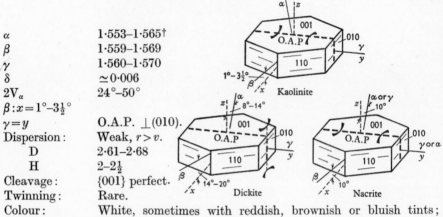

Kaolinite   Dickite   Nacrite

Cleavage :   {001} perfect.
Twinning :   Rare.
Colour :   White, sometimes with reddish, brownish or bluish tints; colourless in thin section.
Pleochroism :   Very slight. Least absorption for vibration direction perpendicular to cleavage plane.
Unit cell :† a 5·15, b 8·95, c 7·39 Å, d_{001} 7·15 Å
$\qquad \alpha$ 91·8°, β 104·8, γ 90°.
$\qquad Z = 1$. Space group $P1$.
$\quad$ Attacked by HCl.

† These values all refer to kaolinite *sensu stricto*.

Kaolinite is the most important of a number of minerals which, because of similarities in composition and/or structure, are classified together as the kaolinite group. The rock or aggregate which contains these minerals is often called china clay and sometimes "kaolin" (a corruption of the Chinese meaning "high ridge", which is the name of a hill where the substance occurs). Among the clay minerals, those of the kaolinite group are perhaps the most restricted in the ranges of composition and properties which they exhibit, and their particle sizes are often large enough for the microscopic and X-ray examination of single-crystals. Other members of the kaolinite group are dickite and nacrite (two rarer polymorphs which yield well formed crystals), anauxite (a mineral with higher $SiO_2 : Al_2O_3$ ratio), halloysite (a hydrated form of kaolinite), and meta-halloysite (the dehydration product of halloysite).[1] Minerals of the kaolinite

[1] The terms halloysite and meta-halloysite are used in this sense throughout the present text, following the proposals by the Clay Minerals Group sub-committee on nomenclature of clay minerals (Brown, 1955). These, or an alternative definition by which they are respectively called "endellite" and "halloysite", have been advocated by various writers (see Alexander *et al.*, 1943; MacEwan, 1947; Faust, 1955).

group are sometimes described as "kaolin minerals" and more recently the term "kandite" has come into use (Brown, 1955). The principal uses of china clay are in the manufacture of ceramic ware. It is also used as a whitening agent for textile and paper manufacture and as a filler or extender for paper, rubber, paints, etc.

STRUCTURE

The essential features of the structures of kaolinite minerals were first described by Pauling (1930). The fundamental unit is an extended sheet which can be regarded as having two constituents. A layer of composition $(Si_4O_{10})^{-4}$ is formed by the linkage of SiO_4 tetrahedra in a hexagonal array, the bases of tetrahedra being approximately coplanar and their vertices all pointing in one direction. The apical oxygens, together with some additional $(OH)^-$ ions located over the centres of hexagons, form the base of a "gibbsite" layer of composition $(OH)_6-Al_4-(OH)_2O_4$. Plan and elevation views of this composite $Al_4Si_4O_{10}(OH)_8$ layer are shown in Figs. 45a, b. Only two out of each set of three available sites are occupied by Al ions so that even a layer of ideal dimensions would not possess three-fold symmetry. A complete structure determination must describe the mode of stacking of successive sheets and attempts were made to determine this by Gruner (1932) and Hendricks (1936). From X-ray powder photographs Gruner deduced for kaolinite a two-layered monoclinic cell with a 5·14, b 8·90, c 14·51 Å and β 100° 12′. Brindley and Robinson (1946) were unable to index all the reflections obtained from kaolinite on the basis of this cell, and found that an adequate cell was triclinic with

a 5·15, b 8·95, c 7·39 Å,
α 91·8°, β 104·5–105·0°, γ 90°

thus containing only one layer. The three alternative sets of two $[Al]^6$ sites which may be occupied are equivalent if only one ideal layer is considered, but when a second layer is superimposed different structures are produced according to the direction of its displacement with respect to the first. It was found that of the several possible combinations of displacement and occupation of octahedral sites only one gave

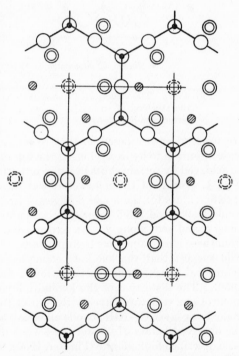

Heights of atoms above (001)

◯ Oxygen at 0　◎ OH at 4·31　⊘ Al at 3·25Å
🅐 Oxygen at 2·19　⬡ OH at 2·19　● Si at 0·60 Å

Fig. 45(a). Projection of idealized kaolinite layer on (001) (after Brindley and Robinson, 1946).

good agreement between observed and calculated X-ray intensities. Investigations of the kaolinite minerals have shown that successive layers

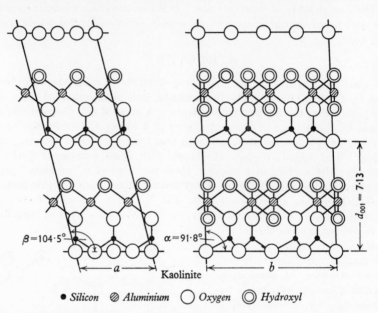

FIG. 45(b). The structure of kaolinite as viewed along y and x axes, showing the stacking of successive layers in the x and y directions respectively (after Brindley, 1951).

are usually superimposed so that oxygens at the base of one are paired by close approach to hydroxyl ions at the top of its neighbour (Fig. 46). This can be achieved by certain shifts in either or both of the x and y directions, which are $\pm (0, \frac{1}{6}, \frac{1}{3}$ or $\frac{1}{2})$ of the relevant repeat distances, and each of these result in specific values for the α and β angles. In an ideal kaolinite structure α and β would be 90° and 103·5° respectively as a result of layer displacements of $-a/3$ along x and zero along y. An explanation of the deviation of α and β angles from these ideal values has been put forward by Brindley and Nakahira (1958a) who suggest that the kaolinite structure involves distorted tetrahedral and octahedral layers similar to those found for dickite (Newnham and Brindley, 1956). The distortion of the kaolinite layer (Fig. 46) modifies the displacement of one structural layer with respect to its neighbour which is required to make inter-layer $O-(OH)$ bonds all equal, and results in α and β angles near to the observed values 91·6° and 104·8°. A different single-layered unit cell has been described for kaolinite (Pinsker, 1950), on the basis of single-crystal electron diffraction patterns which give a 5·14, b 8·92, c 7·34 Å, β 103° 5', and space group Cm. The one-layered triclinic structure of kaolinite is assigned incorrectly in various texts to the space groups Cc or $P\bar{1}$, when its true space group can only be $P1$.

The minerals dickite and nacrite are chemically identical to kaolinite but have their layers stacked in alternative regular sequences. Thus dickite has a 2-layered monoclinic cell (Newnham and Brindley, 1956) and nacrite has a

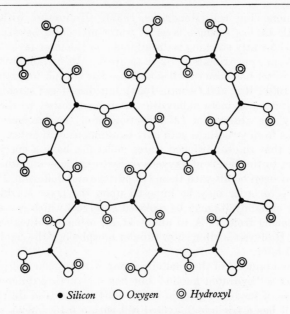

● *Silicon*   ○ *Oxygen*   ◎ *Hydroxyl*

FIG. 46.   Projection on (001) of Si–O network and adjacent
(OH) layer showing pairing of oxygens and hydroxyls
and distortion of six-membered rings in dickite (after
Newnham and Brindley, 1956).

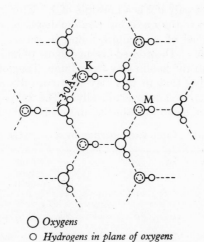

○ *Oxygens*
○ *Hydrogens in plane of oxygens*
◌ *Hydrogens below plane of oxygens*

FIG. 47.   Possible arrangement of oxygens and hydrogens in
layer of water molecules between clay mineral sheets.   One
hydrogen atom in each of the molecules K, L, M is not
involved in bonding within the net, but serves to join the net
to oxygens of the neighbouring silicate layer (after Hendricks
and Jefferson, 1938).

6-layered monoclinic cell (Hendricks, 1938). Halloysite, with formula Al_4Si_4 $(OH)_8O_{10}\cdot 4H_2O$, has a single layer of water molecules between its structural sheets; consequently stacking is disordered and the inter-layer distance (d_{001}) is increased from approximately 7·2 Å to 10 Å. In metahalloysite most of the inter-layer water has been expelled and d_{001} has shrunk to approximately 7·4 Å (Brindley, 1951; Roy and Osborn, 1954), but disordered stacking remains. In both halloysite and meta-halloysite this is manifested in the X-ray powder patterns by the absence of hkl reflections and the presence of "bands" of scattering as from structures with only two-dimensional order. In halloysite it is probable that the sandwiched water molecules have a specific arrangement with respect to the sheets of oxygens or hydroxyl ions on either side (Fig. 47), forming hydrogen bonds with them (Hendricks and Jefferson, 1938); as a result some degree of order may be imposed upon the layer stacking. The inter-layer water of halloysite may be replaced by glycol which causes an increase in the d_{001} spacing from 10 Å to about 11 Å; other kandites show no swelling property. Halloysites often show tubular morphology the significance of which is discussed later.

An unusual mineral of the kaolinite group with tubular morphology has been described as a "hydrated kaolin" but has a structure different from that of halloysite or of kaolinite (Honjo *et al.*, 1954). Electron diffraction diagrams show that it has a triclinic 2-layered cell with a 5·15, b 8·95, $c \sin\beta$ 7·16 Å, α 91·8°, β 83°, γ 90°, and that in some specimens three-dimensional order is well developed. The cylinder axis of the tubes seen in electron micrographs has been identified as [100], [010] or [310]. Certain kaolinite specimens with normal platy morphology give X-ray patterns intermediate between those of kaolinite and halloysite in that sharp reflections occur in addition to basal reflections and certain hk-bands, but only if k is a multiple of 3. This indicates a regularity of stacking with respect to the x axis but random displacements by multiples of $b/3$ along y, and is typical of a kaolinite found in certain fireclays: in this case $\alpha = 90°$, and $\beta = 104\cdot5°$. Disordered arrangements of kaolinite layers frequently occur elsewhere, as in the kaolin clay from Pugu, Tanganyika (Robertson *et al.*, 1954): it is of interest that in this clay the more disordered crystals are not necessarily less well formed macroscopically. The cell parameters of the various kaolinite minerals are listed in Table 31 and each of them has its characteristic

Table 31. CELL PARAMETERS OF KAOLINITE MINERALS

Mineral	aÅ	bÅ	cÅ	$\alpha°$	$\beta°$	$\gamma°$	No. of layers per cell	System	Reference
Kaolinite	5·15	8·95	7·39	91·8	104·5 −105·0	90	1	triclinic	Brindley and Robinson, 1946
Dickite	5·15	8·95	14·42	90	96·8	90	2	monoclinic	Newnham and Brindley, 1956
Nacrite	5·15	8·96	43·0	90	90	90	6	monoclinic	Hendricks, 1938
Fireclay mineral	5·2	8·9	7·39	(layer displacements in y direction)				—	Brindley, 1951
Halloysite	5·2	8·9	10·1	(layer displacements in one or more directions: tubular)				—	Brindley, 1951
Meta-halloysite	5·2	8·9	7·2	(random layer displacements in x and y directions)				—	Brindley, 1951
"Tubular kaolin"	5·15	8·95	7·39	91·8	83	90	2	triclinic	Honjo *et al.*, 1954

X-ray powder pattern (Kerr *et al.*, 1950; Brindley, 1951, and others). However, specimens with structures intermediate between kaolinite and the partially ordered fireclay mineral are not uncommon and it is probable that intermediates between fireclay kaolinite and disordered halloysite also exist (Bramao *et al.*, 1952; Murray, 1954).

Electron micrographs of kaolinite, dickite and nacrite show their platy morphology, but those of halloysite reveal tubular particles (Bates *et al.*, 1950; Bates and Comer, 1959). A structural basis for this morphology can be appreciated when the kaolinite sheet is considered to consist of two parts, an octahedral gibbsite-like layer with repeat distance $b \simeq 8{\cdot}62$ Å and a tetrahedral Si_2O_5 network with $b \simeq 8{\cdot}93$ Å. Because of these unequal dimensions a composite sheet will tend to curve cylindrically about the x axis with the octahedra on the inside. Curvature could alternatively occur about the y axis or some other direction in the plane of the layer, as indeed is the case for the "tubular kaolin" previously described (Fig. 48). In kaolinite, dickite and nacrite it has been suggested that hydrogen bonding between neighbouring layers is

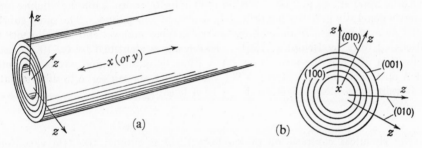

Fig. 48. Proposed relation of morphology to structure in halloysite.
(a). Tube in perspective.
(b). Cross-section showing crystallographic axes and planes
(after Bates *et al.*, 1950).

strong enough to overcome the tendency to curl whereas in halloysite the intervening water molecules and irregular stacking weaken the interlayer forces and allow rolling to relieve the strain inherent in a flat layer. In meta-halloysite the closer approach of layers will favour a tendency for tubes to split longitudinally so that many fractured and partially rolled tubes are formed and can be seen in electron micrographs. The exact structural relationship between "tubular kaolin" and halloysite has not been fully investigated. The tubular morphology of halloysite may be compared with that of chrysotile (see p. 171). In both cases sheet curvature occurs through mis-matching of the components of the sheet, but the curvatures are in opposite senses. Thus for halloysite the tetrahedral, and for chrysotile the octahedral, component lies on the outside of the curve. Bates (1959) assigns a morphological index M which gives a measure of the amount of misfit and which is related to the nature and amount of cation substitution in tetrahedral and octahedral sheets. The values of M range from about $+72$ for chrysotiles to -77 for halloysites. Bates remarks, however, that within the serpentine and kaolinite groups, although cation substitutions play an important role, the amount of hydrogen also provides an important distinction between platy and tubular varieties. In the kaolinite group the hydrogen content probably plays the dominant role in this respect.

Anauxite is the name given to specimens which resemble kaolinite in most respects but which have a higher $SiO_2 : Al_2O_3$ ratio. In structural terms this has been variously attributed to replacement of $[Al]^6$ by Si, or to vacancies in octahedral Al sites. A more plausible suggestion in view of the close similarity in diffraction patterns and d.t.a. curves of kaolinite and anauxite is that excess SiO_2 is present either in an ordered form as irregularly occurring layers of SiO_2 or $4SiO_2 \cdot H_2O$ (Hendricks, 1942), or as amorphous silica. Double layers of silica would occupy approximately 7·1 Å and therefore might not appreciably change the X-ray powder pattern (Brindley, 1951). Allophane is yet another mineral associated with the kaolinite group, which often occurs with halloysite. Its composition is similar to that of kaolinite or anauxite, and X-ray diffraction studies show that it is amorphous.

The kaolinite group can generally be distinguished from other clay minerals by their characteristic powder patterns containing basal reflections at about 7·14 and 3·57 Å, but certain chlorites may give similar patterns and other tests must be applied (see p. 208). Within the kaolinite group, kaolinite, dickite and nacrite generally give distinguishable patterns of sharp lines. The more subtle gradation of pattern from kaolinite to the fireclay mineral and to halloysite is discussed fully by Brindley (1951). Halloysite is identified by its 10 Å basal reflection which reduces to about 7·4 Å when dehydrated and swells to about 11 Å on treatment with glycol. This and other tests can serve to differentiate halloysite from illite which also has a 10 Å basal spacing.

CHEMISTRY

The chemical composition of kaolinite itself is subject to little variation. Analyses (Table 32) show that small amounts of various ions may substitute in the structure, but because of the fine-grained nature of clays it is difficult to be certain that impurities have been eliminated, so that the limits of substitution cannot easily be defined. However, the following averages of minor constituents are derived from a number of published analyses of kaolinite with little impurity:

$$TiO_2 \; 1 \cdot 0, \; Fe_2O_3 \; 0 \cdot 5, \; FeO \; 0 \cdot 1, \; MgO \; 0 \cdot 15, \; CaO \; 0 \cdot 3,$$
$$Na_2O \; 0 \cdot 3, \; K_2O \; 0 \cdot 5 \; \text{per cent.}$$

Titanium, iron and magnesium probably substitute for $[Al]^6$ while calcium, sodium and potassium are present either as adsorbed (exchange) cations, or in impurities of other clay minerals such as illite or montmorillonite. Dickite and nacrite do not differ chemically from kaolinite but halloysite is characterized by its higher content of H_2O^+. While the formula of kaolinite can be written in terms of oxides as $Al_2O_3 \cdot 2SiO_2 \cdot 2H_2O$, that of halloysite is ideally $Al_2O_3 \cdot 2SiO_2 \cdot 4H_2O$. In this fully hydrated form of halloysite, $2H_2O$ corresponds to structural (OH) ions and the remainder occurs as inter-layer water. Most, if not all, of the inter-layer water is not recorded in the H_2O^+ values presented in chemical analyses but appears as H_2O^-. The fact that H_2O^+ is generally somewhat higher for halloysite than for kaolinite may be attributed either to inter-layer water, or to substitution of $(OH)^-$ for O^{-2} within the sheet structure. Although minerals which structurally are tri-octahedral analogues of kaolinite (*e.g.* serpentine, amesite, chamosite, cronstedtite) are well known, substitution in kaolinite of (Mg,Fe) for Al, with or without Al for Si, leading towards tri-octahedral compositions, is negligible.

With the exception of halloysite the kandites show low cation exchange capacity compared with other clays. Because of their close adherence to the ideal chemical formula their structural layers are almost electrically neutral, but additional cations may be adsorbed at unsatisfied valencies at crystal edges and at local imperfections. In the kaolinite minerals a further basis for cation exchange could be the hydrogen ions of terminal $(OH)^-$ groups, and in halloysite some additional exchange may take place with hydrogens of inter-layer water molecules. As would be expected if edge and surface effects are predominant, the exchange capacity of kaolinites increases with decreasing particle size. Its value for kaolinite and meta-halloysite is usually about 10 m.eq./100 gm. dry weight, while an average value for halloysites is about 40 m.eq./100 gm. These may be compared with the values for montmorillonite and illite which are about 100 and 20 m.eq./100 gm. respectively. Measurements of ionization characteristics appear to show that the strength of bonding between kaolinite and exchange cations is rather weak. This, and the fact that the rate of the cation exchange reaction is most rapid for kaolinite, supports the thesis that cations are located at edges rather than between sheets. However, in the case of a kaolinite from Pugu, Tanganyika (Robertson *et al.*, 1954), an association is observed between higher exchange capacity (approximately 7·4 m.eq./100 gm.) and substitution of $[Al]^4$ for $[Si]^4$. While kaolinite shows a lower cation exchange capacity than most clay minerals, its anion exchange capacity is higher, and may be attributed to the presence of replaceable $(OH)^-$ ions on the outsides of the structural sheets. The ability of kaolinite to fix phosphate ions is of great importance in soil science (Haseman *et al.*, 1950; Low and Black, 1950). To the extent that kaolinite particles can adsorb cations, a similar exchange can take place with charged organic ions (*e.g.* organo-substituted ammonium ions), and moreover with neutral organic molecules. The latter (*e.g.* glycol or glycerol) are known to possess a dipole character by which they may be attached to charged sites on crystal surfaces. Halloysite is penetrated freely by organic liquids replacing the inter-layer water, which itself is bound because of the dipole nature of the water molecules. Only one layer of water enters each space as compared with two for vermiculite, perhaps because of the polar nature of the kaolinite sheet as compared with the symmetrical sheet of vermiculite (MacEwan, 1948). Moreover in the latter mineral the presence of inter-layer cations allows the formation of hydration shells which may in turn promote the entry of two layers of water molecules. It appears that the presence of water between the layers facilitates the entry of organic liquids, since partially dehydrated halloysite takes up less organic liquid, and completely dehydrated halloysite (meta-halloysite) and kaolinite itself take up least of all.

Closely related to the adsorption of organic liquids is the property of staining (Faust, 1940; Weil-Malherbe and Weiss, 1948; Milenz *et al.*, 1951). Members of the kaolinite group when pure are not stained by benzidine, whereas montmorillonites are stained blue. Untreated or acid treated kaolinite absorbs the red dye *safranine y* and the green dye *malachite green*, and becomes pleochroic. With *safranine y* the colours adopted are yellow-red and reddish purple perpendicular and parallel to the cleavage respectively. With *malachite green* the corresponding colours are blue and yellow-green. Halloysite absorbs dyes

Table 32.　Analyses of kaolinite minerals

	1.	2.	3.	4.	5.
SiO_2	45·80	46·07	45·72	45·48	46·14
TiO_2	—	0·50	0·42	0·86	—
Al_2O_3	39·55	38·07	39·82	38·84	39·61
Fe_2O_3	0·57	0·33	0·10	0·19	—
FeO	0·18	—	—	—	—
MgO	0·14	0·01	—	0·17	—
CaO	0·41	0·38	—	0·24	—
Na_2O	—	0·27	0·16	0·24	—
K_2O	0·03	0·43	0·36	0·42	—
H_2O^+	13·92	13·47	13·67	13·66	13·91
H_2O^-	0·17	0·43	0·55	0·71	—
P_2O_5	—	—	—	—	—
Total	100·77	99·96	100·80	100·81	99·66
α	1·562	—	—	—	1·560
β	1·566	—	—	—	1·562
γ	1·568	—	—	—	1·566
2V	—	—	—	—	fairly large(+)

Numbers of ions on the basis of 18(O,OH)

Si	3·94	4·02	3·95	3·94	3·98
Al	4·01⎱	3·91⎱	4·05⎱	3·97⎱	4·03⎱
Ti	—	0·03	0·03	0·06	—
Fe^{+3}	0·04 ⎬4·08	0·02 ⎬3·96	0·01 ⎬4·09	0·01 ⎬4·06	— ⎬4·03
Fe^{+2}	0·01	—	—	—	—
Mg	0·02⎰	0·00⎰	—⎰	0·02⎰	—⎰
Ca	0·04	0·04	—	0·02	—
Na	—	0·05	0·03	0·04	—
K	0·00	0·05	0·04	0·05	—
OH	7·98	7·83	7·97	7·90	8·00

1. Hypogene kaolinite, hydrothermal veins of Cu–Pb–Zn ore, Mikawo mine, Niigata, Japan (Nagasawa, 1953).
2. Kaolinite, Mesa Alta, New Mexico, containing 3·61 per cent. impurities (Kerr *et al.*, 1950).　Anal. Ledoux & Co., New York.
3. Kaolinite, Lewistown, Montana, containing 2·56 per cent. impurities (Kerr *et al.*, 1950). Anal. Ledoux & Co., New York.
4. Kaolinite, Murfreesboro, Arkansas, containing 2·81 per cent. impurities (Kerr *et al.*, 1950).　Anal. Ledoux & Co., New York.
5. White to yellowish dickite crystals, Schuylkill Co., Pennsylvania (Honess and Williams, 1935).　Anal. G. A. Brady.

Table 32.   ANALYSES OF KAOLINITE MINERALS—*continued*

	6.	7.	8.	9.	10.
SiO_2	44·87	46·15	45·99	44·46	43·98
TiO_2	0·64	—	—	0·15	0·01
Al_2O_3	38·04	38·93	39·16	36·58	38·46
Fe_2O_3	1·67†	—	0·34	0·36	—
FeO	—	—	—	0·07	0·03
MgO	0·28	0·36	0·09	0·18	—
CaO	0·17	0·27	0·17	0·19	0·32
Na_2O	—	—	0·14	0·01	0·14
K_2O	0·12	—	0·27	0·51	0·48
H_2O^+	14·41‡	14·19‡	13·70‡	13·38	14·59
H_2O^-	—	—	—	4·05	2·58
P_2O_5	—	—	—	0·18	—
Total	100·20	99·90	99·86	100·12	100·59
α	1·560–1·561	1·561	1·560	—	—
β	—	1·563	1·563	—	—
γ	1·566–1·567	1·566	1·566	—	—
2V	50°(+)	—	80°(−)	—	—

NUMBERS OF IONS ON THE BASIS OF 18(O,OH)§

	6.	7.	8.	9.	10.
Si	3·91	3·99	3·97	4·01	3·85
Al	3·91⎫	3·97⎫	3·99⎫	3·89⎫	3·97⎫
Ti	0·04⎪	—⎪	—⎪	0·01⎪	0·01⎪
Fe^{+3}	0·11⎬4·10	—⎬4·02	0·02⎬4·02	0·02⎬3·95	—⎬3·98
Fe^{+2}	—⎪	—⎪	—⎪	0·01⎪	—⎪
Mg	0·04⎭	0·05⎭	0·01⎭	0·02⎭	—⎭
Ca	0·02	0·03	0·02	0·02	0·03
Na	—	—	0·02	0·00	0·02
K	0·01	—	0·03	0·06	0·05
OH	8·00	8·00	8·00	8·04	8·52

6. Massive dickite, with alunite, altered porphyry, Kara-cheku massif, Karkaralinsk, Kazakh steppe (Nakovnik, 1940).   Anal. M. P. Vasilievoi.
7. Dickite, vein in altered porphyrite, Shokozan, Japan (Yoshiki, 1934).
8. White scaly mineral with pearly lustre believed to be nacrite, hydrothermal vein, albite diabase, Eski-Orda, Simferopol, Crimea (Nikogosyan, 1934).
9. White halloysite, Bedford, Indiana (Kerr *et al.*, 1950).   Anal. Geol. Soc. Amer. Rock Analysis Laboratory.
10. Halloysite, Eureka, Utah (Kerr *et al.*, 1950).   Anal. Geol. Soc. Amer. Rock Analysis Laboratory.

† Total iron determined as Fe_2O_3.
‡ Ignition loss.
§ For anals. 6, 7, 8, H_2O^+ was not determined separately; the formula is therefore calculated without using the ignition loss figure, by assuming 10 O's and 8 (OH)'s, *i.e.* on a basis of the equivalent of 14 O's per formula unit.

in a similar but blotchy fashion but does not become pleochroic, while single crystals of dickite and nacrite are not appreciably stained but become weakly pleochroic.   Fine-grained aggregates of dickite and nacrite, however, do take up a stain.   (Montmorillonite stains purple-blue with *safranine y* and orange-yellow with *malachite green*.)   The staining tests are not absolutely conclusive since anomalous behaviour sometimes occurs, and care must be taken over the presence of impurities, for example montmorillonite or non-clay minerals in kaolinite clays.

The solubility of kaolinite in sulphuric acid is very low, but halloysite and poorly crystalline kaolinite are both more readily attacked.

Differential thermal analysis and dehydration experiments are widely used for the characterization and identification of clays.   The dehydration of halloysite proceeds in a number of stages.   Some of its adsorbed water (surface and inter-layer) is lost on heating to 110°C. as with any other mineral, but the remainder comes off gradually and is not completely expelled until about 400°C.   A partially hydrated halloysite may be produced (by dehydration at room temperature in conditions of low humidity) which contains about one instead of four water molecules per formula unit and which is characterized by a basal reflection at about 7·4 Å in its X-ray powder pattern (Brindley and Goodyear, 1948).   The dehydration of halloysite producing meta-halloysite is generally not reversible; once kaolinite layers have been brought into close contact, water cannot re-enter between them, and the split tubular particles cannot be re-assembled.   MacEwan (1946) has shown, however, that the meta-halloysite which is produced by gentle dehydration of halloysite and which probably retains some inter-layer water, can be glycollated, and following this it can be completely re-hydrated, thus regenerating halloysite.   For kaolinite, little or no surface adsorbed water is present and most of the dehydration (loss of con-stitutional OH) takes place between 400° and 525°C. (Ross and Kerr, 1931): the temperature varies with particle size and other experimental conditions, and a similar range is observed for anauxite.   The dehydration process is indicated in a d.t.a. pattern by an endothermic peak occurring for kaolinite and anauxite at 400°–600°C.   For dickite and nacrite this peak occurs at about 100°C. higher and this may be largely a result of greater particle size, rather than an indication of higher stability (Roy and Brindley, 1956).   Similarly the endothermic peak corresponding to loss of (OH) is slightly lower for halloy-site than for kaolinite (Grimshaw *et al.*, 1945) and this may be related to its finer state of subdivision.   Carthew (1955) describes a method for quantitative estimation of kaolinite by differential thermal analysis in which the influence of particle size and crystallinity is minimized.

When the kaolinite minerals are heated so that all water molecules and (OH) ions are driven off (a stage which is almost reached by about 650°C. for the majority of specimens and is complete by 800°C. for all), the products are called meta-kaolinite, meta-dickite, etc.   These are generally highly disordered, but X-ray and electron diffraction patterns show that some order remains (Brindley and Hunter, 1955; Roy *et al.*, 1955).   The nature of the meta phases is not known in detail, but all are similar in that they yield a fairly well ordered kaolinite (not dickite or halloysite) on rehydration by prolonged hydrothermal treatment at 200°–400°C. and at pressures of 2000 to 20,000 lb./in.^{2} (Van Niewenberg and Pieters, 1929; Roy and Brindley, 1956).   An unusual feature of meta-dickite is that its powder pattern shows a strong 14 Å reflection which is not given by dickite itself nor by any of the other kaolinite minerals (Hill, 1955): this behaviour is similar to that found for certain serpentine minerals (Nelson and Roy, 1954; Brindley and Zussman, 1957).

The dehydration corresponding to the endothermic peak which occurs at about 400°–600°C. for kaolinite minerals has been investigated in detail by several workers (Murray and White, 1955; Brindley and Nakahira, 1957). Isothermal weight loss measurements have shown that the rate constants are markedly dependent on factors such as specimen size, shape and compaction. This dependence is attributed to the retention of water vapour within the specimens. For infinitely thin disc-type specimens the reactions are strictly first order and the Arrhenius relation $k = \text{constant} \times \exp(-E/RT)$ is obeyed (k = reaction rate constant, E = activation energy, T = absolute temperature).

When kaolinite minerals are heated beyond 800°C. their layered structures are further disrupted and cannot be reconstituted by rehydration. Many workers have investigated the products of decomposition at various temperatures, and have attempted correlation with the large sharp d.t.a. exothermic peak at 900°–1000°C., and almost as many different conclusions have been reached. Insley and Ewell (1935) attributed the exothermic peak to the formation of γ-Al_2O_3 from amorphous alumina and the later formation of mullite, while others relate it to the crystallization of mullite from meta-kaolinite. The results obtained may vary with the crystallinity of the parent kaolinite and with the nature of the heating process. Thus, well ordered kaolinite, when heated to 1000°C. and then quenched, yields more mullite than does a disordered specimen (Johns, 1953), and for halloysite (which is further disordered) mullite is only apparent after firing at 1100°C. According to Richardson (1951) γ-alumina is formed between 900°C. and 1050°C., cristobalite between 1100° and 1300°C., and mullite between 950° and 1350°C. Mullite often appears as needles which have a definite orientation with respect to the original kaolinite crystal, suggesting that it forms before the kaolinite structure is completely disrupted (Comeforo *et al.*, 1948). It has been suggested that although for disordered minerals no mullite is observed at or beyond the temperature of the exothermic reaction, mullite nevertheless has been formed but is very poorly crystalline: if the high temperature is maintained, crystallization of mullite becomes apparent. More recent observations on the decomposition of kaolinite (Steadman and Youell, 1957; Brindley and Nakahira, 1958b) suggest that at no stage does γ-alumina occur. The substance previously described as γ-alumina is in fact a silicon spinel which has a defect structure in which the number of defects depends upon the Si:Al ratio. Brindley and Nakahira (1958b) represent the reaction sequence as follows:

$$Al_2O_3 \cdot 2SiO_2 \cdot 2H_2O \xrightarrow[500°C.]{} Al_2O_3 \cdot 2SiO_2 + 2H_2O$$
$$\underset{\text{kaolinite}}{} \qquad \underset{\text{meta-kaolinite}}{}$$

$$2(Al_2O_3 \cdot 2SiO_2) \xrightarrow[925°C.]{} 2Al_2O_3 \cdot 3SiO_2 + SiO_2$$
$$\underset{\text{silicon spinel}}{}$$

$$2Al_2O_3 \cdot 3SiO_2 \xrightarrow[1100°C.]{} 2(Al_2O_3 \cdot SiO_2) + SiO_2$$
$$\underset{\text{1:1 mullite-type}}{} \quad \underset{\text{cristobalite}}{}$$
$$\underset{\text{phase}}{}$$

$$3(Al_2O_3 \cdot SiO_2) \xrightarrow[\text{above 1400°C.}]{} 3Al_2O_3 \cdot 2SiO_2 + SiO_2$$
$$\underset{\text{3:2 mullite}}{} \quad \underset{\text{cristobalite}}{}$$

The above interpretation is more satisfactory than one in which alumina and silica are first separated and later recombined to form mullite. Moreover structural coherence, through persistence of oxygen layer arrangements, can be maintained throughout the sequence kaolin–meta-kaolin–silicon spinel–mullite. At temperatures too low for the formation of cristobalite, SiO_2 is believed to be present as amorphous silica. Glass (1954) points out that the varying nature of the results of decomposition experiments may in some cases be attributed to the presence of impurities, such as mica. According to Glass the d.t.a. curves show a second exothermic peak at about 1200°C. corresponding to the formation of mullite and SiO_2, and another at about 1300°C. where excess silica is converted to cristobalite, but these temperatures relate to the precise non-equilibrium conditions of the particular experiments and are only to be taken as sequentially significant.

Synthesis. The hydrothermal synthesis of kaolinite, and in some cases dickite and nacrite, has been achieved by many workers commencing with gels of suitable Al_2O_3–SiO_2 or $Al(OH)_3$–SiO_2 composition at temperatures between 250° and 400°C. (Ewall and Insley, 1935; Permyakov, 1936; Noll, 1944). Kaolinite has also been prepared by treating felspars with dilute HCl at temperatures up to 350°C. (Schwarz and Trageser, 1933; Gruner, 1944; and others), and various clay minerals including kaolinite have been synthesized at low temperatures by mixing very dilute solutions of a silicate, or silicate and aluminate, with dilute solutions of an Mg or Al salt (Caillère and Hénin, 1947; Hénin and Robichet, 1953). The phase equilibrium relationships in the system Al_2O_3–SiO_2–H_2O, under conditions of independently controlled temperature and water-vapour pressure, have been investigated (Roy and Osborne, 1954), the kaolinite minerals being synthesized from co-precipitated Al_2O_3–SiO_2 gels between 150° and 405°C. under varying water pressures. Although positive identification of dickite and nacrite as distinct from kaolinite was not possible, there appeared to be no difference in the upper stability limit for the three minerals. All kaolinite minerals decomposed at approximately 405°C. throughout the range of pressures 2500 to 25,000 lb./in.^{2}. The main product of hydrothermal decomposition of kaolinite is hydralsite, a substance with approximate formula $2Al_2O_3 \cdot 2SiO_2 \cdot H_2O$ which has not been found in nature. Its structure has not been determined but its composition and cell parameters (a 5·14, b 8·90, d_{001} 8·91 Å) suggest a similarity to pyrophyllite. Under certain conditions pyrophyllite itself accompanies hydralsite as a decomposition product of kaolinite. The synthetic investigations throw further light on the question of mullite formation. In hydrothermal equilibrium conditions above 575°C. kaolinite is completely converted to mullite and cristobalite. Equilibrium studies also show that the decomposition temperatures for dickite, nacrite and halloysite are equal to that for kaolinite, so that the differences noted in d.t.a. analyses may be the result of particle size influence only. The synthesis of halloysite or meta-halloysite was not achieved, nor has halloysite been formed from meta-halloysite, but it seems that halloysite has an upper stability limit of about 175°C. at about 5000 lb./in.^{2} and that meta-halloysite is formed only as a dehydration product of halloysite.

OPTICAL AND PHYSICAL PROPERTIES

The kaolinite minerals may occur in compact massive blocks, in vermiform or granular aggregates, as radiating platelets, or as piles of platelets (or "books"), the latter form being particularly common for dickite. The tabular morphology of kaolinite may not be apparent under the microscope when the mineral occurs in fine-grained aggregates, but it can be readily observed in electron micrographs, and occasionally crystals occur as much as 2 mm. in length. Their perfect {001} cleavage yields flexible but inelastic plates which are sometimes large enough for determination of optical properties. Such measurements must, however, be interpreted with care since they may be considerably affected by the presence of impurities and/or adsorbed water. Penetration of the crystals by organic liquid immersion media changes the refractive indices of some clay minerals but does not affect kaolinite or meta-halloysite. Birefringence measurements, however, may vary according to the immersion liquid used, indicating that the particles are small enough for form birefringence to be superimposed upon true birefringence.

Kaolinite and anauxite have similar optical properties and these are compared with the values for dickite and nacrite in Table 33.

Table 33. OPTICAL PROPERTIES OF KANDITE MINERALS

	α	β	γ	δ	2V	Sign	β:x
Kaolinite	1·553–1·565	1·559–1·569	1·560–1·570	0·006	24°–50°	(−)	1°–3½°
Dickite	1·560–1·564	1·561–1·566	1·566–1·570	0·006	50°–80°	(+)	14°–20°
Nacrite	1·557–1·560	1·562–1·563	1·563–1·566	0·006	40°–90°	(+)(−)	10°

For the fine-grained specimens only an average refractive index can be measured, which for halloysite is lower than for kaolinite (approximately 1·530). Meta-halloysite has an average refractive index between 1·55 and 1·56 and a lower birefringence, approximately 0·002 (Correns and Mehmel, 1936). In all of the crystalline varieties γ is parallel to y and the optic plane perpendicular to (010).

Electron micrographs of kaolinite show a high proportion of particles with well defined straight edges and sometimes thin elongated plates with prominent 60° angles. Dickite usually shows still more of these well formed pseudo-hexagonal crystals while nacrite, anauxite and allophane particles are more irregular. There is usually a wide distribution of particle sizes in these minerals but the average dimension for kaolinites is about 0·04 μ. Halloysite has a fibrous rather than platy morphology and moreover the fibres, unlike those of amphibole asbestos, appear in electron micrographs to be tubular or roll-like. Sometimes the appearance is of a ribbon with edges curled up, and sometimes of a roll which has uncurled at its ends giving a spatula shape; the latter occurs particularly for meta-halloysite (Bates *et al.*, 1950; Bates and Comer, 1959). Study of numerous electron micrographs of kandite minerals (Bates, 1959) has shown that there is a complete morphological range from well crystallized hexagonal plates of kaolinite, through elongated plates, laths with definite crystallographic terminations, and curved laths, to tubes of halloysite. Possible explanations of tubular morphology in terms of atomic structure have already been discussed. The tubes have an average outside diameter of 0·04 μ and average wall thickness of 0·02 μ. Tubular morphology has also been observed for some kaolinite specimens (Honjo *et al.*, 1954; Visconti *et al.*, 1956).

The density of a clay mineral cannot easily be determined with precision since it varies considerably with state of hydration. For kaolinite, values of about 2·63 gm./cm.^{3} are usually obtained and are reproducible, but halloysites may vary from 2·55 gm./cm.^{3} for dehydrated material to 2·0 gm./cm.^{3}, according to water content. The density of dickite and of nacrite is approximately 2·60 gm./cm.^{3} which is close to the theoretical value. Halloysite and montmorillonite can be separated from each other and from other natural clay constituents by a method of flotation in a solution of alcohol in bromoform (Loughnan, 1957). In this solution, the apparent specific gravities of halloysite and montmorillonite are approximately 2·2 and 1·85 respectively.

The plastic properties of kaolinite and other clay minerals when mixed with water are well known, but are not fully understood. There is an optimum amount of water required to produce maximum plasticity and various views are held as to the number of layers of water molecules which are adsorbed on clay particles. There is evidence that the water molecules are arranged in a definite pattern rather than in a disordered liquid state, and that they are probably linked by hydrogen bonds to each other and to the oxygen and hydroxyl ions on the outsides of kaolinite layers: the adsorbed water is said to be more dense and more viscous than ordinary water (see Grim, 1943). Various arrangements of water molecules have been suggested and discussed, for example by Hendricks and Jefferson (1938), Barshad (1949), Williamson (1951), and others. The adsorption of water in clays can be considerably influenced by the presence of cations or anions, which in the case of kaolinites may themselves be adsorbed on crystal surfaces.

DISTINGUISHING FEATURES

Optical properties, if available, can be used to distinguish kaolinite from dickite and nacrite. Dickite is optically positive, has a lower refractive index and $\beta:x = 14°–20°$; nacrite is negative but also has a greater extinction angle $\beta:x$. Sericite and montmorillonite have greater birefringence and the latter has a lower refractive index. X-ray powder patterns of untreated and of heated and glycollated specimens may, however, be necessary, in conjunction with d.t.a., staining, and other tests, in order to distinguish fine-grained kaolinite minerals from each other and from other clay and non-clay layered minerals (Brindley, 1951; Kerr *et al.*, 1951; Grim, 1953; Mackenzie, 1957).

PARAGENESIS

Probably the most common of the clay minerals are those of the kaolinite group and they are formed (often accompanied by quartz, iron oxides, pyrite, siderite and muscovite, and by other clay minerals) principally by the alteration of felspars, felspathoids and other silicates either hydrothermally or by weathering. In the hydrothermal alteration of ore deposits there is sometimes a zoning of clay mineral products mostly with kaolinite lying between sericite, which is closest to the vein, and chlorite on the outside. A detailed study of hydrothermal alteration in the Front Range mineral belt, Colorado, has been made by Bonorino (1959). Kaolinite is the only member of the kandite group found in association with veins of this mineral belt, where it appears replacing plagioclase and, to a lesser extent, biotite, hornblende and microcline. Six different patterns of zoning were noted, in four of which kaolinite occurs (other zones are: hydromica, orthoclase, montmorillonite and phlogopite), and their origin is explained in terms of chemical fronts developed by migrating gaseous fluids. The critical changes in fluid composition responsible for zone formation are increase of Si:Al ratio, decrease of K concentration, and increase of pH. Synthetic work indicates that at low temperatures and pressures, acid conditions favour kaolinite formation, and alkaline conditions promote the formation of smectites, or if sufficient potassium is present, mica (above about 400°C. at moderate pressures pyrophyllite is formed.) Field occurrences indicate that the rocks which alter to kaolinite are usually the more acid types (granites, quartz diorites, etc.) while calcium- or sodium-rich rocks generally yield montmorillonite. The kaolin sandstones of Pugu, Tanganyika, for example are derived from migmatites, biotite gneisses and granites. Kaolinite can also be derived from impure limestones and from porphyritic volcanic rocks and is sometimes found in iron ore veins and in cavities in quartz veins. The kaolinite produced by alteration sometimes occurs *in situ* (*e.g.* the hydrothermal deposits of Cornish kaolin), but more often is a product of weathering and transportation. Again non-alkaline conditions are required for kaolinite formation, and weathering by alkaline rather than acid (or pure) water generally yields montmorillonite (Kerr *et al.*, 1951). Primary mica and secondary mica formed by weathering of felspar usually alters to vermicular kaolinites (Sand, 1956). Some indication of the processes involved are given by the synthetic studies previously mentioned. Halloysite frequently occurs with kaolinite, and circumstances sometimes imply that the halloysite was formed first and was replaced by kaolinite. Structurally more plausible are the cases where halloysite is formed later by the action of sulphate-bearing solutions on kaolinite, leading to gel formation and subsequent recrystallization (Ross and Kerr, 1934; Brindley and Comer, 1956). Halloysite may also form independently of associated kaolinite (Sand, 1956) and it is often accompanied by allophane, or by alunite, $KAl_3(OH)_6(SO_4)_2$. Dickite and nacrite do not occur in sediments but usually have a hydrothermal origin; thus dickite is found associated with quartz and with sulphides of hydrothermal origin, and nacrite occurs in a similar environment and has also been found with cryolite and with mica.

REFERENCES

Alexander, L. T., Faust, G. T., Hendricks, S. B., Ensley, H. and McMurdie, H. F., 1943. Relationship of the clay minerals halloysite and endellite. *Amer. Min.*, vol. 28, p. 1.

Barshad, I., 1949. The nature of lattice expansion and its relation to hydration in montmorillonite and vermiculite. *Amer. Min.*, vol. 34, p. 675.

Bates, T. F., 1959. Morphology and crystal chemistry of 1:1 layer lattice silicates. *Amer. Min.*, vol. 44, p. 78.

—— and Comer, J. J., 1959. Further observations on the morphology of chrysotile and halloysite. *Clays and Clay minerals.* Monograph No. 2. Pergamon Press.

—— Hildebrand, F. A. and Swineford, A., 1950. Morphology and structure of endellite and halloysite. *Amer. Min.*, vol. 35, p. 463.

Bonorino, F. G., 1959. Hydrothermal alteration in the Front Range mineral belt, Colorado. *Bull. Geol. Soc. Amer.*, vol. 70, p. 53.

Bramao, L., Cady, J. G., Hendricks, S. B. and **Swerdlow, M.**, 1952. Criteria for the characterisation of kaolinite, halloysite and related minerals in clays and soils. *Soil Science*, vol. 73, p. 273 (M.A. 12–117).

Brindley, G. W., 1951. (Editor). *X-ray identification and crystal structures of clay minerals.* Min. Soc., London.

—— and **Comer, J. J.**, 1956. The structure and morphology of a kaolin clay from Les Eyzies (France). *Proc. Fourth Nat. Conf. Clays and Clay Minerals. U.S.A. Nat. Res. Council publ.*, 456, p. 61.

—— and **Goodyear, J.**, 1948. X-ray studies of halloysite and meta-halloysite. Part II. *Min. Mag.*, vol. 28, p. 407.

—— and **Hunter, K.**, 1955. The thermal reactions of nacrite and the formation of metakaolin, γ-alumina and mullite. *Min. Mag.*, vol. 30, p. 574.

—— and **Nakahira, M.**, 1957. Kinetics of dehydroxylation of kaolinite and halloysite. *Journ. Amer. Ceram. Soc.*, vol. 40, p. 346.

—— —— 1958a. Further consideration of the crystal structure of kaolinite. *Min. Mag.*, vol. 31, p. 781.

—— —— 1958b. A new concept of the transformation sequence of kaolinite to mullite. *Nature*, vol. 181, p. 1333.

—— and **Robinson, K.**, 1946. The structure of kaolinite. *Min. Mag.*, vol. 27, p. 242.

—— and **Zussman, J.**, 1957. A structural study of the thermal transformation of serpentine minerals to forsterite. *Amer. Min.*, vol. 42, p. 461.

Brown, G., 1955. Report of the clay minerals group sub-committee on nomenclature of the clay minerals. *Clay Min. Bull.*, vol. 2, p. 294.

Caillère, S. and **Hénin, S.**, 1947. Formation d'une phyllite du type kaolinique par traitement d'une montmorillonite. *Compt. Rend. Acad. Sci. Paris*, vol. 224, p. 53.

Carthew, A. R., 1955. The quantitative estimation of kaolinite by differential thermal analysis. *Amer. Min.*, vol. 40, p. 107.

Comeforo, J. E., Fischer, R. B. and **Bradley, W. F.**, 1948. Mullitization of kaolinite. *Journ. Amer. Ceram. Soc.*, vol. 31, p. 254.

Correns, C. W. and **Mehmel, M.**, 1936. Über den optischen und röntgenographischen Nachweis von Kaolinit, Halloysit und Montmorillonit. *Zeit. Krist.*, vol. 94, p. 337.

Ewell, R. H. and **Insley, H.**, 1935. Hydrothermal synthesis of kaolinite, dickite, beidellite and nontronite. *Journ. Research Nat. Bur. Standards, U.S.A.*, vol. 15, p. 173.

Faust, G. F., 1940. Staining of clay minerals as a rapid means of identification in natural and benefication products. *U.S. Bureau of Mines, Report.* Invest. 3522.

Faust, G. T., 1955. The endellite-halloysite nomenclature. *Amer. Min.*, vol. 40, p. 1110.

Glass, H. D., 1954. High temperature phases from kaolinite and halloysite. *Amer. Min.*, vol. 39, p. 193.

Grim, R. E., 1953. *Clay Mineralogy.* McGraw Hill, New York.

Grimshaw, R. W., Heaton, E. and **Roberts, A. L.**, 1945. Constitution of refractory clays II. Thermal analysis methods. *Trans. Brit. Ceram. Soc.*, vol. 44, p. 69.

Gruner, J. W., 1932. The crystal structure of kaolinite. *Zeit. Krist.*, vol. 83, p. 75.

—— 1944. Hydrothermal alteration of feldspars in acid solutions between 300 and 400°C. *Econ. Geol.*, vol. 29, p. 578.

Haseman, J. F., Brown, Earl H. and **Whitt, C. D.**, 1950. Some reactions of phosphate with clays and hydrous oxides of iron and aluminium. *Soil Science*, vol. 70, p. 257 (M.A. 11–343).

Hendricks, S. B., 1936. Concerning the crystal structure of kaolinite $Al_2O_3 \cdot 2SiO_2 \cdot 2H_2O$ and the composition of anauxite. *Zeit. Krist.*, vol. 95, p. 247.

—— 1938. Crystal structure of nacrite and the polymorphism of the kaolin minerals. *Zeit. Krist.*, vol. 100, p. 509.

—— 1942. Lattice structure of clay minerals and some properties of clays. *Journ. Geol.*, vol. 50, p. 276.

—— and **Jefferson, M. E.,** 1938. Structure of kaolin and talc-pyrophyllite hydrates and their bearing on water sorption of clays. *Amer. Min.*, vol. 23, p. 863.

Hénin, S. and **Robichet, O.,** 1953. Sur les conditions de formation des minéraux argileux, par voie experimentale, à basse temperature. *Compt. Rend. Acad. Sci. Paris*, vol. 236, p. 517.

Hill, R. D., 1955. 14 Å spacings in kaolin minerals. *Acta Cryst.*, vol. 8, p. 120.

Hofmann, U. and **Hausdorf, A.,** 1942. Kristallstruktur und innerkristalline Quellung der Montmorillonits. *Zeit. Krist.*, vol. 104, p. 265.

Honess, Arthur P. and **Williams, Francis, J.,** 1935. Dickite from Pennsylvania. *Amer. Min.*, vol. 20, p. 462.

Honjo, G., Kitamura, N. and **Mihama, K.,** 1954. A study of clay minerals by means of single-crystal electron diffraction diagrams—the structure of tubular kaolin. *Clay Min. Bull.*, vol. 2, p. 133.

Insley, H. and **Ewell, R. H.,** 1935. Thermal behaviour of kaolin minerals. *Journ. Research Nat. Bur. Standards, U.S.A.*, vol. 14, p. 615.

Johns, W. D., 1953. High temperature phase changes in kaolinites. *Min. Mag.*, vol. 30, p. 186.

Kerr, P. F., Hamilton, P. K. and **Pill, R. J.,** 1950. Analytical data on reference clay materials. Prelim. report no. 7. *Reference clay minerals. Amer. Petroleum Inst., Res. Proj.* 49. Columbia Univ., New York, p. 1.

—— and **others,** 1951. Preliminary reports. *Reference clay minerals. American Petroleum Institute; Research Project* 49. Columbia Univ., New York.

Loughnan, F. C., 1957. A technique for the isolation of montmorillonite and halloysite. *Amer. Min.*, vol. 42, p. 393.

Low, P. F. and **Black, C. A.,** 1950. Reactions of phosphate with kaolinite. *Soil Science*, vol. 70, p. 273.

MacEwan, D. M. C., 1946. Halloysite–organic complexes. *Nature*, vol. 157, p. 159.

—— 1947. The nomenclature of the halloysite minerals. *Min. Mag.*, vol. 28, p. 36.

—— 1948. Complexes of clays with organic compounds. I. *Trans. Faraday Soc.*, vol. 44, p. 349.

Mackenzie, R. C., 1957. (Editor). *The differential thermal investigation of clays.* Min. Soc., London.

Milenz, R. C., King, M. E. and **Schieltz, N. C.,** 1951. Analytical data on reference clay materials. Prelim. report no. 7. *Reference clay minerals. Amer. Petroleum Inst., Res. Proj. 49.* Columbia Univ., New York, p. 135.

Murray, H. H., 1954. Structural variations of some kaolinites in relation to dehydrated halloysite. *Amer. Min.*, vol. 39, p. 97.

Murray, P. and **White, J.,** 1955. Kinetics of the thermal dehydration of clays. *Trans. Brit. Ceram. Soc.*, vol. 54, pp. 137 and 151.

Nagasawa, K., 1953. Kaolinite from the Mikana mine, Niigata prefecture. *Journ. Earth Sci., Nagoya Univ.*, vol. 1, p. 9 (M.A. 12–492).

Nakovnik, N. I., 1940. Dickite from secondary quartzites of the Kazakh steppe. *Mem. Soc. Russe Min.*, vol. 69, p. 472 (M.A. 10–366).

Nelson, B. W. and **Roy, R.,** 1954. New data on the composition and identification of chlorites in clays and clay minerals. *Proc. Second Nat. Conf., U.S.A.*, p. 335.

Newnham, R. E. and **Brindley, G. W.,** 1956. The crystal structure of dickite. *Acta Cryst.*, vol. 9, p. 759.

Nikogosyan, K. S., 1934. Physical and chemical investigations of nacrite. *Trans. Inst. Petrogr. Acad. Sci., USSR*, No. 6, p. 443 (M.A. 7–103).

Noll, W., 1944. New investigations in water–silicate systems. *Koll. Zeits.*, vol. 107, p. 181.

Pauling, L., 1930. The structure of the chlorites. *Proc. Nat. Acad. Sci. U.S.A.*, vol. 16, p. 578.

Permyakov, V. M., 1936. Hydrothermal synthesis of kaolins. *Vernadsky jubilee volume, Acad. Sci. USSR*, vol. 1, p. 563 (M.A. 7–427).

Pinsker, Z. G., 1950. Electronographic determination of the elementary cell and space-group of kaolinite. *Doklady Acad. Sci. USSR*, vol. 73, p. 107 (M.A. 11–451).

Richardson, H. M., 1951. Phase changes which occur on heating kaolin clays, in *X-ray identification and crystal structures of clay minerals*. Min. Soc., London.

Robertson, R. H. S., Brindley, G. W. and **Mackenzie, R. C.**, 1954. Mineralogy of kaolin clays from Pugu, Tanganyika. *Amer. Min.*, vol. 39, p. 118.

Ross, C. S. and **Kerr, P. F.**, 1931. The kaolin minerals. *U.S. Geol. Survey*, Prof. Paper 165E, p. 151.

—— —— 1934. Halloysite and allophane. *U.S. Geol. Survey*, Prof. Paper 185G, p. 135.

Roy, R. and **Brindley, G. W.**, 1956. A study of the hydrothermal reconstitution of the kaolin minerals. *Proc. Fourth Nat. Conf. Clays and Clay minerals, U.S.A.* Nat. Res. Council Publ. 456, p. 125.

—— **Roy, D. M.** and **Francis, E. E.**, 1955. New data on thermal decomposition of kaolinite and halloysite. *Journ. Amer. Ceram. Soc.*, vol. 38, p. 198.

—— and **Osborn, E. F.**, 1954. The system Al_2O_3–SiO_2–H_2O. *Amer. Min.*, vol. 39, p. 853.

Sand, L. B., 1956. On the genesis of residual kaolins. *Amer. Min.*, vol. 41, p. 28.

Schwarz, R. and **Trageser, G.**, 1933. Über die Synthese des Pyrophyllits. *Zeit. anorg. u. allgem. Chem.*, vol. 225, p. 142.

Steadman, R. and **Youell, R. F.**, 1957. Crystallography and thermal transformations of cronstedtite. *Nature*, vol. 180, p. 1066.

Van Niewenberg, C. J. and **Pieters, H. A. J.**, 1929. Rehydration of metakaolin and the synthesis of kaolin. *Ber. deutsch. keram. Ges.*, vol. 10, p. 260.

Visconti, Y. S., Nicot, B. N. F. and **de Andrade, G. E.**, 1956. Tubular morphology of some Brazilian kaolins. *Amer. Min.*, vol. 41, p. 67.

Weil-Malherbe, H. and **Weiss, J.**, 1948. Colour reactions and adsorption of some aluminosilicates. *Journ. Chem. Soc.*, p. 2164.

Williamson, W. O., 1951. The physical relationship between clay and water. *Trans. Ceram. Soc.*, vol. 50, p. 10.

Yoshiki, Bumpei, 1934. Dickite in the rôseki deposits in Shôkôzan. *Proc. Imp. Acad. Tokyo*, vol. 10, p. 417 (M.A. 6–137).

Illite

$K_{1-1.5}Al_4[Si_{7-6.5}Al_{1-1.5}O_{20}](OH)_4$

MONOCLINIC $(-)$

α 1·54–1·57†
β 1·57–1·61
γ 1·57–1·61
δ $\simeq 0·03$
$2V_\alpha$ Generally less than $10°$.
α Approximately $\perp(001)$.
D   2·6–2·9   H   1–2

Cleavage :   {001} perfect.
Colour :   White, and various pale colours; colourless in thin section.
Unit cell : a 5·2, b 9·0, $c \sin\beta$ 9·95 Å.   Z=1.
    Readily attacked by acids.

† These values refer to di-octahedral illites only; tri-octahedral illites have higher values.

Illites, smectites[1] and vermiculites are all clay minerals which are structurally related to the micas, but closest similarity to the micas is shown by the illite group of minerals. Most illites are di-octahedral, like muscovite, but some are tri-octahedral like biotite. The chemical formula most commonly assigned to illite is of the form $K_yAl_4(Si_{8-y},Al_y)O_{20}(OH)_4$ where y is less than 2 and is usually between 1 and 1·5. Thus illite differs from muscovite in having more silica and less potassium; clay minerals which are similar to illite, but which differ from muscovite in other ways, are conveniently regarded as members of the illite group. The name illite is after the State of Illinois, a source of many clay specimens which have been studied. Among the many names which have been used in the past to describe illite minerals (relatively few of which have a precise significance) are sericite, bravaisite, *Glimmerton*, hydrobiotite, hydromuscovite and hydromica. The latter two names are often applied to specimens which appear to have a higher water content than ordinary micas, or to those from which constitutional water is more readily expelled by heating.

STRUCTURE

The structure of illite is essentially that of a mica in that it contains layers with a plane of octahedrally coordinated cations sandwiched between two inward pointing sheets of linked $(Si,Al)O_4$ tetrahedra. The mica structure (which consists of composite sheets of this type alternating with layers of potassium ions) has been more fully described on page 2. A single layer of a di-octahedral illite differs from muscovite only in the chemical substituents

[1] Smectite is the name used for any member of the montmorillonite group of clay minerals.

occupying the well defined atomic sites, but these differences lead to important structural variations when the superposition of layers is considered. Most of the illite minerals have fewer inter-layer cations than muscovite so that forces between layers are weaker and there is consequently less regularity of stacking. The most common polymorph for illites therefore has a disordered one-layered monoclinic cell (1M*d*, see p. 5), and its X-ray powder pattern is similar to that of a mica but has a few broad *hk* diffraction bands replacing the sharp *hkl* reflections given by a well-ordered crystal. These features are observed for hydrous micas as well as for illites, and other polymorphs (1M and 3T) have also been reported (Levinson, 1955; Yoder and Eugster, 1955). Basal reflections are unaffected by stacking irregularities so that illites may be recognized by their strong 10 Å reflection and successive higher orders of varying intensity. Since illites generally contain little or no inter-layer water and are not penetrated by organic liquids the basal reflections are unaffected by heating to 500°C., and an illite which is uncontaminated by a smectite, vermiculite, or halloysite, should show no swelling characteristics when treated with glycol (MacEwan, 1948). For specimens which do contain some randomly distributed inter-stratified layers of water molecules, or which contain small amounts of smectite impurity, the 10 Å basal reflection may be unsymmetrical, with a "tail" towards the low angle side, and the presence of a smectite can be detected by the swelling behaviour with glycol. Swelling of some illites can occur, however, under certain circumstances, for example, after saturation with calcium (Hellman *et al.*, 1943). Nagelschmidt (1944) suggests that illite is unstable in some environments and can in part become more like a smectite by taking up inter-layer water. The mixture of unchanged illite with montmorillonite-type layers leads to a shift of the basal reflection to a lower angle.

A less common illite in which sodium is the inter-layer cation is called bram-mallite (Bannister, 1943). This has a smaller unit cell (see Table 34), thus in powder patterns its basal reflections lie at higher angles. Some specimens classed as illitic (*e.g.* many labelled sericite) are chemically almost identical with muscovite but are extremely fine-grained (Table 36, anal. 1). In these any of the mica stacking polymorphs (1M, 2M$_1$, 3T) may occur (Heinrich *et al.*, 1953; Yoder and Eugster, 1955) but their powder reflections are usually broadened, weakened, or sometimes absent, so that distinction from a true illite is not possible by X-ray methods. Two minerals which give powder patterns of the illite type and exhibit varying degrees of three dimensional order are glauconite (p. 35) and phengite (p. 14). In Table 34 the cell parameters of various illitic specimens are compared with those of muscovite. The table includes the fibrous mica gümbelite (Aruja, 1944), a variety with approximate one-dimensional order in the direction of the fibre axis, predominantly [110]. A coarsely crystal-line tri-octahedral illite with formula $K_{0.66}(Mg_{2.93}Al_{0.06})(Si_{3.30}Al_{0.70})O_{10}(OH)_2$ has been reported, which has *a* 15·9, *b* 9·12, *c* 10·44 Å, β 110°, and super-lattice with $c = 3 \times 10\cdot44$ Å which may arise from the regular positioning of K^+ ions in interlayer spaces (Weiss *et al.*, 1956).

Several substances which were once thought to be homogeneous illites have since been identified as mixed-layer aggregates. Thus hydrobiotite (Gruner, 1934) is a mixture of biotite and vermiculite, and bravaisite (Bradley, 1945) is a mixture of illite and montmorillonite. Such mixed-layer specimens give a basal powder reflection at a position intermediate between 10 Å and the basal spacing of the other constituent, and other peaks occur at spacings which are not submultiples of the first (Brown and MacEwan, 1951).

A mixed-layer clay has been reported (Heystek, 1954) which appears to consist of approximately regularly alternating layers of illite and montmorillonite, since it shows in its powder pattern a basal spacing of 25·8 Å and the second order reflection at 12·4 Å. In a random mixture no *d*-value larger than the average basal spacing (approx. 12·5 Å) would occur, while a mixture of illite and montmorillonite fractions would give their separate peaks at about 10 Å and 15 Å.

Table 34.   Cell parameters of illite and related minerals

	a Å	b Å	Basal spacing Å	$\beta°$	Reference
Muscovite	5·3	9·02	9·98 (002)	95·5	Jackson and West, 1930.
Gümbelite	5·21	9·02	10·0 (002)	96·0	Aruja, 1944.
Glauconite	5·24	9·07	10·01 (001)	100	Gruner, 1935.
Illite	5·2	9·0	9·95		Bannister, 1943.
Brammallite	5·2	9·0	9·60		Bannister, 1943.
Hydromuscovite	5·19	9·03	10·1		Brammall *et al.*, 1937.

The X-ray powder patterns of tri-octahedral illites bear a similar relation to those of biotites as do those of di-octahedral illites to muscovite patterns. Patterns from di- and tri-octahedral illite, differ in the location of the 060 reflection (1·51 Å and 1·53 Å) (Walker, 1950).

CHEMISTRY

The chemistry of the illite group of minerals can be investigated usefully only in conjunction with structural features. Many chemical analyses have been made on specimens of doubtful purity so that formulae quoted for illite may really refer to unrecognized mixtures of illite with smectites, kandites, chlorites, etc. Similarly many X-ray structural identifications of "mica-type" minerals or of "illites", "sericites", etc., have been made without accompanying chemical analyses. The complexity of illite compositions is evident from Table 35 and the ensuing discussion. Table 35 shows chemico-structural variations which could occur in specimens loosely described as di-octahedral illitic clay material.

It seems reasonable to include all of the above categories (except muscovite) in the "illite group" and the name illite may itself be reserved for the specimens in which the principal substitutions are of type 3, *i.e.* substitution of Si for Al and a deficit of potassium as compared with muscovite. Hydromuscovite does not have excess silica, but its deficiency in potassium is compensated either by $(H_3O)^+$ ions in potassium sites (Brown and Norrish, 1952; see also present text p. 15), or by replacement of $(O)^{-2}$ by $(OH)^-$. Both hydromuscovite and

Table 35. Principal variations in illite composition with reference to muscovite

	X	$[Y]^6$	$[Z]^4$	$(OH)^-$	$(O)^{-2}$
1. Muscovite	K_2	Al_4	Si_6Al_2	4	20
2(a) } Hydro-	$[K,(H_3O)^+]_2$	Al_4	Si_6Al_2	4	20
2(b) } muscovite	K_{2-x}	Al_4	Si_6Al_2	$4+x$	$20-x$
3. Illite	K_{2-x}	Al_4	$Si_{6+x}Al_{2-x}$	4	20
4. Phengite	K_2	$Al_{4-x}(Mg,Fe^{+2})_x$	$Si_{6+x}Al_{2-x}$	4	20

illite, because of their deficiency of K ions, tend to have weaker interlayer bonds and therefore have disordered layer stacking, evidence of which is provided by X-ray powder patterns. Similar patterns may, however, be produced by more ordered crystals if particle size is very small, so that specimens with composition 1 (Table 35), *i.e.* that of muscovite, are sometimes reported incorrectly as illites. An important member of the illite group is phengite, in which potassium is not deficient and excess silica is compensated by replacement of $[Al]^6$ by $[Mg,Fe^{+2}]^6$. For this variety the name phengite is preferred to sericite which has a less specific significance. When replacements of type 4 are small, phengites can be considered as substituted muscovites (p. 14). The Mg end-member of this substitution series is leucophyllite or Al-celadonite, $K_2Al_2Mg_2Si_8O_{20}(OH)_4$ (Schaller, 1950), and the magnesium-iron end-member, $K_2Mg_2Fe_2Si_8O_{20}(OH)_4$, is the basis of the glauconite (or celadonite) composition. An additional compositional variation may occur for illite and hydromuscovite (Table 35), as these may contain interspersed layers of water molecules $n(H_2O)$.

Many illites show features of two or more of the variations mentioned above. Thus the term sericite, generally used to describe a fine-grained white mica which may be muscovite or paragonite, is also used for specimens which deviate from the muscovite composition in any or all of the ways previously discussed, and often refers to mixed-layered aggregates. Glauconite, besides having additional water molecules, shows features of illite and of phengite composition with substantial amounts of Fe^{+3}, Fe^{+2} and Mg occurring in Y sites (Table 36, anal. 14). In view of its chemistry and its occurrence in sediments, glauconite may well be regarded as a member of the illite group. For convenience, however, it is discussed in more detail in the section on micas (p. 35).

The complexity of the illite group is increased in several other respects. Tri-octahedral illites have been reported (*e.g.* Walker, 1950; Weiss *et al.*, 1956; see p. 65), and it may be that as many variants on the biotite composition can occur as are shown by di-octahedral illites based on muscovite. Furthermore, there may be intermediates with Mg ions occupying otherwise vacant sites in the octahedral layers (Kerr *et al.*, 1949), but most data indicate that there is little solid solution between di- and tri-octahedral illites.

Some of the characteristic substitutions of illites are in the direction of montmorillonite composition, $Al_2Si_4O_{10}(OH)_2 n H_2O$ with minor replacements, and so the further problem arises as to the completeness of the solid solution series muscovite–illite–montmorillonite. Most illite compositions, however, could also be derived from physical mixtures of muscovite and montmorillonite, and the distinction between these and single intermediate compounds must rest

on X-ray and other evidence (see p. 215).   There is no doubt that many specimens regarded as illite are in fact contaminated with montmorillonite and other
clays either on a coarse scale or in mixed-layer crystals.   For example "bravaisite", which preceded "illite" as the group name, is a mixed-layer clay containing
illite and montmorillonite (Nagelschmidt, 1944), and alushtite is illite plus
dickite (Logvinenko and Frank-Kamenetzky, 1955).   The relations between
di-octahedral micas, illites, montmorillonites, and related minerals are shown in
Fig. 49, where compositions are plotted on the triangular diagram muscovite–

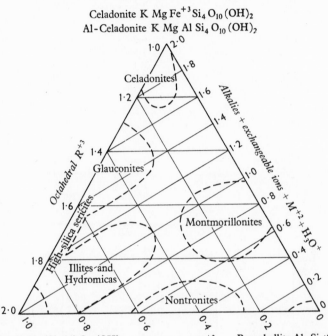

Celadonite K Mg Fe^{+3} Si$_4$ O$_{10}$ (OH)$_2$
Al-Celadonite K Mg Al Si$_4$ O$_{10}$ (OH)$_2$

Muscovite K Al$_2$ (Si$_3$ Al) O$_{10}$ (OH)$_2$ *Tetrahedral R^{+3}*   Pyrophyllite Al$_2$ Si$_4$·O$_{10}$ (OH)$_2$
Fe-Muscovite K Fe$_2^{+3}$(Si$_3$ Al) O$_{10}$ (OH)$_2$ Fe-Pyrophyllite Fe$_2^{+3}$ Si$_4$ O$_{10}$ (OH)$_2$

Fig. 49.   Plot of tetrahedral R^{+3} and octahedral R^{+3} in atomic proportions, for di-octahedral
micas and related minerals (after Yoder and Eugster, 1955).

pyrophyllite–celadonite.   This in effect plots tetrahedral trivalent ions
ranging from zero in pyrophyllite and celadonite to two in muscovite, against
octahedral trivalent ions ranging from four in pyrophyllite and muscovite to
two in celadonite.   These two variables fix the third parameter, namely the
total of potassium, H$_3$O$^+$, divalent cations, and exchangeable cations.

Minerals with intermediate compositions are not easily allocated to either the
illite or the smectite group but those with extreme compositions can readily be
differentiated by X-ray diffraction in conjunction with glycol treatment.

Some chemical analyses of reported illitic minerals are presented in Table 36.
Anal. 1 is of a fine-grained muscovite, and 2 is similar to paragonite. Anals. 3
to 7 are of hydromuscovites, 8 and 9 are illites, 10 and 11 are phengites and 12
and 13 show mixed features of the various illitic minerals.   The chemistry of
glauconite is illustrated by anal. 14, and anal. 15 is of a tri-octahedral illite.   The

Table 36. ILLITE ANALYSES

	1.	2.	3.	4.	5.
SiO_2	46·81	47·30	45·34	46·32	46·54
TiO_2	0·01	—	0·19	0·03	0·17
Al_2O_3	36·09	36·31	31·36	28·79	36·37
Fe_2O_3	—	2·17	0·46	5·74	0·72
FeO	0·25	—	1·57	1·50	0·36
MnO	—	—	0·09	—	0·00
MgO	0·62	—	2·74	tr.	0·50
CaO	0·29	—	0·36	1·09	0·22
Na_2O	0·68	5·27	1·06	0·00	0·46
K_2O	10·24	2·70	9·12	9·31	8·06
H_2O^+	5·00	5·80	6·12	5·81	6·31
H_2O^-	0·42	—	1·13	0·35	0·52
P_2O_5	—	—	—	—	0·06
Total	100·41	99·55	99·54	99·83	100·31
α	1·553	—	1·558	1·559	—
β	1·582	1·58	1·578	1·579	1·575
γ	1·588	—	1·589	1·591	1·580
$2V_\alpha$	30°–40°	—	10°–20°	10°–20°	—
D	—	2·69	—	—	2·65±0·02

NUMBERS OF IONS[†]

	1.	2.	3.	4.	5.
Si	6·14 ⎱ 8·00	6·13 ⎱ 8·00	6·04 ⎱ 8·00	6·36 ⎱ 8·00	6·00 ⎱ 8·00
Al	1·86 ⎰	1·87 ⎰	1·96 ⎰	1·64 ⎰	2·00 ⎰
Al	3·72	3·67	2·97	3·02	3·53
Ti	0·01	—	0·02	—	—
Fe^{+3}	—	0·02	0·05	0·59	0·07
Fe^{+2}	0·03 ⎱ 3·92	— ⎱ 3·69	0·18 ⎱ 3·83	0·17 ⎱ 3·94	0·04 ⎱ 3·76
Mn	—	—	0·01	—	—
Mg	0·12	—	0·55	—	0·10
Ca	0·04	—	0·05	0·16	0·02
Na	0·17 ⎱ 1·88	1·32 ⎱ 1·77	0·27 ⎱ 1·82	— ⎱ 2·07	0·11 ⎱ 1·44
K	1·71 ⎰	0·45 ⎰	1·55 ⎰	1·63 ⎰	1·33 ⎰
$(H_3O)^+$	—	—	—	0·44	—
(OH)	4·38	5·01	5·44	4·00	5·43 ⎱ 5·45
F	—	—	—	—	0·02 ⎰

1. Granular, purple, sericitic muscovite, associated with cleavelandite albite, Rutherford mine, Amelia, Virginia (Glass, 1935). Anal. R. E. Stevens (total iron expressed as FeO).
2. Nodules of soft green sericitic material in conglomerate, Pilot Knob, Ironton, Missouri (Meyer, 1935) (Analysis similar to paragonite; probably brammallite).
3. Hydromuscovite (described as magnesium sericite), greenish sericite clay, Unnan mine, Shimane Prefecture, Japan (Minato and Takano, 1952).
4. Hydromuscovite (described as iron sericite), greenish sericite clay, Unnan mine, Shimane Prefecture, Japan (Minato and Takano, 1952) (Includes SO_3 0·89).
5. Soft, silver white flakes of hydromuscovite, associated with quartz, pyrite and arseno-pyrite, and containing impurities of rutile and apatite, Ogofau, Carmarthenshire, S. Wales (Brammall *et al.*, 1937). Anal. H. Bennett (Includes F 0·02, Li_2O tr.).

† See p. 221.

Table 36. ILLITE ANALYSES—*continued*

	6.	7.	8.	9.	10.
SiO_2	47·55	46·75	51·26	56·91	50·05
TiO_2	0·64	1·15	0·05	0·81	0·14
Al_2O_3	32·45	32·43	30·15	18·50	30·11
Fe_2O_3	0·76	2·98	2·36	4·99	1·47
FeO	1·85	n.d.	0·59	0·26	0·43
MnO	—	—	0·04	—	0·01
MgO	1·70	1·00	1·37	2·07	2·49
CaO	0·06	1·04	0·00	1·59	0·00
Na_2O	1·05	0·94	0·13	0·43	1·97
K_2O	6·22	5·72	7·77	5·10	9·80
H_2O^+	7·73	8·01	6·28	5·98	3·58
H_2O^-	0·00	0·04	0·00	2·86	—
P_2O_5	—	—	—	—	—
Total	100·01	100·06	100·00	99·50	100·05
α	1·572	—	1·568	—	1·560
β	1·587	1·578	1·590	—	—
γ	1·600	—	1·593	—	1·578
$2V_\alpha$	small	5°–10°	—	—	—
D	—	2·913	—	—	—

NUMBERS OF IONS†

	6.		7.		8.		9.		10.	
Si	6·05	8·00	6·16	8·00	6·55	8·00	7·50	8·00	6·70	8·00
Al	1·95		1·84		1·45		0·50		1·30	
Al	2·95		1·60		3·10		2·38		3·45	
Ti	0·05		1·72		—		0·08		0·01	
Fe^{+3}	0·05		0·30		0·25		0·50		0·15	
Fe^{+2}	0·20	3·55	—	3·97	0·05	3·65	0·03	3·62	0·05	4·16
Mn	—		—		—		—		—	
Mg	0·30		0·20		0·25		0·41		0·50	
Ca	—		0·15		—		0·22		—	
Na	0·25	1·25	0·23	2·20	0·05	1·30	0·11	0·97	0·51	2·18
K	1·00		0·96		1·25		0·86		1·67	
$(H_3O)^+$	—		1·01		—		—		—	
(OH)	6·55		4·00		5·4		5·26		3·19	
F	—		—		—		—		—	

6. Hydromuscovite, average analysis of fine fractions from Coal Measures shales of South Wales (Nagelschmidt and Hicks, 1942). Anal. W. N. Adams.

7. Hydromuscovite flakes, fireclay, Tong, Yorkshire, England (Carr *et al.*, 1953).

8. Light greenish yellow soft scales of illite, on decomposed granite, Ballater, Aberdeenshire (Mackenzie *et al.*, 1949). Anal. R. C. Mackenzie (Recalculated after subtraction of impurities).

9. Illite, Fithian, Illinois (Kerr *et al.*, 1950). Anal. Ledoux & Co.

10. Pale green phengite, filling veins in weathered gneiss, near Albbruck, Baden (Jakob *et al.*, 1933).

† See p. 221.

Table 36. ILLITE ANALYSES—*continued*

	11.	12.	13.	14.	15.
SiO_2	49·16	51·22	50·10	49·29	40·87
TiO_2	—	0·53	0·50	0·12	2·13
Al_2O_3	30·81	25·91	25·12	3·17	20·45
Fe_2O_3	—	4·59	5·12	21·72	12·81
FeO	1·43	1·70	1·52	3·19	—
MnO	—	—	—	tr.	0·25
MgO	2·22	2·84	3·93	3·85	6·86
CaO	—	0·16	0·35	0·74	0·89
Na_2O	0·48	0·17	0·05	0·12	0·70
K_2O	10·90	6·09	6·93	6·02	3·25
H_2O^+	4·73	7·14	6·82	7·21	11·84
H_2O^-	0·15	—	—	4·60	—
P_2O_5	—	—	—	0·32	—
Total	100·07	100·35	100·44	100·35	100·05
α	—	1·555	—	1·592	—
β	—	—	—	—	—
γ	—	1·588	1·598	1·614	—
$2V_\alpha$	—	5°	5°	10°	—
D	—	—	—	2·580	—

NUMBERS OF IONS†

	11.	12.	13.	14.	15.
Si	6·54 ⎱ 8·00	6·75 ⎱ 8·00	6·45 ⎱ 8·00	7·63 ⎱ 8·00	6·60 ⎱ 8·00
Al	1·46 ⎰	1·25 ⎰	1·55 ⎰	0·37 ⎰	1·40 ⎰
Al	3·37 ⎫	2·77 ⎫	2·27 ⎫	0·21 ⎫	2·48 ⎫
Ti	—	0·05	0·05	0·01	0·26
Fe^{+3}	—	0·45	0·50	2·53	1·53
Fe^{+2}	0·16 ⎬3·97	0·20 ⎬4·03	0·16 ⎬3·79	0·41 ⎬4·17	⎬5·94
Mn	—	—	—	—	0·04
Mg	0·44	0·56	0·76	0·89	1·63
Ca	— ⎭	— ⎭	0·05 ⎭	0·12 ⎭	0·15 ⎫
Na	0·12 ⎱ 1·97	0·05 ⎫	0·13 ⎱ 1·27	0·04 ⎱ 1·23	0·21 ⎬1·03
K	1·85 ⎰	1·02 ⎬1·83	1·14 ⎰	1·19 ⎰	0·67 ⎭
$(H_3O)^+$	—	0·76 ⎭	—	—	—
(OH)	4·20	4·00	5·86	4·00	4·00
F	—	—	—	—	—

11. Phengite (described as yellow sericite), Amelia, Virginia (Schaller, 1950).   Anal. R. E. Stevens (Includes 0·19 per cent. other components).
12. Illitic material, Pennsylvanian underclay, near Fithian, Vermilion County, Illinois (Grim *et al.*, 1937).   Analysis under supervision of O. W. Rees.
13. Illitic material, Ordovician shale, near Gilead, Calhoun County, Illinois (Grim *et al.*, 1937).   Analysis under supervision of O. W. Rees.
14. Glauconite, sandstone, Whare Flat, East Taieri, Otago, New Zealand (Hutton and Seelye, 1941).   Anal. F. T. Seelye.
15. Tri-octahedral illite, Scottish soil clay (Walker, 1950).   Anal. R. C. Mackenzie.

† See p. 221.

analyses of hydromuscovites 4, 7 and 12 were treated in the way suggested by Brown and Norrish (1952), with $(H_3O)^+$ occupying X sites in the structure. In all other cases numbers of cations were calculated on the basis of $24(O + OH)$, except for nos. 14 and 15 in which $20(O)$ and $4(OH)$ were assumed, and the H_2O^+ figure was disregarded. The sodium illite, brammallite, has not been analysed completely but contains 5·22 per cent. Na_2O and 2·58 per cent. K_2O (Bannister, 1943). The properties of a sericite described by Meyer (1935) suggest that it is a brammallite, and the full analysis is given in Table 36, anal. 2. Kerr and Hamilton (1958) report a "chrome mica-clay" with about 0·4 to 0·6 per cent. Cr_2O_3, which consists of mixed $2M_1$ and $1M$ polymorphs.

The presence of a considerable number of inter-layer potassium ions in illites prevents not only the entry into the structure of water and organic liquids, but also access of other cations, so that illites have a low cation exchange capacity. The exchange that does take place is thought to do so largely at crystal edges (as for kaolinite) where there are unsatisfied valencies. The cation exchange capacity of illites is generally between 10 and 40 m.eq./100 gm. and thus is greater than that for most kaolinites but less than those for halloysite, montmorillonite and vermiculite. The illites in soils, however, are often degraded forms deficient in potassium, and these have a high capacity to take up and fix potassium from fertilizing salts (Stanford, 1947; and others).

The dehydration of illites, whether di- or tri-octahedral, proceeds in a number of stages. Most of the water adsorbed on the surface of particles and the small amount which may be inter-layered with illite sheets comes off rapidly below 110°C., and the remainder more slowly between 110° and 350°C. Water formed by expulsion of $(OH)^-$ ions comes off rapidly at first between 350° and 600°C., but a small amount remains and is given off on further heating (Grim *et al.*, 1937). By contrast, micas have little or no water to lose at the lower temperatures and their constitutional water from $(OH)^-$ ions is driven off at somewhat higher temperatures than that of illite, probably because of larger particle size. Studies of the dehydration and decomposition of illites have yielded varying results depending partly on such factors as purity, particle size and rate of heating. It appears that the loss of $(OH)^-$ ions results in only slight disruption of the crystal structure which remains more or less intact until about 750°C. (Maegdefrau and Hofmann, 1937; Grim and Bradley, 1940). Above approximately 850°C. spinel appears in increasing amounts up to about 1100°C. and it is thought that alkalis combine with silica from the tetrahedral layer to form a glass. At about 1100°C. mullite is formed at the expense of spinel, which has all been resorbed by about 1300°C. The illite which has lost its constitutional water appears to be a stable modification which has a slightly enlarged inter-layer spacing, and gives basal reflections with somewhat changed relative intensities. This modification has slightly lower refractive indices than normal illite, and according to optical studies, final destruction of the structure takes place above about 700°C. If the illite structure has not been too drastically disrupted, rehydration can take place to a limited extent (Grim and Bradley, 1948).

Differential thermal analysis curves of illite show three endothermic peaks, one at about 100°–200°C. representing loss of loosely held water, one at 550°–650°C. corresponding to loss of $(OH)^-$, and one at 850°–950°C. corresponding to disruption of the remaining structure. This is followed by an exothermic peak at 900°–1000°C. when spinel is formed. For coarse-grained muscovite there is only one endothermic peak, at 900°–1000°C. Samples of illite from different localities differ in the precise position of the middle endothermic peak. Thus for the illite from Fithian, Illinois (anal. 12) the peak is at 550°C. while for illite from Ballater, Aberdeenshire (anal. 8) it is at 600°C. An illite described by Mackenzie (1957), with a composition similar to that of anal. 12, has an endothermic peak at each of these temperatures, and is regarded as structurally intermediate between the other two. Mackenzie suggests that different distributions of Al among the available octahedral sites may be responsible for the variation in thermal properties.

Illites show a small capacity for adsorbing organic liquids, and probably hold the polar molecules at crystal surfaces. They give no reaction when treated with benzidine whereas montmorillonite turns purple-blue. The dyes *safranine y* reddish purple) and *malachite green* (green-blue) are adsorbed without change by illite whereas montmorillonite is stained orange-yellow by the latter dye. Mixtures of illite and montmorillonite may be treated with acid prior to staining, when illite is destroyed and the montmorillonite stain results (Grim, 1953; Milenz *et al.*, 1951).

Syntheses of illites have rarely been reported, though it is likely that in experiments to form muscovite some of the products may have been of the illite type. Because synthetic muscovites are usually fine-grained their X-ray patterns are similar to those of illite, and a chemical analysis is necessary for complete identification. Products of laboratory alteration of other minerals have included some which may be illitic, as for example in the partial alteration of nepheline, orthoclase and leucite to sericite (Norton, 1939). Illite has been produced from montmorillonite in the laboratory by treatment with a $1N$ KCl solution and then boiling in a $1N$ KOH solution, and by other methods; this reaction may have considerable relevance to the process of potassium fixation in soils (Caillère and Hénin, 1948; Volk, 1938; Aleshin, 1948).

OPTICAL AND PHYSICAL PROPERTIES

Illite specimens show a rather wide variation of refractive indices owing to the various substitutions possible (refractive indices increase with iron content), the degree of hydration, and interlayering with other minerals. The ranges of refractive indices exhibited are a little below those of the corresponding micas muscovite and biotite. The values given at the head of this section are for di-octahedral illites; for tri-octahedral illites α and γ are 1·58–1·63 and 1·61–1·67 respectively. On gentle heating illites sometimes show a slight increase in indices presumably corresponding to the expulsion of loosely held water: when heating is sufficient to disrupt the structure, driving off (OH) ions, there is a marked decrease in γ by about 0·02. Measurement of optical properties generally cannot be made with great accuracy because of the extremely small size of illite particles. However, a hydrous mica from a fireclay with unusually large particles (Table 36, anal. 7) gave γ 1·578 and $2V_\alpha$ 5°–10° (Carr *et al.*, 1953). "Chrome mica-clay" (Kerr and Hamilton, 1958) has α 1·554, β 1·585, γ 1·592, $2V_\alpha \simeq 30°$.

Pure illites are colourless, but impurities such as fine-grained oxides or hydroxides of iron may colour them yellow, green, or brown, etc., and they may show slight pleochroism. Electron micrographs of illites exhibit very few well-formed particles, the irregularity of shapes being similar to that shown by montmorillonites. Densities, like refractive indices, cannot be precisely defined since they are affected by degree of hydration, and by the presence of fine-grained impurities, but generally they are a little lower than those of corresponding micas.

DISTINGUISHING FEATURES

The extremely fine-grained nature of most illite specimens makes identification by optical methods difficult. Average refractive indices are similar to those for corresponding micas, but 2V is generally smaller than that of muscovite. Reliable identification can only be achieved by combination of chemical analysis, d.t.a., and X-ray diffraction applied to samples before and after treatment by heat and with organic liquids.

PARAGENESIS

Illites are the dominant clay minerals in shales and mudstones, and they also occur in other sediments such as limestones. The illites of sediments may have been deposited as such after their formation by surface weathering of silicates, principally felspars, but in some occurrences they are derived by alteration of other clay minerals, during diagenesis. According to Dietz (1942) and others, illite may be produced from montmorillonite by adsorption of potassium from sea water, but it has been pointed out (Yoder and Eugster, 1952) that the addition of potassium is not the only change required, for there must also be considerable re-distribution of ions between octahedral and tetrahedral sites. In some circumstances the reverse of this reaction takes place, since illite is not a stable mineral under humid conditions and it tends to alter to montmorillonite by hydration. The sodium illite, brammallite, has been found principally in shales associated with coal seams (Bannister, 1943; Endell and Endell, 1943). Illites may also occur through the disintegration of muscovite, or in appropriate conditions by recrystallization of colloidal sediments (Galpin, 1912). Illites may also have a hydrothermal origin, and they are often found in alteration zones around hot springs or metalliferous veins (see, for example, Bonorino, 1959), either pure or as the illite component of a mixed-layer clay. The illite is assumed to derive its potassium from the breakdown of potassium felspar, and so it generally occurs in the inner zone of alteration where temperatures have been high enough for this to take place. Laboratory experiments suggest that for both hydrothermal and sedimentary occurrences the formation of illite is generally favoured by alkaline conditions and by high concentrations of aluminium and potassium. At higher temperatures, however, Gruner (1939) has shown that micas (and presumably illites) can form in acid environments as long as excess potassium is available. The "chrome mica-clays" at Temple Mountain, Utah, described by Kerr and Hamilton (1958) probably had their origin in hydrothermal chromium-bearing solutions.

REFERENCES

Aleshin, S. N., 1948. Changes of montmorillonite into hydro-mica. *Doklady Acad. Sci. USSR*, vol. 61, p. 693.

Aruja, E., 1944.   An X-ray study on the crystal structure of gümbelite.   *Min. Mag.*, vol. 27, p. 11.

Bannister, F. A., 1943.   Brammallite (sodium-illite), a new mineral from Llandebie, South Wales.   *Min. Mag.*, vol. 26, p. 304.

Bonorino, F. G., 1959.   Hydrothermal alteration in the Front Range mineral belt, Colorado.   *Bull. Geol. Soc. Amer.*, vol. 70, p. 53.

Bradley, W. F., 1945.   Diagnostic criteria for clay minerals.   *Amer. Min.*, vol. 30, p. 704.

Brammall, A., Leech, J. G. C. and **Bannister, F. A.**, 1937.   The paragenesis of cookeite and hydromuscovite associated with gold at Ogofau, Carmarthenshire. *Min. Mag.*, vol. 24, p. 507.

Brown, G. and **MacEwan, D. M. C.**, 1951.   X-ray diffraction by structures with random interstratification, in *X-ray identification and structure of the Clay Minerals*.   Min. Soc., London, p. 266.

—— and **Norrish, K.**, 1952.   Hydrous Micas.   *Min. Mag.*, vol. 29, p. 929.

Caillère, S. and **Hénin, S.**, 1948.   Transformation expérimentale d'une montmorillonite en une phyllite à 10 Å type illite.   *Compt. Rend. Acad. Sci. Paris*, vol. 226, p. 680.

Carr, K., Grimshaw, R. W. and **Roberts, A. L.**, 1953.   A hydrous mica from Yorkshire fireclay.   *Min. Mag.*, vol. 30, p. 139.

Dietz, R. S., 1942.   Clay minerals in recent marine sediments.   *Amer. Min.*, vol. 27, p. 219.

Endell, K. and **Endell, J.**, 1943.   Ueber die Bestimmung der Röntgenfeinstruktur mineralischer Bestandeile von Kohlen und Aschen sowie ihre technische Bedeutung.   *Feuerungstech.*, vol. 31, p. 137.

Galpin, S. L., 1912.   Studies of flint clays and their associates.   *Trans. Amer. Ceram. Soc.*, vol. 14, p. 301.

Glass, J. J., 1935.   The pegmatite minerals from near Amelia, Virginia.   *Amer. Min.*, vol. 20, p. 741.

Grim, R. E., 1953.   *Clay Mineralogy*.   McGraw Hill, New York.

—— and **Bradley, W. F.**, 1940.   Investigation of the effect of heat on the clay minerals illite and montmorillonite.   *Journ. Amer. Ceram. Soc.*, vol. 23, p. 242.

—— —— 1948.   Rehydration and dehydration of the clay minerals.   *Amer. Min.*, vol. 33, p. 50.

—— **Bray, R. H.** and **Bradley, W. F.**, 1937.   The mica in argillaceous sediments. *Amer. Min.*, vol. 22, p. 813.

Gruner, J. W., 1934.   Vermiculite and hydrobiotite structures.   *Amer. Min.*, vol. 19, p. 557.

—— 1935.   The structure relationship of glauconite and mica.   *Amer. Min.*, vol. 20, p. 699.

—— 1939.   Formation and stability of muscovite in acid solution at elevated temperatures.   *Amer. Min.*, vol. 24, p. 624.

Heinrich, E. W., Levinson, A. A., Levandowski, D. W. and **Hewitt, C. H.**, 1953. Studies in the natural history of micas.   *Univ. of Michigan engineering research institute.   Project M.978*; final report.

Hellman, N. N., Aldrich, D. G. and **Jackson, M. L.**, 1943.   Further note on an X-ray diffraction procedure for the positive differentiation of montmorillonite from hydrous mica.   *Proc. Soil Sci. Soc. Amer.*, vol. 7, p. 194.

Heystek, H., 1954.   An occurrence of a regular mixed-layer clay mineral.   *Min. Mag.*, vol. 30, p. 400.

Hutton, C. O. and **Seelye, F. T.**, 1941.   Composition and properties of some New Zealand glauconites.   *Amer. Min.*, vol. 26, p. 593.

Jackson, W. W. and **West, J.**, 1930.   The crystal structure of muscovite—KAl_2 $(AlSi_3)O_{10}(OH)_2$.   *Zeit. Krist.*, vol. 76, p. 211.

Jakob, J., Friedlaender, C. and **Brandenberger, E.**, 1933. Über Neubildung von Sericit. *Schweiz. Min. Petr. Mitt.*, vol. 13, p. 74 (M.A. 6–186).

Kerr, P. F. and **Hamilton, P. K.**, 1958. Chrome mica-clay, Temple Mountain, Utah. *Amer. Min.*, vol. 43, p. 34.

—— —— and **Pill, R. J.**, 1950. Analytical data on reference clay materials. Prelim. report No. 7. *Reference clay minerals. Amer. Petroleum Inst., Res. Proj.* 49. Columbia Univ., New York, p. 38.

—— **Kulp, J. L.** and **Hamilton, P. K.**, 1949. Differential thermal analyses of reference clay mineral specimens. Prelim. report No. 3. *Reference clay minerals. Amer. Petroleum Inst., Res. Proj.* 49. Columbia Univ., New York, p. 38.

Levinson, A. A., 1955. Studies in the mica group : polymorphism among illites and hydrous micas. *Amer. Min.*, vol. 40, p. 41.

Logvinenko, N. V. and **Frank-Kamenetzky, V. A.**, 1955. On the so-called alushtite. *Doklady Acad. Sci. USSR*, vol. 105, p. 554 (M.A. 13–146).

MacEwan, D. M. C., 1948. Complexes of clays with organic compounds, I. *Trans. Faraday Soc.*, vol. 44, p. 349.

Mackenzie, R. C., 1957. The illite in some Old Red Sandstone soils and sediments. *Min. Mag.*, vol. 31, p. 681.

—— **Walker, G. F.** and **Hart, R.**, 1949. Illite occurring in decomposed granite at Ballater, Aberdeenshire. *Min. Mag.*, vol. 28, p. 704.

Maegdefrau, E. and **Hofmann, U.**, 1937. Glimmerartige Mineralien als Tonsubstanzen. *Zeit. Krist.*, vol. 98, p. 31.

Meyer, D. B., 1935. A sericite of unusual composition. *Amer. Min.*, vol. 20, p. 384.

Milenz, R. C., King, M. E. and **Schieltz, N. C.**, 1950. Analytical data on reference clay materials. Prelim. report No. 7. *Reference clay minerals. Amer. Petroleum Inst., Res. Proj.* 49. Columbia Univ., New York, p. 135.

Minato, H. and **Takano, Y.**, 1952. On the iron sericites and magnesium sericite from Unnan mine, Shimane Prefecture, Japan. *Sci. Papers College General Education, Univ. Tokyo*, vol. 2, p. 189 (M.A. 12–221).

Nagelschmidt, G., 1944. X-ray diffraction experiments on illite and bravaisite. *Min. Mag.*, vol. 27, p. 59.

—— and **Hicks, D.**, 1943. The mica of certain coal-measure shales in South Wales. *Min. Mag.*, vol. 26, p. 297.

Norton, F. H., 1939. Hydrothermal formation of clay minerals in the laboratory. *Amer. Min.*, vol. 24, p. 1.

Schaller, W. T., 1950. An interpretation of the composition of high-silica sericites. *Min. Mag.*, vol. 29, p. 406.

Stanford, G., 1947. Fixation of potassium in soils under moist conditions and on drying in relation to the type of clay mineral. *Proc. Soil Sci. Soc. Amer.*, vol. 12, p. 167.

Volk, G., 1938. Nature of potash fixation in soils. *Soil. Sci.*, vol. 45, p. 263.

Walker, G. F., 1950. Trioctahedral minerals in soil clays of northeast Scotland. *Min. Mag.*, vol. 29, p. 72.

Weiss, A., Scholz, A. and **Hofmann, U.**, 1956. Zur Kenntnis von trioktaedrischem Illit. *Zeit. Naturforsch.*, Vol. 11b, p. 429.

Yoder, H. S. and **Eugster, H. P.**, 1955. Synthetic and natural muscovites. *Geochim. et Cosmochim. Acta.*, vol. 8, p. 225.

Montmorillonite Group (Smectites)

$$(\tfrac{1}{2}\text{Ca,Na})_{0\cdot7}(\text{Al,Mg,Fe})_4(\text{Si,Al})_8\text{O}_{20}(\text{OH})_4.n\text{H}_2\text{O}$$

MONOCLINIC $(-)$

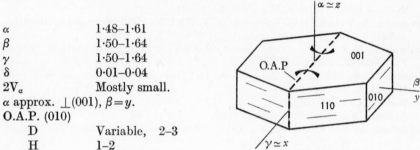

α	1·48–1·61
β	1·50–1·64
γ	1·50–1·64
δ	0·01–0·04
$2V_\alpha$	Mostly small.

α approx. $\perp(001)$, $\beta=y$.
O.A.P. (010)

D	Variable, 2–3
H	1–2

Montmorillonite, Beidellite, Nontronite

Cleavage: {001} perfect.

Colour: Commonly white, yellow or green; colourless, yellow, green in thin section.

Unit cell: Layer parameters: a 5·23, b 9·06 Å, stacking disordered; d_{001} variable.

Attacked by acids.

The name montmorillonite (after Montmorillon, Vienne, France) was originally applied to a clay mineral with composition similar to that of pyrophyllite except for the presence of excess water, $\text{Al}_4\text{Si}_8\text{O}_{20}(\text{OH})_4 \cdot n\text{H}_2\text{O}$. Chemical variation of this basic formula yields a group of clay minerals which are related by a common structure and by similarity of chemical and physical properties, and are therefore classed as the "montmorillonite group." According to present usage one member of this group is itself called montmorillonite and has the formula $(\text{Na})_{0\cdot7}(\text{Al}_{3\cdot3}\text{Mg}_{0\cdot7})\text{Si}_8\text{O}_{20}(\text{OH})_4 \cdot n\text{H}_2\text{O}$. An alternative term once used for this type of clay is "smectite", and this has now been revived to describe the group as a whole (Mackenzie, 1957a), which contains the following principal members: montmorillonite, beidellite, nontronite, saponite, hectorite and sauconite. The latter three are tri-octahedral smectites which are based on the formula and structure of talc rather than pyrophyllite. All are "swelling" clay minerals in that they can take up water or organic liquids between their structural layers, and all show marked cation exchange properties. They occur in sedimentary and metamorphic rocks, in deposits of hydrothermal origin, and in soils, and are useful, as are most other clay minerals, in the preparation of ceramics, drilling muds, paper, rubber, paints and moulding sands. The smectites are the principal constituents of bentonite clays which have exceptionally high water absorbing and cation exchange capacities.

STRUCTURE

The structure first suggested for montmorillonite (Hofmann *et al.*, 1933; Marshall, 1935; Hendricks, 1942) is based on that of pyrophyllite (Fig. 28, p. 116). The latter mineral consists of superimposed layers each of which contains a plane of Al ions sandwiched between two inward pointing sheets of linked SiO_4 tetrahedra. The central section may be regarded as a layer of gibbsite, $Al_2(OH)_6$, in which two out of every three (OH) ions are replaced by apical oxygens of an Si_4O_{10} pseudo-hexagonal network. In pyrophyllite itself there is no replacement of either Si or Al ions so that the composite sheets are electrically neutral and there are no cations between them. In smectites the charge balance is upset by substitutions in both octahedral and tetrahedral sites and is redressed by the presence of a small number of interlayer cations, usually Na or Ca. Values of b parameters ($b \simeq a\sqrt{3}$) typical for smectites are listed in Table 37. These vary slightly according to the substitutions which occur, and MacEwan (1951) tentatively suggested an equation relating the b parameter with various substitutions, but pointed out that it is more useful in

Table 37. b CELL PARAMETERS FOR SMECTITES, PYROPHYLLITE AND TALC

Mineral	b Å	Reference
Pyrophyllite	8·88	Hendricks, 1938.
Montmorillonite	8·94–9·00	Nagelschmidt, 1938; Earley *et al.*, 1953.
Beidellite	$\simeq 9·00$	Nagelschmidt, 1938.
Nontronite	9·10–9·12	Nagelschmidt, 1938.
Talc	9·13	Hendricks, 1938.
Saponite	$\simeq 9·2$	Mackenzie, 1957b.
Hectorite	9·16	Nagelschmidt, 1938.

the beidellite–nontronite rather than the montmorillonite–beidellite range of composition. The cell parameters are affected mostly by substitution of Fe or Mg for Al in Y sites, and by the total number of Y ions, so that increases are evident in the direction montmorillonite–nontronite–saponite. Electron diffraction studies on montmorillonite gave a 5·17 $\pm$ 0.02, b 8·94 $\pm$ 0·02, c 9·95 $\pm$ 0·06 Å, β 99° 54′ $\pm$ 30′, space group $C2/m$ (Zvyagin and Pinsker, 1949).

For pyrophyllite the inter-layer spacing d_{001} is approximately 8·9 Å and for the micas and illites it is about 10 Å. In smectites the basal spacing can vary over a wide range, with a minimum corresponding to the fully collapsed state at about 9·6 Å. Water is readily adsorbed between the structural layers and it is believed by some workers to enter as integral numbers of complete layers of water molecules arranged in a specific manner with relation to their neighbouring tetrahedral networks (Bradley *et al.*, 1937). The number of layers of water molecules is influenced to some extent by the nature of the inter-layer cation, calcium montmorillonites (the most common in nature) usually having two layers per cell and $d_{001} \simeq 15 \cdot 5$ Å, and the sodium varieties having one ($d_{001} \simeq 12 \cdot 5$ Å), two (15·5 Å), three (19 Å) or more layers per cell. Since specimens may contain randomly mixed cells with various water contents the range of effective basal spacings that may be recorded is continuous between 10 and about 21 Å (Hofmann and Bilke, 1936) and can vary with humidity and the nature of the cation.

Smectites are so poorly crystalline that single-crystal X-ray data are unobtainable; detailed structural information cannot be obtained from powder photographs alone. Powder patterns show only basal reflections and two-dimensional scattering bands indicating a lack of stacking order, so that a three-dimensional cell cannot be strictly defined. Vermiculite, however, is in many respects similar to montmorillonite and occurs in crystals large enough for a structure determination to be achieved (Mathieson and Walker, 1954). The details of its structure (see p. 247) may therefore be relevant to some or all of the smectite minerals. As for many other layered silicates the position of the 060 reflection can be used to indicate the di-octahedral or tri-octahedral nature of a smectite (see p. 6). The powder patterns of dehydrated montmorillonite and saponite are similar to those of pyrophyllite and talc respectively.

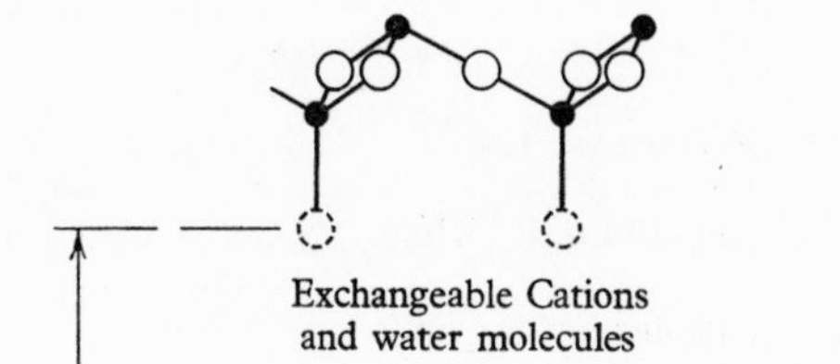

The inter-layer cations of smectites are mostly exchangeable but it has been noted that the cation exchange capacity is sometimes in excess of that expected on the basis of the positive charge deficiency within the composite sheets. Some additional exchange could take place through unsatisfied surface valencies as in the case of kaolinite, but two other explanations have been offered. The first (Edelman and Favjee, 1940) involves a radically different structure for montmorillonite (Fig. 50). This has a proportion of its SiO_4 tetrahedra inverted with respect to their neighbours and having their apical oxygens, which now point away from the central Y ions, replaced by $(OH)^-$ ions the hydrogens of which are then available for exchange with other cations. A less drastic possible modification of the montmorillonite structure (McConnell, 1950) is that in which some oxygens at the bases of SiO_4 tetrahedra are replaced by (OH) ions and this substitution compen-

Exchangeable Cations and water molecules

$c \simeq 14$Å

2(OH)

2 Si
6 O
2 Si

4(OH)+2O

4 Al

4(OH)+2O

2 Si
6 O
2 Si

2(OH)

— *y axis* —

Montmorillonite $(OH)_{12} Al_4 Si_8 O_{16} \cdot n H_2 O$

FIG. 50. Alternative to pyrophyllite structure for montmorillonite suggested by Edelman and Favjee (1940).

sated by a deficit of silicon ions. The poor crystallinity of smectites, and difficulties of ensuring purity and homogeneity, make it hard to discriminate between the various possibilities, but some X-ray evidence (Brown, 1950) favours a pyrophyllite type of structure rather than that proposed by Edelman and Favjee.

The inter-layer spaces in smectites can be penetrated not only by water and exchange cations but also by certain organic cations and by various organic liquids. Substituted ammonium ions in the form of simple amines or even complex proteins, are taken up by the clays and result in interplanar spacings ranging from 12 to 48 Å (Gieseking, 1939; Hendricks, 1941; Sedletzky and Yussupova, 1945). Polar organic liquids such as glycol are adsorbed in integral numbers of layers and yield regular layer sequences with characteristic basal spacings (Bradley, 1945; MacEwan, 1948): glycerol gives rise to a basal reflection at 17·7 Å and an integral series of higher orders. The only other common swelling clay constituents are halloysite, which expands with glycerol to about 11 Å, and vermiculite to 14 Å (Brindley, 1951). The adsorption and retention of organic materials in the presence of water have been studied by Brindley and Rustom (1958). In these circumstances either one layer of organic molecules, or two layers, are regularly taken in by montmorillonite according to the concentration of organic material in the water, and at intermediate concentrations mixtures of one- and two-layer complexes are formed.

On heating at between 100° and 200°C. smectites lose their interlamellar water reversibly, and the basal spacing shifts from between 12 and 15 Å to about 10 Å. With heating at 500°C., d_{001} is reduced further to about 9·6 to 10 Å depending upon the nature of the inter-layer cation, and at higher temperatures, where detachment of (OH) ions takes place, the X-ray pattern deteriorates considerably. Rowland *et al.* (1956) report that on heating, calcium, magnesium, manganese, lithium and hydrogen montmorillonites pass through two stable hydrates, with basal spacings at 14·5 Å and 11·5 Å (see vermiculite, p. 247). Montmorillonites of sodium and potassium, however, have a regular one-water-layer configuration at 12·4 Å which is distinctly different from the 11·5 Å hydrate of the smaller ions. Similar though not identical results were obtained by Midgley and Gross (1956), who also found intermediate structural states during the dehydration of smectites and noted different behaviour according to the nature of the exchangeable ion.

X-ray powder patterns are presented by Brindley (1951) for all the principal smectites, and a useful table is also given describing the features of X-ray patterns of various clay minerals before and after treatment by heat and by organic liquids.

Many clay samples (*e.g.* bentonites) prove to be mixtures of more than one clay mineral which may be either regularly or randomly interstratified, and the two cases can be distinguished by the X-ray powder pattern (see p. 215). X-ray methods may also be used to estimate quantitatively the proportions of two constituents in a random mixture (Méring, 1949; Brown and MacEwan, 1951; Weaver, 1956), and similar methods may be employed to estimate a mixture of swollen and unswollen layers (Brown and Greene-Kelly, 1954) or a mixture of different hydrates (McAtee, 1956). A regularly interstratified montmorillonite-chlorite has been reported by Earley *et al.* (1956).

CHEMISTRY

The chemical formulae of all smectites are similar to those of either pyrophyllite or talc in which substitutions in octahedral or tetrahedral sites by ions of lower valency are accompanied by the addition of an equivalent number of inter-layer cations. The average extent of such substitution requires about 0·66 additional monovalent cations (or their equivalent) per formula unit, and these ions are in general exchangeable. The smectites are subdivided according to the substitutions involved (Ross and Hendricks, 1945) and these are illustrated in an idealized manner in Table 38. Thus in montmorillonite and hectorite substitution is almost entirely in the Y sites, while in beidellite and saponite it takes place principally in the Z sites. Several specimens of beidellite (including the type specimen) have proved to be mixtures of clay minerals (Grim and Rowland, 1942) and its validity as a true species has been doubted. However, there now appear to be sufficient analyses of pure material to include it as a specific member of the group. In addition to the comparatively rare lithium-bearing mineral, hectorite (Table 39, anal. 16), and the zinc mineral, sauconite (Table 39, anals. 17 and 18; see also Faust, 1951), occurrences of chromiferous (Ross and Hendricks, 1945) and cupriferous (Chukhrov and Anosov, 1950) montmorillonites have been reported. As can be seen from the list of representative analyses, substitutions other than those shown in the simplified table (Table 38) commonly occur. Tetrahedral positions may be occupied by small numbers of titanium ions (but small amounts of rutile impurities are often present) and possibly also by ferric ions, and in addition to the constituents

Table 38. SMECTITES, PYROPHYLLITE AND TALC

	Z	Y	X (exchange cations)
	Di-octahedral		
Pyrophyllite	Si_8	Al_4	—
Montmorillonite	Si_8	$Al_{3.34}Mg_{0.66}$	$(\tfrac{1}{2}Ca,Na)_{0.66}$
Beidellite	$Si_{7.34}Al_{0.66}$	Al_4	$(\tfrac{1}{2}Ca,Na)_{0.66}$
Nontronite	$Si_{7.34}Al_{0.66}$	Fe_4^{+3}	$(\tfrac{1}{2}Ca,Na)_{0.66}$
	Tri-octahedral		
Talc	Si_8	Mg_6	—
Saponite	$Si_{7.34}Al_{0.66}$	Mg_6	$(\tfrac{1}{2}Ca,Na)_{0.66}$
Hectorite	Si_8	$Mg_{5.34}Li_{0.66}$	$(\tfrac{1}{2}Ca,Na)_{0.66}$
Sauconite	$Si_{6.7}Al_{1.3}$	$Zn_{4-5}(Mg,Al,Fe^{+3})_{2-1}$	$(\tfrac{1}{2}Ca,Na)_{0.66}$

already mentioned, octahedral sites may contain minor amounts of Fe^{+2}, Mn and Ni. Furthermore, intermediates may exist possessing features of two or more of the groups of Table 38. Thus, montmorillonite often has some replacement of Si by Al, and there is usually some Mg in octahedral coordination in beidellite and in nontronite, so that montmorillonite–beidellite–nontronite appear to form a continuous series. The total number of Y ions seems to lie within the ranges 4·00–4·44 and 5·76–6·00 so that there does not appear to be a solid solution series between the di- and tri-octahedral members. In the tri-octahedral minerals, saponite (Table 39, anals. 12–15) usually contains some trivalent ions in Y sites and has correspondingly more Al replacing Si; hectorite usually has some replacement of (OH) by F. A green iron-rich saponite (Fe_2O_3 7·85, FeO 5·32 per cent.) occurring in amygdales in altered basalt has been reported by Miyamoto (1957) and a mineral, griffithite, once regarded as a chlorite, is similarly an iron-rich saponite (Ross, 1946; Faust, 1955).

Cation exchange. The most commonly occurring exchangeable cations are sodium and calcium, but smectites can be prepared containing potassium, caesium, strontium, magnesium, hydrogen and other inter-layer cations which are to varying degrees exchangeable. In several analyses of di-octahedral smectites the total of Y ions exceeds four and it is likely that some of the Mg ions occupy inter-layer sites and contribute to the cation exchange capacity (Foster, 1951). The inter-layer cations of smectites may be already in the specimen when it is formed, or may be the result of subsequent exchange, since some cations are more readily substituted than others. The cation exchange capacity is usually in the range 80–150 m.eq./100 gm. but varies with the concentration of the clay, particle size, and the nature of the cation, usually being greater for Ca than for Na. Generally the replacing power of ions with higher valency is greater and their replaceability is less, so that calcium is more firmly held. The principal cause of cation exchange in smectites is the un-balance of charge in the fundamental layers, and not the presence of unsatisfied surface valencies. Weaver (1958) drew a distinction between smectites derived from volcanic material and those derived by the alteration of micas. The latter can be fully "collapsed" by mild treatment with $1N$ KOH, to a 10 Å phase which corresponds more or less to regeneration of the original mica. These smectites may be referred to as "expanded micas" and are further characterized by having a greater cation exchange capacity (> 150 m.eq./100 gm.). The more common smectites have a lower cation exchange capacity, and when treated with KOH remain partially expanded and show spacings of 11 to 12·4 Å. Those clays in which a large proportion of the inter-layer charge originates in the octahedral layer are less easily collapsed than those in which the charge has a tetrahedral origin, but the former may be more fully collapsed by more drastic treatment with KOH.

The mineral stevensite, $Mg_{5·76}Mn_{0·04}Fe_{0·04}Si_8O_{20}(OH)_4 \cdot M^+_{0·30}$, is closely related to the tri-octahedral smectites, but its cation exchange capacity is unusually low and compensates a deficiency in total Y ions rather than replace-ments in tetrahedral or octahedral components. Brindley (1955) described stevensite as a talc-saponite inter-layered mineral, whereas Faust and Murata (1953) and Faust *et al.* (1959) regard it as a smectite with a defect structure in which a small proportion of layers with the "attributes of talc" play only a minor role.

Inter-layer molecules. The amount of inter-layer water adsorbed varies according to the type of smectite, the nature of the inter-layer cations and the physical conditions. Calcium smectites usually take up two layers of water molecules in each space, while the amount taken by sodium compounds appears to be continuously variable and in general they show a greater swelling capacity.

Table 39. SMECTITE ANALYSES

	1.	2.	3.	4.	5.	6.
SiO_2	53·98	51·14	51·52	49·90	51·90	59·75
TiO_2	0·08	—	0·48	—	0·23	tr.
Al_2O_3	15·97	19·76	17·15	20·23	18·61	24·41
Fe_2O_3	0·95	0·83	5·65	1·23	2·81	3·73
FeO	0·19	—	0·32	0·21	0·95	—
MnO	0·06	—	—	—	0·03	—
ZnO	—	—	—	—	—	—
MgO	4·47	3·22	2·80	2·20	3·29	3·10
CaO	2·30	1·62	1·72	2·41	3·52	3·36
Na_2O	0·13	0·11	0·15	0·25	0·64	} 1·44
K_2O	0·12	0·04	0·85	0·06	1·59	
H_2O^+	9·12	7·99	8·55	8·84	6·05	3·93
H_2O^-	13·06	14·81	11·22	14·58	10·40	—
Total	100·43	99·52	100·41	99·91	100·02	99·82
α	1·494	—	1·503	—	1·513–1·520	—
β	1·512	—	1·534	—	1·515–1·525	—
γ	1·512	—	1·534	—	—	—
n	—	—	—	1·501–1·513	—	1·517–1·519
D	—	—	—	2·057	—	2·23

NUMBERS OF IONS[†]

	1.	2.	3.	4.	5.	6.
Si	8·08 } 8·08	7·81 } 8·00	7·69 } 8·00	7·66 } 8·00	7·60 } 8·00	7·46 } 8·00
Al	—	0·19	0·31	0·34	0·40	0·54
Al	2·82	3·37	2·71	3·32	2·71	3·05
Ti	0·01	—	0·05	—	0·03	—
Fe^{+3}	0·11	0·09	0·64	0·14	0·31	0·35
Fe^{+2}	0·02 } 3·97	— } 4·19	0·04 } 4·06	0·03 } 3·99	0·12 } 3·89	— } 3·98
Mn	0·01	—	—	—	—	—
Zn	—	—	—	—	—	—
Mg	1·00	0·73	0·62	0·50	0·72	0·58
Ca	0·37	0·27	0·28	0·40	0·55	0·45
Na	0·04 } 0·43	0·03 } 0·31	0·04 } 0·48	0·07 } 0·59	0·18 } 1·03	0·17 } 0·73
K	0·02	0·01	0·16	0·12	0·30	0·11
(OH)	4·00	4·00	4·00	4·00	4·00	4·00
H_2O	2·56	2·05	2·26	2·53	—	—
M[‡]	0·80	0·58	0·76	0·99	1·48	1·18

1. Pink montmorillonite, altered rhyolitic and andesitic tuff, Santa Rita, New Mexico (Kerr *et al.*, 1950). Anal. Ledoux and Co. (Contains 3 per cent. impurities including some MnO, felspar, quartz and limonite).

2. Pink montmorillonite from shale, Montmorillon, France (Ross and Hendricks, 1945). Anal. R. C. Wells.

3. Dark coloured montmorillonite clay, Amory, Mississippi, containing carbonaceous inclusions, glass shards, quartz, limonite, orthoclase, pyrite, and calcite (Kerr *et al.*, 1950). Anal. Ledoux & Co.

4. Spheroids of montmorillonite, Stritez, near Skuteč, eastern Bohemia (Rost, 1944).

5. Montmorillonite clay, fault fissure between quartz poryphyry and dolomite, Vallortigara-Posina, Schio, Venezia, Italy (Andreatta, 1949) (Includes CO_2 in H_2O^+ value).

6. White montmorillonite, Triassic limestone, near Baratka, Transylvania (Dittler and Hofmann, 1945) (Includes SO_3 0·10).

[†] Nos. 5 and 6 were calculated assuming 20(O) and 4(OH), and ignoring the listed value of H_2O^+. The remainder were calculated according to the method of Mackenzie (1957b).
[‡] M = total charge on inter-layer cations.

Table 39.   SMECTITE ANALYSES—*continued*

	7.	8.	9.	10.	11.	12.
SiO$_2$	45·32	45·83	47·28	39·92	40·25	53·88
TiO$_2$	—	0·46	—	0·08	0·03	0·25
Al$_2$O$_3$	27·84	22·79	20·27	5·37	5·50	4·47
Fe$_2$O$_3$	0·70	5·71	8·68	29·46	29·44	0·60
FeO	—	0·28	—	0·28	0·00	—
MnO	—	—	—	—	—	—
ZnO	—	—	—	—	—	—
MgO	0·16	0·86	0·70	0·93	0·53	31·61
CaO	2·76	1·41	2·75	2·46	2·29	—
Na$_2$O	0·10	0·16	0·97	tr.	0·00	0·01
K$_2$O	0·12	0·09	tr.	tr.	0·00	0·05
H$_2$O$^+$	14·48	9·79	—	—	7·25	9·28
H$_2$O$^-$	8·16	12·55	13·07	14·38	15·09	
Total	99·64	99·93	100·37	99·88	100·38	100·15
α	—	—	—	1·567	1·580	—
β	—	—	—	—	—	1·486–1·493
γ	1·540	—	1·589	1·605	1·625	—
n	—	1·501–1·513	—	—	—	—
D	—	1·998	—	—	—	—

NUMBERS OF IONS[†]

	7.		8.		9.		10.		11.		12.	
Si	6·92	8·00	7·08	8·00	7·16	8·00	6·92	8·00	7·00	8·00	7·23	7·94
Al	1·08		0·92		0·84		1·08		1·00		0·71	
Al	3·92		3·23		2·78		0·02		0·12		—	
Ti	—		0·06		—		0·01		—		0·03	
Fe^{+3}	0·08		0·66		1·00		3·84		3·84		0·06	
Fe^{+2}	—	4·04	0·04	4·19	—	3·94	0·04	4·15	—	4·10	—	6·09
Mn	—		—		—		—		—		—	
Zn	—		—		—		—		—		—	
Mg	0·04		0·20		0·16		0·24		0·14		6·32	
Ca	0·46		0·23		0·44		0·46		0·86		—	
Na	0·04	0·52	0·05	0·30	0·28	0·72	—	0·46	—	0·86	—	0·44
K	0·02		0·02		—		—		—		0·12	
(OH)	4·00		4·00		4·00		4·00		4·00		4·00	
H$_2$O	—		3·05		—		2·05		—		2·16	
M[‡]	0·98		0·53		1·16		0·92		1·72		0·76	

7. Beidellite, Black Jack mine, Carson district, Owyhee County, Idaho, U.S.A. (Shannon, 1922).

8. Beidellite, Velka Kopan, near Chust, Carpathian Ukraine (Rost, 1944).

9. Beidellite, Beidell, Saguache County, Colorado (Larsen and Wherry, 1917) (Includes SO$_3$ 6·65).

10. Green-yellow nontronite, joint fillings in diabasic basalt, Garfield, Washington, U.S.A. (Kerr *et al.*, 1950) (Includes SO$_3$ 7·00).

11. Yellow-green nontronite in veins associated with weathered basalt, Colfax, Whitman County, Washington, U.S.A. (Allen and Scheid, 1946).   Anal. N. Davidson.

12. White soapy saponite, chrysotile asbestos mine, Krugersdorp, Transvaal, associated with serpentine and chlorite (Schmidt and Heystek, 1953).   Anal. D. Sampson.

[†] Nos. 7, 9 and 11 were calculated assuming 20(O) and 4(OH), and ignoring the listed value of H$_2$O$^+$.   The remainder were calculated according to the method of Mackenzie (1957b).

[‡] M = total charge on inter-layer cations.

Table 39. Smectite analyses—*continued*

	13.	14.	15.	16.	17.	18.
SiO$_2$	43·62	50·01	40·46	53·95	33·40	38·59
TiO$_2$	0·00	<0·04	—	tr.	0·15	0·31
Al$_2$O$_3$	5·50	3·89	10·15	0·14	7·45	13·36
Fe$_2$O$_3$	0·66	0·21	3·56	0·03	1·73	3·41
FeO	—	—	4·89	—	—	—
MnO	0·06	—	0·24	—	tr.	—
ZnO	—	—	—	—	36·73	23·50
MgO	24·32	25·61	20·71	25·89	0·78	1·18
CaO	2·85	1·31	1·94	0·16	1·92	0·94
Na$_2$O	0·08	—	0·25	3·04	0·22	0·01
K$_2$O	0·04	—	0·32	0·23	0·27	0·18
H$_2$O$^+$	5·48	12·02	4·24	5·61	7·14	8·05
H$_2$O$^-$	17·42†	7·28	13·33‡	9·29	9·78	10·39
Total	100·03	100·37	100·23	99·56	99·70	99·92
α	1·490	1·511	1·513	1·489	1·564	1·570
β	1·531	—	—	1·499	—	—
γ	1·534	1·514	1·536	1·510	1·605	1·605
n	—	—	—	—	—	—
D	—	—	—	—	—	—

NUMBERS OF IONS§

	13.	14.	15.	16.	17.	18.
Si	7·00 ⎫ 8·00	7·49 ⎫ 8·00	6·32 ⎫ 8·00	7·78 ⎫ 7·80	6·54 ⎫ 8·00	6·78 ⎫ 8·00
Al	1·00 ⎭	0·51 ⎭	1·68 ⎭	0·02 ⎭	1·46 ⎭	1·22 ⎭
Al	0·04	0·17	0·19	—	0·24	1·56
Ti	—	—	—	—	—	—
Fe^{+3}	0·08	0·03	0·42	—	0·26	0·46
Fe^{+2}	— 5·94	— 5·95	0·64 6·00	— 6·28‖	— 6·00	— 5·40
Mn	0·01	—	0·03	—	—	—
Zn	—	—	—	—	5·28	3·08
Mg	5·81	5·75	4·84	5·57	0·22	0·30
Ca	0·49	0·21	0·33	0·02	0·40	0·18
Na	0·02 0·52	— 0·21	0·08 0·59	0·85 0·91	0·04 0·48	— 0·22
K	0·01	—	0·06	0·04	0·04	0·04
(OH)	4·00	4·00	4·00	4·00	4·00	4·00
H$_2$O	0·93	4·00	1·97	0·70	—	—
M¶	1·01	0·42	1·04	0·93	0·88	0·40

13. Pale blue saponite, lava vesicles, Allt Ribhein, Fiskavaig Bay, Skye, Scotland (Mackenzie, 1957b). Anal. J. B. Craig.
14. Saponite, veins in dolomitic limestone, near Milford, Utah (Cahoon, 1954). Anal. W. Savournin.
15. Saponite, Caslav, Czechoslovakia (Konta and Sindelar, 1955) (Includes P$_2$O$_5$ 0·14).
16. White hectorite, Hector, California (Kerr *et al.*, 1950). Anal. Ledoux & Co. (Includes Li$_2$O 1·22).
17. Reddish brown sauconite, Coon Hollow Mine, Boone County, Arkansas (Ross, 1946). Anal. M. K. Carron (Includes CaO 0·13).
18. Reddish brown sauconite, Liberty Mine, Meekers Grove, Wisconsin (Ross, 1946). Anal. M. K. Carron.

    † At 300°C.
    ‡ At 160°C.
    § Nos. 17 and 18 were calculated assuming 20(O) and 4(OH), ignoring the listed value of H$_2$O$^+$. The remainder were calculated according to the method of Mackenzie (1957b).
    ‖ Includes Li 0·71.
    ¶ M = total charge on inter-layer cations.

Various suggestions have been made to explain the values of basal spacings exhibited at different stages of hydration. Some may be related directly to an integral number of water molecule layers repeating regularly throughout the structure (Bradley *et al.*, 1937), while others indicate a continuously variable amount of water (Hofmann and Bilke, 1936) which may be attributed to randomly mixed layers of two or more different hydrates. Some workers suggest that initially at least the inter-layer water is essentially water of hydration surrounding the replaceable cation, and that this leads to a characteristic basal spacing (Méring, 1946; Mackenzie, 1950). Among the many cations which can enter the inter-layer spaces of smectites, an important one is the ammonium ion, and a large number of organic substances which contain an amino radical such as amines, pyrimidines, purines, etc., are also easily substituted. Organic molecules with planar configurations such as the purines lie parallel to the clay mineral sheets and may be adsorbed in single or double layers (Hendricks, 1941). Another group of organic substances readily adsorbed are the polyhydric alcohols such as glycol and glycerol, and more complex compounds, the molecules of which have some polar character. Because of these marked adsorption properties, smectites (the principal constituent of fuller's earths) are extensively used as decolorizing agents, for purifying fats and oils, and in the refinement of petroleum. Extensive studies have been made of the amounts of various liquids adsorbed under various conditions (*e.g.* Gieseking, 1939; Grim *et al.*, 1947). It is believed that polar molecules are held by a C–H–O bond (MacEwan, 1948), and the fact that large numbers of (OH) ions are required to form these bonds is used to support the Edelman and Favjee model for the montmorillonite structure. The structure proposed by McConnell (see p. 228), however, is consistent with both X-ray and chemical data.

It has been found that the substitution of lithium (or magnesium) as exchange cation in montmorillonite makes it less expandable with glycerol after moderate heating. The effect is more marked with increasing lithium substitution but does not occur with beidellite and nontronite. Greene-Kelly (1955) suggests that when the net charge on a layer is due to octahedral substitution, heating can cause migration of the Li and Mg ions into octahedral sites, and that the absence of inter-layer cations then prevents swelling.

Structural formula. Various methods have been used in calculating formulae from chemical analyses, and in the absence of additional information such as cell volume and density, all necessarily make some fundamental assumption. For smectites, the value of H_2O^+ can be used to derive the number of $(OH)^-$ ions assuming that $(O)+(OH)=24$. The difficulty of distinguishing adsorbed from constitutional water, however, leads some workers to ignore the H_2O^+ figure and to calculate other ions on the basis of 22 oxygen equivalents. Mackenzie (1957b) shows how a formula may be calculated using the H_2O^+ figure assuming that all hydrogen present is in the 4(OH) ions and in the adsorbed water.[1] The latter two methods have been used to derive the numbers of ions shown in Table 39, so that where a number of water molecules per formula unit is given, this corresponds to water held beyond the temperature at which H_2O^- was determined, in most cases 105°–110°C. Minor constituents are in most cases allocated to some role in the structure although the samples were

---

[1] This method, though less simple, yields the same results as that based on 22 oxygen equivalents.

known to contain small amounts of impurity. Further difficulty arises in the dual role of Mg as an octahedral and an exchange cation, but although the total of Y ions is greater than its ideal value in several cases, only in anal. 16 (Table 39) is Mg designated in part as an exchange cation.

Thermal effects. On heating, the inter-layer water of smectites is lost mostly between 100° and 250°C. but some remains to about 300°C. at which temperature slow loss of constitutional (OH) water begins. Rapid loss of (OH) water takes place at about 500°C. and is complete at about 750°C. It is reported (Earley *et al.*, 1953) that at this stage the basal spacing has shrunk to about 9·8 Å and that the a and b parameters and the crystal symmetry have changed; heating to 870°C. enhances these effects. Midgley and Gross (1956) describe the heating of a saponite for which shrinkage to 9·7 Å occurs at 550°C., but further shrinkage takes place with heating to 600°–750°C. yielding a minimum basal spacing of 9·5 Å; this corresponds to the inter-layer distance in talc. The dehydration of montmorillonite is at least partly reversible as long as it is not taken to completion, and even after heating to 600°C. some inter-layer water can be regained slowly (Grim and Bradley, 1948). Examples of dehydration curves of smectites are presented by Ross and Hendricks (1945). Decomposition of the structure generally occurs between 800° and 900°C. and beyond this the phases formed vary according to initial composition. The most important products are spinel, α or β quartz, or cristobalite, and, at the highest temperatures (1200°–1300°C.), mullite or cordierite depending upon the amount of Mg present. The fibrous saponite from the Lizard, Cornwall (Midgley and Gross, 1956), is transformed at 950°C. to enstatite and amorphous silica. Differential thermal analysis curves of smectites (*e.g.* Grim, 1951) show an endothermic peak at low temperatures corresponding to the loss of inter-layer water, and another corresponding to loss of (OH) water beginning at 450°–500°C., with a maximum at about 700°C. With some smectites the first endothermic peak appears to be double, perhaps indicating that the exchangeable ion is hydrated (Kerr *et al.*, 1950; Midgley and Gross, 1956). Doubling of the second endothermic peak also occurs for some specimens, possibly due to the presence of two slightly different montmorillonites, but alternatively it may be attributed to the expulsion of differently bonded (OH) ions at slightly different temperatures. Replacement of Al by Mg or Fe lowers the temperature of the second endothermic peak. Yet another endothermic peak sometimes occurs at about 800°–900°C. and is generally attributed to the final breakdown of the structure which can retain a considerable degree of order even after all (OH) has been expelled. Other explanations of the third endothermic peak include that by Page (1943) who associates it with Mg octahedrally coordinated by (OH) ions, and McConnell (1950) who associates it with the expulsion of (OH) ions which had replaced oxygens in the tetrahedral parts of the composite layer. Earley *et al.* (1953), however, present evidence that this third endothermic peak does not involve (OH) ions, and is related entirely to the final breakdown of the structure.

The first exothermic peak given by smectites which have little substitution in Z sites and which are low in iron corresponds to the formation of quartz, while spinel is formed if there is appreciable $[Al]^4$ and $[Fe^{+3}]^6$ (Earley *et al.*, 1953). High magnesium and low iron content tend to raise the temperature of the first exothermic peak and in such cases enstatite, sillimanite or anorthite are formed at about 1000°C. depending upon the amount of Mg and Ca present in the original compound. In the case of nontronite, spinel forms as fast as the structure breaks down so that the exothermic effect masks the highest endothermic peak (Kerr *et al.*, 1951). An additional exothermic peak usually occurs for all smectites at about 1200°C. which is due to the formation of mullite or cordierite. The specimens which yield spinel at first, subsequently form cristobalite, and spinel disappears at about 1200°C. (Bradley and Grim, 1951). The d.t.a. curves of montmorillonite, beidellite, nontronite and hectorite are distinguishable (Kerr *et al.*, 1949) and curves for montmorillonites differ from those of illites in the position of the second endothermic peak (Grim and Rowland, 1942). Some examples of d.t.a. curves of smectites are illustrated in Fig. 51.

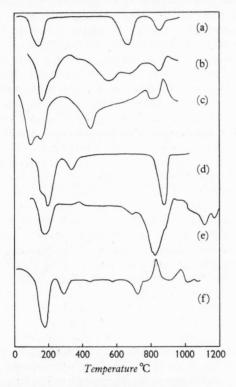

FIG. 51. Illustration of d.t.a. curves for some smectites:
    (a) Montmorillonite, Santa Rita, New Mexico (after Earley *et al.*, 1953).
    (b) Beidellite, Beidell, Colorado (after Grim and Rowland, 1942).
    (c) Nontronite ("chloropal"), Hungary (after Grim and Rowland, 1942).
    (d) Saponite, Krugersdorp, Transvaal (after Schmidt and Heystek, 1953).
    (e) Hectorite, California (after Schmidt and Heystek, 1953).
    (f) Sauconite, Coon Hollow mine, Arkansas (after Faust, 1951).

Experimental. Alteration of montmorillonites has been effected in the laboratory using $MgCl_2$ and $NH_4(OH)$ to form a chlorite-like substance, and using KCl and KOH to produce an illite; partial alteration to kaolinite has also been achieved (Caillère and Hénin, 1947, 1949). Smectites have been synthesized in many different ways. Noll (1936), for example, heated mixtures of oxides with water in a bomb to 300°C. at 87 atmospheres. The most favourable proportions of oxides were $X : Al_2O_3 : SiO_2 = 0.2 : 1.0 : 4.0$ where X was MgO, CaO, Na_2O or K_2O. At higher oxide concentrations, using Na_2O, analcite was formed, and using K_2O, mica, kaolinite and potassium felspar resulted. At lower oxide concentrations the product was mostly kaolinite. Montmorillonite was obtained by Sedletzky (1937) by leaching sodium silicate and sodium aluminate with $MgCl_2$ for 4 years, and by Strese and Hofmann (1941) by boiling $MgCl_2$ and hydrated silica with KOH or $Ca(OH)_2$ or NaOH.

Montmorillonite has also been prepared from bentonitic glasses at 300°C. (Hauser and Reynolds, 1939) and from illite by treatment with sodium cobalti-nitrite or $MgCl_2$ (White, 1951). Beidellite was prepared by using alumino-silicates, albite and CO_2–charged water (Norton, 1939), and nontronite by heating dilute solutions of Na_2SiO_3 in $FeCl_3$ and neutralizing with NaOH (Hamilton and Furtwängler, 1951). In general terms the formation of mont-morillonite may be said to be favoured by alkaline conditions and the presence of magnesium. Nontronite has been synthesized also from silica gel and ferric oxide at 350°C. and 167 atmospheres (Ewell and Insley, 1935).

Studies in the systems Al_2O_3–SiO_2–H_2O, MgO–Al_2O_3–SiO_2–H_2O and Na_2O–Al_2O_3–SiO_2–H_2O by various workers have resulted in the synthesis of many smectites, with the advantage that chemical and physical properties could be determined for pure homogeneous substances, and related to the controlled variation of chemical composition. Ames and Sand (1958) studied synthetic smectites of various compositions most of which had sodium as exchange cation. Maximum hydrothermal stability is achieved when optimum substitution occurs in either octahedral or tetrahedral sites, producing maximum exchange capacity. For di-octahedral smectites (montmorillonite and beidellite) the highest temperature of stability is 480°C. and for tri-octahedral members (saponite and hectorite) 750°C. at 1000 atmospheres. Lower stability tem-peratures result from deviations from optimum composition, a pure magnesium saponite ($Na_{0.66}Mg_{6.00}Si_{8.00}$), for example, breaking down at 255°C. at 1000 atmospheres (see also Roy and Roy, 1955; Sand, 1955; Sand *et al.*, 1957). Similarly the absence of an inter-layer alkali cation causes low decomposition temperatures. An unusual beidellite, in which the exchangeable ions are $Al(OH)_2^+$, has been prepared from high purity $Al_2O_3 : (SiO_2)_4$ gels, and gives the smectite type of X-ray pattern, but in this d_{001} increases to only 14 Å with glycerol (see vermiculite). This phase does not form above about 420°C. and it is assumed to be stable down to atmospheric temperature and pressure (Roy and Osborn, 1954). Additions of Na, Mg and Ca to the above composition yield typical beidellites. Saponites, sauconites and chromium and nickel mont-morillonites have also been synthesized (Roy and Sand, 1956).

OPTICAL AND PHYSICAL PROPERTIES

Smectites occur most commonly in fine-grained aggregates which may be vermiform, lamellar or spherulitic. Sometimes the constituents of such aggre-gates are well oriented and give the appearance of well formed crystals, but examination under the electron microscope reveals that the fundamental particles are extremely thin platelets, which for montmorillonite and saponite are mostly irregular in outline. A fibrous saponite with α 1.520, γ 1.535 has been described by Midgley and Gross (1956), and another fibrous saponite by Caillère and Hénin (1957). Nontronite particles tend to be lath-like while those of hectorite are still more elongated, in the direction of the *x* axis (Mackenzie, 1957a). More rarely, montmorillonite specimens exhibit well formed pseudo-hexagonal plates (Nixon and Weir, 1957) and occasionally a fibrous texture (Caillère *et al.*, 1953). The most common colours of montmorillonites are pink, buff, grey or light brown, and many are white, while nontronites are usually bright green. Those which are coloured show distinct pleochroism, the colours for nontronite being green parallel to (001), and yellow perpendicular to (001). Because of their fine-grained nature, detailed optical properties cannot easily be determined, but oriented aggregates, and thin films of clay material, can yield useful measurements approximating to correct values (Grim, 1934). A further difficulty, however, is that optical properties are affected not only by compositional changes, but by state of hydration, and sometimes by the immersion liquid itself (Vendel, 1945): Table 40, however, gives the approximate ranges

Table 40. OPTICAL PROPERTIES OF SMECTITES

	α	γ	δ	$2V_\alpha$
Montmorillonite–beidellite series	1·48–1·57	1·50–1·60	0·02–0·03	0°–30°
Nontronite	1·56–1·61	1·57–1·64	0·03–0·045	25°–70°
Saponite	1·48–1·53	1·50–1·59	0·01–0·036	moderate
Hectorite	$\simeq 1\cdot49$	1·52	0·03	small
Sauconite	1·55–1·58	1·59–1·62	0·03–0·04	small

within which the optical constants of the various smectites lie. Refractive indices are only slightly influenced by the substitutions Si–Al, and Al–Mg, but are considerably dependent upon iron content (Winchell, 1945). Fig. 52 illustrates the approximately straight line relationship for γ and α when plotted against percentage of FeO. All smectites are optically negative, but $2V_\alpha$ is variable over a wide range. The increase of refractive index with loss of inter-layer water has been demonstrated directly, and indirectly by its increase with temperature as water is driven off. Dehydrated montmorillonite and saponite have refractive indices similar to those of pyrophyllite and talc respectively.

Specific gravities are also affected considerably by degree of hydration, one sample showing variation from 1·77 for 46 per cent. water content to 2·35 in the dry state (DeWit and Arens, 1950). "Dry state" values as high as 2·7 and 2·3 have been found

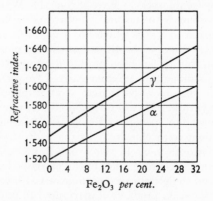

FIG. 52. Refractive indices of montmorillonite plotted against Fe_2O_3 content (after Ross and Hendricks, 1945).

for nontronite and saponite respectively.   The infra-red absorption spectra of talc, saponite and hectorite have been studied and compared by Farmer (1958) using oriented specimens.   The three related minerals give similar spectra but the bands of the smectites are more diffuse because of isomorphous substitutions in the talc structure.   The smectites show strong broad absorption bands in the region corresponding to the stretching modes of inter-layer water; these bands have three components, one of which corresponds to a very weak hydrogen bond.

DISTINGUISHING FEATURES

The average refractive indices for smectites are similar to those for illites and kaolinites, but minerals of the kaolinite group have lower birefringence than most smectites, and illites generally have higher birefringence.   Dehydrated montmorillonites and saponites which have low iron content have refractive indices similar to those of pyrophyllite and talc respectively but birefringences are lower.   Optical methods alone are in general not reliable for the identification of smectites and it is usually necessary to observe several other properties, such as d.t.a. curves, dehydration curves, and X-ray powder patterns before and after treatment by heating and by organic liquids.   A method for separating kaolinite from smectites has been described (Rodda, 1952) in which kaolinite floats in Clerici solution of specific gravity 2·70 whereas montmorillonite and sauconite sink at 3·55.   Flotation in a mixture of alcohol and bromoform has been used for separating mixtures of montmorillonite and halloysite (Loughnan, 1957).

PARAGENESIS

Montmorillonite and beidellite are the principal constituents of bentonite clay deposits.   These have been formed by the alteration of basic igneous eruptive rocks, usually tuffs and volcanic ash, and contain in addition varying amounts of cristobalite, zeolites, biotite, quartz, felspar and other minerals found in volcanic rocks.   Except for the Wyoming bentonites, calcium rather than sodium is the naturally occurring exchange cation.   "Fuller's earth" is a name given to a clay which has a high adsorptive capacity (see p. 229); its principal clay mineral constituent is usually montmorillonite.   Most of the fuller's earth in Europe has been produced by weathering of basic igneous rocks, or occurs in a sedimentary product derived from them.   The name is also used in England to denote a particular stratigraphical formation.   Smectites also occur as hydrothermal alteration products around metalliferous veins or deposits, and near hot springs and geysers, sometimes as the outer part of a zoned deposit along with chlorite.   In the hydrothermal alteration of plagioclase associated with ore veins in the Front Range mineral belt (Bonorino, 1959) montmorillonite occurs, mainly in the marginal zone, either alone or mixed with kaolinite, and sometimes as a regular mixed layer illite-montmorillonite.   The zoning of alteration products is attributed to migrating gaseous fluids, the composition of which changes through reaction with the wall rock.   The critical changes are increase of Si:Al ratio, decrease of K concentration, and increase of pH.   In calcareous sediments a smectite may be derived by reaction between the magnesium and silica of silicified dolomitic rocks.   Ames *et al.* (1958), in a study of the bentonite deposits at Hector, California, describe their formation as being related to hot spring activity.   The hectorite at this locality is formed through the alteration of the zeolite clinoptilolite, which itself was derived from tuff and volcanic ash having a high content of glass.   Smectites are widely found (often mixed with illites) in soils and in shales which have resulted from the weathering of basic rocks.   Probably the most important single factor in determining that montmorillonite shall form in any of the environments mentioned above is the availability of sufficient magnesium.   Thus montmorillonite results from the weathering of basic rocks mainly in conditions of poor drainage when magnesium is not removed.   In good drainage conditions magnesium is leached and kaolinite results.   Other factors which favour the formation of smectites are an alkaline environment, availability of calcium, and paucity of potassium.   Alteration of basic igneous rocks yields mostly montmorillonite, and acid rocks tend to yield illites unless Mg and Ca are high and K low in concentration.   Weaver (1958) points out that "expanded mica" clays (*i.e.* smectites derived from muscovite and biotite), which are easily collapsed by treatment with potassium, are unlikely to be found in marine sediments.   Most of the smectites, smectite-illite, and smectite-chlorite intergrowths found in marine sediments were derived from non-micaceous material.   Saponite occurs mainly associated with mineral veins, but also in amygdaloidal cavities in basalt along with celadonite (see p. 37).   Nontronite is found both in mineral veins (often with opal and quartz) and as an alteration product of volcanic glasses. Smectites are probably not the most stable of the clay mineral products of weathering, since with prolonged leaching by water kaolinite would tend to form.   They are frequently found along with kaolinites particularly in soil clays, and with illites, detrital micas and other layered minerals.   Random or regular mixed layer aggregates are not uncommon.   Smectites are sometimes found also as alteration products of olivine.

REFERENCES

Allen, V. T. and **Scheid, V. E.**, 1946.   Nontronite in the Columbia River region. *Amer. Min.*, vol. 31, p. 294.
Ames, L. L. and **Sand, L. B.**, 1958.   Factors effecting maximum hydrothermal stability in montmorillonites.   *Amer. Min.*, vol. 43, p. 641.
—— —— and **Goldich, S. S.**, 1958.   A contribution on the Hector, California, bentonite deposit.   *Econ. Geol.*, vol. 53, p. 22.
Andreatta, C., 1949.   Studio di un interssante giacimento di riempimento di argille montmorillonitiche idrotermali (Vallortigara-Posina, Schio).   *Mem. Accad. Sci. Ist. Bologna, Cl. Sci. Fiz. Sez. Sci. Nat.*, ser. 10, vol. 5 (M.A. 11–547).
Bonorino, F. G., 1959.   Hydrothermal alteration in the Front Range mineral belt, Colorado.   *Bull. Geol. Soc. Amer.*, vol. 70, p. 53.
Bradley, W. F., 1945.   Molecular associations between montmorillonite and some poly-functional organic liquids.   *Journ. Amer. Chem. Soc.*, vol. 67, p. 975.
—— and **Grim, R. E.**, 1951.   High temperature thermal effects of clay and related minerals.   *Amer. Min.*, vol. 36, p. 182.
—— —— and **Clark, W. C.**, 1937.   Study of the behaviour of montmorillonite upon wetting.   *Zeit. Krist.*, vol. 97, p. 216.
Brindley, G. W., 1951.   *X-ray identification and crystal structures of clay minerals.* Min. Soc., London.

Brindley, G. W., 1955. Stevensite, a montmorillonite-type mineral showing mixed layer characteristics. *Amer. Min.*, vol. 40, p. 239.

—— and **Rustom, M.**, 1958. Adsorption and retention of an organic material by montmorillonite in the presence of water. *Amer. Min.*, vol. 43, p. 627.

Brown, G., 1950. A Fourier investigation of montmorillonite. *Clay Minerals Bull.* No. 4, p. 109.

—— and **Greene-Kelly, R.**, 1954. X-ray diffraction by a randomly interstratified clay mineral. *Acta Cryst.*, vol. 7, p. 101.

—— and **MacEwan, D. M. C.**, 1951. X-ray diffraction by structures with random interstratification, in *X-ray identification and crystal structures of clay minerals.* Min. Soc., London, p. 266.

Cahoon, H. P., 1954. Saponite near Milford, Utah. *Amer. Min.*, vol. 39, p. 222.

Caillère, S. and **Hénin, S.**, 1947. Formation d'une phyllite du type kaolinique par traitement d'une montmorillonite. *Compt. Rend. Acad. Sci. Paris*, vol. 224, p. 53.

—— —— 1949. Experimental formation of chlorites from montmorillonite. *Min. Mag.*, vol. 28, p. 612.

—— —— and **Mathieu-Sicaud, A. O.**, 1953. Sur une montmorillonite à texture fibreuse. *Compt. Rend. Acad. Sci. Paris*, vol. 236, p. 1581.

—— —— 1957. Sur la presence à Dielette d'une saponite à texture fibreuse. *Bull. Soc. franç. Min. Crist.*, vol. 80, p. 543.

Chukhrov, F. V. and **Anosov, F. Y.**, 1950. Medmontite, a copper mineral of the montmorillonite group. *Mém. Soc. Russe Min.*, vol. 79, p. 23.

DeWit, C. P. and **Arens, P. L.**, 1950. Moisture content and density of some clay minerals and some remarks on the hydration pattern of clay. *Trans. 4th Internat. Congr. Soil. Sci.*, vol. 2, p. 59.

Dittler, E. and **Hofmann, U.**, 1945. Ein neues Montmorillonitvorkommen. *Chem. Erde*, vol. 15, p. 406 (M.A. 11–172).

Earley, J. W., Brindley, G. W., McVeagh, W. J. and **Vanden Heuvel, R. C.**, 1956. A regularly interstratified montmorillonite-chlorite. *Amer. Min.*, vol. 41, p. 258.

—— **Milne, I. H.** and **McVeagh, W. J.**, 1953. Thermal, dehydration and X-ray studies on montmorillonite. *Amer. Min.*, vol. 38, p. 770.

—— **Osthaus, B. B.** and **Milne, I. H.**, 1953. Purification and properties of montmorillonite. *Amer. Min.*, vol. 38, p. 707.

Edelman, C. H. and **Favjee, J. C. L.**, 1940. On the crystal structure of montmorillonite and halloysite. *Zeit. Krist.*, vol. 102, p. 417.

Ewell, R. H. and **Insley, H.**, 1935. Hydrothermal synthesis of kaolinite, dickite, beidellite and nontronite. *Journ. Res. U.S. Nat. Bur. Standards*, vol. 15, p. 173.

Farmer, V. C., 1958. The infra-red spectra of talc, saponite, and hectorite. *Min. Mag.*, vol. 31, p. 829.

Faust, G. T., 1951. Thermal analysis and X-ray studies of sauconite and of some zinc minerals of the same paragenetic association. *Amer. Min.*, vol. 36, p. 795.

—— 1955. Thermal analysis and X-ray studies of griffithite. *Journ. Wash. Acad. Sci.*, vol. 45, p. 66.

—— **Hathaway, J. C.** and **Millot, G.**, 1959. A re-study of stevensite and allied minerals. *Amer. Min.*, vol. 44, p. 342.

—— and **Murata, K. J.**, 1953. Stevensite redefined as a member of the montmorillonite group. *Amer. Min.*, vol. 38, p. 973.

Foster, M. D., 1951. The importance of exchangeable magnesium and cation exchange capacity in the study of montmorillonite clays. *Amer. Min.*, vol. 36, p. 717.

Gieseking, J. E., 1939. The mechanism of cation exchange in the montmorillonite-beidellite-nontronite type of clay minerals. *Soil. Sci.*, vol. 47, p. 1.

Greene-Kelly, R., 1955. Dehydration of the montmorillonite minerals. *Min. Mag.,* vol. 30, p. 604.

Grim, R. E., 1934. Petrographic study of clay minerals—a laboratory note. *Journ. Sed. Petr.,* vol. 4, p. 45.

—— 1951. *Clay mineralogy.* McGraw-Hill, New York.

—— **Allaway, W. H.** and **Cuthbert, F. L.,** 1947. Reaction of different clay minerals with organic cations. *Journ. Amer. Ceram. Soc.,* vol. 30, p. 137.

—— and **Bradley, W. F.,** 1948. Rehydration of the clay minerals. *Amer. Min.,* vol. 33, p. 50.

—— and **Rowland, R. A.,** 1942. Differential thermal analyses of clay minerals and other hydrous materials. *Amer. Min.,* vol. 27, p. 746.

Hamilton, G. and **Furtwängler, W.,** 1951. Synthese von Nontronit. *Tschermaks Min. Petr. Mitt.,* ser. 3, vol. 2, p. 397 (M.A. 12–84).

Hauser, E. A. and **Reynolds, H. H.,** 1939. Alteration of glasses to montmorillonite. *Amer. Min.,* vol. 24, p. 590.

Hendricks, S. B., 1938. On the crystal structure of talc and pyrophyllite. *Zeit. Krist.,* vol. 99, p. 264.

—— 1941. Base exchange of the clay mineral montmorillonite for organic cations and its dependence upon absorption due to van der Waals forces. *Journ. Phys. Chem.,* vol. 45, p. 65.

—— 1942. Lattice structure of clay minerals and some properties of clays. *Journ. Geol.,* vol. 50, p. 276.

Hofmann, U. and **Bilke, W.,** 1936. Ueber die innerkristalline Quellung und das Basenaustauschvermögens des Montmorillonits. *Koll. Zeit.,* vol. 77, p. 239.

—— **Endel, K.** and **Diederich, W.,** 1933. Kristallstruktur und Quellung von Montmorillonit. *Zeit. Krist.,* vol. 86A, p. 340.

Kerr, P. F., Kulp, J. L. and **Hamilton, P. K.,** 1949. Differential thermal analyses of reference clay mineral specimens. Preliminary report No. 3. *Reference clay minerals. Amer. Petroleum Inst., Res. Proj.* 49. Columbia Univ., New York.

—— and **others,** 1950. Analytical data on reference clay materials. Preliminary report No. 7. *Reference clay minerals. Amer. Petroleum Inst., Res. Proj.* 49. Columbia Univ., New York.

Konta, J. and **Sindelar, J.,** 1955. Saponite from the fissure fillings of the amphibolites of Caslav. *Univ. Carolina (Prague), Geol.,* vol. 1, p. 177.

Larsen, E. S. and **Wherry, E. T.,** 1917. Leverrierite from Colorado. *Journ. Washington Acad. Sci.,* vol. 7, p. 213 (M.A. 2–133).

Loughnan, F. C., 1957. A technique for the isolation of montmorillonite and halloysite. *Amer. Min.,* vol. 42, p. 393.

MacEwan, D. M. C., 1946. The identification and estimation of the montmorillonite group of clay minerals with special reference to soil clays. *Journ. Soc. Chem. Ind.* (London), vol. 65, p. 298.

—— 1948. Complexes of clays with organic compounds, I. *Trans. Faraday Soc.,* vol. 44, p. 349.

—— 1951. The montmorillonite minerals (montmorillonoids), in *X-ray identification and crystal structures of clay minerals.* Min. Soc., London.

Mackenzie, R. C., 1950. Some notes on the hydrations of montmorillonite. *Clay Min. Bull.,* vol. 1, p. 115.

—— 1957a (Editor). *The differential thermal investigation of clays.* Min. Soc., London.

—— 1957b. Saponite from Allt Ribhein, Fiskavaig Bay, Skye. *Min. Mag.,* vol. 31, p. 672.

McAtee, J. L., Jr., 1956. Determination of random interstratification in montmorillonite. *Amer. Min.,* vol. 41, p. 627.

McConnell, D., 1950. The crystal chemistry of montmorillonite. *Amer. Min.*, vol. 35, p. 166.

Marshall, C. E., 1935. Layer lattices and base-exchange clays. *Zeit. Krist.*, vol. 91, p. 433.

Mathieson, A. McL. and **Walker, G. F.**, 1954. Crystal structure of magnesium-vermiculite. *Amer. Min.*, vol. 39, p. 231.

Méring, J., 1946. The hydration of montmorillonite. *Trans. Faraday Soc.*, vol. 42B, p. 205

—— 1949. X-ray interference by disordered layer lattices. *Acta Cryst.*, vol. 2, p. 371.

Midgley, H. G. and **Gross, K. A.**, 1956. Thermal reactions of smectites. *Clay Min. Bull.*, vol. 3, p. 79.

Mitsuda, T., 1957. Long spacing clay mineral from the Uku mine, Yamaguchi Prefecture, Japan. *Min. Journ. (Japan)*, vol. 2, p. 169.

Miyamoto, N., 1957. Iron-rich saponite from Mazé, Niigata Prefecture, Japan. *Min. Journ. (Japan)*, vol. 2, p. 193.

Nagelschmidt, G., 1938. On the atomic arrangement and variability of the members of the montmorillonite group. *Min. Mag.*, vol. 25, p. 140.

Nixon, H. L. and **Weir, A. H.**, 1957. The morphology of the Unter-Rupsroth montmorillonite. *Min. Mag.*, vol. 31, p. 413.

Noll, W., 1936. Zynthese von montmorilloniten. Ein Beitrag Zur Kenntniss der Bildungsbedingungen und des Chemismus von Montmorillonit. *Chemie der Erde*, vol. 10, pp. 129, 154.

Norton, F. H., 1939. Hydrothermal formation of clay minerals in the laboratory. *Amer. Min.*, vol. 24, p. 1.

Page, J. B., 1943. Differential thermal analyses of montmorillonite. *Soil Sci.*, vol. 56, p. 273.

Rodda, J. L., 1952. Anomalous behaviour of montmorillonite clays in Clerici solution. *Amer. Min.*, vol. 37, p. 117.

Ross, C. S., 1946. Sauconite, a clay mineral of the montmorillonite group. *Amer. Min.*, vol. 31, p. 411.

—— and **Hendricks, S. B.**, 1945. Minerals of the montmorillonite group. *U.S. Geol. Surv., Prof. Paper* 205B.

Rost, R., 1944. Contribution to the knowledge of clay minerals. *Rozpravy České Akad.*, vol. 54, No. 15 (M.A. 10–22).

Rowland, R. A., Weiss, E. J. and **Bradley, W. F.**, 1956. Dehydration of monoionic montmorillonites. *Proc. 4th Nat. Conf. on Clays and Clay Minerals (U.S.A.)*, p. 85.

Roy, R. and **Osborn, E. F.**, 1954. The system Al_2O_3–SiO_2–H_2O. *Amer. Min.*, vol. 39, p. 853.

—— and **Sand, L. B.**, 1956. A note on some properties of synthetic montmorillonites. *Amer. Min.*, vol. 41, p. 505.

Roy, D. M. and **Roy, R.**, 1955. Synthesis and stability of minerals in the system MgO–Al_2O_3–SiO_2–H_2O. *Amer. Min.*, vol. 40, p. 147.

Sand, L. B., 1955. Montmorillonites stable at high temperatures. *Bull. Geol. Soc. Amer.*, vol. 66, p. 1610 (abstract).

—— **Roy, R.** and **Osborn, E. F.**, 1957. Stability relations of some minerals in the Na_2O–Al_2O_3–SiO_2–H_2O system. *Econ. Geol.*, vol. 52, p. 169.

Schmidt, E. R. and **Heystek, H.**, 1953. A saponite from Krugersdorp district, Transvaal. *Min. Mag.*, vol. 30, p. 201.

Sedletzky, I. D., 1937. Genesis of minerals from soil colloids of the montmorillonite group. *Doklady Acad. Sci. USSR*, vol. 17, p. 375.

—— and **Yussupova, S. M.**, 1945. Variation in parameters of montmorillonite as affected by petroleum. *Doklady Acad. Sci. USSR*, vol. 46, p. 27 (M.A. 10–25).

Shannon, E. V., 1922.   Notes on the mineralogy of three gouge clays from precious metal veins.   *Proc. U.S. Nat. Mus.*, vol. 62, art. 15, p. 4 (M.A. 2–134).

Strese, H. and **Hofmann, U.**, 1941.   Synthese von Magnesium-Silikatgelen mit zweidimensional regelmässiger Struktur.   *Zeits. anorg. Chem.*, vol. 247, p. 65.

Vendel, M., 1945.   Zur Bestimmung der Lichtbrechung silikatischer Tonminerale. *Chemie der Erde*, vol. 15, p. 325.

Weaver, C. E., 1956.   The distribution and identification of mixed layer clays in sedimentary rocks.   *Amer. Min.*, vol. 41, p. 202.

—— 1958.   The effects and geologic significance of potassium "fixation" by expandable clay minerals derived from muscovite, biotite, chlorite and volcanic material.   *Amer. Min.*, vol. 43, p. 839.

Wells, R. C., 1937.   Analyses of rocks and minerals.   *U.S. Geol. Surv., Bull.* 878, p. 108.

White, J. L., 1951.   Transformation of illite into montmorillonite.   *Proc. Soil Sci. Soc. Amer.*, vol. 15, p. 129 (M.A. 11–546).

Winchell, A. N., 1945.   Montmorillonite.   *Amer. Min.*, vol. 30, p. 510.

Zvyagin, B. B. and **Pinsker, Z. G.**, 1949.   Electrographic investigations of the structure of montmorillonite.   *Doklady Acad. Sci. USSR*, vol. 68, p. 65.

Vermiculite $(Mg,Ca)_{0\cdot7}(Mg,Fe^{+3},Al)_{6\cdot0}[(Al,Si)_{8\cdot0}O_{20}](OH)_4\cdot8H_2O$

MONOCLINIC $(-)$

α	1·525–1·564
β	1·545–1·583
γ	1·545–1·583
δ	0·02–0·03
$2V_\alpha$	0°–8°

α approx. $\perp(001)$; O.A.P. (010).

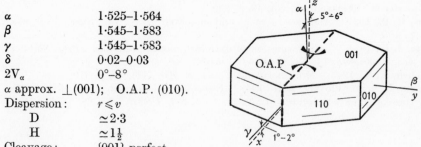

Dispersion:	$r \leqslant v$
D	$\simeq 2·3$
H	$\simeq 1\frac{1}{2}$
Cleavage:	{001} perfect.
Colour:	Colourless, yellow, green, brown; colourless in thin section.
Pleochroism:	α paler shades than β and γ.
Unit cell:	$a \simeq 5·3$, $b \simeq 9·2$, c 28·9 Å, β 97°.
	$Z = 2$. Space group Cc.

Readily attacked by acids, leaving silica with laminated texture.

Vermiculite could well be regarded as a tri-octahedral member of the smectite group but its special characteristics warrant its description as a separate mineral. The name, which is derived from the Latin *vermiculare*, to breed worms, alludes to the peculiar exfoliation phenomenon exhibited when specimens are rapidly heated. Many other names (jefferisite, kerrite, protovermiculite, vaalite, etc.) have been used in the past to describe minerals of the vermiculite group. In its natural state the mineral has little useful application, but when exfoliated it provides a low density material with excellent thermal and acoustic insulation properties which can form a constituent of lightweight concretes and plasters. It also finds use as a filler or extender in the manufacture of papers, plastics, and paints, and as a packing material.

STRUCTURE

The structure of vermiculite is basically that of talc since it contains a central octahedrally coordinated layer of (Mg,Fe) ions which lies between two inward pointing sheets of linked SiO_4 tetrahedra. As in talc and phlogopite, the central part of this composite layer may be regarded as one of brucite in which two out of three (OH) ions on each side are replaced by the apical oxygen of an SiO_4 tetrahedron. In talc the layers as a whole are electrically neutral, no inter-layer cations occur, and cohesion between successive sheets is very slight. In vermiculite the principal changes from the talc composition, $Mg_6Si_8O_{20}(OH)_4$, are a replacement of Si by Al, compensated by the presence of inter-layer cations, mainly magnesium.   A further difference from talc is the occurrence of water molecules between the structural layers.   The structure of vermiculite was first studied by Gruner (1934) who gave the unit cell as monoclinic with a 5·3 Å, b 9·2 Å, c between 28·57 and 28·77 Å and β 97° 09′.   The existence of inter-layer cations as well as water was recognized in the subsequent structure work by Hendricks and Jefferson (1938), Barshad (1948), and Walker (1951), and a complete structure determination was achieved from single-crystal X-ray data by Mathieson and Walker (1954) and Mathieson (1958).   The latter workers have shown that the inter-layer water molecules and cations occupy definite positions with respect to the oxygens of neighbouring talc-like layers.   The water molecule sites form a distorted hexagonal pattern such that each molecule is linked by a hydrogen bond to an oxygen on the silicate layer surface, and in a naturally occurring Mg-vermiculite two of these hexagonal networks occur in each inter-layer space.   Weak hydrogen bonding links together water molecules in the same plane, and the pairs of water planes are held together by the exchangeable cations which lie midway between them: the cations thus have a hydration shell of water molecules around them.   Not all available sites are in fact occupied by water molecules in normal atmospheric conditions and many of the water molecules do not enclose a cation.   Those which do not surround a cation may be referred to as unbound water, and this water is readily expelled below 110°C. The basal spacing (d_{002}) at ordinary temperatures and humidity is approximately 14·4 Å, but on dehydration successive changes occur (accompanied by endothermic peaks on a d.t.a. curve) which result in basal spacings of 13·8 Å, 11·6 Å and 9 Å.   The 13·8 Å stage is transitory and corresponds to displacement of the cations across one water layer to sites adjacent to the "talc" layer.   The 11·6 Å phase corresponds to replacement of the double water molecule layers by a

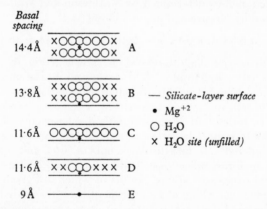

FIG. 53.   Diagrammatic view of inter-layer region in Mg-vermiculite at various stages of dehydration:

A—normal Mg-vermiculite in which 12 out of 16 water molecule sites are occupied.   B—reorganization of double sheet with about 8 of the 16 water molecule sites occupied.   C—replacement of double sheet by single sheet of water molecules.   D—removal of a further 5 water molecules leaving 3 in contact with the cation.   E—all inter-layer water removed leaving only the cation between the silicate layers (after Walker and Cole, 1957).

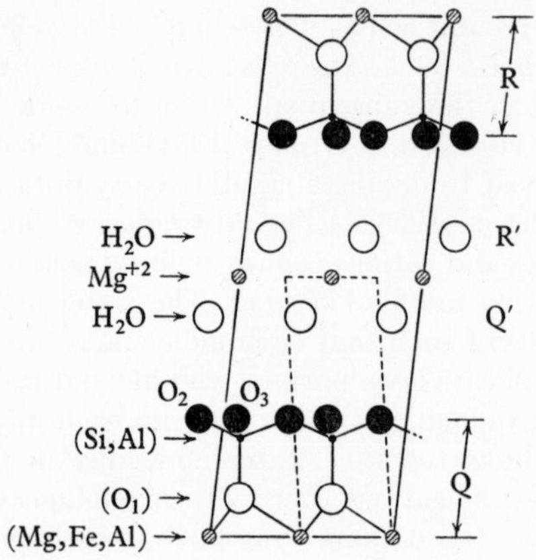

FIG. 54. The crystal structure of Mg-vermiculite projected on (010). Q and R refer to silicate half-layers, Q′ and R′ to sheets of water molecules (after Mathieson and Walker, 1954).

single sheet in which there are about eight water molecule sites per cation instead of the original sixteen. In the reverse direction, formation of the 11·6 and 13·8 Å phases can be observed under the microscope in ordinary light; the phase boundaries are seen converging on the centre of a partially dehydrated vermiculite flake as water is allowed to enter at its edges (Walker, 1959). The final stage of dehydration which is reached at about 650°C. results in the 9 Å basal spacing corresponding to the talc structure. (Immediately following the 11·6 Å stage, Walker and Cole (1957) report the appearance of a peak at about 20·6 Å which is said to be derived from a regular interstratification of 11·6 Å and 9 Å layers.) The structural interpretation of the dehydration process is illustrated in Fig. 53. Using the "oscillating-heating" method of studying thermal transformations Weiss and Rowland (1956) observed changes in structure at 80°C. and 215°C. which are associated with the dehydration process.

The cell parameters determined by Mathieson and Walker (1954) are similar to those given by Gruner and are as follows:

$$a\ 5{\cdot}33\ \text{Å},\ b\ 9{\cdot}18\ \text{Å},\ c\ 28{\cdot}90\ \text{Å},\ \beta\ 97°,\ \text{space group } Cc.$$

The structure as seen along the y axis is shown in Fig. 54, and Fig. 55 shows projected on (001), (a) half of a "talc" layer and (b) the sites of water molecules and exchange cations referred to the same axes and origin. It is seen from Fig. 55 (a) that the silicate layer is distorted from the ideal arrangement of regular hexagons. In order that α may be 90°, displacements of successive "talc" layers parallel to y must be either zero or alternately $+b/3$ and $-b/3$, if the structure is ordered. In fact displacements of $+b/3$ and $-b/3$ occur randomly and give rise to diffuse reflections when $k \neq 3n$. A possible arrangement of water molecules and exchange cations, details of which are given by Mathieson and Walker, involves the filling of two thirds of the sites available for water molecules, and a ratio of one exchangeable cation to approximately 12 H_2O. These relationships are consistent with the experimental data for Mg-vermiculite.

The layer occupied by water molecules and hydrated cations under atmospheric conditions is approximately 5 Å in thickness and this is similar to the thickness of a brucite layer, so that vermiculite and chlorite powder patterns are similar. The structure of Mg-vermiculite resembles that of a chlorite in many respects but differs mainly in the reduced occupation of the interlamellar atomic sites; the "brucite" sheet of chlorite is replaced by a partially filled H_2O–Mg^{+2}–H_2O double sheet in vermiculite (Mathieson, 1958). The strong 14 Å

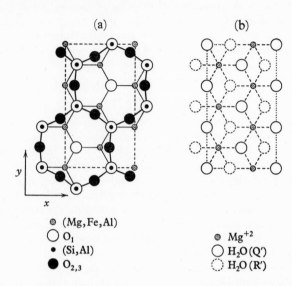

(a) (b)

⊘ (Mg,Fe,Al)
◯ O_1
• (Si,Al)
● $O_{2,3}$

⊘ Mg^{+2}
◯ $H_2O(Q')$
◌ $H_2O(R')$

FIG. 55. (a). Section of the crystal structure of Mg-vermiculite from $z = 0.0$ to 0.114 (*i.e.* half-layers Q, Fig. 54) projected on the base of the cell. (b). Section of the crystal structure from $z = 0.213$ to 0.287, *i.e.* sites of water molecules in the sheets Q' and R' and sites of exchangeable Mg^{+2} cations (after Mathieson and Walker, 1954).

basal reflection serves to distinguish Mg-vermiculite from all other layered silicates except chlorites and smectites. For vermiculite, however, the 7 Å peak is weaker than that at 14 Å, while for most chlorites the two peaks are of similar intensity, and on heating to 700 °C. the 14 Å peak of vermiculite is replaced by the 9 Å peak of talc, while the 14 Å peak of chlorite is enhanced. After boiling with an ammonium salt the 14 Å peak of vermiculite is replaced by one at 10 Å but the chlorite peak is unaffected. Smectites are distinguished by treatment with glycerol (see below).

It is clear from the above structural concepts that the nature of the exchange cation will influence the degree of hydration and consequently the observed basal spacings. Potassium and ammonium ions have no hydration shell and are probably partially embedded in the bases of the tetrahedral layers. (K-vermiculite is very similar to biotite.) The values of d_{002} for vermiculite with various exchange ions (Barshad, 1948) are:

Mg 14·33 Å, Ca 15·07 Å, Ba 12·56 Å, Li 12·56 Å, Na 12·56 Å, K 10·42 Å, NH₄ 11·24 Å, Rb 11·24 Å, Cs 11·97 Å.

When the inter-layer water is replaced by a single layer of glycol molecules a spacing of about 14 Å results. This means that little change is noted for Mg-vermiculite, a contraction for Ca, and an expansion for Ba, Li and Na. No change is noted for K-, NH₄-, Rb- and Cs-vermiculites because their layers are in contact and glycol does not penetrate. Similar behaviour with glycerol serves to distinguish vermiculite from a smectite, since the latter swells to 17 Å :

pre-treatment with a magnesium salt may be advisable, however, if conclusive results are to be obtained (Walker, 1957).

Structural studies of regularly and randomly interstratified vermiculite and chlorite layers have been described (Bradley and Weaver, 1956; Weaver, 1956).

CHEMISTRY

Vermiculites are chemically very similar to tri-octahedral smectites, since both consist of talc-like layers in which a deficiency of positive charge is compensated by the presence of some inter-layer cations. In montmorillonite and hectorite this deficiency is caused principally by substitution in the octahedral part of the composite layers and is compensated on the average by 0·66 monovalent ions or their equivalent. The most common inter-layer ions in smectites are sodium and calcium, though magnesium sometimes occurs in this role. In vermiculites a larger charge deficiency is caused principally by tetrahedral substitution as in beidellites and saponite (Al or Fe^{+3} for Si) and is compensated generally by about 0·7 divalent cations, or their equivalent, between the layers. In natural specimens these are most commonly magnesium ions, though calcium and very rarely sodium also occur. Accordingly the cation exchange capacity of vermiculites (between 100 and 260 m.eq./100 gm.) is greater than that of smectites, and indeed is the highest of all the clay minerals. According to Weaver (1958) vermiculites can be subdivided into two main types. One type is derived from the alteration of biotite or phlogopite, contracts to a 10 to 10·3 Å phase when treated with K^+ (in KOH for 15 hrs., and subsequently dried at room temperature), and has a cation exchange capacity of 260 to 150 m.eq./100 gm. The other type is derived from non-mica minerals, contracts to 11 to 12·7 Å on treatment with K^+, and has an exchange capacity of less than 150 m.eq./100 gm. The latter type can be made to contract further only by less mild treatment with KOH. Fixation of potassium in soils, probably by mica-derived vermiculites, has been reported frequently (*e.g.* Kunze and Jeffries, 1953; Van der Marel, 1954). Some chemical analyses of vermiculites are given in Table 41.

The naturally occurring inter-layer cations can be exchanged for others, so that vermiculites with Mg, Ca, Na, K, Rb, Cs, Ba, Li, H and $(NH_4)^+$ as inter-layer cations can be prepared. Some cations are replaced more readily than others; for example an ammonium vermiculite may be prepared from a natural specimen (Gruner, 1939) and ammonium ions may be replaced by sodium or calcium but not by potassium (Allison *et al.*, 1953; Barshad, 1954). In general it may be stated that Na, Ca, Mg and K are interchangeable but K, NH_4, Rb and Cs are not. The octahedral sites in vermiculites are occupied mainly by Mg and Fe^{+2}, but appreciable substitution by Al and Fe^{+3} occurs, and in minor amounts Ti, Li, Cr, Ni and other ions are often present. A vermiculite with exceptionally high nickel and iron content (NiO 8·60, Fe_2O_3 19·22, FeO 5·03 per cent.) has been described by Nikitina (1956). Di-octahedral clay minerals with vermiculite-like characteristics have been reported as formed by the alteration of muscovite (Brown, 1953; Rich and Obershain, 1955).

Vermiculites and tri-octahedral smectites both contain water molecules between their talc-like layers but the amount of water taken up by natural vermiculites is less variable, and the maximum for them corresponds to two layers of water molecules in each available space. Even when soaked with water for 144 hours a vermiculite sample took up no more than this amount (Cano-Ruiz and Lopez Gonzalez, 1955). The ranges of substitution which occur in most natural vermiculites are indicated by the formula:

$$(Mg,Ca)_{0\cdot7-1\cdot0}\underbrace{Mg_{3\cdot5-5\cdot0}(Fe^{+3},Al)_{2\cdot5-1\cdot0}}_{6\cdot0}\underbrace{Al_{2\cdot0-3\cdot5},Si_{6-5\cdot5}}_{8\cdot0}O_{20}(OH)_4{\cdot}(H_2O)_{7\cdot0-9\cdot0}$$

Vermiculites also show the property of adsorbing organic liquids between their layers, but take up less than do the smectites. For most vermiculites (*e.g.* Mg, Ca, Na, Li, H) a single layer of glycol molecules replaces a double layer of water molecules in each space, but vermiculites with $(NH_4)^+$, K, Rb or Cs are contracted and take up no glycol. The amount of water or other liquid which is accommodated in the vermiculite structure is influenced by a number of factors such as the size, charge, and abundance of the inter-layer cation, and the dipole moment and dielectric constant of the liquid (Barshad, 1952). Ca-, Mg- and H-vermiculites have two layers of water molecules, Ba-, Li- and Na- have one, and $(NH_4)^+$-, K-, Rb- and Cs-vermiculites have none at all (Barshad, 1948). The above factors also influence the detail of the dehydration process, but for most natural vermiculities the dehydration curve has the following features. On heating to 110°C. roughly half the inter-layer water (corresponding to "unbound" molecules) is driven off, and most of the remainder is expelled between 250° and 400°C. Loss of water from (OH) ions takes place mostly between 500° and 850°C. (Walker, 1951). The expulsion of inter-layer water can be reversed after heating to temperatures as high as 550°C., and only beyond 700°C. is it certain that none can be regained. The unusual phenomenon of exfoliation occurs when vermiculite is heated suddenly to about 300°C. or more, and is due to the rapid generation of steam which cannot escape without buckling and separating the structural layers. Exfoliation, which may cause as much as a thirty-fold expansion in the direction perpendicular to the cleavage planes, can also be brought about by treatment with H_2O_2 and it is thought that in this case oxygen is liberated by chemical action with inter-layer magnesium ions. Vermiculite does not exfoliate if the water is driven off slowly, even at 250°C.

Differential thermal analysis curves of vermiculites generally show three principal endothermic peaks corresponding to the expulsion of inter-layer water, and a further two due to the disruption of the structure by loss of (OH) ions. There is a further small endothermic peak at about 550°C. which indicates that a small amount of inter-layer water is held very tenaciously (Walker and Cole, 1957). For vermiculites, d.t.a. curves are complex, and clearly may be different for specimens with different cations and consequently different initial hydration states. Thus curves for vermiculite saturated with NH_4^+, K, Rb or Cs show very small low temperature endothermic effects. Exothermic peaks occur at various temperatures according to the chemistry of the initial material, one at about 800°C. possibly being associated with the formation of enstatite (Walker, 1951).

Mixed layer clays with vermiculite as a constituent are not uncommon, the most well known being "hydrobiotite", a random mixture of vermiculite and biotite (Gruner, 1934). Hydrobiotite exfoliates with H_2O_2 and, as would be expected, its cation exchange capacity lies between that of biotite and of vermiculite. Regular and random interstratifications of vermiculite and chlorite layers have been identified (Bradley and Weaver, 1956).

Table 41. VERMICULITE ANALYSES

	1.	2.	3.	4.	5.
SiO_2	34·76	36·54	36·13	32·97	34·60
TiO_2	—	—	0·24	—	n.d.
Al_2O_3	14·86	16·96	13·90	17·88	13·63
Fe_2O_3	2·74	2·78	4·24	4·76	4·15
FeO	0·41	0·95	0·68	0·57	1·80
MnO	—	—	tr.	tr.	—
NiO	11·25	2·32	0·28	—	n.d.
MgO	18·18	19·78	24·84	22·36	22·88
CaO	0·40	0·06	0·18	0·00	0·04
Na_2O	—	—	—	0·00	0·39
K_2O	—	—	—	0·00	0·05
F	—	—	—	—	0·05
H_2O^+	}17·80	11·16	}18·94	10·05	11·68
H_2O^-		9·24		11·42	9·80
	100·40	99·79	99·43	100·01	99·07
$O \equiv F$	—	—	—	—	0·02
Total	100·40	99·79	99·43	100·01	99·05
α	1·542	—	1·525	—	1·540
$\beta = \gamma$	1·573	—	1·545	—	1·560
$2V_\alpha$	—	—	—	—	6°–8°
D	—	—	—	—	2·29

NUMBERS OF IONS ON THE BASIS OF 22 OXYGEN EQUIVALENTS†

	1.	2.	3.	4.	5.
Si	5·61 }8·00	5·81 }8·00	5·68 }8·00	5·30 }8·00	5·68 }8·00
Al	2·39	2·19	2·32	2·70	2·32
Fe^{+3}	—	—	—	—	—
Al	0·50	0·99	0·25	0·70	0·31
Ti	—	—	0·03	—	—
Fe^{+3}	0·33	0·33	0·50	0·58	0·51
Fe^{+2}	0·06 }6·00	0·13 }6·00	0·09 }6·00	0·08 }6·00	0·25 }6·00
Ni	1·46	0·30	0·04	—	—
Mn	—	—	—	—	—
Mg	3·65	4·25	5·09	4·64	4·93
Mg	0·72	0·43	0·73	0·71	0·66
Ca	0·07 }0·79	0·01 }0·44	0·03 }0·76	— }0·71	0·01 }0·80
K	—	—	—	—	0·01
Na	—	—	—	—	0·12
M^{+2}	0·78	0·44	0·76	0·71	0·73
H_2O	7·58	8·82	7·96	9·52	9·75
(OH)	4·00	4·00	4·00	4·00	4·00

1. Green nickeliferous vermiculite, Webster, North Carolina (Ross and Shannon, 1926).
2. Greenish yellow vermiculite, Webster, North Carolina (Ross *et al.*, 1928).
3. Pale yellow-green vermiculite, Bare Hills, Maryland (Shannon, 1928).
4. Yellowish brown vermiculite, Corundum Hill, North Carolina (Chatard, 1887).
5. Vermiculite, Röhrenhof, Fichtberg, Bavaria (Matthes, 1950).

† M^{+2} = No. of inter-layer divalent cations (or equivalents).
  H_2O = No. of water molecules per formula unit, corresponding to total water content less amount required for 4(OH).

Table 41.   VERMICULITE ANALYSES—*continued*

	6.	7.	8.	9.
SiO_2	34·04	33·82	34·86	35·92
TiO_2	—	1·84	0·61	—
Al_2O_3	15·37	15·82	14·46	10·68
Fe_2O_3	8·01	7·51	6·17	10·94
FeO	—	1·12	2·60	0·82
MnO	—	—	0·22	—
NiO	—	—	—	—
MgO	22·58	19·17	27·25	22·00
CaO	0·00	0·56	0·27	0·44
Na_2O	0·00	0·29	0·19	—
K_2O	0·00	0·10	0·02	—
F	—	—	—	—
H_2O^+	19·93	}20·25	12·11	9·34
H_2O^-	—		1·49	10·50
	99·93	100·48	100·25	100·64
$O \equiv F$	—	—	—	—
Total	99·93	100·48	100·25	100·64
α	—	—	1·564	—
$\beta = \gamma$	—	—	1·583	—
$2V_\alpha$	—	—	0°	—
D	—	—	—	2·31

NUMBERS OF IONS ON THE BASIS OF 22 OXYGEN EQUIVALENTS[†]

	6.	7.	8.	9.
Si	5·44 ⎫8·00	5·44 ⎫8·00	5·23 ⎫	5·77 ⎫
Al	2·56 ⎭	2·56 ⎭	2·56 ⎬8·00	2·02 ⎬8·00
Fe^{+3}	—	—	0·21 ⎭	0·21 ⎭
Al	0·32 ⎫	0·44 ⎫	— ⎫	— ⎫
Ti	—	0·22	0·07	—
Fe^{+3}	0·96	0·92	0·48	1·11
Fe^{+2}	— ⎬6·00	0·16 ⎬5·68	0·33 ⎬6·00	0·11 ⎬6·00
Ni	—	—	—	—
Mn	—	—	0·03	—
Mg	4·72 ⎭	3·84 ⎭	5·09 ⎭	4·78 ⎭
Mg	0·64 ⎫	0·76 ⎫	1·00 ⎫	0·49 ⎫
Ca	— ⎬0·64	0·10‡ ⎬0·76	0·04 ⎬1·10	0·08 ⎬0·57
K	—	—	—	—
Na	—	—	0·06 ⎭	—
M^{+2}	0·64	0·76	1·07	0·57
H_2O	8·64	8·86	4·81	8·63
(OH)	4·00	4·00	4·00	4·00

6. Vermiculite, Kenya. (Mathieson & Walker, 1954; used for the crystal structure determination.)

7. Vermiculite, West Chester, Pennsylvania (Walker & Cole, 1957). Anal. H. V. Hueber.

8. Olive- to green-brown vermiculite in lenses of metamorphosed limestone, Maaninka, Posio, north Finland (Volborth, 1954).

9. Yellowish brown vermiculite, Pilot, Maryland (Ross *et al.*, 1928).

[†] M^{+2} = No. of inter-layer divalent cations (or equivalents).
H_2O = No. of water molecules per formula unit, corresponding to total water content less amount required for 4(OH).

[‡] Walker and Cole (1957) state that no calcium occurs as exchangeable cation and therefore allocate Ca to octahedral sites.

Hydrobiotite, which has probably been derived by partial alteration of biotite either hydrothermally or by weathering, can be readily converted to vermiculite by leaching with $MgCl_2$, but the similar alteration of fresh biotite proceeds more slowly (Barshad, 1948). The partial alteration of phlogopite to vermiculite has been accomplished using $MgCl_2$ solution, excessive treatment resulting in montmorillonite (Caillère and Hénin, 1949).

Hydrothermal studies of vermiculite under equilibrium conditions (Roy and Romo, 1957) show that under 10,000 lb./in.^{2} of water pressure the first dehydration reaction occurs at 550°C. and that non-expanding structures are formed only above 650°C. At 300°C., however, a migration of magnesium from octahedral to inter-layer sites appears to take place giving rise to a "pseudochlorite" structure. It is suggested, therefore, that no vermiculite can have formed above 300°C. Since vermiculites are rich in iron it is argued also that they are derived from biotite rather than phlogopite and that the leaching of potassium, for example by weathering, is compensated in the first place by low temperature oxidation of ferrous to ferric iron.

OPTICAL AND PHYSICAL PROPERTIES

Although vermiculite occurs with minute particle size as a constituent of soil clays, it is also found in large crystalline plates, principally when it is an alteration product of biotite. Optical properties may therefore be measured

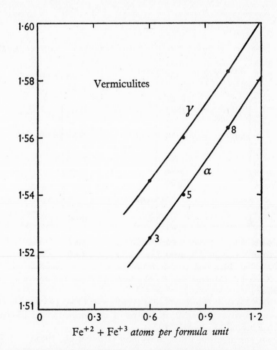

Fig. 56. Refractive indices of vermiculites plotted against number of iron atoms per formula unit. Numbers refer to analyses in Table 41.

more easily than for other clay minerals, but again variable hydration and cation content lead to a range of optical parameters. Some vermiculites contain considerable amounts of iron and these have the higher refractive indices. (Fig. 56, based on only three analyses, gives some indication of this trend.) The larger flakes are sometimes pseudo-hexagonal in outline, resembling the mica from which they have been derived, but they are soft and pliable, dull in appearance, and opaque: fibrous vermiculite has also been reported (Weiss and Hofmann, 1952).

DISTINGUISHING FEATURES

Vermiculites generally have lower refractive indices than biotite or hydrobiotite and higher refringence than chlorites. Their birefringence is lower than that of either biotite or talc. X-ray powder patterns of vermiculites which have been treated with an ammonium salt and glycerol, serve to distinguish vermiculite from montmorillonite and chlorite. The principal differences between vermiculites and smectites may be summarized as follows: 1. Vermiculites generally have a larger grain size. 2. Vermiculites have higher cation exchange capacity and greater substitution of $[Al]^4$ for Si. 3. In vermiculite the deficiency of positive charge in the "talc" layers lies mainly in the tetrahedral component. 4. Vermiculites take up at most one layer of glycol molecules, giving a basal spacing of about 14 Å, whereas smectites take double layers, the basal spacing swelling to 17 Å. 5. Smectites dehydrate more readily, and vermiculites re-hydrate more readily. 6. Vermiculites are formed mainly by the weathering of large flakes of biotite.

The distinction between the two groups, however, is not precise, and some smectites (*e.g.* saponites) possess several of the above characteristics. (For detailed discussion see Weaver, 1956; Walker, 1957.)

PARAGENESIS

One of the two main types of occurrence of vermiculite is as an alteration product of biotite either by weathering or by hydrothermal action. Derived in this way it is found sometimes as large crystal pseudomorphs after the mica, but it is also widespread as a clay constituent of certain soils (*e.g.* Walker, 1949, 1950). The second major occurrence of vermiculite is in the region of contact between acid intrusives and basic or ultra-basic rocks such as pyroxenites, peridotites, dunites, etc. (Williams and Skerl, 1940; Varley, 1948). In these circumstances it is found associated with corundum, apatite, serpentine, chlorite and talc. Weaver (1958) states that those vermiculites which are derived from mica-type minerals are comparatively rare in marine sediments since the potassium of sea water readily contracts them. Those which do occur in marine sediments are derived from non-micaceous sources such as volcanic material, chlorite and hornblende. Vermiculites are also found associated with carbonatites, and in metamorphosed limestones (Volborth, 1954). Laboratory hydrothermal studies (Roy and Romo, 1957) show that primary vermiculite is unlikely to form at a temperature above 200°–300°C. Hydrobiotite is in most cases produced hydrothermally and not by weathering, and occurs with apatite in pyroxenite. Less iron-rich hydrobiotites occur sometimes in metamorphosed limestone, or in serpentine–magnetite–apatite rock (Gevers, 1949).

REFERENCES

Allison, F. E., Roller, E. M. and **Doetsch, J. H.**, 1953. Ammonium fixation and availability in vermiculite. *Soil Sci.*, vol. 75, p. 173.

Barshad, I., 1948. Vermiculite and its relation to biotite as revealed by base exchange reactions, X-ray analyses, differential thermal curves and water content. *Amer. Min.*, vol. 33, p. 655.

—— 1950. The effect of interlayer cations on the expansion of the mica type of crystal lattice. *Amer. Min.*, vol. 35, p. 225.

—— 1952. Factors affecting the interlayer expansion of vermiculite and montmorillonite with organic substances. *Proc. Soil Sci. Soc. Amer.*, vol. 16, p. 176.

—— 1954. Cation exchange in micaceous minerals : II—Replaceability of ammonia and potassium from vermiculite, biotite and montmorillonite. *Soil Sci.*, vol. 78, p. 57.

Bradley, W. F. and **Weaver, C. E.**, 1956. A regularly interstratified chlorite-vermiculite clay mineral. *Amer. Min.*, vol. 41, p. 497.

Brown, G., 1953. The dioctahedral analogue of vermiculite. *Clay Min. Bull.*, vol. 2, p. 64.

Caillère, S. and **Hénin, S.**, 1949. Experimental formation of chlorites from montmorillonite. *Min. Mag.*, vol. 28, p. 612.

Cano-Ruiz, J. and **Lopez Gonzalez, J. de Dios**, 1955. Imbibición de agua par silicatos de estructura laminar. *Anales de Edafología*, vol. 14, p. 249 (M.A 13–444).

Chatard, Th. M., 1887. The gneiss–dunite contacts of Corundum Hill, N.C., in relation to the origin of corundum. *U.S. Geol. Survey*, Bull. 42, p. 45.

Gevers, T. W., 1949. Vermiculite at Loolekop, Palabora, north east Transvaal. *Trans. Geol. Soc. South Africa*, vol. 51, p. 133 (M.A. 11–64).

Gruner, J. W., 1934. The structure of vermiculites and their collapse by dehydration. *Amer. Min.*, vol. 19, p. 557.

—— 1939. Ammonium mica synthesized from vermiculite. *Amer. Min.*, vol. 24, p. 428.

Hendricks, S. B. and **Jefferson, M. E.**, 1938. Crystal structure of vermiculites and mixed vermiculite-chlorites. *Amer. Min.*, vol. 23, p. 851.

Kunze, G. W. and **Jeffries, C. D.**, 1953. X-ray characteristics of clay minerals as related to potassium fixation. *Proc. Soil Sci. Soc. Amer.*, vol. 17, p. 242.

Mathieson, A. McL., 1958. Mg-vermiculite : a refinement and re-examination of the crystal structure of the 14·36 Å phase. *Amer. Min.*, vol. 43, p. 216.

—— and **Walker, G. F.**, 1954. Crystal structure of magnesium vermiculite. *Amer. Min.*, vol. 39, p. 231.

Matthes, S., 1950. Vorkommen von Vermiculit in mitteldeutschen Serpentiniten. *Neues Jahrb. Min., Monatshefte*, p. 29 and p. 49.

Nikitina, A. P., 1956. Nickel vermiculite from the crust of weathering in the Ukraine. *Crust of weathering, Acad. Sci. USSR*, No. 2, p. 188 (M.A. 13–514).

Rich, C. I. and **Obershain, S. S.**, 1955. Chemical and clay mineral properties of a red-yellow podzolic soil derived from muscovite schist. *Proc. Soil Sci. Soc. Amer.*, vol. 19, p. 334.

Ross, C. S. and **Shannon, E. V.**, 1926. Nickeliferous vermiculite and serpentine from Webster, North Carolina. *Amer. Min.*, vol. 11, p. 92.

—— —— and **Gonyer, F. A.**, 1928. The origin of nickel silicates at Webster, North Carolina. *Econ. Geol.*, vol. 23, p. 542.

Roy, R. and **Romo, L. A.**, 1957. Weathering studies. I. New data on vermiculite. *Journ. Geol.*, vol. 65, p. 603.

Shannon, E. V., 1928. Vermiculite, optical data. *Amer. Journ. Sci.*, vol. 15, p. 21.

Van der Marel, H. W., 1954. Potassium fixation in Dutch soils: mineralogical analyses. *Soil Sci.*, vol. 78, p. 163.

Varley, E. R., 1948. Vermiculite deposits in Kenya. *Bull. Imp. Inst. London*, vol. 46, p. 348 (M.A. 11–63).

Volborth, A., 1954. Vermiculite aus Maaninka, Posio, Nordfinnland. *Comptes Rend. 19th Internat. Géol. Congr., Algiers*, 1952. Fasc. xv., p. 367.

Walker, G. F., 1949. The decomposition of biotite in soils. *Min. Mag.*, vol. 28, p. 693.

—— 1950. Trioctahedral minerals in soil clays of north-east Scotland. *Min. Mag.*, vol. 29, p. 72.

—— 1951. Vermiculites and some related mixed-layer minerals, in *X-ray identification and structures of Clay Minerals*. Min. Soc., London. Chap. VII, p. 199.

—— 1957. On the differentiation of vermiculites and smectites in clays. *Clay Min. Bull.*, vol. 3, p. 154.

—— 1959. Diffusion of interlayer water in vermiculite. *Nature*, vol. 177, p. 239.

—— and Cole, W. F., 1957. The vermiculite minerals, in *The differential thermal investigation of clays*. Min. Soc., London. Chap. VII, p. 191.

Weaver, C. E., 1956. The distribution and identification of mixed-layer clays in sedimentary rocks. *Amer. Min.*, vol. 41, p. 202.

—— 1958. The effects and geological significance of potassium "fixation" by expandable clay minerals derived from muscovite, biotite, chlorite, and volcanic material. *Amer. Min.*, vol. 43, p. 839.

Weiss, A. and Hofmann, U., 1952. Fäserig Vermikulit von Kropfmuhl bei Passau. *Acta Albertina Ratisbonensia*, vol. 20, p. 53 (M.A. 12–531).

Weiss, E. J. and Rowland, R. A., 1956. Effect of heat on vermiculite and mixed-layered vermiculite-chlorite. *Amer. Min.*, vol. 41, p. 899.

Williams, G. J. and Skerl, A. F., 1940. Mica in Tanganyika Territory. *Bull. Geol. Div. Dept. Lands & Mines Tangan. Terr.*, No. 14 (M.A. 8–43).

Apophyllite

$KFCa_4[Si_8O_{20}]8H_2O$

TETRAGONAL (+)

ω 1·534–1·535

ϵ 1·535–1·537

δ 0·002

Dispersion: High, sometimes anomalous.   D 2·33–2·37   H 4½–5

Cleavage: {001} perfect, {110} poor.

Colour: Colourless, white, pink, pale yellow or green; colourless in thin section.

Unit cell: a 9·00, c 15·84 Å.

Z=2.   Space group $P4/m\ nc$.

Decomposed by HCl, leaving silica.

Apophyllite is an uncommon mineral which is of interest largely because of its unusual atomic structure. Although it often occurs together with zeolites, and like them has a high content of water, in other respects it is more akin to the micas. The name apophyllite is derived from the Greek *apo*, away from, *phullon*, leaf, and alludes to the way in which it exfoliates on heating.

STRUCTURE

The structure of apophyllite (Taylor and Náray-Szabó, 1931) bears some relationship to that of the micas in that a basic part of it is a sheet of composition Si_8O_{20}. This is formed as in the micas by linkage of SiO_4 tetrahedra, but is different in two important respects. Instead of forming an approximately hexagonal network the tetrahedra are arranged in four-fold and eight-fold rings, as shown in Fig. 57, and alternate rings of four tetrahedra point in opposite directions. The plane which approximately contains the bases of tetrahedra pointing one way is not the same as that passing through the bases of the others. Linking these unusual puckered sheets and lying on horizontal mirror planes between them are Ca, K and F ions distributed as shown in Fig. 58; oxygens of water molecules lie in the plane of tetrahedral apices. Each calcium is seven-fold coordinated by four oxygens (each of which is linked to one silicon), by one fluorine ion in the same plane, and by two oxygens of water molecules. Each fluorine ion is surrounded by four calcium ions. The potassium ions are eight-fold coordinated by the water molecules, four in a plane above and four below. A direct determination of the role of the hydrogen atoms in this structure has not been made but there is strong evidence from the interatomic distances that each water molecule is hydrogen bonded to an oxygen of the Si_8O_{20} sheet. The second hydrogen of the water molecule could also lie on

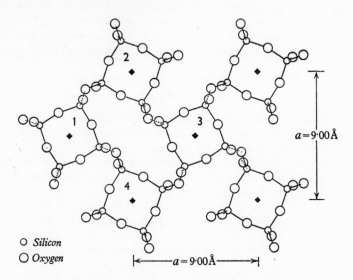

O *Silicon*
O *Oxygen* |←——*a* = 9·00Å——→|

FIG. 57. (001) projection of silicon-oxygen sheets of apophyllite; tetrad axes pass through the corners and centre of the unit cell. In rings numbered 1 and 3, tetrahedral point upwards, and in those numbered 2 and 4, tetrahedra point downwards (after Taylor and Náray-Szabó, 1931).

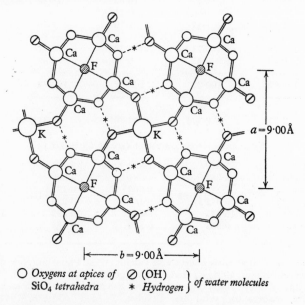

|←——*b* = 9·00Å——→|

O *Oxygens at apices of*   ⊘ *(OH)*
SiO₄ tetrahedra   * *Hydrogen* } *of water molecules*

FIG. 58. (001) projection showing apical oxygens of SiO₄ tetrahedra, and K, Ca, F and H₂O which link the silicon–oxygen sheets. K, Ca and F ions lie on the reflection plane at the base of the unit cell. Oxygens and hydroxyls lie 1·5 Å above and below this plane (after Taylor and Náray-Szabó, 1931).

a line towards an oxygen at the base of an SiO_4 tetrahedron. The existence of hydrogen-bonded water molecules is consistent with the process of dehydration since most water is lost at about 250°C., a temperature higher than that for unbound water molecules, but lower than that for structural (OH) ions.

CHEMISTRY

Of the few chemical analyses of apophyllite which are available, five are listed in Table 42. These conform quite well with the ideal formula but show that some sodium may substitute for potassium; other analyses show that some aluminium may replace silicon. The specimens with highest and lowest water content are those with lowest and highest fluorine respectively, suggesting that deficiencies of fluorine below one atom per formula unit are compensated by substitution of (OH) ions. The role of water in this mineral seems to be different from that in zeolites since the structure determination and dehydration

Table 42.   APOPHYLLITE ANALYSES

	1.	2.	3.	4.	5.
SiO_2	52·24	52·41	51·90	52·21	52·21
CaO	25·11	25·28	25·24	25·16	25·58
Na_2O	0·27	0·39	0·53	0·63	1·60
K_2O	5·05	5·09	4·69	4·82	3·52
H_2O^+	16·41	16·37	16·53	16·49	17·06
H_2O^-	—	—	0·14	—	—
F	1·51	1·17	1·70	1·40	1·16
	100·70	100·71	100·73	100·71	101·13
$O \equiv F$	0·63	0·49	0·71	0·59	0·43
Total	100·07	100·22	100·02	100·12	100·70
D	2·373	2·373	2·361	2·371	2·346

NUMBERS OF IONS ON THE BASIS OF 29(O,OH,F)

	1.	2.	3.	4.	5.
Si	7·891	7·842	7·832	7·874	7·789
Ca	4·064	4·053	4·081	4·066	4·089
Na	0·080 $\}$	0·113 $\}$	0·903 $\}$	0·185 $\}$	0·462 $\}$
K	0·972 $\}$ 1·05	0·972 $\}$ 1·09	0·155 $\}$ 1·06	0·928 $\}$ 1·11	0·671 $\}$ 1·13
H	16·536	16·341	16·642	16·592	16·982
F	0·721	0·554	0·810	0·668	0·547

1. Apophyllite, associated with quartz and calcite, West Paterson, New Jersey, U.S.A. (Gossner and Kraus, 1928) (Includes 0·11 MgO).
2. Large crystals of apophyllite, Cape Blomidon, Nova Scotia (Gossner and Kraus, 1928).
3. Apophyllite, fissures in pyrite ore, Boliden, Sweden (Ödman, 1941). Anal. T. Berggren.
4. Colourless crystals of apophyllite, St. Andreasberg Harz, Germany (Gossner and Kraus, 1928) (Includes 0·46 Al_2O_3).
5. Pale red crystals of apophyllite, on quartz, Guanajuato, Mexico (Gossner and Kraus, 1928).

experiments show that it is most probably hydrogen-bonded to oxygen atoms in the Si_8O_{20} network. Treatment with dilute acids leaves behind a skeleton of silica with apophyllite morphology; in nature similar alteration products are sometimes found and these may be hydrous silica (Bailey, 1941), kaolinite, or calcite.

OPTICAL AND PHYSICAL PROPERTIES

The sheet-like structure of apophyllite leads to perfect cleavage on its {001} faces. Crystals may be tabular, prismatic or granular and when well formed exhibit prisms and bipyramids. Basal cleavage faces have a pearly iridescent lustre. Optical properties are often anomalous, some specimens being isotropic, uniaxial negative, or even biaxial with crossed dispersion of optic axial planes. Table 43 gives refractive indices for different types according to Wenzel (1917), although these conflict somewhat with earlier results.

Table 43. APOPHYLLITE REFRACTIVE INDICES

λ	positive			isotropic			negative		
	ω	ϵ	δ	ω	ϵ	δ	ω	ϵ	δ
Li	1·532	1·534	0·002	1·5381	1·5384	0·0003	1·5415	1·5415	0·0000
Na	1·535	1·537	0·002	1·5418	1·5418	0·0000	1·5433	1·5429	0·0004
Tl	1·537	1·539	0·002	1·5438	1·5438	0·0000	1·5448	1·5439	0·0009

Those specimens for which δ varies with wavelength show anomalous interference colours which are said to disappear on heating at about 275°C., roughly the temperature at which the hydrogen bonded water molecules are driven off.

DISTINGUISHING FEATURES

Apophyllite is characterized by its tetragonal habit and often by marked anomalous interference colours. It may be distinguished from the zeolites, even though some of these are uniaxial, by its higher refractive indices and perfect basal cleavage. The tetragonal zeolite ashcroftine has similar refractive indices and good {001} cleavage but has higher birefringence.

PARAGENESIS

The main occurrences of apophyllite are as a secondary mineral in amygdales or druses in basalts where it is often accompanied by zeolites, datolite, pectolite, and calcite. Less frequently it is found in cavities in granites, in fissures in metamorphic rocks bordering granite, and in limestone or calc-silicate rock associated with calcite, sometimes as an alteration product of wollastonite. It has been reported with stilbite on serpentine at a marble contact and in crevices in aplite. Apophyllite has been recorded from natrolite veins in aegirine–alkali amphibole–nepheline-syenite associated with lamprophyllite, arfvedsonite, microcline, apatite, eucolite, fluorite, calcite, catapleiite and opal (Barabanov, 1957).

REFERENCES

Bailey, E. H., 1941. Skeletonized apophyllite from Crestmore and Riverside, California. *Amer. Min.*, vol. 26, p. 565.

Barabanov, V. F., 1957. Apophyllite from the Gakman ravine, Khibin Tundra. *Doklady Akad. Nauk. SSSR*, vol. 114, p. 876.

Gossner, B. and **Kraus, O.**, 1928. Über die chemische Zusammensetzung von Apophyllit. *Zeit. Krist.*, vol. 68, p. 595.

Ödman, O. H., 1941. Geology and ores of the Boliden deposit, Sweden. *Årsbok Sveriges Geol. Undersokning*, vol. 35, no. 1 (M.A. 8–311).

Taylor, W. H. and **Náray-Szabó, St.**, 1931. The structure of apophyllite. *Zeit. Krist.*, vol. 77, p. 146.

Wenzel, A., 1917. Untersuchung der Beziehung zwischen der Dispersion der Doppelbrechung und den Interferenzfarben an Apophylliten im polarisierten Licht. *Neues. Jahrb. Min.*, Bl. Bd. 41, p. 565.

Prehnite

$Ca_2Al[AlSi_3O_{10}](OH)_2$

ORTHORHOMBIC ($+$)

α	1·611–1·632
β	1·615–1·642
γ	1·632–1·665
δ	0·022–0·035
$2V_\gamma$	65°–69°
O.A.P.	(010); $\alpha = x$, $\gamma = z$.
Dispersion:	Usually $r > v$.
D	2·90–2·95
H	6–6½
Cleavage:	{001} good, {110} weak.
Twinning:	Fine lamellar twinning may occur.
Colour:	Pale green, yellow, grey or white; colourless in thin section.
Unit cell:	a 4·61, b 5·47, c 18·48 Å.
	$Z=2$. Space group $P2cm$.

Slowly gelatinized by HCl.

Prehnite is a common hydrothermal mineral in cavities in igneous rocks often occurring as small radiating crystals in the form of rosettes: it is also found in metamorphosed limestones. The name is after Col. von Prehn who first found the mineral at the Cape of Good Hope.

STRUCTURE

The cell dimensions and space group of prehnite were first determined by Gossner and Mussgnug (1931), who showed that the unit cell contains two formula units of composition $H_2Ca_2Al_2(SiO_4)_3$. The structure has not been fully determined, but Nuffield (1943) on the basis of a detailed morphological, physical and chemical study confirmed the cell constants and indexed the X-ray powder pattern. Berman (1937) included prehnite in the brittle mica family since it contains Ca and has a good platy cleavage. A formula suggesting a layered structure has been given by Malčić and Preisinger (1960).

CHEMISTRY

Prehnite does not show any marked variation in composition; the alkalis, manganese and magnesium are usually low, and the only appreciable substitution is iron for aluminium. As noted by Nuffield (1943), however, there is often a small replacement of silicon by aluminium. Selected analyses of prehnites and the numbers of ions calculated on the basis of 24(O,OH) are given in Table

44, and the relative constancy of composition is apparent. The water content is slightly variable, but most probably is related to analytical difficulties due to the fibrous nature of most samples. Gruner (1933) has shown that when prehnite is treated with anhydrous liquid ammonia it loses some water and may absorb ammonia in its place. Most of the water is only lost at red-heat; a dehydration curve obtained by Gallitelli (1928) shows a loss of about 0·2 per cent. of water at 230°C., the remainder being retained until between 600° and 750°C. Prehnite cannot therefore be classed with the zeolites with which it is often associated.

Table 44. PREHNITE ANALYSES

	1.	2.	3.	4.	5.	6.	7.
SiO_2	42·76	44·04	42·86	42·78	43·7	41·67	43·08
TiO_2	—	0·03	0·01	—	tr.	0·12	—
Al_2O_3	24·83	24·77	24·41	25·37	24·05	24·44	24·55
Fe_2O_3	0·13	0·20	0·52	0·87	0·93	1·03	1·40
FeO	1·12	0·00	0·28	—	0·03	0·32	—
MnO	0·05	0·00	0·06	—	0·00	—	0·02
MgO	0·07	0·01	0·03	tr.	0·11	0·25	0·12
CaO	26·84	26·99	26·89	26·95	26·85	27·25	26·65
Na_2O	0·03	0·00	0·32	0·30	0·04	0·18	—
K_2O	0·18	0·00	0·01	tr.	0·00	0·18	0·38
H_2O^+	4·24	}4·20	4·45	4·18	4·54	4·44	3·28
H_2O^-	—		0·08	—	0·03	0·00	—
Total	100·25	100·25	99·92	100·45	100·36	99·88	100·52
α	1·613	—	1·613	1·612	1·615	1·615	—
β	1·622	—	1·624	1·617	1·624	1·624	—
γ	1·637	—	1·638	1·644	1·643	1·644	—
$2V\gamma$	68°50′	—	68°	—	69°	69°	—
D	2·928	—	2·936	2·900	—	2·915	—

NUMBERS OF IONS ON THE BASIS OF 24(O,OH).

	1.	2.	3.	4.	5.	6.	7.
Si	5·909 }6·00	6·036	5·930 }6·00	5·884 }6·00	5·989 }6·00	5·786 }6·00	6·043
Al	0·091	—	0·070	0·116	0·011	0·214	—
Al	3·953	4·002	3·900	3·998	3·874	3·786	4·060
Fe^{+3}	0·013	0·021	0·050	0·090	0·096	0·106	0·148
Mg	0·014 }4·12	0·002 }4·03	0·003 }4·00	— }4·09	0·022 }4·00	0·051 }3·99	0·025 }4·23
Ti	—	0·003	0·001	—	—	0·013	—
Fe^{+2}	0·130	—	0·033	—	0·003	0·038	—
Mn	0·006	—	0·008	—	—	—	—
Na	0·008	—	0·081	0·079	0·010	0·050	—
Ca	3·973 }4·01	3·965	3·973 }4·06	3·970 }4·05	3·943 }3·95	4·055 }4·14	4·006
K	0·032	—	0·001	—	—	0·032	—
OH	3·908	3·840	4·096	3·830	4·150	4·114	3·070

1. Spherulitic hydrothermal prehnite, amphibolite, Markovice, Čáslav, Bohemia (Kratochvíl, 1934).
2. Brown to flesh-coloured prehnite, zoned pegmatite associated with quartz monzonite cutting magnesian limestones, Crestmore, California (Burnham, 1959). Anal. W. F. Blake (Includes P_2O_5 0·01).
3. White fibrous prehnite, rodingite, Pastoki, Hindubagh, Pakistan (Bilgrami and Howie, 1960). Anal. R. A. Howie.
4. Cream-yellow radiating prehnite, crevice in Keweenawan traps, Lake Nipigon, Ontario (Walker and Parsons, 1926). Anal. H. C. Rickaby.
5. Translucent, very pale green, botryoidal prehnite, cavities in dolerite, Prospect Quarry, New South Wales (Coombs et al., 1959). Anal. A. M. Taylor and J. A. Ritchie (Includes P_2O_5 0·02, Ag 0·01, Pb 0·04, SnO 0·01).
6. Colourless prehnite crystals, fissure in peridotite, E. side of Bonaparte river, Ashcroft, British Columbia (Nuffield, 1943). Anal. E. W. Nuffield.
7. Prehnite, phlogopite deposit, Emel'dzhak, South Yakutia, Siberia (Galyuk, 1956) (Includes a remainder of 1·04 per cent.).

The synthesis of prehnite by the hydrothermal treatment of a glass of prehnite composition at about 3000 bars pressure and 350°C. has been reported by Fyfe et al. (1958), who noted that prehnite will form rapidly at relatively low tem-

peratures only if pressures are well above 3000 bars. Prehnite was reported also
to be stable up to 450°C. at 4000 bars: at higher temperatures it is converted to
anorthite and wollastonite (Coombs *et al.*, 1959). The d.t.a. curve of prehnite
shows a double endothermic effect with peaks at 787° and 868°C. which are
related to the loss of water from the structure in two distinct processes (Mc-
Laughlin, 1957). Norin (1941), however, obtained a relatively large exothermic
peak after a single endothermic one, and found that melting began at 1225°C.
Prehnite may be altered to garnet and epidote by metamorphism (M'Lintock,
1915), or changed by low-temperature alteration to scolecite or to a chloritic
material.

OPTICAL AND PHYSICAL PROPERTIES

The sign of elongation of prehnite crystals depends on the habit, but in
prismatic crystals it is positive. The refractive indices and birefringence in
general increase with the amount of iron. Optical anomalies are often found,
many specimens having wavy or incomplete extinction and abnormal interference colours. In these examples crossed dispersion is sometimes observable.
Dana has suggested that two systems of thin layers may be superimposed in this
type of crystal, giving rise in addition to lamellar banding parallel and normal
to {100}.

Distinct individual crystals are relatively rare; tabular groups, barrel-shaped
aggregates and reniform globular masses being more common, often giving a
characteristic imperfectly columnar "bow-tie" appearance, which has been
alternatively termed "hour-glass" structure (Shannon, 1924). Richmond (1938)
has recorded from optical evidence that, in addition to the crystals consisting
of segments in a plane parallel to (001), normal to that plane the crystals are
composed of layers rotated 90° to each other; the hour-glass appearance is due
to this assemblage in conjunction with a medial band with simple orthorhombic
orientation.

DISTINGUISHING FEATURES

Prehnite differs from many hydrothermal minerals in its relatively high
relief and its strong birefringence. Lawsonite has lower birefringence and
slightly higher refractive indices; datolite, which may be found associated with
prehnite, has only a very poor cleavage and a stronger birefringence, while
danburite, andalusite, topaz and wollastonite all have lower birefringence.

PARAGENESIS

Prehnite occurs chiefly in basic volcanic rocks as a secondary or hydrothermal
mineral in veins, cavities and amygdales (*e.g.* Table 44, anal. 4), and is frequently
associated with zeolites. It is also found in veins in granite, monzonite and
diorite, etc., and as pseudomorphs after such minerals as laumontite, axinite
and clinozoisite. In metamorphic rocks it is found in contact-altered impure
limestones and marls, and in rocks which have suffered calcium metasomatism
such as rodingites (Table 44, anal. 3) or garnetized gabbros. It may be formed
by the alteration of felspars, and is stable in the greenschist and zeolite facies

(Coombs, 1954; Coombs *et al.*, 1959). Brothers (1956) has recorded prehnite as a product of incipient metamorphism in schistose greywackes and Coombs *et al.* have shown that prehnite-bearing rocks are of regional extent in New Zealand, where they occur in a zone characterized by pumpellyite and/or prehnite.

REFERENCES

Berman, H., 1937. Constitution and classification of the natural silicates. *Amer. Min.*, vol. 22, p. 342.

Bilgrami, S. A. and Howie, R. A., 1960. The mineralogy and petrology of a rodingite dike, Hindubagh, Pakistan. *Amer. Min.*, vol. 45, p. 791.

Brothers, R. N., 1956. The structure and petrography of graywackes near Auckland, New Zealand. *Trans. Roy. Soc. New Zealand*, vol. 83, p. 465.

Burnham, C. W., 1959. Contact metamorphism of magnesian limestones at Crestmore, California. *Bull. Geol. Soc. Amer.*, vol. 70, p. 879.

Coombs, D. S., 1954. The nature and alteration of some Triassic sediments from Southland, New Zealand. *Trans. Roy. Soc. New Zealand*, vol. 82, p. 65.

—— Ellis, A. J., Fyfe, W. S. and Taylor, A. M., 1959. The zeolite facies; with comments on the interpretation of hydrothermal syntheses. *Geochim. et Cosmochim. Acta*, vol. 17, p. 53.

Fyfe, W. S., Turner, F. J. and Verhoogen, J., 1958. Metamorphic reactions and metamorphic facies. *Mem. Geol. Soc. Amer.*, no. 73.

Gallitelli, P., 1928. Sulla prehnite di Toggiano. *Atti Soc. Toscana Sci. Nat.*, vol. 38, p. 267 (M.A. 4–319).

Galyuk, V. A., 1956. Prehnite from the Emel'dzhak phlogopite deposit (South Yakutia). *Trudy Moskov. Geol. Razvedoch Inst. in S. Ordzhonikidze*, vol. 29, p. 73.

Gossner, B. and Mussgnug, F., 1931. Röntgenographische Untersuchung an Prehnit und Lawsonite. *Centr. Min., Abt. A.*, p. 419 (M.A. 5–186).

Gruner, E., 1933. Untersuchungen an Alkali-Aluminium-Silikaten. VII. Das Verhalten einiger mineralischer Zeolithe zu flussigem Ammoniak. *Zeits. anorg. Chem.*, vol. 211, p. 385.

Kratochvíl, F., 1934. Prehnites from the environs of Čáslav. *Rospravy České Akad., Class II*, vol. 44, no. 17 (M.A. 6–129).

McLaughlin, R. J. W., 1957. Other minerals, in *The Differential thermal investigation of clays*. Min. Soc., London.

M'Lintock, W. F. P., 1915. On the zeolites and associated minerals from the Tertiary lavas around Ben More Mull. *Trans. Roy. Soc. Edin.*, vol. 51, p. 1.

Malčić, S. and Preisinger, A., 1960. Struktur des Prehnits. *Fortschr. Min.*, vol. 38, p. 45 (abstract).

Norin, R., 1941. Tillämpning av termisk analys på leror och vattenhaltiga mineral. *Geol. För. Förh. Stockholm*, vol. 63, p. 203.

Nuffield, E. W., 1943. Prehnite from Ashcroft, British Columbia. *Univ. Toronto Stud., Geol. Ser.*, no. 48, p. 49.

Pauling, L., 1930. The structure of the micas and related minerals. *Proc. Nat. Acad. Sci. U.S.A.*, vol. 16, p. 123.

Richmond, W. E., Jr., 1938. Paragenesis of the minerals from Blueberry Mountain, Woburn, Massachusetts. *Amer. Min.*, vol. 22, p. 290.

Shannon, E. V., 1924. The Mineralogy and petrology of intrusive Triassic diabase at Goose Creek, Loudoun County, Virginia. *Proc. U.S. Nat. Mus.*, vol. 66, p. 62.

Walker, T. L. and Parsons, A. L., 1926. Zeolites and related minerals from Lake Nipigon, Ontario. *Univ. Toronto Stud., Geol. Ser.*, no. 22, p. 15.

INDEX

Mineral names in **bold** type are those described in detail; page numbers in **bold** type refer to the principal descriptions or definition of the mineral. Entries other than minerals are in *italic* type.

Adamsite, 11
Age determinations, 23, 40, 86
Al-celadonite, 216, 217
Allophane, 191, **200**, 207, 209
γ-Alumina, 205
Aluminian serpentine, 174, 177, 179
Alunite, 209
Alurgite, 15
Alushtite, 217
Amblygonite, 90
Amesite, 135, 146–9, **164–9**, 181, 200
Anauxite, 191, 194, **200**, 204, 207
Annite, **42**, 57, 61, 65, 66, 67, 68
Anomite, 70, 100
Antigorite, 170–90
Aphrosiderite, 138, 142, **146**
Apophyllite, 258–62
  Structure, 258
  Chemistry, 260
  Optics, etc., 261
  Paragenesis, 261
Asbestos, 170, 185
Attapulgite, 191, 193

Base exchange, 37
Bastite, 186
Bavalite, 142, 146
Beidellite, **226–45**, 250
Bentonite, 226, 229, 240
Benzidine, 222
Berthierine, 150, 164
Biotite, 1, 7, 42, **55–84**, 214, 216, 222, 249, 254
  Structure, 55
  Chemistry, 57
  Optics, etc., 70
  Paragenesis, 71
Brammallite, 31, 32, 34, 191, **214**, 215, 218, 221, 223
Brandisite, 100
Bravaisite, 213, 214, **217**
Brittle micas, 7, **95**
Brunsvigite, **137**, 144, 152

Cat gold, 11
Cat silver, 11
Cation exchange, 37, 221, 226, 228, 231, 250

Celadonite, 35, **37**, 157, 158, 191, 216, **217**
Chamosite, 136, 137, 139, **150**, 152, 153, 158, **164–9**, 175, 200
China clay, 194
Chlorine-rich biotite, 64
Chlorite, 69, **131–63**, 164, 165, 215, 248, **249**
  Structure, 131
  Chemistry, 136
  Optics, etc., 151
  Paragenesis, 153
Chlorite-montmorillonite, 136
Chlorite polymorphs, 133
Chlorite-vermiculite, 136
"Chloropal", 237
Chrome mica-clay, 221, 222, 223
Chromian phengite, 14
Chromian talc-chlorite, 144
Chromiferous clinochlore, 142, 146
Chrysotile, 148, 149, **170–90**, 199
"Clay biotite", 48, 65, 70
"Clay mica", 48
Clay minerals, 191–257
  Introduction, 191–3
Clinochlore, 135, **137**, 142, 143, 146, 147, 148, 149, 151, 165
Clino-chrysotile, 172, 173
Clintonite, 7, 96, **99–102**
  Structure, 100
  Chemistry, 100
  Optics, etc., 100
  Paragenesis, 102
Common mica, 11
Cookeite, 145, 147
Corrensite, 136
Corundophilite, **137**, 139, 152, 157, 165
Cronstedtite, **164–9**, 200
Cuspidine, 50

Daphnite, **137**, 142, 146, 150, 156, 157
Delessite, **137**, 139, 152, 156
Diabantite, **137**, 144, 152, 165
Dickite, 191, 192, **194–212**, 217
Didymite, 11
Di-octahedral micas, 5, 6, **7**, 43, 61, 65

Eastonite, **42**, 44, 57, 61, 65
Endellite, 194